PATRICK CHAMOISEAU

CARIBBEAN STUDIES SERIES
Anton L. Allahar and Shona N. Jackson
Series Editors

Patrick Chamoiseau:
A Critical Introduction

Wendy Knepper

University Press of Mississippi   Jackson

www.upress.state.ms.us

The University Press of Mississippi is a member
of the Association of American University Presses.

Copyright © 2012 by University Press of Mississippi
All rights reserved
Manufactured in the United States of America

First printing 2012

∞

Library of Congress Cataloging-in-Publication Data

Knepper, Wendy.
  Patrick Chamoiseau : a critical introduction / Wendy Knepper.
    p. cm. — (Caribbean studies series)
  Includes bibliographical references and index.
  ISBN 978-1-61703-154-0 (hardback) — ISBN 978-1-61703-155-7 (ebook) 1. Chamoiseau, Patrick—Criticism and interpretation. 2. Creole dialects in literature. 3. Creole dialects—Caribbean Area. I. Title.
  PQ3949.2.C45Z75 2012
  843—dc23   2011032669

British Library Cataloging-in-Publication Data available

For Roseann and Lee

CONTENTS

Acknowledgments   ix

Chronology   xi

Abbreviations   xv

1. Contexts and Intertexts   3

2. Insurgent Performance Works   32

3. Vernacular Forms and Wandering Genres   59

4. *Créolité*, Community, and the Word Scratcher   95

5. Autoethnographic Fictions of Childhood   130

6. Initiating the Warrior of the Imaginary   154

7. Visual Texts and the Revolutionary Epic   185

8. Activism and Tales of Initiation   212

Notes   239

Select Bibliography   261

Index   271

ACKNOWLEDGMENTS

This project has been supported by a Social Sciences and Humanities Research Council of Canada postdoctoral fellowship, which enabled me to research and write an early draft of this book in affiliation with New York University and Harvard University (2003–2005). Part of this text was written while I was a visiting fellow at the Institute for the Study of the Americas, University of London (2008).

I would like to thank the many individuals who have supported this work. A word of special thanks goes to Michael Dash, who has been encouraging throughout the project; I particularly appreciate his advice and feedback on the initial draft of the manuscript. Ted Chamberlin and Roseann Runte supported my application for a postdoctoral fellowship as well as supervised my thesis, which includes a discussion of the utopian dimensions of Patrick Chamoiseau's *Texaco*. For their encouragement and advice during the early part of this project, I would like to thank Pierre Pinalie and Raphaël Confiant. Lorna Burns offered helpful feedback on the introductory chapter to the work. The librarians at Schoelcher Library in Martinique helped me to source early manuscripts by Chamoiseau and other resources. On the occasion of my first visit to Martinique, Madame and Monsieur Aratus were very hospitable; they introduced me to many aspects of Martinican culture and life, including the art of riddles. Martine Gardeux and Marybeth Timmerman have offered valuable advice on translation issues. I would especially like to thank Tamara O'Callaghan, Heidi Knepper, and Lee Koenig for their personal support. Finally, Patrick Chamoiseau has graciously responded to my many e-mail queries about various aspects and phases of his writing. Out of respect for the author's privacy, I have included only those details pertinent to his writing career.

Aspects of my textual analysis have been previously discussed in published essays and articles, including "The *Émerveille*: Initiating the Warrior of the Imaginary," *The Caribbean Writer as Warrior of the Imaginary— L'Écrivain caribéen, guerrier de l'imaginaire*, ed. Kathleen Gyssels and Bénédicte Ledent (Amsterdam: Rodopi, 2008), 51–72; "Patrick Chamoiseau's Field of Play: Fostering a New World Imaginary," *To See the Wizard:*

Politics and the Literature of Childhood, ed. Laurie Ousley (Newcastle: Cambridge Scholars Publishing, 2007), 337–59; "Remapping the Crime Novel in the Francophone Caribbean: The Case of Patrick Chamoiseau's *Solibo Magnifique*," PMLA 122, no. 5 (2007): 1431–46; and "Patrick Chamoiseau's Seascapes and the Trans-Caribbean Imaginary," *Constructing Vernacular Culture in the Trans-Caribbean*, ed. Holger Henke and Karl-Heinz Magister (Lanham, MD: Lexington Books, 2008), 155–77.

Unless otherwise noted, all translations are my own.

CHRONOLOGY

1946	Martinique becomes an Overseas Department of France
1953	Patrick Chamoiseau born
1963	Cyclone Edith hits Martinique
1971	Brutal repression of student protests in Fort-de-France results in death of a student named Gérard Nouvet
Circa 1972–1975	Artistic director for M.G.G. (Martinique Guadeloupe Guyane), a monthly comic produced by Tony Delsham
1973–1975	Teaches at Collège Lamennais
1973	Production of *Solitude la mulâtresse* at the Avignon Festival, Chamoiseau freely adapts André Schwarz-Bart's novel for the stage
1974	*L'Époque Delgrès*
1975	Writes a play entitled *Une manière d'Antigone*
	Publication of Édouard Glissant's *Malemort*
	Publication of Frankétienne's *Dézafi*
	Leaves Martinique to study and work in France
Circa 1975	Writes a play entitled *Misère et misère double*
1976	First novel, *Notre dernière chance*, is rejected by the publisher
1981	*Les Antilles sous Bonaparte: Delgrès* published with text by Chamoiseau
1982	Publishes *Manman Dlo contre la fée Carabosse*
1984	*Le retour de Monsieur Coutcha* (in collaboration with Tony Delsham) published
1984–1986	*Le bourreau d'Antigone* is performed under the direction of Marie-Line Ampigny with subsequent tours in France, Belgium, and the French Caribbean
1986	Returns to Martinique, works for Ministry of Justice as an educator in the area of juvenile justice at the Tribunal de Fort-de-France
	Chronique des sept misères

	Wins Prix Kléber Haedens as well as Prix de l'île Maurice for *Chronique des sept misères*
1986–1987	Contributes to *Histoire des Antilles-Guyane par l'image* (Editions Désormeaux)
1988	*Au temps de l'antan: Contes du pays Martinique* published with illustrations by Mireille Vautier
	Awarded Grand prix de la littérature de jeunesse for *Au temps de l'antan*
	Publishes *Solibo Magnifique*
	Oral presentation of *Éloge de la Créolité* in France (read aloud by Jean Bernabé, Patrick Chamoiseau, and Raphaël Confiant), May 1988 "Festival caraïbe de la Seine-Saint-Denis"
1989	Co-publishes *Éloge de la créolité* in a bilingual edition
1990	Publishes *Antan d'enfance*
	Awarded Grand Prix Carbet de la Caraïbe for *Antan d'enfance*
1991	*Lettres créoles. Tracées antillaises et continentales de la litterature: Haiti, Guadeloupe, Martinique, Guyane: 1635–1975*
1992	500th anniversary of Christopher Columbus's discovery of the Americas
	Publishes *Texaco*
	Awarded the Prix Goncourt for *Texaco*
	Cofounded MODEMAS (Mouvement des Démocrates et des Ecologistes pour une Martinique Souveraine) on September 11, 1992, along with Garcin Malsa and Raphaël Confiant
	Dictionnaire encyclopédique Désormeaux, sous la direction de Jacques Corzani, Martine Allain et Patrick Chamoiseau, dessins de José Chantalou et Robert Hamparian (*Dictionnaire encyclopédique des Antilles et de la Guyane*)
1993	Writes an episode entitled "Au nom du coq" for the TV program *Les cinq dernières minutes*
1993–1996	Contributes a semi-regular column to *Antilla*
1994	Publishes *Chemin-d'école*
	Contributes "Le dernier coup de dent d'un voleur de banane" and "Que faire de la parole? Dans la tracée

	mystérieuse de l'oral à l'écrit" to *Écrire la «parole de nuit»; la nouvelle littéraire antillaise*
	Publishes *Guyane: Traces-mémoires du bagne*
	Release of *L'Exil du roi Béhanzin* by Guy Deslauriers for which Chamoiseau wrote the screenplay
	Release of *Les oubliés de la liberté* by Guy Deslauriers and Patrick Chamoiseau
1995	Release of *Femmes-Solitude* (3 parts) directed by Guy Deslauriers for which Claude Chonville and Patrick Chamoiseau wrote the screenplay
	Publishes a guide to the island, entitled *Martinique*
1996	Release of *Un siècle d'écrivains: Édouard Glissant* directed by Guy Deslauriers and text by Claude Chonville and Patrick Chamoiseau
	50th anniversary of departmentalization in Martinique
	Contributes "Postface" for Raphaël Confiant's *La baignoire de Joséphine*
1997	Publishes *Écrire en pays dominé*
	Publishes *L'Esclave vieil homme et le molosse*
	Publishes tribute to Louis Laouchez
1998	150th anniversary of the abolition of slavery
	Publishes *Émerveilles*, which includes illustrations by Maure
	Publishes *Elmire des sept bonheurs: confidences d'un vieux travailleur de la distillerie Saint-Etienne* with photos by Jean-Luc de Laguarigue
1999	Publishes *Métiers créoles* with photos by Jean-Luc de Laguarigue
2000	Publishes *Cases des îles* with photos by de Laguarigue
	Publishes "Dans la Pierre-Monde"
	Release of Guy Deslauriers's *Passage du milieu* for which Chamoiseau wrote the screenplay
2001	"Taubira" law ratified in France, recognizes slavery as a crime against humanity
	Interview with Chamoiseau in *Landscape and Memory: Martinican Land-people-history*, a film produced by Renée Gosson and Eric Faden
2002	Publishes *Biblique des derniers gestes*

	Awarded Prix Spécial du Jury RFO for *Biblique des derniers gestes*
	Publishes *Livret des villes du deuxième monde*
	Release of *Biguine* directed by Guy Deslauriers for which Chamoiseau wrote the screenplay
	Chamoiseau contributes introduction to *Les bois sacrés d'Hélénon*
	Le commandeur d'une pluie suivi de L'accra de la richesse published with illustrations by William Weaver
	Patrick Chamoiseau participates in the film entitled *Un imaginaire pour une mondialité à faire* by Federica Bertelli
2003	Release of *Nord-Plage* directed by José Hayot for which Chamoiseau wrote the screenplay
2004	Release of *La tragédie de la mangrove* directed by Guy Deslauriers with text by Patrick Chamoiseau
2005	Publishes *À bout d'enfance*
2007	Publishes *Un dimanche au cachot*
	Édouard Glisssant and Chamoiseau publish *Quand les murs tombent. L'identité nationale hors la loi?*
2009	Release of *Aliker*, directed by Guy Deslauriers and for which Chamoiseau writes the screenplay
	L'Intraitable beauté du monde: Adresse à Barack Obama and *Manifeste pour les "produits" de haute nécessité*
	Publishes *Encyclomerveille d'un tueur, 1. L'Orphelin de cocoyer grands-bois* with Thierry Ségur
	Les neuf consciences du Malfini

Note: The dates for films refer to original screenings. Official release dates may be later.

ABBREVIATIONS

Abbreviated references in the text are to Chamoiseau's manuscripts and published works as well as to translations of certain works. The initials given are followed by a page number and both references appear in parentheses.

AE	*Antan d'enfance*
AT	*Au temps de l'antan*
BDG	*Biblique des derniers gestes*
BE	*À bout d'enfance*
CE	*Chemin-d'école*
CF	*Creole Folktales*
CH	*Childhood*
CSM	*Chronique des sept misères*
CSS	*Chronicle of Seven Sorrows*
E	*Émerveilles*
EC	*Éloge de la créolité*
EPD	*Écrire en pays dominé*
EV	*L'Esclave vieil homme et le molosse*
IB	*L'Intraitable beauté du monde: Adresse à Barack Obama*
LC	*Lettres créoles*
LD	"L'époque Delgrès"
LDM	*Livret des villes du deuxième monde*
M	*Les neuf consciences du Malfini*
MA	"Une manière d'Antigone"
MD	*Manman Dlo contre la fée Carabosse*
MPHN	*Manifeste pour les "produits" de haute nécessité*
QM	*Quand les murs tombent: L'identité nationale hors-la-loi?*
SD	*School Days*
SLM	"Solitude, la mulâtresse"
SM	*Solibo Magnifique*
StM	*Solibo the Magnificent*
T	*Texaco*
TX	*Texaco* (translation)
UDC	*Un dimanche au cachot*

PATRICK CHAMOISEAU

CHAPTER ONE

Contexts and Intertexts

In Caribbean culture and literature, the storyteller has long been a figure who encodes the mysteries of community. Wilson Harris describes the Caribbean artist as a masquerading figure, a trickster, and a truth-teller who stands at the gateway "at the heart of the lie of community and the truth of community" where he or she discovers the potential for "a profoundly compassionate society committed to freedom within a creative scale."[1] While the trickster truth-teller figure emerges in the context of plantation society with its creolization of cultures and carnivalesque tradition of Caribbean masquerade,[2] he continues to have a role in a postcolonial world where neocolonial relations persist and new forms of imperialism, particularly through globalization, are emerging. In his 2007 novel *Un dimanche au cachot* (*A Sunday in Confinement*), Patrick Chamoiseau attests to the importance of masquerade as a means of relational expression:

> Du Marqueur de Paroles au Guerrier de l'Imaginaire *(ces masques dont je m'affuble pour décrocher les autres)*, chacun de mes livres a fixé des dimanches. [. . .] La dérive est totale. Je m'abandonne à ces ego que je fabrique, et que j'habite, et qui me squattent plus que nécessaire: ils vont en moi, et je vis en eux, pour explorer ce que le monde nous fait en dehors, en dedans. Je suis explosé d'écriture. En mots et en images. Chaque mot: un univers à inventer. Chaque image: un pays à trouver sans territoire et sans frontière. (*UDC*, 23; the emphasis is mine)

> (From the Word Scratcher to the Warrior of the Imaginary *[the masks I don in order to divest myself of others]*, each of my novels took place on Sunday. [. . .] The departure is absolute. I abandon myself to these egos I fabricate, and that I inhabit, and that squat inside me more than need be: they enter me, and I live in them, in order to explore that which the world makes of

us, outside and in. I am bursting with writing. In words and images. Each word is a universe to invent. Each image is a country to find, without territory and without frontiers.) (emphasis is mine)

For Chamoiseau, the invention of identities, such as Word Scratcher or Warrior of the Imaginary, serves as an authorial strategy for exploring the interactions among the world, the self, and the word through the activity of "la dérive" or imaginative wandering. This post-abolition wanderer (*le driveur*) is heir to the maroon slave and the freed slave: he is someone on the move who has moved beyond the forced migration and flight from slavery into a kind of creative wandering through time and space in order to articulate a new sense of place and dwelling (squatting) in the world.[3] As Chamoiseau suggests, this ongoing activity takes on a kind of genesiac potential as the writer's word has the potential to invent a new universe as well as to find new imagined countries without territories or borders. Yet, the very necessity of engaging in strategies of masquerade and wandering indicates that the task is at best an ambivalent one, carried out in the face of histories of dispossession and uneven power dynamics in the Caribbean and the wider world. Thus, Chamoiseau suggests that there is a need to both adopt and divest himself of masks as he works through the various guises and complexities of Martinican identity.

Patrick Chamoiseau: A Critical Introduction explores the ways in which the author's use of masks and phases of writing serve to interrogate contemporary postcolonial horizons as well as reenvision the Caribbean through creolization and the long history of globalization, which dates back to the age of exploration and colonial conquest. Tensions between fluidity and fixity are embodied in the dynamics of the narrative where the storyteller emerges as a figure who takes an active role as an agent and subject in highly politicized, unfolding storytelling processes and methods of textual transmission. The presence of the narrator as a trickster–truth-teller figure who serves as a mediator for the interplay of identities, often in an unreliable fashion, may begin with a quest to master the world through investigative narrative modes or pacts, but the instabilities of memory, place, relations to others, and cultural formation induce a fluid discursive world where concretely imagined details, persons, and events appear to be in flux. The shifting narrative ground defies certain knowledge and the formation of fixed identities in favor of a poetics where the negotiation and rerouting of identities, genres of narrative, languages, histories, and places enter into new imaginative fields of interactive, transformative relations.

More generally, *Patrick Chamoiseau: A Critical Introduction* presents an introduction to Chamoiseau's oeuvre and the growing field of related critical studies.[4] While the author is best known for his novel *Texaco* (1992), for which he was awarded the *Prix Goncourt*, theories of creolization, fictionalized memoirs of childhood, and novels relating to the creolization of culture, many of which have been translated into English and other languages, less attention has been given to Chamoiseau's recent fiction as well as his other writings as a dramatist, screenplay writer, comic book artist, activist, journalist, and educator. By taking into account the various facets of Chamoiseau's output and experience, this work aims to offer a broad overview of his accomplishments and contributions to postcolonial writing. This chapter provides a brief overview of the author's strategies of masquerade in Martinican and Caribbean contexts, main phases of writing as defined through role-play, and an overview of his reputation as an artist and activist. Subsequent chapters offer close readings of the author's work in a roughly chronological order except for the discussion of the author's autoethnographic fictional narratives of childhood and visual narratives, which are grouped together for the purposes of generic interpretation. Neglected or lesser-known works are brought into dialogue with the author's best-known fictions in order to investigate his poetics in a holistic fashion.

Chamoiseau's Strategies of Masquerade in a Martinican Context

The sense that Martinique is a land of disguise and riddling identities surfaces in Édouard Glissant's "Dispossession" where he questions the usefulness of offering an official account of Martinique's history: "Once this chronological table [see below] has been set up and completed, the whole history of Martinique remains to be unraveled. The whole Caribbean history of Martinique remains to be discovered."[5] For Chamoiseau, as for Glissant, a recognition of the illusion of a chronological history of Martinique's historical formation through conquest and slavery to departmentalization invites attempts to explore the masks and guises of its identity as well as to work toward the unraveling of identity formation in postcolonial terms. Chamoiseau's use of masks can be situated as a response to the "chronological illusion," which has been shaped through and by colonial discourses, as well as the landmarks or places and spaces that shape Martinican identity. Consequently, the author's encounters with and representations of postcolonial history, identity, spatiotemporality and language find an aesthetic correlative in various forms of narrative masquerade.

Table 1.   Landmarks: The Chronological Illusion

It is possible to reduce our chronology to a basic skeleton of "facts," in any combination. For instance:

1502	"Discovery" of Martinique by Columbus.
1635	Occupation by the first French colonizers. Beginning of the extermination of the Caribs. Beginning of the African slave trade.
1685	Proclamation of the *Code Noir*.
1763	Louis XV surrenders Canada to the English and retains Guadeloupe, Martinique, and St. Dominique (Haiti).
1789–1797	Occupation of Martinique by the British.
1848	Abolition of slavery.
1902	Eruption of Mt. Pelée. Destruction of St. Pierre.
1946	Departmentalization.
1975	Doctrine of "economic" assimilation.[1]

1. Glissant, "Dispossession," 13.

From a psychoanalytic perspective, masquerade is often intrinsic to the process of working through the unresolved traumas associated with the colonial past, specifically through the belated return of trauma in a disguised form. Dominick La Capra calls attention to traumatic masquerade when he observes that "what is denied or repressed in a lapse of memory [through trauma] does not disappear; it returns in a transformed, at times disfigured and disguised manner."[6] The many names, guises, and titles Chamoiseau has invented for himself can be seen as efforts to defy the trauma associated with the colonial imposition of slavery, language, and identity: Abel (the son of Adam and Eve, the brother Cain kills), *Oiseau de Cham* ("the Bird of Ham," a reference to the son Noah cursed, which was interpreted in the colonial context as a justification for slavery, which might also be a pun on Bird of the Field), *Chamgibier* (fieldgame, meaning where wild animals are present and presumably open to being killed), *Chamzibié, Ti-Cham, Fils de la Parole* (Son of the Spoken Word), ethnographer, investigator, *Marqueur de paroles* (Word Scratcher), *Guerrier de l'imaginaire* (Warrior of the Imaginary) and *l'éducateur* (educator). In adopting these names, Chamoiseau suggests the ways in which he remains both bound to and free from the constraints of the colonial past. The name *Oiseau de Cham* suggests a tendency to take flight from the slave past, but it also bears witness to the constitutive influence of slavery on identity (re)formation. In this context, Maeve McCusker's emphasis on the stretching of memory in Chamoiseau's oeuvre through its "nexus of interrelations, echoes and doublings" and practices of "linguistic camouflage" might be seen as symptomatic of traumatic displacement and disguise as well as of ongoing efforts to work through the past in the uncertain quest for postcolonial identity.[7] In this context, Chamoiseau's mystifying language games serve as efforts to initiate a sense of interpretive possibility and disclose the (dis)locations of meaning through (post)coloniality. Through his adaptation of the Glissantian notion of an opaque language of resistance, which represents an otherness that cannot be assimilated, and detours through space and time, the author works through the guises of trauma as well as the various triggers that serve to disclose relations among traumatic episodes in Martinique.

Any consideration of Chamoiseau's use of masquerade as an authorial strategy needs to take into account the long history of creolization in the Caribbean, which emerged through the interaction of indigenous, French, African, Asian, and other peoples and cultures in (post-)plantation environment and continues today in and beyond the region. Creolization refers to "a syncretic process of tranverse dynamics that endlessly reworks and transforms the cultural patterns of varied social and historical experiences and identities,"[8] which defies a sense of unitary origins or stable, fixed identity. Michaeline Crichlow suggests that through masquerade Creole subjects "seek to enlarge and transfigure their place in the world through the liminal state and the liminal performative."[9] Chamoiseau's account of his ongoing efforts to decipher, challenge, and renew identity through narration might be seen as embodying the transformative potential of Creole masquerade: "J'écris pour comprendre des choses. Je fais le point avec moi-même. Je n'essaie pas de refaire *Chronique des sept misères*, de refaire des recettes de *Solibo*, de refaire du *Texaco*. On peut voir l'évolution comme cela, ça change tout le temps, je cherche . . ."[10] ("I write in order to understand things. I take stock of myself. I do not try to remake *The Chronicle of Seven Sorrows*, or redo *Solibo*, or remake *Texaco*. One can see evolution in this way; it's constantly changing, I am searching . . ."). The author's quest for self-articulation takes place through unfinished processes of Creole masquerade: evident in his use of narrative masks, generic intermixtures, renaming, and creative wordplay. For Chamoiseau, the processes of creolization, which take place through deculturation, acculturation, and interculturation, together with the postcolonial rewriting of the past from a creolizing perspective open up rich possibilities for exploring the continuous, ambiguous unfolding of identity and culture. Thus, the pluralism, ambiguity, and instabilities of Creole masquerade form the basis for a wide-ranging, relational exploration of the postcolonial condition, and more recently, of worldly relations in a globalizing era; this rich signifying potential also enables the inscription of ambivalence, difference, and alternatives to prevailing paradigms for cross-cultural identity in and beyond the Caribbean.

Masquerade speaks to the duplicity, multiplicities, and incertitude of identity in spatiotemporal, sociopolitical, economic, and cultural terms. In the context of Caribbean culture, Gerard Aching argues that masking processes "articulate degrees of recognition, misrecognition and nonrecognition between masked subjects and viewing subjects."[11] Chamoiseau himself observes that Martinicans have inherited a complex set of hierarchical values as a result of colonization, which has contributed to an often conflicted sense of identity and spatiality.[12] Drawing on the work of Julie Lirus, who cites that of Albert Memmi and Frantz Fanon, Lorna Milne suggests that Eurocentric colonial discourses and practices led to a sense of role-playing and alienation in Martinique: individuals came to see the self as other, such as in the ways described by Fanon's *Peau noire, masques blancs* (*Black Skins, White Masks*).[13] In the context of colonialism and the postcolonial reclamation of history, we might consider Martinique's situation in relation to other Caribbean islands and communities.

Notably, a sense of ambivalence about past-present horizons is particularly acute in Martinique as a result of its specific history of accommodation to colonial powers. Martinique is a comparatively small Caribbean island whose size was not conducive to the establishment of maroon communities, such as those established in Jamaica or Haiti. As a result, it is sometimes said that Martinique suffers from a "Toussaint complex"[14] vis-à-vis Haiti, the first black republic, which has long demonstrated a tenacious drive for self-sufficiency. Yet, Martinique's current economic and political situation stands in direct contrast to the poverty and ongoing sociopolitical unrest in Haiti, which further complicates a sense of anxiety about the past-present horizons of resistance. Despite the recent strike action in Martinique (2009), with demands for higher wages and improved standards of living, Caryl Phillips describes the contemporary socioeconomic situation (during his travels to Guadeloupe, which is also an overseas department of France) when he observes that "the French Caribbean is the First World in tropical clothes."[15] Notably, the 2010 referendum, which held out the promise of greater autonomy for Martinique, was rejected by 80 percent of the population. Compared to other Caribbean and colonial struggles for independence in the twentieth century, Martinique's history can be read as one of accommodation, driven by a sense of pragmatism.

In 1946, Martinique opted for departmentalization, a decision that has subsequently rendered problematic and even hindered the processes of decolonization. Writing in 1962, V. S. Naipaul referred in a typically vituperative fashion to the "French colonial monkey-game"[16] of Martinique where "the myth of non-separation is carried to the extent that *routes nationales*, which presumably lead to Paris, wind through the Martiniquan countryside."[17] While Naipaul suggests both that processes of mimicry and disguise are evident in terms of identity and spatiality, Justin Daniel suggests that departmentalization itself raises the issue of masquerade: "la départmentalisation correspond-elle à une forme hétérodoxe de décolonisation ou au contraire au simple travestissement d'une phénomène colonial poursuivant *nolens volens* son devenir historique?" ("does departmentalization correspond to a heterodox form of decolonization or, on the contrary, is it a colonial phenomenon simply in disguise as it pursues, willingly or unwillingly, its historical becoming?").[18] H. Adlai Murdoch has made a convincing case for reading Chamoiseau's autobiographical works under departmentalization as examples of doubled discourse: "a joint product both of remembering and fictionalization, where memory is strategically placed as the service of complex fictional framework that seeks to create a distanced, doubled re-citation of real events and subjects."[19] More generally, Chamoiseau's techniques of masquerade might be seen as attesting to the displacements and detours of Martinican identity. Strategies of distancing, the fracturing of identities and motifs of circulation and displacement reflect the author's acute and ambivalent awareness of Martinique's (neo)colonial identity.

Furthermore, Chamoiseau extends the experimental processes of postcolonial rewriting and representation to the reader by inviting him or her to engage in the activity of deciphering the borderlands between genres, between narrative and authorial presences, between story and history, and between languages, such as French, Creole, and poetic language. Through allusions to the colonial archive, methods of transcription, mediation, and translation, Chamoiseau conveys a sense of the uneven, shifting grounds of history, community, and self-inscription: he fosters, disrupts, and renews the illusion of presence by inviting the reader to engage imaginatively in the narrative processes of articulation. Disruptive poetic techniques elicit a new encounter with past-present horizons by encouraging the reader to scrutinize the processes of transmission, knowledge, and power that shape the discourses of identity. In this sense, masquerade is an essential strategy for Chamoiseau because it enables him to reveal the various guises of Caribbean identity and history. While the author might put aside a given masque, the masquerade continues, fueled by the ongoing processes of traumatic recovery, energies of creolization, and the need to articulate a relational identity. Consequently, Chamoiseau's work might be seen as a contribution to the Martinican tradition of revolutionary poetics and political thought: the Negritude movement, struggles for decolonization, the critique of racial thinking, theories of creolization, and postcolonial poetics owe much to the work of Aimé Césaire, Fanon, and Glissant. According to Milne, Chamoiseau's poetics of displacement emphasize a relational sense of identity and way of being in the world—the Glissantian sense of a *mise-en-relation*—as opposed to the territoriality of empire.[20] His work can also be situated in relation to local writers who continue to unravel the dynamics of Creole culture, notably Raphaël Confiant and Tony Delsham, as well as writers from the wider Caribbean, especially Saint-John Perse[21] and Frankétienne, French, and world literatures. Unlike some of his peers, however, his creolizing poetics may be grounded in vernacular culture, but they are also open to the wider world through intertextual allusion and affiliation. Chamoiseau's techniques for masquerade potentially draw on a rich range of sources for (mis)recognizing and revealing Martinique's relational place and identity in the world, whether in light of Third World struggles, imperialism, or globalization.

A Rebel Comes of Age

Born in 1953, just seven years after the departmentalization of Martinique in 1946, Chamoiseau grew up in the urban environment of Fort-de-

France where he was witness to the modernizing transformations of Creole culture. His childhood coincided with the pivotal years of 1958–1964, which are as Richard Burton notes "without doubt the fulcrum of recent French West Indian history" marking the transition from the traditional agriculture-based economy of the past to "the massive tertiarized, consumer-oriented economy of the contemporary DOM" (Département d'Outre Mer).[22] As beet sugar became popular in Europe, the Martinican sugar industry entered into a decline from which it has never recovered. In the decade following departmentalization, as work on plantations declined dramatically, people migrated to urban environments, particularly Fort-de-France, in search of employment. The modernization of the city, including the decimation of the vegetable market, the declining use of the Creole language, the increase in French and American consumer goods and imports,[23] the influence of television, attempts to sanitize certain quarters in the city, problems with drug trafficking and other changes associated with departmentalization took place. Martinique began a process of *bétonisation* or urban development, which has eroded the natural landscape and undermined the ecosystems of the island.

Today, Fort-de-France is a lively center with markets, crowded inner-city pedestrian traffic (from Monday to Saturday), where tourists bump elbows with the local population, bars, restaurants, and shops. The colonial past and neocolonial present are inescapable in the city center with its monuments and statues that serve as reminders of colonization, slavery, abolition, service during the wars, and resistance to neocolonization, including the decapitated statue of Josephine in the Savane (1991), the statue of Victor Schoelcher in front of the *Palais de Justice*, the monument to those who served in the World Wars and the Algerian wars, the looming presence of the fort itself, the statue of Belain d'Esnambuc, and the Bibliothèque Schoelcher, a library whose inner walls are framed by the names of French Classical writers. The impact of tourism, which is especially evident in the southern part of the island, also touches Fort-de- France with its tourist market on the Savane and souvenir shops scattered throughout the city center. For some, the closure of the cinema on the Savane (as people flock to the air-conditioned comfort of Madiana's multiplex mall environment), and the suburban way of life led by many Martinicans attest to an increasingly French consumer society. Chamoiseau's writing has been touched in many ways by the contrast between the city of his childhood and present. His accounts of childhood document the transition toward the neocolonial French economy while his journalistic articles often show an intense sense of outrage at the ways in which departmentalization has undermined the local economy and its accompanying sense of self-sufficiency. In other instances, Chamoiseau's descriptions of the energies of the market culture in pre-departmental Martinique show signs of nostalgia for an era when there appeared to be wider scope for decolonization.

Patrick Chamoiseau is the youngest of five children. His father worked as a cobbler and then postman. He grew up in the center of the city in a street with a high concentration of inhabitants of Syro-Lebanese descent, Rue François-Arago. Symbolically, it seems that Chamoiseau's mother represented the maternal language of Creole while his father was associated with the paternal influence of proper French as well as French literature, particularly the fables of La Fontaine. In *Écrire en pays dominé*, Chamoiseau (the narrator of the autobiographical fiction) claims that his mother played an important role in forming his democratic reading habits and tastes. She bought books cheaply from a *djobeur* at the market: these could be sold at reduced prices, provided the covers were ripped off the works (*EPD*, 41). He records with delight the free intermixing of high and low genres of literature:

> Romans policiers ou recueils de poèmes, photos-romans italiens ou essais sans-images, bandes dessinées ou classiques littéraires... tout cela lui était égal-même-prix-ici. Son principe était d'activer les centres d'intérêt. (*EPD*, 43)

(Detective novels or collection of poems, Italian photographic novels or essays without images, comic books or literary classics... all of this had the same value for her. Her principle was to activate centers of interest.)

In an interview with Philippe Lançon, he offers another account of his childhood library and reading habits:

> Mes frères et mes soeurs avaient ramené de tas de prix de l'école sous forme de livres. Notre bibliothèque contenait ainsi tous les classiques. J'ai lu, enfant, les prix des mes aînés, tout en parlant créole avec ma mère et mes voisins. Je me récitais aussi *La légende des siècles*, de Hugo, et les poésies de François Villon. Ils sont toujours présents quand j'écris. Ma musique interne reste l'alexandrin, volte musicale de la langue française. J'ai aussi

lu très jeune *Alice aux pays des merveilles*, qui m'a donné le sens du merveilleux; puis *Germinal*, qui m'a donné le goût des petits gens.²⁴

(My brothers and sisters brought back many prizes from the school in the form of books, so our library contained all of the classics. I read, as a child, the prizes of my older siblings while at the same time speaking creole with my mother and neighbors. I also recited *The Legend of the Centuries* by Hugo and the poetry of François Villon. They are still present when I write. My internal music remains the alexandrine, the musical turn of the French language. While very young, I also read *Alice in Wonderland*, which gave me a sense of the marvelous, and *Germinal*, which gave me a taste for the concerns of the working class.)

His neocolonial education placed emphasis on canonical works of Western literature and the acquisition of standard French; at school, children were not permitted to speak Creole. Although he mastered written French, impressing his teachers with his written analysis and juvenile fiction, Chamoiseau claims he was often hesitant when speaking in French because he continued to think in Creole.²⁵ However, by early adolescence, he began to write poetry in French. Gradually though, partly through his friendship with Tony Delsham, he became interested in local literature and language, exploring new forms and genres as well as the use of Creole in the fictional work. This early confluence of languages and cultural influences, including local, French, and world literatures, has subsequently become a hallmark of Chamoiseau's poetics.

Chamoiseau came of an age during a period of unrest during which various efforts were made to acknowledge and foster a sense of Martinican identity. This era (the mid-1960s to mid-1970s) saw the formation of local theater troupes, storytelling groups, the creation of a school to teach a curriculum that would include Antillean subjects (Glissant's I.M.E. in 1967–1970), and the founding of GEREC-F (*Groupe d'Études et de Recherches en Espace Créolophone et Francophone*) at the Université des Antilles-Guyane in 1973. By the mid-1960s, anti-French feeling started to find expression in protests, including a 1965 protest organized by O.J.A.M. (*Organisation de la Jeunesse Anticolonialiste de la Martinique*) during which students were arrested for their pro-independence views. From 1965 to 1974, there were demonstrations, protests, riots, and strike actions. In 1971, a student protestor died as a result of a police beating, and in 1974, two banana workers were killed and many wounded during a strike at Chalvet plantation. Culturally, the flowering of Negritude created a globally self-conscious theater and artistic scene in which works of protest proliferated. It is against this backdrop that we can understand Chamoiseau's early rebel period as one of negotiating his artistic identity in the face of the dualities of the French-Creole language and neocolonial experience. He sought to find ways to integrate the realities of his Creole cultural identity and experiences. In the late 1960s and early 1970s, Chamoiseau experimented with science fiction, comic strips, and theatrical works. Chamoiseau has referred to this as a schizophrenic period when he attempted to become a French poet while also exploring a Creole self through his illustrations for comic books.

For Chamoiseau, the rebel is someone who is engaged in an oppositional struggle to a dominant system of oppression.[26] During his early rebel phase of writing (a term Chamoiseau uses), the author engaged in ardent expressions of anticolonialism and wrote poetry inspired by Aimé Césaire. Césaire's influence as poet, mayor, and anticolonialist thinker have had a formative and ongoing influence on the author, beginning with his early work as a would-be poet and aspiring activist until today.[27] Many of Chamoiseau's early writings—poems, plays, and comic books—reflect the influence of Negritude as well as the lyricism of Césaire's poetic voice. Despite his later opposition to Negritude, Césaire remains a key literary influence for Chamoiseau in terms of an experimental approach to poetic language, interest in the figure of revolt or anticolonial resistance, and the rewriting of canonical literary works of Western literature. In particular, Chamoiseau's engagement with *Et les chiens se taisaient* is evident from his earliest works in which a rebel figure is often present to his more recent fiction with the Warrior of the Imaginary as an alternative to the doomed rebel figure. As well, the idea of "les armes miraculeuses" or "miraculous weapons" seems to have inspired Chamoiseau's concept of writing as a form of battle. Moreover, as a Caribbean who combines the poet, the politician, the international spokesperson, and the theorist, Césaire provided a model for Chamoiseau's own multifaceted identity.

During his late adolescence, Chamoiseau's friend and occasional collaborator, Tony Delsham, played a significant role in the author's life. Delsham seems to have encouraged his younger friend to experiment with language at the interfaces of French-Creole. From 1972 to 1975, Chamoiseau worked with Delsham as the artistic director for Editions M.G.G. (Martinique Guadeloupe Guyane). Chamoiseau collaborated with

Delsham on a number of comics written in Creole and French, creating such characters as Monsieur Coutcha, Kadack, Papa Totone, Django, and Lulu. These comic works included Creole and creolized language, reflecting the kind of ribald vernacular touch that characterizes much of Delsham's proliferate novelistic writing and pervades some of Chamoiseau's own texts, notably *Solibo Magnifique* and *Texaco*. Indeed, the character of Bouaffesse in *Solibo* first emerges in the comic strip work. Throughout Chamoiseau's career, Delsham has done much to promote his friend's writing; in his role as editor of *Antilla*, a weekly magazine for the francophone Caribbean, he has given him the space to publish journalistic musings on local politics, culture, and other topics. Delsham offers an interesting counternarrative to Chamoiseau's rise to authorial fame because he founded his own press (Éditions M.G.G., known today as Martinique Éditions); he has a very loyal local readership in Martinique, but remains primarily a local literary and cultural figure. Delsham's works are firmly grounded in the everyday concerns of the local; he is attentive to contemporary concerns and issues such as unemployment, racial hierarchies, religious and ethnic differences, relations to the *metropole*, generational difference, economic migration, and so on. The specificity of his political concerns and his conversational prose style may perhaps account in part for a lack of readership beyond the Martinican audience.[28] Delsham's political ideas, humor, orality, and resistant modes of the imaginary are indications of a shared interest in the contours of urban space and the intimate as a highly contested, politicized sphere. The author also makes an appearance in *À bout d'enfance* in the guise of Tony, a member of the Antillean knights of the round table. An account of Chamoiseau's sense of locality and the role of vernacular culture needs to take into account Delsham's early and ongoing influence in the author's personal and professional life.

Upon graduation from the lycée, Chamoiseau taught French, geography, and history at Collège Lamennais.[29] In 1975, he left his post in Martinique and, like many Martinicans of his generation, participated in the exodus to France in search of better opportunities. Given his French citizenship and migration to France for education and work, Chamoiseau's career might be seen as influenced by the generation of 1968. While living in France, Chamoiseau completed a degree in law and sociology and worked as a social worker with prison inmates. In *Écrire en pays dominé*, he provides an account of this time period, including the enormous influence of Édouard Glissant's *Malemort* and Frankétienne's *Dézafi*. Combined with his experiences working in the French prison system, he claims to have undergone a kind of *prise de conscience* in 1976 at the age of twenty-three (*EPD*, 103). He observes: "Ma lutte contre la domination avait porté des fruits rebelles. Mais ces fruits militants m'avaient laissé stérile" ("My struggle against domination produced rebellious fruits. But these militant fruits left me sterile," *EPD*, 103). Among the works he describes from his rebel period are poems, comic books, and theater works, including works that critique modernization and the ill effects of departmentalization. For instance, his theater work entitled *Supermarché* deals with a couple who undergoes a kind of decomposition as the supermarket starts to take form (*EPD*, 78–79). He also wrote *Une tempête*, a play inspired by Aimé Césaire's adaption of Shakespeare's *The Tempest*. In his modern, anticolonial theatrical work, a cyclone provides the stormy environment for the confrontation between a storekeeper (the Prospero figure) and the *djobeur* (Caliban) who works as a stock boy for him (*EPD*, 79).

Despite Chamoiseau's claims that this early rebel period led to a sense of sterility, one can see the works themselves as a testing ground for poetic and political ideas that have continued to shape his career as a novelist. Theater proved to be the medium through which Chamoiseau negotiated a new relationship between his French-Creole selves. He began writing theatrical works, primarily in the form of a *pièce contée* where the storyteller plays an important role in the drama and as a narrator of the action. Among the theatrical works Chamoiseau wrote during this period, the best known are *L'Époque Delgrès* (1974), *Une manière d'Antigone* (1975), *Solitude la mulâtresse* (performed in 1976), and *Misère et misère double* (circa 1975). *L'Époque Delgrès* dramatizes the slave revolt in Guadeloupe while *Une manière d'Antigone* transposes Sophocles's Greek tragedy to the Antilles. *Solitude la mulâtresse* (a theatrical adaptation of André Schwarz-Bart's *La mulâtresse, Solitude*) was performed by the *Théâtre Fer de Lance* troupe at the thirtieth Festival of Avignon (1976). Narrating the story of this famous slave, maroon, and rebel, Chamoiseau explores the role of mother-daughter relations and violence under slavery. This performance work integrates songs, stories, drumming, and dance in representing the tale of the slave, maroon, and rebel. In 1984, this play was adapted and produced by *Théâtre de l'Air Nouveau* troupe at the Théâtre Noir in Paris and afterward in Guyana, Martinique, and Belgium. Luc Saint-Éloy provides a sense of this rebel phase when he describes the play *Antigone* as a response to the period during which Pierre Messmer was the minister, during which there were a number of student demonstrations, spontaneous uprisings, and even victims as one lycéen was killed (1971). In these works, Chamoiseau strives to use theater to foster a sense of heroic resistance through a history of revolts and *marronnage* and thereby to develop a collective consciousness.

In France (1975–1986), Chamoiseau's writing underwent a transformation, moving from ideologically driven protest fiction to works of greater poetic and political complexity. *Notre dernière chance*, a protest novel written in response to the wounding and deaths of Martinicans during an agricultural strike, was rejected by the publisher Seuil in 1976. Chamoiseau's anticolonial performance work (*pièce contée*), *Manman Dlo contre la fée Carabosse* was also written during this time and performed in Paris. Chamoiseau collaborated with the comic book illustrator, Georges Puisy (whom he had met through their work at Éditions M.G.G.) to create a pedagogical comic book history of the slave revolt in Guadeloupe, titled *Les Antilles sous Bonaparte: Delgrès* (1981). Written in French and Creole, the comic book is written in less vituperative style than the earlier play, *L'Époque*, upon which it is based.

Finally, Chamoiseau's formative years need to be situated in the context of worldwide colonial struggles for independence. France, like many other colonial powers, underwent a period of decolonization during the author's childhood, including wars and violent struggles in Algeria (1954–1962) and Indochina (modern-day Vietnam gained independence from France in 1954). The influence of these anticolonial struggles on his writing resonates in the future of the rebel. His epic novel, *Biblique des derniers gestes*, whose protagonist participates in various guerrilla struggles for freedom, revives a phase of postcolonial resistance, which seems to have greatly inspired the author. More generally, political radicalism is evident in his earlier works, which examine the negative effects of departmentalization and bear witness to the difficulties of decolonization that result from continued economic dependence on France. In particular, Frantz Fanon's *Damnés de la terre* (*Wretched of the Earth*) infuses the approach to decolonization in *Biblique* where it is presented as an ongoing struggle and the psychiatric ill effects of colonial legacies are cataloged. In many ways, the novel can be seen as an effort to revive the radicalism of the 1960s in the context of globalization, which is positioned by some as the latest wave of imperialism to threaten local identities. Even in these early years, however, one might situate Chamoiseau's engagement with anticolonial resistance, experiments in postcolonial drama, and interest in vernacular forms as part of a wider current of decolonizing Third World poetics.

Ethnography, Creolization, and the Word Scratcher

In the 1980s, Chamoiseau writes two novels that deal with the erosion of Creole vernacular traditions, including folklore, storytelling, the market tradition, and the Creole language, in face of departmentalization: *Chronique des sept misères* (1986) and *Solibo Magnifique* (1988). These novels can be seen as nostalgic to the extent that they return to the Martinique of Chamoiseau's youth and present a mournful perspective of the postcolonial present, but they also signal a destabilizing poetics through the metafictional interventions of the ethnographic narrator. These narratives of return engage in vital investigations of colonial Martinique, the residual influences of colonialism in the postcolonial era and document the rise of neocolonialism under departmentalization. *Chronique des sept misères* traces the years from colonization to departmentalization, following the migration from the country into the city of Fort-de-France. The energy of the markets and the *djobeurs* (those who make a living doing odd jobs, primarily in the markets) vitalize a novel that draws on oral storytelling, forms of dance, Creole language, and folklore. Recounting the story of Pipi through a myriad of related personal narratives, the novel traces Martinique's own transformation as the society moved from colonization to departmentalization. In *Solibo Magnifique*, Chamoiseau appears as a fictional character present in the unfolding story. This witness and murder suspect is described in the police report as a self-described Word Scratcher who is actually unemployed:

> Patrick Chamoiseau, surnommé Chamzibié, Ti-Cham ou Oiseau de cham, se disant "marqueur de paroles," en réalité sans profession, demeurant 90 rue François-Arago. (*SM*, 30)

> (Patrick Chamoiseau, nicknamed Chamzibié, Ti-Cham [Little Field] or Oiseau de cham [Bird of the field], calling himself the Word Scratcher, in reality has no profession, lives at 90 Francois-Arago Street. (*StM*, 11–12)

The novel presents the writer as an ethnographer in the markets who attempts to understand local culture and to record popular traditions. The history of the market presented in the *Chronique* and the decline of folk traditions recounted in *Solibo* as well as the author's address from his childhood home are indications that these novels revive memories in fictional form. According to Dominique Chancé, the Word Scratcher is rather paradoxically a type of author who does not write.[30] His posture is that of the *bricoleur*: "d'un chercheur désoeuvré qui ne sait pas vraiment ce qu'il cherche, d'un personnage embarassé de lui-même et se dissimulant" ("an idle searcher who does not really know what he is looking for, a character who is ill at ease with himself and who closes his eyes to certain things").[31] The notion of a deceptive person, perhaps someone who hides things from others because he is concealing them from himself, is suggestive of a profoundly ambivalent identity where disguise has become a way of life. The Word Scratcher may thus embody the everyday duplicities at work in a neocolonial society, but at the same time the adoption of this guise enables the author Chamoiseau to interrogate critically Martinican society.

With his return to Martinique in 1986, Chamoiseau began a more affirmative reconstitution of history through memory and Creole culture. His interest in Creole folktales and storytelling as forms of resistance is reflected in the collection *Au temps de l'antan: contes du pays Martinique*. In *Martinique* (a tourist guide), he offers a first articulation of the tenets of the Creolist movement: "la culture créole résulte du contact de l'Europe, de l'Afrique, de l'Asie, elle est une mosaïque de valeurs et de ethnies"[32] ("the creole culture results from the contact of Europe, Africa, Asia; it is a mosaic of values and ethnicities"). As a Creolist, Chamoiseau helped to launch the most important theoretical and creative movement in the francophone Caribbean at the end of the 1980s and throughout much of the 1990s. In 1988, together with Raphaël Confiant and Jean Bernabé, the authors presented *Éloge de la Créolité* at the *Festival caraïbe de la Seine-Saint-Denis*. This oral presentation was followed by a dual-language (English/French rather than French/Creole) edition. Despite criticism on many fronts (which I discuss later in this work), *Éloge* sparked productive debates about creolization and postcolonial aesthetics as well as fostered new directions in francophone Caribbean fiction, particularly during the 1990s.

Specifically, the claims concerning the reconstitution of collective memory through personal narrative and the reactivation of Creole vernaculars inspired a number of important works. Chamoiseau and Confiant cowrote *Lettres créoles. Tracées antillaises et continentales de la littérature: Haiti, Guadeloupe, Martinique, Guyane: 1635–1975* (1991). This literary history highlights the importance of the *conteur* (storyteller) on the plantation as a figure of resistance and attests to the importance of Glissant's in outlining new directions for postcolonial writing, particularly as incarnated in the figure of the *Marqueur de paroles* (Word Scratcher). The *Marqueur* is able to disclose new historical horizons through the presentation of a narrative composed of alternative chronologies, multiple stories, and the "voices" of many storytellers. For Chamoiseau, the Word Scratcher first appears in *Solibo Magnifique*, but it is not until *Texaco* that this narrative presence comes to the foreground in a fully developed way. Nonetheless, Glissant recognized the incipient presence of the *Marqueur* in Chamoiseau's work when he wrote a preface to the 1988 edition of *Chronique des sept misères* in which he observes:

> Dans l'univers multilingue de la Caraïbe, il nous avertit lui-même qu'il se considère comme un "marqueur de paroles," "oiseau de Cham" ou "Chamgibier," à l'écoute d'une voix venue de loin, dont l'écho plane sur les lieux de notre mémoire et oriente nos futurs. C'est reconnaître qu'il marche à cette lisière de l'oral et l'ecrit ou se joue une des perspectives actuelles de la littérature. (*CSM*, 6)

> (He himself informs us that in the multilingual world of the Caribbean, he sees himself as *"marqueur de paroles,"* a *"Chambgibier"* or *"oiseau de Cham,"* listening to a distant voice whose echo hovers over the scenes of our collective memory and guides our future. This is an acknowledgment that he walks the line between the spoken and the written word, one of the crucial perspectives in literature today.) (*CSS*, ix)

Glissant's tribute ends with the invocation to take pleasure in listening to Chamoiseau. This account of *oraliture* orients us toward Chamoiseau's accomplishments (already thematized in *Manman Dlo* as a written version of an oral performance). Although Chamoiseau's sometimes unreliable *Marqueur* rejects the notion of *oraliture* (*SM*, 169–70) in favor of collecting and transmitting stories in written form, his textual interventions serve to introduce oral accounts and testimonial evidence in *Solibo Magnifique* and in *Texaco*. Inevitably, the Marqueur negotiates multiple fields (*champs*) of discourse in both written and oral form (or at least gives the reader an illusion of orality).

The importance of Creole language, culture, and community is explored in his first two narratives of childhood, *Antan d'enfance* (1990) and

Chemin-d'école (1994). The latter work examines the role of the educational system in repressing Creole language and culture and can be read as an urban response to Joseph Zobel's *La rue Case-Nègres* (*Black Shack Alley*), published in 1950. Zobel's work deals with childhood as experienced between the World Wars through an account of a child who moves from the rural environment of the declining plantation economy to Fort-de-France. The quest for literacy, education, and upward mobility are shown in direct contrast to the colonial imperatives still at work in society and its institutions. Unlike Zobel's chronological approach, which is closer to a testimonial narrative, Chamoiseau's autobiographical project leapfrogs throughout his life, dividing it up into epochs and shifts that reflect the child's own phenomenological, linguistic, and biological changes. *Antan d'enfance* (1990) and *Chemin-d'école* (1994) record the early years. *Écrire en pays dominé* (1997) picks up his life story in the mid-1970s and *À bout d'enfance* (2005) finally returns to the end of childhood and burgeoning adolescence.

Chamoiseau has collaborated in a number of visual arts and multimedia projects. *Guyane: Trace-mémoires du bagne* (1994) is an essay on memory, monuments, and history that accompanies Rodolphe Hammadi's photos. Photographic books with Jean-Luc de Laguarige include: *Elmire des sept bonheurs: confidences d'un vieux travailleur de la distillerie Saint-Etienne* (1998), *Métiers créoles* (1999), and *Cases des Îles Pays-Mêlés* (2000). *Émerveilles* (1998), an illustrated collection of stories for children (and adults), was created with the painter Maure. Two of the stories from *Au temps de l'antan* were reprinted as a book for children with illustrations by William Wilson in *Le commandeur d'une pluie suivi de L'Accra de la richesse* (2002). He has written the text for a beautifully illustrated postcolonial graphic novel, entitled *Encyclomerveille d'un tueur* (2009). Five feature-length screenplays have been released, including *L'Exil du roi Béhanzin* (1994), *Passage du milieu* (2000), *Biguine* (in cinemas in 2004), and *Aliker* (2008) under the direction of Guy Deslauriers as well as *Nord-Plage* (2003/2004) under the direction of José Hayot. As an art critic, Chamoiseau has expressed his admiration for Louis Laouchez and Serge Hélénon—two of the most important contemporary Martinican artists and founders of "L'École Négro-Caraïbe"—in tributes to the artists, titled *Laouchez: Traces caraïbes* (1997) and *Les bois sacrés d'Hélénon* (2002). The text he wrote for *Trésors cachés et patrimoine naturel de la Martinique vue du ciel* (2007) reflects his interests in a geo-poetical/political reading of the island.

Activism and the Warrior of the Imaginary

Ecological concerns, urban development, and the impact of tourism inform Chamoiseau's concerns with the places and histories that shape the real and imagined spaces of this tiny island. While an interest in ecocritical perspectives is evident already in the 1980s with *Manman Dlo* and *Chronique*, he did not immediately turn to ecological activism. In 1992, he became one of the founding members of MODEMAS (Mouvement des Démocrates et des Écologistes pour une Martinique Souveraine), an eco-political party that regularly comments on developments in the built and natural environment. By 1993, this spirit of activism is evident in his column for *Antilla*, a weekly edited by Delsham. Launched under the title "Une semaine en pays dépendent,"[33] he changed the title in the subsequent issue to "Une semaine en pays dominé."[34] In this column, Chamoiseau mixes together observations about current events in Martinique, book reviews, acerbic remarks about certain individuals, discussions about the role of literature, and thoughts on modes of resistance. A mixture of pragmatism and poetics, it foregrounds some of the themes that are more fully articulated in *Écrire en pays dominé* (1997). During this decade, Chamoiseau would also become more vocal in his political views. For instance, in response to the 150th anniversary of the abolition of slavery (1988), he denounced slavery as a crime against humanity.[35] In 2001, partly due to Chamoiseau's influence, the French government officially adopted this position when it ratified the Taubira law, which declared slavery to be a crime against humanity.

In 1993, the *guerrier* consciousness emerges in Chamoiseau's journalism where he seeks to critique and attack the various signs and traces of a dominated imaginary. The first image of this warrior appears in *L'Exil du roi Béhanzin* (1994), where the African warrior is envisioned as a kind of prophet for a postcolonial view of creolization and diasporic identities. In 1997, with the publication of *L'Esclave vieil homme et le molosse* and *Écrire en pays dominé*, the Warrior of the Imaginary or *Guerrier de l'imaginaire* is born in narrative and theoretical form. He observed that "le guerrier est plus large que le marqueur de paroles" ("the warrior is greater than the Word Scratcher").[36] Claiming we live in a world where we can no longer master the real and where the unexpected is all that we can count on, Chamoiseau described the new domain of fiction and the creative writer's role in this field as follows:

La fiction que nous devons imaginer est une fiction particulière, à la fois intime et ouverte. Intime, parce qu'il faut construire le lieu et qu'on a une mythologie personnelle, et ouverte, parce que nous sommes agis par la totalité monde. Le grand débat, le grand drame que nous vivons aujourd'hui, c'est ça. Le marqueur de paroles était dans une problématique qui est quand même ouverte, une problématique d'oral/écrit: organiser le relais et rassembler les deux—plus de domination de l'un sur l'autre, ou de prééminence—, ça nous a donné l'oral et l'écrit, donc il faut faire avec, ça concerne tous les écrivains du monde. Mais le guerrier prend plus de choses en compte, les gestes, les formes de domination, silencieuse, enfin, beaucoup de choses.[37]

(The fiction that we should imagine is a particular fiction, at once intimate and open. Intimate, because it is necessary to construct the setting and because one has a personal mythology, and open, because we are acted upon by the totality-world. This is the great debate, the great drama that we live today. The Word Scratcher dealt with a problematic that is nevertheless open, a problematic of the oral/the written: to organize the relay points and to reassemble both—no longer a case of domination by one or the other, or of preeminence—this gave us the oral and the written; so we must work with both, and this concerns all writers in the world. But the warrior takes more things into account, gestures, forms of domination, which are silent, basically, many things.)

With the transition from the Word Scratcher to the Warrior of the Imaginary, Chamoiseau seeks to address relations among various forms of domination throughout history. Increasingly, he is attentive to the rise of globalization and shifting definitions of empire.

With his theory of the *Pierre-Monde*, which echoes the Glissantian *Tout-Monde*, and his descriptions of creolization as a model for globalization, Chamoiseau has increasingly come to sound like an adherent of Glissant. Chamoiseau's writing, particularly since 1997, contains Glissantian echoes and intertextual references: examples include *L'Esclave vieil homme et le molosse* (1997), *Écrire en pays dominé* (1997), *Biblique des derniers gestes* (2002), *Un dimanche au cachot* (2009), and *Les neufs consciences du malfini* (2009). In *Biblique*, Glissant is depicted in a pantheon of Third World heroes and theorists of decolonization, alongside Frantz Fanon and others. This might seem somewhat surprising, but Glissant is also an important activist in the Caribbean. With the foundation of the *Institut Martiniquais d'Études* in the late 1960s, Glissant established a curriculum that reflected local Caribbean contexts and subjects of study. Glissant also played a strong role in local culture and politics, founding the journal *Acoma* in 1971, arguing for independence and critiquing Martinican neocolonization. This kind of activism inspired Chamoiseau and their recent works together, such as the coauthored texts entitled *Quand les murs tombent* (2007) and *L'Intraitable beauté du monde: Adresse à Barack Obama* (2009) and their contribution to *Manifeste pour les "produits" de haute nécessité* (2009), affirm a sense of postcolonial solidarity in a changing world order.

Since the latter half of the 1990s, Chamoiseau often turns to the marvel (*Émerveilles, Écrire en pays dominé, L'Esclave vieil homme et le molosse, Biblique de derniers gestes, À bout d'enfance, Un dimanche au cachot,* and *Les neufs consciences du Malfini*) as a genre suited to the location of Martinican identity in relation to the wider world. In the afterword to *Émerveilles*, Chamoiseau describes this as a poetics that goes beyond marvelous realism as it is already known in Haiti, the Antilles, and Latin America (*E*, 126). The *émerveille* functions through admixture and juxtaposition to mobilize legends, myth, fables, inexplicable events, and stories by mixing and cutting them together in a strange and fantastic manner (*E*, 126). Quotations are used more often as a way of establishing a multilevel text or introducing points of relay to other writers. Inspired by Glissant's reading of Gilles Deleuze and Félix Guattari, the narrative increasingly takes a rhizomatic form in which multiple points of entry are possible. The texts themselves come to mirror the constructs of nature: the forest, the waters, and the sedimented layers of rock and earth serve as ways of envisioning and writing these new textual landscapes. The self is constructed in dialogue and often through creative intersections with the Other. This *bricolage* (creolizing intermixture) of the self is evident in all of the works during this period. A sense of place is construed as both the product and process of criss-crossed narratives, which reflect the material flows in, through, and out of the region as well as networks of affiliation to other places in the world.

Nonetheless, Chamoiseau's poetics remain attentive to creolizing processes and the "wounds of locality," to borrow a phrase from Richard Watts.[38] The return of the rebel figure in *Biblique*, the rootedness of this vision in the Martinican imaginary and the emphasis on the geo-poetical perspective form part of a politicized aesthetic that is grounded in locality. At the same time, one might refer to Arjun Appadurai's theory of "-scapes" to describe Chamoiseau's attentiveness to the ways in which Martinique has participated in the long history of globalization. Specifically, Chamoiseau's interest in the Warrior of the Imaginary attests to his growing concern with what Appadurai refers to as *"the imagination as a social practice."*[39] In Chamoiseau's view, the cultural shock and the flows of creolization serve as forerunners to the processes of globalization. Moreover, creolization is a form of world interaction that offers a positive alternative to forms of social injustice the author sees as associated with global capitalism and new forms of imperialism. Chamoiseau remains guardedly optimistic about the possibilities for resistance, pointing to the history of creolization and the poetics of relational thinking as alternatives to the proliferation of global inequities.

To summarize, Chamoiseau's writing incorporates various, shifting storytelling masks and guises, such as the rebel, the *Fils de la parole* (Son of the Spoken Word), the *Marqueur de paroles* (Word Scratcher), the *Guerrier de l'imaginaire* (Warrior of the Imaginary), and the *l'éducateur* (Educator). As a correlative to this narrative trope of masquerade, Chamoiseau's poetics can be seen as shaped by complex strategies of disguise and transformation. In giving expression to the interfaces among genres, languages, and cultural forms, the rich poetics of masquerade and experimentation infuses both form and content. While his writing bears the imprint of the complex legacies of colonialism, the ambivalent conditions associated with departmentalization and the malign effects of globalization, it also fosters a sense of productive alternatives that emerge through multiple, shifting relations among peoples, vernaculars, places, times, and discourses. Consistently, Chamoiseau's poetics challenge ways of imagining the flows, routes, displacements, and creative metamorphoses of Caribbean identities.

Chamoiseau's Literary Reputation and Influence

Recognition of the excellence and importance of Chamoiseau's work has come in the form of numerous literary prizes, the widespread translations of many of his works, and recognition from fellow writers. *Chronique des sept misères* won the *Prix Kléber Haedens* and the *Prix de l'île Maurice*. Chamoiseau was awarded the *Grand prix de la littérature de jeu-*

nesse for *Au temps de l'antan* (1988) and the *Prix Carbet de la Caraïbe* for *Antan d'enfance* (1993). For *Texaco*, he won the prestigious Prix Goncourt in 1992. In 2002, he won the *Prix Spécial du Jury RFO* for *Biblique des derniers gestes*. Today, thanks to translation in over thirty languages, Chamoiseau's readership consists of a truly global audience. In addition to *Texaco*, works such as *Éloge de la Créolité*, *Solibo Magnifique*, *Antan de l'enfance*, and *Chemin-d'école* hold a place in world literature through translation. Milan Kundera's laudatory essay, entitled "The Umbrella, the Night World, and the Lonely Moon," which appeared in the *New York Review of Books* (1991), signaled Chamoiseau's success as a world author. Nonetheless, he remains a vital source for fellow Caribbean authors in the francophone, hispanic, and anglophone Caribbean. Austin Clarke acknowledges Patrick Chamoiseau's *Texaco* as the source of inspiration for *The Polished Hoe*, stating, "I wanted to be able to do for Barbados what Chamoiseau did for Martinique."[40] Junot Díaz credits Chamoiseau's *Texaco* as a source of inspiration for his Pulitzer-Prize-winning novel, *The Brief Wondrous Life of Oscar Wao*. Both the footnotes and the subject of Díaz's novel, which features the spectral presence of a subject who dies an unexpected death as occurs in *Solibo*, can be seen as tributes to the author.

Chamoiseau plays with and at the interfaces of French and Creole. Like James Joyce or Rabelais (whom Chamoiseau admires), he is concerned with the creative spaces between languages and the interplay among linguistic registers. Caryl Phillips compares Chamoiseau to Salman Rushdie in "Patrick Chamoiseau: Unmarooned" where he observes that the author "tells the history of his people in great polyphonic rushes of words and ideas, all the while reveling in name play, punning, parenthetical asides, strange but effective metaphors and a highly effective penchant for affecting the stuttering rhythms of speech."[41] In works that celebrate the polyphony of language and genres, his prose self-consciously explores the alchemy of language: the poetic, political, and philosophical implications of the various spaces and registers of linguistic interplay. Phillips's description of this tradition's distinct techniques and rhythmic patterns might well be applied to Chamoiseau's novels and stories:

> Its restlessness of form, its polyphonic structures, its yoking together of man and nature, of past and present, its linguistic dualities and its unwillingness to collapse into easy narrative closure appeared to me to be characteristics that had grown out of something specific to the Caribbean region.[42]

In his quest to demonstrate the power of the imaginary as a vehicle for radical critique and self-creation, Chamoiseau has simultaneously transformed the French-Caribbean novel and forged a distinctive vernacular tradition.

While most readers revel in Chamoiseau's creolized language style, his approach to Creole language and identity has been a contentious subject. When Raphaël Confiant, Jean Bernabé, and Chamoiseau collaboratively authored *Éloge de la créolité*, they sparked heated discussions about the role of language, cultural identity, racial constructs, and Caribbean identity. Rejecting Aimé Césaire's Negritude, they recognize Édouard Glissant's Antillean concept of identity as the basis for an affirmation of creolization. They argued for the need to recover interior vision through a reconnection to Creole language and culture. Chamoiseau's collection of Creole folktales, *Au temps de l'antan* (1988) and subsequent history of Creole literature, *Lettres créoles* (cowritten by Confiant and Chamoiseau, 1991), demonstrated the role of Creole storytelling as a form of resistance. The influence of creolist theory can be measured in part by the many thoughtful (sometimes virulent) debates it has provoked. In "A Letter to Chamoiseau," Derek Walcott observes that he remains unconvinced by the eulogy to Creoleness, but praises *Texaco* as a great novel. Speaking of its relevance for Caribbeans, Walcott writes:

> I would press the book into the hands of every West Indian as if it were a lost heirloom, even on those who cannot read. After that formality, I would run through the markets with vendors in the shade of huge umbrellas, past abandoned fountains, stopping traffic with an uplifted hand, entering dark retail stores selling fading ledgers and disintegrating chalks, preaching "You have to read this book, it is yours! It has come to reclaim you!"[43]

Maryse Condé makes ironic reference to Chamoiseau in *Traversée de la mangrove* as the "gifted Martinican writer" who deconstructs the "French-French language."[44] Elsewhere she has stated her opposition to the need to see the Creole language as essential to a resistant poetics. In recent years, Chamoiseau has stated his support for a Glissantian appreciation of the ongoing process of creolization as opposed to an essentialist celebration of Creole culture.

Chamoiseau's contributions to the francophone Caribbean film industry and the promotion of Caribbean visual arts stem from the desire to foster local forms of self-expression. Rejecting externally imposed visions of the Caribbean, such as those projected through colonialism or via tourism, he works actively to foster alternative images and vernacular visions of the francophone Caribbean islands and their peoples. This work covers a number of genres: the tourist guide (*Martinique*), comic books, screenplays, children's literature, and collaborations with photographers. *Émerveilles* presents a map of Martinique as a space of marvels; educational comic books, such as *L'Époque Delgrès*, celebrate histories of colonial resistance; collections of photographs offer a prosaic look at images of Martinicans and Guadelopeans in their daily lives or celebrate the diverse ecosystem of the island from a geopolitical perspective (*Martinique vue du ciel*). In addition to his work in French film, Walter Mosley's loosely translated version of *Passage du Milieu*, which is distributed as *The Middle Passage* in North America, has extended the film's influence to North American viewers. As a judge at the Cannes film festival, Chamoiseau has played a role in the fostering of World Cinema. In the realm of the fine arts, Chamoiseau has written tributes to members of *L'École Négro-Caraïbe*, Serge Hélénon, and Louis Laouchez.

An opinionated social critic and sometimes strident political activist, Chamoiseau is keenly interested in ecological issues, theories of globalization and other sociopolitical concerns. A former student of law and socioeconomics, he currently works as a social worker with juvenile delinquents and troubled youth in Martinique for the Ministry of Justice. In his acerbic journalistic writings (published primarily in *Antilla*) and through his work as an ecologically minded political activist, Chamoiseau contributes in more pragmatic ways to Martinican society. Along with Raphaël Confiant and Garcin Malsa, he is a founding member of MODEMAS, a political party with a strong interest in preserving the ecological balance of Martinique. Like Édouard Glissant and Aimé Césaire before him, Patrick Chamoiseau combines poetic thinking with a keen interest in effecting cultural and sociopolitical change in Martinican society. Rejecting the tenets of Negritude, the author's political thought is grounded in a Creolist sensibility, but shaped in a rather paradoxical fashion by the Glissantian sense of a relational and fluid identity. If, as Chamoiseau suggests, the great challenge today is to bring the poetic and the pragmatic together, his life and literature might arguably be said to offer an example of how this task might be accomplished.

Nonetheless, the author and his work are not without detractors at home and abroad. Some postcolonial and francophone literary critics see the author's ideas, politics, and writing as embodying the perils associated with a reactionary quest for a resistant space of identity through nostalgic essentialism or folkloric motifs. Referring to Chamoiseau's novels, J. Michael Dash poses the issue of resistance in provocative terms when he observes that "Martinique risks being the privileged site of metropolitan tropical fantasy with which even those who appear to resist are involuntarily complicit."[45] In these contexts, Chamoiseau's emphasis on a return to the colonial past in an effort to recuperate history from below or investigate past-present relations, is often seen as predetermined by a sense of unease regarding Martinique's complicit role in colonial and neocolonial processes. The author is seen as engaging in acts of imaginative marooning[46] in defiance of contemporary realities. Chamoiseau is seen by some as favoring a *passéiste* perspective[47] and critics question his uses and representations of history, arguing that the Creolist is heavily biased by a willful desire for a resistant identity. Writing in 1997, Richard and Sally Price observe that there "is a tendency for the literary works of the créolistes to be complicitous with the celebration of a museumified Martinique," which "promotes a 'feel good' nostalgia for people who are otherwise busy adjusting to the complexities of a rapidly modernizing lifestyle."[48] In particular, the mythic dimensions of Chamoiseau's historical narratives can be seen as a problematic attempt to recuperate idealized or heroic histories in order to prop up or foster a sense of postcolonial resistance. Lucien Taylor summarizes these kinds of criticism when he notes that critics take the Creolists to task for promoting a "long-lost Creole plenitude, before the deluge of departmentalization" and argues that "Créolité offers little more than a post-modern pastiche of Creole culture, a vision of the Antilles riddled with alienated exoticisms, designed to appeal to the *doudouesque* desires of foreigners."[49] In response to these and other critical perspectives about Chamoiseau's colonial nostalgia, McCusker's *Patrick Chamoiseau: Recovering Memory* and Milne's *Patrick Chamoiseau: Espaces d'une écriture antillaise* present nuanced analyses of the author's complicated engagement with colonial spaces as well as the traumatic legacies of slavery.

While Chamoiseau has never been as contentious a figure as some Caribbean author, such as V. S. Naipaul, he has nonetheless provoked debate and entered into public squabbles. As a spokesman and writer in the activist tradition, Chamoiseau has often been criticized for failing to offer sufficiently nuanced perspectives. Some critics see binaries at work in his fiction or view oppositional patterns as part of an ongoing desire for narratives of resistance.[50] As a Creolist, Chamoiseau has been criticized alongside Bernabé and Confiant for harboring a fixed, essentialist understanding of identity rather than an attitude of openness to the ongoing processes of creolization.[51] Chamoiseau's gender politics are seen as problematic by those who argue that he advances an erotic, exoticizing image of the Caribbean, particularly Martinique.[52] The author's activism and attacks on literary critics often take an overly strident form in certain instances, which leads some to question his judgment and willingness to engage in an open critical dialogue about his work.[53] Some Martinicans see contradictions between Chamoiseau's neo-Marxist political views and his elitist, highly literate and densely wrought poetics; they also question the viability of the author's proposals for eco-friendly economic development.[54] Following these various critical perspectives, some might argue that Chamoiseau's global popularity is fueled in part by a metropolitan desire for narratives of local resistance, emancipation, erotic otherness, and exotic locales. His depictions of Martinique represent a version of the postcolonial condition that is least troubling or even most appealing to the metropolitan reader. However, other critical perspectives suggest that the author is seen as deconstructing the very images he represents through the creolizing dynamics of his narrative discourses. To my mind, careful distinctions need to be made about Chamoiseau's earlier and more recent works as well as between his activism and his writing. Chamoiseau began writing in an oppositional way, which he describes as his early rebel phase. Yet, even in his early work, he has begun to develop techniques of masquerade and metafiction and introduce the motifs of conversion, initiation, and ongoing transformation. Although Chamoiseau often adopts the position of strategic essentialism when it comes to politics, his techniques of masquerade and disguise serve to resist fixity and invite ambivalent explorations of the postcolonial dynamics of Martinique.

Chamoiseau participates in the pan-Caribbean and diasporic literary movements that emerged in the twentieth century and persist today as writers confront the challenge of creating a literary tradition and fostering a vernacular that gives adequate expression to the dynamics of the postcolonial experience. Like Glissant, Derek Walcott, Frankétienne, Kamau Brathwaite, and Wilson Harris, Chamoiseau brings a cosmic but worldly perspective to the Caribbean imaginary, which he seeks to articulate through writing as an act of ongoing and incomplete genesis. In recent years, his engagement with the local postcolonial concerns of Martinique, particularly manifest in the processes of creolization and the challenges inherent in decolonization, also touches on concerns relevant to the globalizing world of transnational flows and transcultural formation. In this respect, Chamoiseau's work which might be read at the interfaces of the local and the global through his ongoing concerns with the extended work of creolization as well as shifting experiences and conceptions of empire.

CHAPTER TWO

Insurgent Performance Works

Patrick Chamoiseau has described his early writing as his rebel phase. He sees the rebel as someone who revolts in tactical rather than strategic ways: "dépendant de l'oppression dont il est victime—il est dépendant de l'agresseur, il réagit à l'attaque de l'agresseur" ("the rebel remains dependent on the oppression of which he is a victim—he is dependent on the aggressor, he reacts to the attack of the aggressor").[1] Opposed to the (neo)colonial present, the rebel remains caught in a fight-or-flight response. While Chamoiseau celebrates the insurgent impulse in all its forms, he is opposed to the rebel as a figure who seeks to evade or retreat from history, such as is the case with the maroon whose nostalgic yearnings for an African past lead to a regressive form of community. A rebel may reject the colonial system, but that does not mean that he envisions a world beyond colonial discourses; even when a measure of freedom is achieved, the rebel has yet to work through the trauma of colonization and engage fully in efforts to decolonize the imaginary. Chamoiseau's rebels are marooned slaves or other heroic figures of protest, including Louis Delgrès (the Martinican-born soldier who led a slave revolt in Guadeloupe), Antigone (transposed to Martinique), Solitude the mulatto, and Manman Dlo, who defy slavery, oppression, and colonization. Chamoiseau's early theatrical works attest to the author's shifting strategies for rebellion as he experiments with tenets of Negritude, *Antillanité*, and an emerging Creolist sensibility. However, even in these early works, Chamoiseau moves from rebellion toward a more complicated poetico-political drama of decolonization. The rebel is situated in contexts that call into question strategies of resistance, representation, and processes of decolonization. By incorporating various modes and genres of performance (such as dance, music, drumming, storytelling, and other modes of vernacular performance), Chamoiseau's drama can be seen as aspiring to a total performance. Together his performance works offer a fascinating look at how he develops the playfully self-conscious narrative techniques, which are characteristic of his mature work. Chamoiseau focuses on narratives that entail transformations of consciousness as individuals and communities experience the destabilizations of consciousness associated with the uneven dynamics of Creole culture in (neo)colonial contexts. In this early body of work, the trope of the anticolonial rebel initiates a symbolic *j'ouvert* (meaning *jour ouvert* or opening day of carnival) for the revolutionary postcolonial that has yet to unfold.

Two of the most important developments during this period are the introduction of the storyteller as a mediating figure and articulation of the imaginary as a field of transformation. One could apply one of Chamoiseau's own axioms to this period: "The domain of the imaginary is an absolutely fundamental theater for resistance."[2] Chamoiseau's work during this period inverts this axiom for the theatricality of the *pièce contée* (story performance), and the comic book provided Chamoiseau with the means to articulate the work of the imaginary as a domain of resistance. Chamoiseau claims to have written many plays during the 1970s, many of which were produced in Martinique as well as some in France. Unfortunately, only one play is readily available in print, *Manman Dlo contre la fée Carabosse* (published in 1982, written in 1977). Two theatrical works are available in manuscript form at the Schoelcher library in Fort-de-France: *L'Époque Delgrès* (manuscript, 1974) and *Solitude, la mulâtresse* (undated manuscript, performed in 1976 at the Festival d'Avignon). *Une manière d'Antigone* (manuscript, 1975) is available in manuscript form while *Misère et misère double* is not to be found easily in manuscript form despite references to the work in the 1982 edition of *Manman Dlo*. Together, these works offer a sense of the poetic and political issues that shaped the author's early artistic development.

The comic books, particularly in the oppositional use of French-Creole language, provide evidence of a rebel sensibility. Chamoiseau has referred to this early period as one that was "a bit schizophrenic," during which he had two personalities, including "a superego that was very French, and another part that was freer, more secret, more underground, which found expression in the cartoons."[3] In the comic book *Antilles sous Bonaparte* (1981), Chamoiseau juxtaposes French and Creole, but he is not yet practicing the Chamoisification of languages. Creole is set against French and used for emphatic purposes, to express emotion, as a mode of resistance to the colonial and as a means of expressing solidarity within the community of rebels. This sense of liberty is also evident in the illustrations that Chamoiseau as a comic strip illustrator and in producing the illustrations for *Maman Dlo*. In the Martinique Hebdo and M.G.G., Chamoiseau's characters appeared, including Monsieur Coutcha, Kadack, Lulu, and Papa Totone. In the illustrations for *Manman Dlo* (1982), *Colik* (Éditions M.G.G. reprinted it in 1982), and *Le retour de Monsieur Coutcha* (1972 in Le journal M.G.G.), one sees Chamoiseau's playful humor quite literally illustrated. These antirealist drawings capture the wit, whimsy, and satire that permeate Chamoiseau's writing. *Le retour de Monsieur Coutcha* is particularly noteworthy for it contains a brigadier named Bouafesse, instances of police violence, and a critique of colonial ideologies that resonated in the police attitudes toward Antillean citizens during this time period. Monsieur Coutcha represents the Martinican archetype of the "Major": a local figure who crystalizes the "la révolte de tous" or the rebellion of all in face of the *déveine* (rotten luck or misfortune) of postcolonial life. Coutcha also seems to be part *driveur*, a kind of modern-day urban maroon and figure of resistance. Finally, he is a carnivalesque figure, embodying a comic celebration of Caribbean culture. Chamoiseau created the cartoon drawings, which accompanied Tony Delsham's text (who was responsible for the Creole-French dialogue). This antecedent to *Solibo Magnifique* introduces elements central to the novel, such as the interplay of languages, the comic treatment of the characters, and the presence of Bouafesse (different spelling of the name from the novel) in an earlier part of his police career.

The theatricality of Chamoiseau's novels owes much to these early experiments with performance works, which often focus on the imagination as a site of resistance. In a 1999 interview, when asked about the use of dialogue in his works, Chamoiseau observed: "D'une manière générale dans mon écriture, il y a toujours une situation théâtrale" ("In a general way, in my writing, there is always a theatrical situation").[4] He envisions narrative scenes in a cinematic way, and these traces are evident in his use of techniques such as fades, cuts, close-ups, and flashbacks in his prose works.[5] Chamoiseau often divides the novel into digestible portions, which are shorter than chapters or stories, and function like scenes in a longer drama. As will be seen, Chamoiseau's writing for the stage serves as a kind of theater of the imaginary for the author, by which I mean that his meta-theatrical approach to performance, which brings together storytelling, dance, drumming, and song, incorporates textual and linguistic hybridity, and introduces experimental approaches to modes of narration, can be seen as a "rehearsal" of the polyphonic performative techniques that come to characterize his approach to prose. Moreover, the discovery of the rebel figure, which he focuses on during this period, is a subject to which he will return, albeit in more sophisticated ways, throughout his career. By developing a meta-theatrical approach to telling the story of the rebel, Chamoiseau discovers ways to go beyond the tactics of anticolonial resistance and begins to engage in more productive strategies of postcolonial inscription.

Resistance and Riddles

Chamoiseau turns to the subject of Louis Delgrès in two of his early works, including the play *L'Époque Delgrès* (1974) and a pedagogical comic book, *Les Antilles sous Bonaparte* (1981). During this rebellious phase, Delgrès is an appealing subject: a heroic spokesman for anticolonial resistance, abolition, and Revolutionary principles of "equality, fraternity and liberty" in the Caribbean. Born in St. Pierre, Martinique, Delgrès served in the French military during the Napoleonic reign, a period that saw slavery abolished (1794) and reinstated in the French colonies (1802). Opposed to slavery, he led a rebel force that committed mass suicide rather than be captured. This narrative also allows Chamoiseau to explore the notion that it was another Martinican, Josephine, who was instrumental in persuading Napoleon to reinstate slavery.

Divided into twenty-one scenes, *L'Époque Delgrès* is structured by a number of framing elements, including an opening dialogue between Papa Aboul and his son Mano. Presented in question-response format, this exchange deals with questions of identity and ancestral memory in a manner that is somewhat reminiscent of the dialogue between Papa Longoué and Mathieu that serves as the opening to Glissant's *Le quatrième siècle* (1964). The Creole riddle is also evident in this exchange. Papa Aboul begins with praise for the paradoxical identity of "ceux qui vont de l'avant mais qui guardent racines" ("those who forge ahead but keep their roots") and "ce qui s'élancent endroite vers le soleil" ("that which heads straight for the sun") (*LD*, 1). This kind of a person is like the coconut tree. Mano responds by praising the "force des racines" (1) or the "power of roots" (rootedness). Papa Aboul then rehearses the riddling script of identity with his son:

Papa Aboul: Que diras-tu au monde quand il te faudra parler de ton pays?"
Mano: Je dirai l'Afrique.
Papa Aboul: Et s'il te fait parler de ton cœur...
Mano: Je parlerai des Îles. (*LD*, 2)

(Papa Aboul: What will you say to people when you are required to speak of your country?
Mano: I will say Africa.
Papa Aboul: And if they make you speak about your heart...
Mano: I will speak about the Islands.)

In this brief exchange, Chamoiseau's drama mixes theories of Negritude and Antillanité. The son, however, has his own lesson to share, a theme that is of importance for Chamoiseau in his defense of youth as a time when one is more open to the world. The son says that he wants to leave his home in the Caribbean for the following reasons:

Je pars parce qu'il faut partir Papa Aboul.
Je pars aussi parce que le monde est là
que le monde est à voir
que le monde est à connaître
et que je suis de ceux qui doivent faire
beaucoup plus que les autres. (*LD*, 1)

(I leave because it is necessary Papa Aboul
I depart also because the world is there
The world is there to be seen
The world is to there to be known
And because I am among those who have to do
Much more than others.)

From a literary perspective, this citation introduces an important theme during this period of writing: the relationship between the parental figure and the child. The child is seen as questioning the parent's perspectives and orientation in the world. While such a thematic is common enough in juvenile literature, the theme was particularly relevant for Chamoiseau's generation, many of whom migrated to France in search of employment. This movement to the metropolitan center marked a step further away from the rural past and daily connections to folk culture. These dynamics are reflected in this father-son dialogue which moves from the Creole riddle to the desire to explore the world.

This dialogue introduces the frame for the play in the form of the *conteur* who addresses the audience directly in the prelude to the drama and gestures toward the audience at the end of the play. Paradoxically, the *conteur* is represented as outside history and embedded in the unfolding historical action. In both situations, the *conteur* is depicted as a figure of resistance, a rebel in the anticolonial struggle. Addressing the audience, the storyteller argues that the history of Europe should only serve to better understand "our history and ourselves" (*LD*, 3). This entails rescuing history from the "jeu du colon" ("colonizer's game") that has obscured Caribbean history with its silencing effects and lies (*LD*, 4). Prefiguring the Creolist motto that the first thing on the agenda is collective memory, the storyteller says: "Je dis qu'un travail de recuperation s'impose / un travail de fondations / un travail de contact avec nous-mêmes" ("I say that a labor of recovery is necessary / a labor of foundations / a labor to make contact with ourselves") (*LD*, 3). In the drama, the storyteller is most closely associated with the maroon community for whom he is a spokesperson, bringing their concerns to the government. Here too he is identified as the one who preserves collective memory:

> Le marron (au conteur)
> C'est toi l'homme de la mémoire?
> Le conteur
> C'est moi
> Celui qui se souviendra! (*LD*, 12)

> (The marooned slave (to the storyteller):
> Are you the man of memories?
> The storyteller:
> Is me.
> The one who will remember.)

The storyteller is a witness to history and its herald, saluting Ignace as a king, a chief (chef), and a god (49). He is a witness to Solitude's role as a bloodied, rebel figure, and functions as a linking character to Chamoiseau's *Solitude, la mulâtresse*, a play whose heroine is a marooned slave.

This early example of intertextual referencing, which is evident throughout his oeuvre, serves to link the works and foster a larger imagined community of resistance.

The *conteur* is affiliated with the old man whose presence in the work serves to foreground the need for an intensely emotional witnessing of history and reclamation of cultural memory. As with many of Chamoiseau's figures of resistance, this older man retains ties to Africa; notably this man seems to prefigure the protagonist of the fleeing slave in *L'Esclave vieil homme et le molosse*. The older man represents an archetypal figure in Chamoiseau's fiction: the guardian of memory. Specifically, this old man calls out for justice when he laments the crime of making a man kill his brother (*LD*, 45). While his protest remains politically impotent, he plays an important role in the redemptive rhetoric of the piece, which aims to recuperate forgotten or obliterated moments in history. For instance, the old man bears witness to Delgrès' response as to whether or not they shall win the battle: "Vaincre? / Pas dans la bataille / dans l'Histoire / les vainqueurs seront nous dans les coeurs des frères à venir" ("Conquer? / Not in battle / in History / the conquerors will be us in the hearts of our brothers to come") (*LD*, 47). In *L'Époque Delgrès*, Chamoiseau introduces another motif central to his prose works: the sacred rock. This rock symbolizes a foundational moment in the community's history and identity, a motif that appears in *Texaco*, *L'Esclave vieil homme et le molosse*, *Écrire en pays dominé*, and *Un dimanche au cachot*. At the outset of the play, echoes of Césaire's poetics are evident in the description of Delgrès as one of "des hommes volcans à sang de lave" ("the volcanic men with blood of lava") (*LD*, 3). Delgrès perceives this death as a foundational act of heroism, which will add "notre pierre" ("our stone") to the foundation already established with Makandal, Boukman, and Toussaint (53).[6] Acts of heroism will contribute to the materials needed to cement culture and community. For Delgrès, dying represents a means to cement the home (*case*) and fortify its foundations (*LD*, 53). Thus, collective memory is imagined as a kind of foundation to be made and poured, an artifice to be improved on through heroic deeds and not simply inhabited.

The heroic rhetoric of the play and the morality of good (anticolonialism) versus evil (colonialism) are elements that most clearly identify this work as part of Chamoiseua's rebel phase of writing. Chamoiseau criticizes this early sensibility when he describes himself as a rebel and the rebel as follows:

"il a bien identifié son ennemi, et son problème c'est de montrer qu'il y a un système d'oppression [...] il casse le système de domination sans l'avoir interrogé profondément."[7]

("he has clearly identified his enemy, and his problem is to show that there is a system of oppression [...] he breaks the system of domination without having questioned it very thoroughly.")

While Chamoiseau may criticize the failure to reflect on the system of domination and one might fault this early work for lacking the metatextual sophistication and distancing techniques employed in later fictions, this play remains a significant work in his fiction. Not only does it introduce many of the key concepts, ideas, and symbolic references found throughout his fiction, it offers a glimpse into the kennel narrative of rebellious confrontation that recurs throughout his writing.

(Neo)Colonial Resistance and New Forms of Consciousness

Against the backdrop of departmentalization, Chamoiseau explores the importance of vernacular forms of resistance in his early theatrical works. In 1975, Chamoiseau wrote *Une manière d'Antigone* in response to recent events in Martinican history. From the late 1960s to the early 1970s, Martinicans engaged in demonstrations and protests against the French government, which were often brutally repressed. In 1971, a student by the name of Gérard Nouvet died as a result of state attempts to put down the protest. In adapting Sophocles's *Antigone*, Chamoiseau precociously reworked world literature for local purposes. While he might be seen as following Aimé Césaire's lead in rewriting a classic work of Western literature (*The Tempest*) in a Caribbean context, he introduced his own unique set of poetics concerns and perspectives. Chamoiseau began with the idea that in order to punish this rebellion among the youth, Creon ordered that the body of the youth be left lying in the public space. Antigone opposes this command and is imprisoned. The main action of the play takes place in the prison of Fort-de-France during a period of five days leading up to Carnival. Stéphanie Bérard calls attention to the maroon as a figure of past-present resistance, noting that Chamoiseau raises the question of whether or not the guard will become a "nègre marron" (maroon) following his encounter with Antigone.[8] Furthermore, she sees the guard's masquerades in the role of Creon as subversively mimicking French power and suggests that Antigone's suicide on the first day of Carnival is symbolic of the reversal of dominant culture.[9] The drama examines the possibility of carnivalesque reversal and signals the potential for a *marronage* of consciousness.

Equally, the emphasis on the fate of Antigone also introduces a postcolonial feminist perspective, which takes aim at the debilitating effects of patriarchy. Under the direction of Marie-Line Ampigny, the work was staged with the title of *Le bourreau d'Antigone*. First performed by *Théâtre de l' A.I.R.* (Artistes Immigrés Réunis) in 1984, the production subsequently went on tour in France, Belgium, and the French Caribbean. Luc Saint-Éloy (who played the role of the executioner/guard in the production) describes the original conception of the relationship between Antigone and the guard/executioner as follows:

> Ce qui est original, c'est que le bourreau était le versant populaire: c'est par le bourreau que vivait la population martiniquaise. Antigone était plus la sagesse, la conscience. Faire opposer ces deux personnages était tout à fait original parce qu'il fallait faire se confronter l'insouciance et la conscience de nos populations. Créon était le prétexte, mais en même temps c'était aussi affirmer qu'on savait dire non à l'inacceptable, non à certaines formes d'injustice, non à un certain processus colonial. C'est un spectacle qui a très bien marché également. On l'a créé à Paris, on l'a joué pendant quatre semaines au Théâtre Noir, ensuite on l'a joué en Guyane, en Martinique, en Belgique. C'est vrai que c'est une pièce engagée politiquement.[10]

> (What is original is that the executioner represented the popular voice: the Martinican populace lived through the executioner. Antigone represents wisdom and conscience. Having these two personages face one another was completely original because it meant that our populus's lack of concern would be confronted by its conscience. Creon was the pretext, but at the same time, it was also a way of affirming that we know how to say no to the unacceptable, no to certain forms of injustice, no to a certain colonial process. The play was also a very big success. We initially staged it in Paris, where it ran for four weeks at the Théâtre Noir, after which it played in Guyana, Martinique and Belgium. It is true that it is a politically engaged work.)

Saint-Éloy's commentary suggests that the pairing of Antigone and the guard appealed to Chamoiseau because it presented an opportunity to forward a critique of complacency and compromise in Caribbean society; thus, the drama can be read as an early example of Chamoiseau's critique of the malign effects of departmentalization. Equally, this pairing is significant because it highlights the author's interest in feminine presence as both literally and symbolically resistant to imperialism. Antigone is the figure of wisdom and resistance who embodies the revolutionary spirit that might resist patriarchy and transform the community.

For his part, Chamoiseau focuses on the conversion narrative and the poetics of initiation as a means for eliciting change within society:

> En lisant l'*Antigone* de Sophocle, j'avais été frappé par le personnage du garde, bref mais riche. Il m'avait paru étrange que ce garde puisse côtoyer la terrible détermination d'Antigone sans en être lui-même modifié d'une manière ou d'une autre. C'est pourquoi j'ai voulu développer le côtoiement d'un garde et d'une Antigone. Montrer que la force brutale et aveugle pouvait être affecté par une foi simple et forte. Et dire surtout comment l'apparent défaite d'Antigone aurait pu acquérir une dimension nouvelle si son garde avait par elle été changé.[11]

(Upon reading Sophocles's *Antigone*, I was struck by the figure of the guard, [which was] briefly described but rich. It seemed strange to me that this guard could come into contact with the terrible determination of Antigone without being changed in some manner or another. This is why I wanted to develop the coming together of a guard and an Antigone: to show that brutal and blind force could be affected by a simple and strong faith. And above all [I wanted] to show how the apparent defeat of an Antigone could acquire a new dimension if her guard could be changed through contact to her.)

The emphasis on a transformation of consciousness is particularly striking. Significantly, Chamoiseau chose a feminine rebel figure as a protagonist. This choice of a strong woman as the spokesperson for the community recurred in subsequent theatrical works as well as in later novels, most notably with the figure of Marie-Sophie in *Texaco*. At the same time, the guard represents the ambivalent Caribbean who is both part of the French system and apart from it. This kind of figure appears again in the police of *Solibo Magnifique*, but neither Pilon nor Bouaffesse undergo a comparable transformation of consciousness. Perhaps, a better point of reference is the figure of the guard in *L'Exil du roi Béhanzin* in the film directed by Guy Deslauriers. In *L'Exil*, Chamoiseau once again evokes an ambivalent figure at the interfaces of political systems and cultures and shows how someone might undergo a transformation when confronted by a rebellious conscience. In many ways, the dynamics of the Warrior of the Imaginary also take inspiration from this kind of confrontation with a rebel consciousness who serves as an initiatory figure. Such a reading is reinforced by Chamoiseau's more recent comments on the play (2006) in which he remarked that he wanted to see how an act of revolt, a gesture of freedom, could alter the adverse lines, even without defeating them.[12] Rather than measuring the success of resistance in terms of the short-term outcome, Chamoiseau calls attention to the diffuse workings of the imaginary and the potential for change through a slow transformation of consciousness through a longer account of historical transformation. Moreover, he once more attests to the power of reading as a transformative activity that is passed on by the reader-writer who seeks to author a new vision of the original work and the world through the processes of adaptation and rewriting.

Chamoiseau turned to another female rebel when he adapted André Schwarz-Bart's *La mulâtresse, Solitude* (1972) for his theatrical work entitled *Solitude la mulâtresse*. This historical fiction tells the story of the slave, maroon, and rebel who was executed in 1802, following the defeat of Louis Delgrès and the birth of her child (whom the state claimed as property). This performance text dramatizes the psychic and emotional life of the child as she succumbs to madness and serves to ground the rebelliousness of the woman in the trauma of suffering. The mother-daughter relationship is at the heart of this drama, which marks a turn toward Creolist genres through the introduction of storytelling, song, and dance into the performance. In keeping with the theme of embodiment, the language of the play is highly rhythmic.

The theme of *souffrance* (suffering) is explored in various ways. In the opening scene, we learn that Manman Bobette is unable to accept her enslavement, with the result that she is aging rapidly and becoming increasingly suicidal. Her daughter Rosalie is the child she conceived as a result of rape during the Middle Passage. Nicknamed *Deux-âmes* (Two Souls), Rosalie's eyes are different colors and thus reflect her mixed heritage. Manman Bobette soon flees the plantation to join a maroon community, leaving her daughter Rosalie behind. Rosalie becomes a servant in the household and a kind of companion to the *béké*'s daughter. She too breaks down as she confronts the pressures of maternal abandonment and the threat of torture if she fails to please her new mistress. This madness manifests itself in barking, cries, and sighs as if she had become one of the dogs who are sent to chase down marooned slaves. Consequently, Rosalie or Deux-âmes becomes a zombie, without a soul (Sans-âme). She is traded from one master to another, which leads to her new name, that of Solitude. Like her mother, Solitude also joins a community of maroons. This community becomes caught up in the rebellion led by Delgrès. Although Solitude has regained her soul in the community of maroons, the return to battle throws her back inside herself. Her heroic actions in battle are not simply heroic, but presented as aspects of the return to her solitary self. Solitude becomes pregnant. Ignoring the father's pleas that she should protect the child and retreat from battle, Solitude continues on. When the father is killed by shrapnel, she is left alone to struggle on. The play comes to a close with a vision of the three figures who have dominated her life: her mother, Sango the maroon leader, and her lover. Suicide, glorious death, and motherhood are the three alternatives they present. Solitude rejects suicide until she is captured and condemned to be executed, following the birth of her child. Her search for a nuclear family and efforts to bring about a liberated community are thwarted. In exploring these aspects of suffering, this political theater of decolonization confronts the psychic trauma of slavery and colonization through the fragmentation of consciousness, family, and community.

The drama offers a sustained comparison of the role of slaves on the plantation and the maroon community. Pilon, a slave on the plantation, views displacement and loss of memory as part of a process of adaptation as well as a means to gain a more expansive sense of community:

Paix et Paix
Ici nous apprenons que notre patrie est plus grande que notre village.
Que notre peuple est plus grand que notre tribu.
Ici ceux-là même qui ont un village apprennent à l'oublier.
Alors, négresse je te dis
Paix et paix
Car ma patrie n'est plus dans mon village. (*SLM*, 5)

(Peace and Peace
Here we learn that our country is bigger than our village.
That our people are more than our tribe.
Here even those who have a village learn to forget . . .
So, Negress I say to you
Peace and Peace
Because my homeland is no longer in my village.)

By contrast, the representation of the maroon community is both multiply situated and more ambivalent. Polycarpe describes the maroon community (based on a report from a slave who marooned and then returned to the plantation) as one that persists in tribal ways of life with an emphasis on chiefs, gods, and kings (*SLM*, 24). The colonizer's daughter repeats the colonial patriarchal views of her father, who believes that the maroons have signed a pact in blood with the devil as they do not seem to suffer under torture, but continue to smile in a distant, insulting way (*SLM*, 22). Solitude's encounters with the maroons highlight both the regressive and rebellious tendencies of the maroon community. Sanga, the leader, and his wife, Euphrosine, sing of their desire to return to Africa (*SLM*, 43). At the same time, Sanga is a spokesperson for colonial resistance as is evident when he denounces blacks who fight alongside colonial powers in order to suppress revolt; he sees such accommodating figures as lost in the mysterious ways of "la pensée blanche" (*SLM*, 50) ("white ways of thinking"). Chamoiseau's critique of unreflective rebelliousness is evident through Sanga's conversion of consciousness. Initially, Sanga fights instinctively (without knowing why) against the English, the soldiers of Victor Hugues, aristocrats, the white landowners, the more important whites, the mulattos, the quadroons, and the negroes (*SLM*, 37): "Sans savoir! San comprendre!" ("Without knowing! Without understanding!"), Sanga exclaims (*SLM*, 37). However, Sanga eventually learns to understand the meaning of his struggle in ideological and imaginative terms (*SLM*, 37). He presents a Glissantian defense of *errance* and the need for detours of the imaginary in the form of a riddle: that to ascend to the heights, one must descend to the depths (*SLM*, 37). Instead of glorifying the French revolutionary model of liberty, equality, and fraternity, Sanga offers an ironic, poetic view of death as the great equalizer and thus a form of liberty. His revolutionary poetics place emphasis on the role of vernacular performance as a way of remembering the past and sustaining the communal voice. Upon his death, he asks that the community use his skin to create a drum. In this way, his "voice" will continue to drum on and be heard in the community (*SLM*, 45). The regenerative and revolutionary energies of the community find embodiment in the vernacular traditions of the community, which resonate through and beyond the life of the individual.

The question of a maroon identity and marooning haunts the mother-child relationship. The mother sets an example that liberty from suffering is more important than the filial bond. Solitude asks and discovers that many mothers take their children along when they maroon. Solitude's own marooning of consciousness, her zombification, occurs when Xavière reports that she has been told by her father that black mothers kill their children. To her questions about the ways that black motherhood functions, Deux-âmes replies:

> Oh, pas avec les mains
> Ou avec les gestes
> Ou avec les mots
> Ma-mais avec le coeur
> Le cœur est les yeux
> Et puis les bonnes paroles
> Les paroles qui donnent courage d'être nègre
> Les paroles qui se battent avec la vie
> Les paroles bonnes!
> Et si elles tuent
> C'est que le bateau est dans les bois
> Pour le retour, le vrai!
> Si elles tuent c'est qu'elles aiment. (*SLM*, 19)

> (Oh, not with the hands
> Or with gestures
> Or with words
> Bu-but with the heart
> The heart and the eyes
> And then with the right words
> Words that give one the courage to be a Negro
> Words that fight with life
> The right words!
> And if they kill
> It is because the boat is in the woods

For the return, the real one!
If they kill it is because they love.)

Motherhood is associated with arming the child with the right words to defend oneself and live courageously. Like Toni Morrison's *Beloved*, the enslaved or colonized mother may also kill her daughter to protect her from greater suffering. This dilemma of motherhood is repeated when Solitude herself is pregnant and must choose between a retreat to safety to preserve her child or battle. Like her mother before her, she chooses liberty. Her bio-political aspirations for a life that combines political activism and parenthood are crushed when Maimoun, her partner, is killed and she is condemned to death. With its strong characterization, use of Caribbean genres, and emotional pathos, the play marks a significant step forward in Chamoiseau's theatrical vision.

Performed in 1976 at the Festival of Avignon, the play was chosen to represent the theme of "cultural minorities" at the thirtieth anniversary of this theatrical event. *Théâtre Fer de Lance*, established by Yvan Labéjof in 1972, led a troupe of Antillean performers. According to a review of the performance, it seems that the script was somewhat modified as the "story unfolds in a series of vignettes which are first introduced by the narrator, a contemporary Caribbean dock worker, and then re-enacted by friends whom he has called together to celebrate her legacy."[13] This narrative structure is comparable to the use of the framing device in *L'Époque Delgrès*, where Chamoiseau bridges the distance between past and present through dialogue. Doll-like marionettes were suspended on the necks of the actors playing the slaves to symbolize white masters, and life-sized effigies were used to represent French soldiers. Creole songs and drumming were introduced. Overall, the performance, the story, and the acting were positively reviewed.[14]

The Creolized Landscape of the Postcolonial Imaginary

Manman Dlo contre la fée Carabosse turns from the realm of historical fiction and the rewriting of Western classics to a theater based in the traditions of Caribbean folklore and storytelling. Manman Dlo, a sorceress who inhabits water, represents the central rebel figure who is pitted against the evil witch of European folklore, called la fée Carabosse. The witch silences and imprisons figures of Martinican folklore whose sufferings come to represent the malign effects of colonial domination. Manman Dlo fights back and demonstrates how the vernacular can be mobilized in the quest for liberation when she conquers the European witch figure in a laghia-like[15] battle of powerful words and blows. The drama closes with a celebration of Manman Dlo's daughter, Algoline, who takes up the enchanted ring of memory and its techniques (*MD*, 139). This whimsical drama marks a departure from the serious tone of other early theatrical works. Indeed, the mood of the drama is closer to the wit and satire of Chamoiseau's comic strip collaborations with Delsham: this is heighted through the introduction of humorous illustrations by Chamoiseau. Despite the fact that *Manman Dlo* is the only theatrical work readily available in print, it is often neglected or dismissed by critics. J. Michael Dash suggests that the play is a "pointedly nationalistic allegory" about a colonizing project that is "foiled when the divinity, who is not only indigenous but autochthonous, unleashes the forces of nature, sweeping all before them."[16] According to Dash, the work lacks the "aesthetic inventiveness and linguistic extravagance" of the author's later novels, and he views the work as "a naïve exercise in wishful thinking" to the extent that it depicts Martinique as an organic community that preexisted the "invasive forces of modernity."[17] When the play is interpreted as an allegory of history, and emphasis is placed on the role of Manman Dlo as a rebel, these criticisms of the drama hold true.

However, the meta-theatricality of *Manman Dlo*, which features the use of narrative masks, serves to displace a mimetic (merely representational) approach to history and narrative in favor of performative dynamics. The problematic role of the storyteller, the whimsical interplay between French and Creole, the invocation of Caribbean folklore motifs, and the introduction of the poetics of the marvel are among this play's several noteworthy innovations. In the context of Chamoiseau's oeuvre, this is a groundbreaking work because it introduces the author as a metafictional character in a drama about interculturation and the decolonization of the imaginary. Moreover, *Manman Dlo* offers a critique of oppositional identities through the interventions of Algoline, the daughter of Manman Dlo who serves as a spokesperson for a relational sense of identity. Through Algoline's presence in the drama and the emergence of a new kind of narrator, the Son of the Spoken Word, Chamoiseau shifts his artistic focus from figures of anticolonial resistance to revolutionary figures in search of a sense of place in a creolizing world. Thus, he turns to one of the most significant and persistent themes in his work: the freedom of the imaginary in the face of domination. The folkloric struggle for liberation is mirrored by the narrator's quest for aesthetic emancipation. In *Manman Dlo*, Chamoiseau dramatizes the precarious situation in which the author under departmentalization finds himself. Dominique Chancé describes the tensions for the author caught between the oral and literary traditions, between the scribe and the oral storyteller: while the storyteller takes on the role of narrating stories, which need to be reclaimed from the abyss of memory in order to foster a sense of communal identity, the writer transposes the oral tradition into written French, which constitutes a double betrayal of the vernacular traditions from plantation culture.[18] The farcical aspects of the drama and the narrator's masquerade can be seen as the embodiment of the author's tricky situation as he attempts to find a viable means of writing past-present horizons. The contradictions and fractures of the narrative are symptomatic of this politico-aesthetic struggle, but they also serve to open up new narrative possibilities.

With *Manman Dlo*, Chamoiseau turns from neorealistic depictions of the historical past to the realm of fantasy in order to consider the role of the imaginary in a (neo)colonial society. When the publication of this performance work was first announced in *Antilla*, it was described as a "conte symbolique qui rogne sur notre veille déveine" ("a symbolic tale that rages against our night of misfortune").[19] Chamoiseau excerpted a portion of the theatrical work that highlights the need to explore the quest for self in a postcolonial context:

> La parole qui va suivre, raconte le dérouelement de la colonisation dans le Monde de la Merveille. [. . .] Mais pour vaincre elle [Maman dlo] devra opérer une Grande Recherche, sorte de quête de Soi.[20]

> (The words that will follow, tell of the unfolding of colonization in the World of Marvels . . . but to vanquish, she must undertake a Great Study, a sort of quest of the Self.)

Placing emphasis on the colonization of the imaginary, he calls for a critique of the production of the communal self through narrative. In the foreword or "Avant la parole," the narrator observes:

> Quand il y a colonisation, il y a non seulement colonisation d'un peuple par un autre, d'hommes par d'autres hommes, mais aussi domination d'une culture par une autre.

> Le Monde de la Merveille de la culture dominante (ses contes, ses légendes, ses mythes) soumettra celui de la dominée.
> Aux Antilles, les colons sont venus, porteurs de leur Imaginaire.
> Les Africains aussi.
> [. . .] La bataille était inévitable. (*MD*, 6)

> (When there is colonization, there is not only the colonization of one people by another, of men by other men, but also the domination of one culture by another.
> The World of Marvels of the dominant culture (its stories, its legends, its myths) subjugates that of the dominated.
> In the West Indies, the colonizers came, bearing their Imaginary.
> The Africans also.
> A battle was inevitable.)

In his drama, the showdown between the French colonial imaginary and African diasporic presence results in the dispersion of both influences and the ascendancy of Creole culture. In this respect, the questions, which haunt the narrator in *Écrire en pays dominé*, "Comment écrire alors que ton imaginaire s'abreuve, du matin jusqu'aux rêves, à des images, des pensées, des valeurs qui ne sont pas les tiennes? [. . .] Comment écrire dominé?" (*EPD*, 17) ("How can you write when, from the break of day to dreams at night, your imaginary drinks in images, thoughts and values that are not your own? [. . .] How can you write dominated?"), are nascent in *Manman Dlo*.

This "théâtre conté" ("theater in story form") makes use of meta-theatrical techniques, hybrid theatrical traditions (Creole and French), and language games. These aesthetic techniques subvert the binaries at work in the dramatic encounter between the forces of domination and resistance. For example, the *conteur* (storyteller) is described as the Son of the Spoken Word (*MD*, 5) who has abandoned the world of oral storytelling and social gatherings in order to "ECRIRE ses contes" ("write his tales") (*MD*, 5). The writer occupies a liminal position for he is both inside and outside the world of folklore. He belongs to this world and is subject to its laws; he has been brought to a tribunal (the co-op for the safety of the spoken word) on charges of high treason. In a Derridean sense, the storyteller and his assistant, called La-po-figue, have broken "the law of genre" by combining the oral and the written in the form of an oraliture.[21] In defense of this act of transgression, they argue that the theater is both an oral and a written medium, thus permitting the "fils de la parole" to enter a new world of textuality without leaving the folkloric oral world behind. Thus, they claim the right to both participate in and depart from vernacular traditions. In transgressing the laws of genre, Chamoiseau opens up past-present horizons for the invocation of the folkloric and discloses new spaces for postcolonial articulation between French traditions of writing and Creole/French oral traditions. In a manner comparable to the kind of metaleptic rupture found in postmodern drama, Chamoiseau disrupts the frame of the performance text, which results in the sense of an elision of represented/implied storytellers and imagined/actual audience members.

Chamoiseau's metafictional approach to narrative thwarts a sense of linear history and defies mimetic approaches to the representation of identity. Notably, he undermines the fiction of the "storyteller / Son of the Spoken Word." At the end of the tale, the *conteur* runs offstage in pursuit of Marianne while the Son of the Spoken Word steps forward and presents himself as a kind of acrobat who has been catapulted into the drama (*MD*, 141). In the stage directions, the Son of the Spoken Word confesses: "J'étais là aussi. Et c'est là-même qu'une calotte de joie m'a voltigé sur ce papier pour ECRIRE toutes ces paroles . . . moi, Fils de la Parole!" ("I was there too. And it was right then and there that a joyful box to the ears catapulted me onto the paper to WRITE all these words . . . me, the Son of the Spoken Word!) (*MD*, 141). This "voltige" or example of narrative acrobatics calls attention to the transformative potential of the text as a performative work so that the illusion of presence (that this is a story being told to children) is both disrupted and displaced: the act of telling a story to children serves as one that propels the Son of the Spoken Word into the narrative world. Thus, the dynamic processes of the Creole world are shown to produce a writer who is heir to the oral tradition. Consequently, the motif of masquerade come to the foreground through the presence of the Storyteller-Son of the Spoken Word who is listed as a single character in the cast but who (as noted previously) appears onstage as two separate characters. The storyteller is a duplicitous figure who plays a double role, appears in different guises and engages in acts of concealing and revealing his shifting identities. The world of folklore thus provides a domain for a theater of the imaginary where transformations of identity might be enacted.

Two epigraphs to *Manman Dlo*, which introduce the call-response logic of the play, prefigure the tropes of disguise and deception. The call begins with a quote by René Menil and the response comes in the form of a short verse by Patrick Chamoiseau. Menil's text invokes the motif of masking and unmasking through reference to the quest for a "vrai visage" ("real face") (*MD*, 4) and the imperative to look into the mirror of the marvelous to see "l'image sûre de toi-même" (*MD*, 4) ("the certain image of yourself"). Menil challenges the reader to integrate the marvelous (*le Merveilluex*) into everyday life in order to achieve grandeur; his quote ends with the axiom, "Le Merveilleux est l'image de notre Liberté absolue" (*MD*, 4) ("The Marvelous is the image of our absolute Liberty"). Chamoiseau's verse extract follows Menil's text and can be interpreted as a kind of response to Menil: "Et ta parole embillit / sur nos virer" (*MD*, 4) ("And your spoken word embellishes on our change in direction"). Addressed to the sacred, patient "flaireur" (someone who senses danger) who allows "us" (presumably the "nous" of Menil who are looking for their true image) to leave behind the path in order to pursue what will be, Chamoiseau's verse response reinforces the related themes of masking, marvels, and transformation.

Similarly, within the larger work, the split subject of the narrative and the split image of the marvelous Storyteller / Son of the Spoken Word result—which take the form of masking and unmasking identities—emerge as a result of the encounter with the marvelous world of folklore. Like the characters in the play, the Storyteller and Son of the Spoken Word undergoes a process of dissipation and liberation. In fracturing the image of a single true self, Chamoiseau underscores the impossibility of recuperating a sense of wholeness. Instead, he celebrates the appearance of a new self who emerges as a result of the processes and possibilities of gazing into the mirror of the marvelous. In this respect, the masquerade of the self operates in a manner that might be described in terms of Homi Bhabha's account of the Third Space of enunciation, which he derives from Wilson Harris's sense of the void of misgiving in the textuality of colonial history. Bhabha notes that the importance of what Harris terms the "assimilation of contraries" as a prequel to creating "that occult instability which presages powerful cultural changes."[22] In this case, the masquerade derived from colonial narrative forms produces an oppositional dynamic and a sense of paradoxical performativity whereby the Son of the Spoken Word becomes a mediator for the generation of the self who is always already *in media res*. The orature in process has already been prefigured through the assimilation of oral and literary, European and African, influences in a creolizing context. The intercultural apprehension of identity is posited as elusive and shifting, elicited through the processes of narration and dialogue in everyday life and embellished through the mediating processes of the imaginary. While Algoline functions as the rebellious figure of hybridity in the drama, the storyteller's processes of masking/unmasking serve as a metafictional correlative: the emergence of hybrid narrative presences and techniques attests to the writer's need for an ongoing space of articulation where he continuously works through the thirdness of Caribbean culture. For Chamoiseau, masquerade thus becomes a means to highlight the open, ongoing in-between space of a drama performed by and for the people of Martinique.

The piece humorously dramatizes a psychic landscape where sociocultural memory and language are repressed through the introduction of characters/caricatures of colonial and anticolonial thinking. With a laugh that sounds like classical music (Beethoven's fifth symphony), the Fée Carabosse is a kind of walking-talking "Code Noir" who creates laws to establish her power in this world by delimiting the definitions of "culture" and "humanity" as a means of determining who can be colonized and enslaved. Surveying the landscape, she can be seen as a spokesperson for the colonizing gaze when she says:

> Hé hé hé hé
> Nous allons prendre possession de ce pays
> Dominer les rivières
> Domestiquer les vents
> Classer les végétaux pouvant servir aux philtres énergétiques
> [...].
> Enfin, tout ce que rampe, marche, court ou vole sera traité,
> domestiqué, mis sous Etat-Civil, pour une domination totale
> de ce bout de terre. (*MD*, 16–17)
>
> (Hee Hee Hee Hee
> We will take possession of this country
> Dominate the rivers
> Domesticate the winds
> Classify the vegetables that can be used for magic potions
> [...].
> Finally, all that crawls, walks, runs or flies will be dealt with
> Domesticated, put under the Civil State for a total domination
> Of this piece of earth.)

Chamoiseau brings together the discourses of witchery and colonialism, suggesting that the colonial is a form of malevolent enchantment. He satirically undermines the witch's "natural" desires to cast spells, to make potions, and so on. As a (post)modern witch who belongs to the contemporaneous world order as well as the colonial one, she considers the merits of the "new-fangled" brooms on the market; that is, the carpet sweeper versus the vacuum cleaner. Her broom is anthropomorphized as a "cheeky" and somewhat dim-witted servant with whom she has discussions about the need to sanitize the Martinican landscape. Through satiric socio-psychological realism and anachronistic references, the realm of fairytales is shown to be ideologically motivated in the past-present horizons of the (neo)colonial imaginary.

Chamoiseau plays at (and with) the interfaces of spoken and written language in order to subvert colonial discourses and establish postcolonial perspectives. The play begins with a dialogue between the witch and her broom, which serves as a vehicle for transporting her and a secretary who is meant to convey her intended meaning to the wider world. The colonial transcription process quickly turns to farce as the broom introduces a number of telling errors, which subvert the witch's imperialistic claims to rule the New World. Through techniques of disruption (such as the witch's continuous exclamations of pain as she says "ouille" or "ouch" in the midst of her dictation), Chamoiseau suspends meaning. Notably, the prolonged emphasis on the multiple possibilities for interpreting the meaning of the word "le vol" (depending on the context, the word "le vol" can mean either "flight" or "theft" in French) in a colonial context (*MD*, 12–15). Inadvertently, the witch reveals that her imperialistic desire to take possession of the land depends on painful manipulations of language. Similarly, the transcription of the word "humanity" comically undermines the witch's self-perceptions as the broom suggests that she is not as attractive as she believes herself to be. Biological features, skin color, language, and pronunciation, clothing, and the cult and rules of sorcery practices are defining features for the witch's own identity and Othering of the new world. The witch places emphasis on skin color: in her view, those who are human should have the same white "fond de teint" ("shade of skin") as Carabosse rather than "fond teint" ("dark skin") (*MD*, 23). These farcical transcription processes call attention to the fallacies and strategic misuses of language which underpin discourses of race and slavery. Through the disclosure of counter-hegemonic hermeneutic possibilities in language, Chamoiseau subverts colonial discourses of interpretation.

Metafiction and marvels (the *merveille*) serve as means to rewrite the literal places, plants, and waters of Martinique in vernacular terms. In this geo-poetical work, nature is not merely a backdrop to the action but an active site of transformation. In the opening speech of the play, the narrator asks who can claim to have not heard of Manman Dlo: "sans que Manzè-marie ne ferme sa porte/qui peut prétendre ne pas connaître une histoire de Manman dlo?" ("would Manzè-marie's door remain open to someone/who claimed not to not know a story about Manman Dlo?") (*MD*, 7). Manzè-Marie is a character in the play so one might argue that she literally closes the door on people who lie to her. However, the reference to Manzè-Marie might seem puzzling for anyone unfamiliar with the fact that this name refers to a kind of plant that retracts its leaves when touched. In a footnote, the author explains this reference and notes that the closing of her door is a way of referring to the plant's retraction (*MD*, 7). The footnote also provides an alternative etymology for the name of the plant, which is referred to in French as "Marie-la-honte" ("la honte" means shame) and in Latin as *mimosa pudica*. Through renaming, Chamoiseau playfully revitalizes the landscape in a Creole cultural context. Although no other footnotes are found in this text, Chamoiseau introduces the trope of footnotes, which present counter-historical perspectives and disrupt the illusion of transparency.[23] In this instance, the identity of Manzé-Marie is disclosed as multireferential: she is a plant, an etymology, and a character. Her biological, lexical, and dramaturgic presence introduces multiple registers of meaning, embodies various forms of knowledge, and presents layers of interpretative possibility. Animism, playful etymology, and magic all come together in the handling of the role of this combined plant-etymology-character in the drama. Rather than associate the land with the botanical systems of universal knowledge, Chamoiseau invokes local traditions for envisioning, renaming, and laying claim to the land through imagined experience. Notably, he does so by showing that the landscape is also engaged in the activity of masquerade through its shifting, cross-cultural negotiation of multiple identities.

The mother-daughter relationship offers an inverted tale of development whereby the daughter plays a nurturing role and comes to be seen as the truly revolutionary figure in the drama. While many representations of Manman Dlo situate her as a creolized figure in the Caribbean world, Chamoiseau's depiction of the character in this work places emphasis on her isolationist stance and resistance to interculturation. According to the descriptions of the cast of characters, she represents an African diasporic figure (*MD*, 5), reminiscent perhaps of Mami Wata, whose presence is evident throughout the Caribbean in South American in various guises, such as Yemanja and Dona Janayna. In this representation of Manman Dlo, Chamoiseau tends to associate her with the essentialist desire to resist the transformative influences of interculturation. When Algoline asks her mother why they must remain in the water, Manman Dlo responds, "Nous devons rester pures" (*MD*, 33) ("We must remain pure"). While the mother celebrates purity, the daughter longs for intermixture: she dislikes isolation and longs for friends. The mother responds that her only friend is the river (*MD*, 34) and that anything outside their watery sphere will spoil her. When the daughter laments that the river has eaten one of her human friends, the mother replies that it is not the river but fails to explain that it is she (Manman Dlo) who consumes others. In this context, Manman Dlo might be seen to represent the ways in which a sense of nostalgia threatens to devour and destroy the diasporic subject. As a subject who is about to evaporate, Manman Dlo represents an African diasporic worldview on the verge of extinction while Algoline's resistance to her isolationist stance can be seen as indicative of a shift in the (neo)colonial world order on the part of Creole persons born in the Caribbean.

Manman Dlo engages in the rebel's attempt to bring about and celebrate anticolonial inversions while the daughter looks to a world of intermixture. Manman Dlo instructs her daughter to invert the binary oppositions at work in colonial hierarchies rather than to defy them: small blue clouds are bad and dark or black ("noir") clouds are beautiful and good (*MD*, 36). She provides her daughter with a catalog of all the objects and people that have nothing to do with her, including children of humans, butterflies, bamboo, and so forth. "Préserve toi de tout / Ferme-toi tout / Reste pur: ta seule amie, c'est l'eau!" ("Preserve yourself from everything / Close yourself up completely / Remain pure: your only friend is the water!") (*MD*, 38). At the same time, Manman Dlo catalogs all the forms of admixture that are taking place in the forest. She warns her daughter that she risks ending up walking like the "sans-tête-le-crabe" (headless crab) (*MD*, 39). This reference to the headless crab is interesting for there are folktales that explain why the crab does not have a head, which suggest that this is so because they try to protect a young girl from being devoured by a malevolent maternal figure.[24] Thus, the reference to the actual landscape might also be seen as a reference to the textual landscape of Creole storytelling, but it also signals a darker interpretation of Manman Dlo's own maternal role. Significantly, Manman Dlo represents a closed worldview; she believes that she and her daughter belong to the domain of the water and must uphold their role in giving the land its children and its blood (MD, 38). Meanwhile, Algoline encourages her mother to view the world in a more relational way. Thus, Chamoiseau effectively raises the question of "nature versus nurture" through the introduction of characters representing symbolic aspects of nature, but these representations of nature and naturalized worldviews are shown to be culturally constructed through diasporic representations of the land in narrative form.

Just as the metaphorical cric-crac of the mother-daughter dialogue projects a world where creolizing processes are emergent, the theatrical work as a whole dramatizes a shift from oppositional politics to dispersed, mediated, and assimilative ways of conceiving the processes of creolization. Battles or laghia-like encounters between the witch and the folklore figures give way to the logic of diffusion. For instance, when Papa Zombi is defeated, he does not die but is dispersed throughout the Caribbean world. When Carabosse is defeated, her magic continues to infuse the Caribbean world as Algoline inherits the ring. Algoline is given the ring from Carabosse and mother tells her to immerse herself in the ring without being engulfed by it and to enter into a relation with the entire world (MD, 139). This marks a turning away from the nationalist motif of purity toward creolization as a process. The play is indicative of Chamoiseau's desire to move away from the tenets of Negritude and toward Glissantian ideas of creolization and relation. The *théâtre conté* is staged as a performance for an imagined audience of children who are addressed by the *conteur* in the opening and closing scenes of the work. The storyteller attempts to end with a series of moral lessons: "La Première / c'est qu'avec ce qu'il y a dans ton propre sac / tu peut chanter et rêver / et faire chanter et rêver tes enfants" (MD, 140) ("The first moral lesson / is that with what you have in your own sack, / you can sing and dream / and make your children sing and dream"). This interrupted moral lesson underscores the notion that childhood is a time of self-creation, often overshadowed by the "colonizing" influences of elders. Through the example of Algoline, Chamoiseau dramatizes the ways in which children might interrogate the colonial legacies passed down through the family and wider culture, participate critically and actively in their own/communal coming-of-age narrative, and emerge as leaders in a creolizing world.

The figure of Algoline reflects Chamoiseau's own shifting poetics as he too takes the magic ring of his Creole inheritance forward in creating fictions that explore the imaginary of the culture, less in a spirit of rebelliousness and more in a kind of open, satirical, and marvelous vein. Rather than relying solely on spokespersons to articulate a politics and poetics of resistance, Chamoiseau expresses interest in the legacies of colonialism and the ways in which creolization works as a process of dialogic transformation through strategies of appropriation, rewriting, and adoption. In the drama, the production of self/selves functions according to the logic of call-and-response dialogue whereby the act of storytelling becomes a reproductive activity: the Son of the Spoken Word emerges as a kind of response to the call of the Storyteller. This external projection of an internalized, psychic call-and-response mechanism serves to foreground the simultaneous effects of narrative performance, which transform both the community and the self. While the call-and-response dynamic of the storyteller places emphasis on the storytelling traditions of the colonial past, Chamoiseau highlights the projected effects of narrative on the self and community in the contemporaneous world. In this respect, he calls attention to the lag and the leap between the colonial past and the self questing for a postcolonial identity who seeks to revive the vernacular traditions of the colonial past in the present. Through the acts of masking and revealing identities in past-present vernacular contexts, Chamoiseau's work expresses both anxiety and hope about the renewal of Creole cultural traditions in departmental Martinique.

Through the meta-performative presentation of masquerading narrative personae, Chamoiseau takes the performative dynamics of Creole storytelling as the basis for a postcolonial performance that initiates a new sense of community and self through fractured spatiotemporalities. By disrupting temporality, the domains of the "fictional" and the "real" and mixing genres, the imaginary itself emerges as a performative space for acts of communal and self-inscription. With *Manman Dlo*, Chamoiseau discovers the poetic principles he will continue to explore throughout the 1980s in such works as *Chronique des sept misères*, *Solibo Magnifique*, and *Au temps de l'antan* and anticipates the poetics of marveling and initiation to come in the *Émerveilles* and *Biblique des derniers gestes*.[25] Already one can trace in this early rebel stage an emerging poetics for the roles of the storyteller, the importance of oraliture and Creolist poetics.

Performative poetics enable new forms of revolt for the young writer and artist as he moves through and beyond his rebel phase of anticolonial resistance.

CHAPTER 3

Vernacular Forms and Wandering Genres

Throughout the Caribbean, the anxiety of cultural influence, the quest for vernacular forms, the reclamation of history, and the crisis of writing were significant issues during the 1970s and 1980s. Where writers in the anglophone Caribbean pursued strategies of nation language, such as outlined in Kamau Brathwaite's *A History of the Voice* (1979), and articulate new forms of postcolonial identity, such as the notion of a creolized national identity found in Derek Walcott's *The Star-Apple Kingdom* (1979), Chamoiseau confronted a different set of postcolonial conditions under departmentalization. Édouard Glissant's *Le discours antillais* (1981) as well as his fiction, notably works such as *Malemort* (1975) and *La case du commandeur* (1981), highlighted the barriers to speaking as a collective and call attention to the neurotic tendencies of alienated individual speech and discourse. At the same time, Raphaël Confiant was writing in Creole, but finding it difficult to gain a readership for his work, while Tony Delsham's work in media, journalism, and fiction addressed to a local audience because he is attentive to the need to bring together the fragmented discourses and concerns of the francophone Caribbean. The sense of anxiety and malaise concerning national and communal identity for Martinique found expression in both the form and content of Chamoiseau's writing as did the hope of renewal through creative, critical interrogations of its possibilities for communal dialogue. *Chronique des sept misères* and *Solibo Magnifique* bring related but distinctive narrative strategies to the inscription of a shared set of concerns about Martinique's sense of community, the role of vernacular culture, and the role of neoimperialism.

Chronicle of Seven Sorrows (*Chronique*) presents the tale of Martinique, with a particular focus on the role of the market in Fort-de-France, through much of the twentieth century, including the periods before and after World War II and departmentalization while *Solibo Magnifique* takes the form of a crime novel, influenced by the American and French models for *noir*, procedural, and hard-boiled genres, which introduces Chamoiseau as a narrator, witness, and investigative figure. In terms of narrative masquerade, there are significant differences between *Chronique des sept misères* (1986), which features the chorus of narrators and an ethnographer, and *Solibo Magnifique* (1988), which sees the emergence of the Word Scratcher, who writes at the interface of oral and written cultures as well as standard French and Creole. Nonetheless, these two novels are similar in several ways: both converge on Fort-de-France, interrogate the role of vernacular culture in Martinican culture, and address the need for a new kind of realism. Chamoiseau describes the relationship between the *Chronique* and *Solibo* as follows:

> L'idée est de recréer l'univers urbain que j'ai connu. Et dans cet univers urbain, moi, je vois encore, c'est l'avantage de vieillir dans son pays natal, dans sa ville, c'est que je vois des gens, que je vois depuis mon enfance, qui vieillissent. Donc des gens, qui à un moment donné avaient une importance, ils disparaissent, comme Pipi qui est au centre de *Chronique* et dans *Solibo* on le voit passer au loin; dans *Texaco* on entend parler de lui. J'aime bien cette idée là, c'est exactement la vie réelle.[1]

> (The idea is to recreate the urban universe that I knew. And in this urban universe, I am still a witness—this is the advantage of growing old in one's native country, in one's city—I see the people whom I have seen since my childhood, who are growing old. Thus, the people who at a certain moment were important start to disappear, like Pipi who is at the center of *Chronique*, and in *Solibo* you see him passing in the distance; in *Texaco*, you hear people talking about him. I like this idea, it is exactly like real life.)

Reading these two novels in dialogue offers an effective way to highlight Chamoiseau's quest for a new form of narration that would represent creatively and critically the dislocated realities and guises of life and culture in Martinique under colonization and departmentalization. Where *Chronique* explores the demise of market culture in the twentieth century, *Solibo* interogates the erosion of vernacular culture, especially oral storytelling traditions. Through authorial and textual strategies of masquerade, both works depict and defy the moribund tendencies of (neo)colonialism and open up vital new perspectives concerning the articulation of postcolonial society. By strategically reworking vernacular traditions (including storytelling and local language) and creolizing genres, Chamoiseau's interwoven novels explore past-present relations in a critical and productive manner while highlighting the dangers of nostalgic regression.

Through the genres of the chronicle and the detective novel, Chamoiseau investigates the everyday lives of Martinicans, incorporating testimonial accounts as part of a more expansive inscription of history from below. When Chamoiseau started working on *Chronique*, he began by writing short stories about the market as well as poems that led to portraits of characters; he brought these fragments together to create a first draft of what eventually became a novel. The notion of fiction-making as a process of establishing points of connection, building relations between and among genres and "voices," is a powerful model for what is dramatically presented in *Solibo*. The presence of the same characters in both works and the interrelated spatiotemporalities of the novels create the illusion that the reader is learning about the ongoing life of a real community. The appended material to *Chronique* refers to Solibo's presence outside the market and makes reference to his calamity. Characters such as Man Goul, Man Elo, and Chinotte are first introduced in *Chronique* and reappear as characters in *Solibo*. From a temporal perspective, the story of Solibo's death is included among the many tragedies of modernization and departmentalization that take place in the *Chronique*. Pipi's folly, Alcide-Victor's murder, and the complete decimation of the market seem to have not yet taken place in the timeline of *Solibo*, which suggests that the novel is a subset of *Chronique*. The novels can be seen as engaging in a kind of cric-crac dialogue with each other: *Solibo Magnifique* "interrupts" or supplements *Chronique des sept misères* because its events take place at a time before the death of Zozor Alcide-Victor and Pipi, who appear as witnesses and suspects in the case of Solibo's mysterious death. *Chronique* interrogates *Solibo* by offering a counter-response to the prevailing views of the neocolonial order: where *Solibo* asserts the lack of value placed on the labors of the *djobeurs* (odd-job men) in a society under departmentalization (they are described in a police report as having no occupation), *Chronique* offers an account of the vital role they play in the market. Together these entangled narratives explore the interplay between the lives of individuals and sociopolitical circumstances, offering both a chronicle and a critical investigation of Martinique's history in the twentieth century.

Through the displacement of the fictional self in time and space, Chamoiseau counterfeits the illusion of presence and slyly calls attention to the role of the narrator as a mediator who constructs "reality." In *Solibo Magnifique*, Chamoiseau refers to himself as an ethnographic researcher who is producing a work on the role of the *djobeurs* (*SM*, 222) as well as refers to himself as the author of *Manman Dlo* (*SM*, 52). The trope of the observer whose very act of observation alters the realities he or she captures recurs in his writing.[2] Where the ethnographer observes, collects, and transmits what has been lost from the history of the people and their folk traditions, the *Marqueur* self-consciously plays upon the effects of intervention in remediating and reconstructing the narrative. With the Word Scratcher, Chamoiseau takes the disruptive effect of ethnography as the basis for creative expansiveness and a renewal of the vernacular tradition. Dominique Chancé eloquently describes the difference the *Marqueur* introduces when she says: "La belle unicité de 'nous' est perdue, comme l'innocence d'une énonciation collective"[3] ("The beautiful uniqueness of 'us' is lost as is the innocence of a collective enunciation"). The question of the relationship of the "I" to the "us" of community is rendered ambiguous by the marginal figure of the *Marqueur* who belongs to the community and the unfolding narrative, but who is also outside of it as an observer.

This *Marqueur* disrupts one illusion of presence only to introduce another. While the ethnographer acknowledges the difficulties of transcribing orality and of classifying human behaviors, the *Marqueur* exploits the potential lapses and creative possibilities in deconstructive ways. Referring to *Solibo*, Chris Bongie notes that "Chamoiseau simultaneously conjures up this strategic illusion [or oral narration] and deconstructs it in a series of metafictional gestures that remind his readers of the author's distance from the oral narrations that he is (re)presenting."[4] As with *Manman Dlo*, the author (in both *Chronique* and *Solibo*) elicits a metafictional field of play for ethnographic investigation and postcolonial critique. The contributions of other professions (such as *djobeurs*, the women in the markets, the bar owners, the vendors of fabrics, the postman, and a host of other *métiers* or trades) are also presented as reflecting and contesting social norms. Chamoiseau both fosters and disrupts the illusion of presence by playing the role of participant-narrator. Given his emphasis on the ways in which Martinican life is prescribed by colonization and departmentalization, authorial intrusions can be seen to signal the need for greater local intervention and participation in the drama and inscription of everyday life on the island.

Performativity and narrative masquerade play an important role in *Chronique* and *Solibo*. Chamoiseau "stages" the processes of storytelling, transcription, and transmission. He introduces stories within stories, includes playfully erudite footnotes, and experiments with identity in the form of metaleptic disruptions of the framed narrative structure. As a result, the immediacy of the storytelling performance is subverted; techniques of distancing, repetition, and unreliable narration call attention to the processes of fictional production. In *Chronique*, Chamoiseau creates the illusion that the *djobeurs* "step forward" to tell the reading audience their tales of tribulation and sorrow. The author appends texts and introduces ethnographic observations, undermining the illusion of presence. In *Solibo Magnifique*, Chamoiseau in the guise of the Word Scratcher or *Marqueur de paroles* "tells" the story of how he as a suspect-turned-detective becomes the author of the novel. This metafictional crime story posits the death of the storyteller as the symbolic birth of the creolizing novelist. At the same time, his playful reworking of crime fiction forges a new genre of postcolonial investigation. In both works, Chamoiseau extends the creolization of culture from the mimetic world of Martinique as represented in the narrative to the meta-narrative exploration of storytelling itself.

The blending of the marvelous with historical and sociological perspective, the mixed modes of drama and comedy, evident in the performance works, and techniques of masquerade prove to be indispensable elements in shaping the novelistic discourse. In an article titled "Que faire de la parole?" Chamoiseau explains the complexities of his use of multiple oral, written, and performative genres:

> Il s'agit de mobiliser à tout moment le génie de la parole, le génie l'écriture, mobiliser leurs lieux convergences mais aussi leurs lieux ivergences, leurs oppositions et leurs paradoxes, conserver à tout moment cette amplitude totale, qui traverse toutes les formes de la parole, mais qui traverse aussi tous les genres de l'écriture, du roman à poésie, de l'essai au théâtre.[5]
>
> (It is a matter of mobilizing the genius of the spoken word, the genius of writing, mobilize their spaces of convergence but also their spaces of divergence, their oppositions and their paradoxes, conserving all the time a

total amplitude, which traverses all forms of the word, but that traverses also all the genres of writing, from the novel to poetry, from the essay to theater.)

For Chamoiseau, the ambiguities and paradoxes of transmission (from oral to written, among genres, between French and Creole, etc.) mobilize and renew the imaginary. Police reports, oral stories, dialogues, street language, poetry, and genres of language contribute to the polyphonic qualities of his writing. Expressing as well as contesting the constructs of the real through magic realism, folklore, folktales, and other genres, the discursive space is fraught with comic, ethical, linguistic, socio-critical, and creative possibilities.

Strategies of linguistic camouflage met with mixed reviews. In Martinique, Chamoiseau's creative use of French and Creole languages in *Chronique des sept misères* and *Solibo Magnifique* sparked controversy. While *Chronique* exploits the interplay between French and Creole, *Solibo* takes this innovation further through the sophisticated interplay of linguistic and textual hybridity. Raphaël Confiant expressed ambivalence about the use of language in *Chronique des sept misères*. While he admired the interplay between languages, he argued that Creole was being violated by the French; similar concerns were expressed during a special session organized by GEREC to discuss *Chronique* in February 1987. *Solibo Magnifique*, which was inspired in part by the populist language found in the crime fiction of San Antonio and Simenon,[6] also provoked debates about language, such as Jean Bernabé expresses in an essay entitled "Les universitaires et les critiques répondent: Faut-il brûler Patrick Chamoiseau?"[7] Like Confiant, Bernabé worries that Chamoiseau was enriching the French language at the expense of Creole, thus enabling a new form of linguistic imperialism. Yet at the same time, Chamoiseau's use of Creole is also seen to highlight incidents of emotional intensity, detours from French ways of thinking, and thus as injecting a sense of poetic realism. Notably, Pierre Pinalie's very fine linguistic analysis of *Chronique des sept misères* offers a thoughtful inquiry into the effects of poetic language. Citing Jean Bernabé, he notes that the use of Creole should be interpreted not as a matter of exoticism, but as an impulse toward an alternative form of realism. Pinalie observes that many Martinican writers' use of the French language at the time often served to mask and conceal Creole presence, thus projecting a kind of double consciousness:

> le réel est vécu en créole, mais est assumé par la langue française, ce qui fait que la domination et l'éviction du créole plonge les écrivains dans une contradiction socio-linguistique et socio-littéraire dans laquelle ils se débattent, et d'où ils sortent par des procédés diversifies.[8]
>
> (the real is experienced in Creole, but taken up by the French language, which means that the domination and eviction of Creole plunges writers into a socio-linguistic and socio-literary contradiction, where they struggle, and from which they emerge by different procedures.)

By contrast, Chamoiseau was seen to embark on the more trangressive path of articulating himself through an entangled route of French-Creole lexical selections. Pinalie notes that forty-seven out of sixty times Chamoiseau offers translations from Creole into French, implying a non-Creole speaking audience of French readers is being addressed and included by this textual strategy.[9] While Creole words at times reflect the language of the marketplace, the presence of Creole elsewhere, such as in folktales, motifs, and proverbs, suggests that the novel is to be understood as a kind of oral storytelling event.[10] If *Chronique* conceals and unmasks hidden meaning through the incorporation of the vernacular and accompanying translations, *Solibo* suggests another linguistic strategy, one poised between French and Creole as well as between spoken and written uses of language in the metropolitan center and Martinique.[11] Language becomes a medium for introducing a hybrid perspective at the interfaces of French-Creole society.

Chamoiseau's linguistic and discursive strategies for exploring (post)colonial identity can be situated in the context of debates about Creole language and culture, which emerged in Martinique during the 1980s but were already in evidence in other parts of the Caribbean. Despite efforts by GEREC-F and fictional works by authors in Creole, the language was (and is) primarily spoken. In *Chronique* and *Solibo*, Chamoiseau's mixture of language is part of a wider strategy for defying the opposition of oral and written culture, particularly as embodied in the opposition of spoken Creole and written French. Chamoiseau has claimed that Glissant's *Malemort* inspired him to introduce new forms of language (*EPD*, 88). Whether he was aware of it or not, these linguistic experiments echoed techniques already present in the English-speaking Caribbean, such as the word play found in dub poetry, the code-switching present in works by Derek Walcott, and the experiments with nation language found in Kamau Brathwaite's poetry. English-speaking Caribbeans point to the "doggerel" nature of English itself, a language already shaped through the processes of creolization. Through nation language and creolized English, English Caribbean writers introduced oral language into written texts and found ways of deconstructing as well as stretching the English language. Thus, Chamoiseau's innovations participate in pan-Caribbean narrative traditions that take language itself as a site of resistance and transformation. In the French-speaking world, presided over by its linguistic guardian the *l'Académie française*, the spirit of linguistic impropriety, unrest, and revolt is all the more keenly felt when the French language is spoken through and transformed by other voices, such as Creole. It is important to note that Martinican Creole is a distinctly different language from French; therefore, French-only speakers must learn another language in order to understand fully Chamoiseau's creolized use of language. At the same time, for the Creole speaker, the transcription of an oral language produces a kind of distancing effect. Thus, Chamoiseau's free play with French-Creole languages is utopian to the extent that it projects a nonexistent shared psycho-social reality. It can also be seen as an erudite art that requires hermeneutic skills on the part of both French and Creole readers, thus signaling the need to decipher Martinique's deeply ambivalent sociopolitical conditions.

Chronique des sept misères

The title, *Chronique des sept misères* or *Chronicle of Seven Sorrows*, refers to the lives and sorrows of seven *djobeurs* or odd-job men working in the markets of Fort-de-France. While the novel weaves in and out of the *djobeurs'* activities in the market, the narrative of these men is to a large extent obscured by story about the fate of an apprentice and master *djobeur*, Pipi, whose narrative is further entangled with the tales about persons he encounters. The first part of the novel, entitled "Inspiration," narrates events preceding and after World War II while the latter part of the work, entitled "Expiration," offers an account of life under departmentalization. Stylistically, the energetic prose of the first part of the work mimics the progress of a wheelbarrow through the market, taking detours and moving among people with spontaneous energy. This motion is reflected in a very unusual approach to temporality as the narrative moves forward in tracing the life of Pipi, but then digresses and moves backward when new characters are introduced and their genealogies are presented. This back-and-forth spatiotemporal motion fosters a sense of community through interrelated narratives and shared incidents, which are presented through shifting viewpoints. "Expiration," the second half of the novel describes the life energy going out of Martinique under departmentalization as if the collective breath drawn in is now being exhaled. Indeed, it seems in many ways like a dying breath, ending with the extinction of the *djobeurs* as a social reality and the *djobeurs*' expiring voice as the oral narrative comes to a close. The latter half of the novel marks a retreat from the plurality of characters as Pipi becomes obsessed with recovering a buried colonial treasure. The *djobeurs*' narrative is tinged by nostalgia as they trace the effects of departmentalization on Martinique. This part of the novel is a response to the *djobeurs* who appear in Édouard Glissant's *Malemort*.[12] Characters such as Pipi and Bidjoule take inspiration from Glissant's *djobeurs* who are "obsessed by treasure hunts, delusions of grandeur and the senseless impulse to violence."[13] Increasingly, the novel takes on an absurd and mournful tone as the influence of departmentalization encompasses most facets of life.

When the novel was published in 1986, the response to it both at home and abroad was resoundingly positive; the novel was awarded both the *Prix Kléber Haedens* and the *Prix de l'île Maurice*.[14] In an article entitled, "*Chronique des sept misères*: la mémoire restituée," Raphaël Confiant praises the novel for restoring to memory this aspect of cultural life before the advent of Monoprix (a symbol of departmentalization and French consumerism).[15] He observes that the novel is "une grande oeuvre, une oeuvre a lire et a relire sans tarder" ("a great work to be read and reread without delay")[16] and admires the nonlinear, energetic prose style with its genealogies, folklore, and plethora of character types. Referring to the novel as a quasi-ethnographic testimonial, Confiant suggests that Chamoiseau depicted a world derided by many in contemporary Martinique, but which had certainly left an indelible impression on the collective unconscious,[17] particularly the depiction of the *djobeurs* and emphasis on the important role played by women who worked in the markets. Confiant claims that all Martinicans are to some extent *djobeurs* because they do not want to undertake the kind of meaningless, highly compartmentalized labor that has been imposed as a result of the modernization,[18] but long for liberating forms of work.[19] Similarly, Richard Burton sees the novel as demonstrating the enterprising nature of Martinicans who oppose the systems of power from within,[20] while Valérie Loichot sees the inspiration and expiration of the novel as part of a bio-rhythmic renewal of life.[21] Other critics emphasize the moribund aspects of the novel. Notably, Maeve McCusker read the work as a trauma narrative, claiming that this work lays the strongest claim to a tragic status in the author's oeuvre,[22] while Renée Gosson's ecocritical reading of the novel focuses on the ironic disintegration of the Creole garden as evidence of the corrosive influence of dominant French systems of rationalization.[23] Lorna Milne's nuanced account of *Chronique* situates the work in the context of the decline of the traditional market culture in Martinique under departmentalization but also recognizes the possibility for a renewal of the imaginary through techniques of narration and the recuperation of histories of place.[24] The tensions between representation and narration contribute to a reading of the novel as an ambiguous disclosure of a society in transition.

Chronique takes the form of a tragic-farce, which embodies the Marxist principle that history repeats itself so that "all great events and characters of world history occur, so to speak twice [. . .]: the first time as tragedy, the second time as farce."[25] By calling attention to the ways in which Martinique's colonial culture returns in the form of neocolonialism, this sense of the tragi-farcical cuts both ways, showing the dark, absurd legacies of the colonial impinging on the present and highlighting the tragedies of the present through farcical returns to the colonial past. Indeed, the closing description of the fate of the wheelbarrow and the odd-job man is a good indicator of the wobbly tone of the narrative as the narrators turn from an account of the extinction of memories about their place in society to a description of the wheelbarrow's demise:

> Elles ont si peu à charroyer! De plus, le gardien municipal a livré nos brouettes au camion de la voirie, amer peut-être de nous imaginer dans cette belle vie de France où alluvionnent les disparus, et—messieurs et dames bonsoir—il nous est très agréable de ne pas le détromper. (*CSM*, 240)

> These vendors bring so little to sell! Besides, the municipal guardian packed our wheelbarrows off in the garbage truck, embittered, perhaps, by thoughts of us living the fine life in France, where those who vanish from here fetch up, and—ladies and gentlemen good night—it's a real pleasure for us not to set him straight. (*CSS*, 173)

The issue of cultural extinction under departmentalization takes a comic turn at the prospect that the odd-jobbers have moved to France and are enjoying themselves, but this fantasy is soon undercut by the reality of the odd-jobbers precarious existence in Martinique. The tragic-farcical dimensions of the narrative are heightened through the interventions of the narrators who wish to conceal their fates from the municipal guardian, the representative of departmentalization, but nonetheless disclose their fate to an illusory listening audience whose named presence masks the role of the reading audience. Thus, techniques of narrative masquerade are intrinsic to the depiction and re-presentation of the instabilities of life in Martinique through history's tragic-farcical repetitions. More generally, *Chronique* can be seen as farcical through its presentation of unlikely, extravagant, and improbable situations, disguise and mistaken identity (names of characters are subject to change), and verbal humor, which includes both sexual innuendo and word play. While the first half of the work increases in pace as is typical of farce, the latter part of the work slows down so that by the time that the novel ends in an elaborate scene of pursuit (typical of farce), the reader is prepared for the tragic end of Pipi, who is caught and consumed by diabolical, underground forces at work in Martinique.

For Glissant, *Chronique* is an example of what Jacques-Stephen Alexis's terms "le réalisme merveilleux" or magical realism,[26] which gives expression to the details of Martincian life, language, and history; Glissant observes that Chamoiseau elicits "le débroussaillage de notre antillanité"[27] ("the clearing a space for our Caribbeanness"). Similarly, the *djob* ("odd job") represents a marevlous reality: the possibility for inventing life at each turn in the road.[28] The market, the natural habitus of the *djobeur*, is described as the prodigious stomach of the world.[29] The novel does not simply describe but expresses that unimaginable appetite for errancy that introduces its rhythms into the mechanisms of existence: "l'inimaginable appétit d'errance qui rythme la mécanique d'existence" ("the unimaginable appetite for errancy that unfolds in the rhythms of the mechanics of existence").[30] In *A Companion to Magical Realism*, Lois Parkinson Zamora observes that the magical realism has a capacity to integrate various kinds of otherness without reconciling their contradictions,[31] while the editors, drawing on the work of Franz Roh, suggest that magical realism offers an intuitive representation of the interior figure of the exterior world.³² The magical view tends to function as an allegorical coding of history from a creolized perspective so that the often tragic dimensions of the colonial experience are represented in a disguised way. While the effects may be associated with resistance and liberation, as is the case with Mackandal's lycanthropic power, the figure of the *dorlis* or *soucouyant* suggest that they may also represent disguised ways of representing traumatic acts of violence and abuse in colonial society. Wen-chin Ouyang puts the matter succinctly when she observes:

> magical realism is inherently political[,] concerned not only with the continuing influence of empire but also with the corruption of political authority set up in the post-independence nation-states, not to mention the attendant cultural politics that partake in the formulation of a plausible postcolonial identity.³³

These shifting political contexts suggest that the role and function of magical realism is itself subject to fluctuation. For Martinique, where the transition from colonialism to self-sufficiency was curtailed by the rise of departmentalization, magical realism signals shifting apprehensions of power relations, cultural forms of expression, and the role of production/consumption.

Magical realism functions differently in the two halves of the *djobeurs'* narrative account. "Inspiration" incorporates magic as part of the characters' life histories, emotional experiences (particularly traumatic events or sorrow), and perceptions of the real. A tragic-farcical view is evident when Théophile's corpse becomes unbearably heavy for the pallbearers as they approach the grave (*CSM*, 47). Manman-Doudou is married to a fisherman who is said to have a pact with the devil because he catches so many fish (*CSM*, 42). Likewise the *dorlis* is a coded, symbolic figure whose presence attests to the threat of rape in Caribbean society, making the figure a bearer of tragedy. However, the figure of the *dorlis* is also comically presented and pragmatically dealt with by women who have their own counter-magical means of protecting themselves, which introduces a farcical dimension. Beverley Ormerod notes that this use of folklore is consistent with the Creole story as there is "the same mixture of trickery, humour and plausibility."³⁴ The characters inhabit a reality that is perceived and experienced as magical. The magical offers an indirect, coded way of articulating events or subjects that might otherwise be difficult to mention, discuss, or express fully. The magical perspective reflects and expresses lived realities.

By the second half of the novel, everyday life is narrated increasingly through the challenges and changes that departmentalization brings, including a rationalized approach to work, migration, goods in the market, and even familial relationships. Chinotte's Antichrist, which is perceived by the *djobeurs* as real in the first part of the narrative, is represented as a form of delusion in the second half. Chinotte rejects the magical reading of her life as someone who has acquired a treasure and can conquer a *quimboiseur* (sorcerer, practitioner of Afro-Creole spiritual traditions), stating that she has worked hard throughout the Caribbean to scrape together a living. Odibert hears about "her" death on the radio, which prompts her to disappear magically into the public fountain in a fulfillment of this announcement (*CSM*, 174). When *quimboiseurs* come to collect this magical water, the fountain is turned off because the costs of supplying so much water are too high for the municipality. The magical real narrative exposes how rational measures are transforming public spaces. This changing perspective represents a mode of resistance to the increasingly rationalized public sphere. In the second part of *Chronique*, belief in the magical increasingly serves as a means to avoid facing economic realities. At the same time, the interrogation of the magical from a realistic perspective, on the part of the narrators, serves to disclose the malign effects of departmentalization, thus restoring magical realism's potential to bring together multiple interpretations of events.

The rise of departmentalization is accompanied by a growing sense of disenchantment, delusion, and disillusionment. Pipi's mordant longings for instant wealth take him away from contemporary realities; he becomes obsessed with the quest for treasure and enters into dialogue with Afoukal, the *zombi*. This turn from entrepreneurial energy to a regressive fantasy about the past serves to strengthen the novel's critique of the lack of viable employment in departmental Martinique. Even when Pipi shows initiative in developing a Creole garden, this success is quickly quashed as scientists move in and try to turn this art form into a rational method of production. In the process of rationalizing the garden, it is destroyed. In this context, the realistic (rather than magical) aspects of the narrative function as an allegory for the erasure of Creole culture under departmentalization. Other forms of sociocultural extinction or "ethnocide" (as Chamoiseau refers to them) are depicted. The decline of the markets is chronicled by the *djobeurs* who describe its consequences for themselves and others; they have less and less work to do and are gradually replaced by professional transporters. Mam Joge's abandoned son, Bidjoule the *djobeur*, goes mad. Riot police quell student protests through the use of violence, resulting in the death of Mam Joge's second son Emile (a repetition of a story that is presented in *Une manière d'Antigone*). Her husband dies in a fire that consumes the bar Chez Chinotte, a fire started by sailors who are angry about the riots in the city. Pipi's love, Anastase, murders the man she loves, Zozor Alcide-Victor, who is emotionally and sexually mistreating her. Rats, ants, and zombie-sellers (ghostly presences that the police try to arrest) invade the markets. Rather than relying on his wit and his skill, Pipi reverts to a listless fantasy world and a zombified fascination with the past that leads to his destruction. Likewise, the narrative returns to the tale of the dorlis, Anatole-Anatole, and in an ironic reversal: the playfulness of magical realism from within creolized culture is turned inside-out (like the skin of the dying *dorlis*) in a mimetic reflection of socio-psychological alienation. In the end, Anatole-Anatole's double name signals the ways in which his tragic death is resituated in the context of the farcical transformations of departmental Martinique:

> *La fin tragique du dorlis.* [. . .] on retrouva son cadavre blanchi comme une peau de touriste, castré, écorché sur toute la face ventrale, avec sur le visage l'horreur indiscriptible qui saisit les damnés aux abords du grand saut. Le médecin légiste, peu au fait des mystères de la vie, diagnostiqua un cancer de la peau et une mort par infarctus. (*CSM*, 233–34)

> *The tragic fate of the dorlis.* [. . .] the corpse they found was bleached as white as a tourist, castrated, flayed all down its front, and wearing the expression of indescribable agony that comes from the damned poised on the edge of an abyss. The forensic pathologist, poorly informed about the mysteries of life, diagnosed skin cancer and death by coronary thrombosis. (*CSS*, 167–68)

Calcified, the whitened corpse of the *dorlis* is associated with the white skin of the tourist as well as with the failings of French departmental approaches to the realities of life in Martinique. Magical realism thus becomes a means to highlight interpretive differences in a neocolonial context.

Under departmentalization, magical realism comes to signal a flight from the real as characters turn away from history and escape into magical explanations of the real or are consumed by the desire to inhabit an enchanted reality. Such is the case when Pipi becomes obsessed with recovering Afoukal's treasure. Rather than learning to unlock the resources of the past in order to confront more effectively the challenges of the present, he engages in a regressive and deluded quest for instant wealth. Through Afoukal's narrative, the reader is presented with a retelling of Martinican colonial history in eighteen parts. This history traces the capture of slaves, the Middle Passage, the creolization of language through forgetfulness, the idea of nicknames as a form of resistance, a description of a typical day of slave labor, the horrors of the sugar mill when a person is caught in its teeth, harvesting, the use of leisure time for dancing and dice, the constant hunger, colonial religious conversion, disease and folk medicine, abortion practices under slavery, suicide, the use of poisons, marooning, and Afoukal's own sense of strange loyalty to the *béké*. This narrative bridges past and present, showing how certain social practices can be traced back to colonial forms of resistance. Instead of the quest for capital or the treasure of profits gained through the plantation system and slavery, the narrative valorizes the hunt for collective memory as a meaningful form of recuperation.

A critique of nostalgia is embedded in a self-consciously reflective nostalgic novel. Pipi embodies the narcissistic aspects of nostalgia through his melancholic retreat from the world and entry into a disabling state of existence, which leads to alienation and death, while the *djobeurs* embody a mournful attitude in that their sorrows are part of a larger process of giving voice and working through grief. Between these nostalgic and reflective forms, Chamoiseau's narrative also manifests nostalgia for a time when autonomy was possible, which finds representation in the Creole garden, the Creole city, Creole language, and Creole culture. However, the moment of Creole plenitude is also shown to have been extinguished in a tragic-farcical way through departmentalization. At the end of "Inspiration," the *djobeurs* refer to the "wave of nostalgia" that washes over them when they consider the energy and struggles of the postwar period, a time when self-sufficiency was still possible (*CSM*, 128; *CSS*, 91). Reflecting on the date of Pipi as well as their own, they discuss the processes and purposes of memory:

> Quant à nous, Didon, Sirop, Pin-Pon, Lapochodé, un autre genre de diablesse nous dévore. Epuisés sur les caisses, serrés les uns aux autres pour conjurer un froid lancinant, nous disons et redisons ces paroles, ces sou-

venirs de vie, avec la certitude de devoir disparaître. Vous en donner cette version nous a fait un peu de bien, si vous venez demain vous en aurez une autre, plus optimiste peut-être, quelle importance? Cela se maintenant: l'Histoire ne compte que par ce qu'il en reste; au bout de celle-là rien ne subsiste, si n'est pas nous—mais c'est bien peu. A la disparition de Pipi, la douleur nous mit en grappe, comme nous le sommes maintenant, incapables du *Je*, du *Tu*, de distinguer les uns des autres, dans une survie collective et diffuse, sans rythme interne ni externe. (*CSM*, 240)

(As for us, Didon, Sirop, Pin-Pon, Sifilon, Lapochodé, we're being devoured by another sort of *jablesse*. Worn out on our crates, huddled together to ward off a piercing chill, we say these words over and over again, these memories of life, certain we must disappear. Giving you this version has done us a bit of good, and if you come by tomorrow you'll get a different one, more cheerful perhaps—what does it matter? This much is known, now: History only counts through what remains when the story's done. There is nothing left at the end of this one, except us, and that's not much. When Pipi vanished, pain bunched us all together, as we are now, incapable of saying I or you, or telling one from another, lumped in a collective, diffuse survival without rhyme or reason.) (*CSS*, 172–73)

In the case of the *djobeurs*, the magical real (represented by the *jablesse*) can be seen as a thinly veiled reference to uneven, all-consuming power dynamics in the modern era. While the *jablesse* (she-devil) who consumes Pipi represents a narcissistic form of nostalgia, the *djobeurs* confront the she-devil of departmentalization. Through their ruminations, Chamoiseau shows the ways in which both the colonial past and the neocolonial present threaten life on the island. The vanishing of the *djobeurs* from use, observation and memory and supposed reappearance in France makes ironic reference to the illusion that life is better in the *metropole* as well as points to the massive migration of workers to France. Unlike Pipi, whose life is extinguished by the destructive tendencies of narcissistic nostalgia, the *djobeurs*, who juxtapose the tragic (colonial) and farcical (neocolonial) effects of French intervention, engage in a reflective form of nostalgia, which "dwells on loss, ruins, and dreams, and acknowledges imperfection"[35] but also introduces the possibility of a more cheerful account of events, which might be rendered on another day. The emphasis on the affective qualities of life (its sorrows) is a means to acknowledge the bodily, material conditions of life and the economic imperatives that shape histories of dispossession. The narrators claim that history only counts through what remains when the story is done, and since nothing of Pipi and not much of themselves remains by the end of the narrative account, they suggest that their account may be of little worth. Thus, the chronicle shifts from the affective symptoms of dispossession (sorrow) to underlying socioeconomic continuities and discontinuities, disclosing the primacy of physicality and the ineluctability of embodied history.

The related motifs of disappearance, apparition, and embodiment call attention to the social themes of mobility and drifting. The theme of mobility is repeated in varying forms, including the Middle Passage, the history of those who entered into indentured servitude, marooning, the travels of those who served in the army during World War II, migration from the country into the urban centers, migration from Martinique to France, migration throughout the Caribbean in search of employment, the flow of goods and imports, and the mobility of those who drift through society. The presence of the *driveur* or the person who drifts through society is a particularly important and recurring theme for Chamoiseau. In an article titled "Les nègres marrons de l'en-ville: à propos du driveur" (1992) and in *Écrire en pays dominé*, Chamoiseau explains his theory in more detail. "La langue créole appelle Drive une situation peu reluisante durant laquelle on erre sans fin" ("Drive in the Creole language refers to a far from brilliant situation in which one errs [wanders] incessantly") (*EPD*, 204). The *driveur* has experienced misfortune and is constantly on the move. While the marooned slave is the original *driveur*, the freed slave and the indentured servant who has fulfilled his/her contract are often also *driveurs*. Chamoiseau's genealogies in *Chronique* show the ways in which the modern *driveur* is literally heir to the colonial and post-emancipation *driveur*. Chamoiseau observes that "Le djob c'est la Drive dans le travail. On va de services en services, et chaque jour le service est différent" ("The *djob* is drifting in the form of work. One goes from job to job, and each day the job is different").[36] Chamoiseau's view of the drifter or *driveur* is positive in that he sees such a person as open to creolization and the world as well as opposed to *bétonisation* and rootedness, but negative to the extent that the resistance tendencies of the *driveur* fail to translate into political consciousness or action. Unconsciously, the *driveur* may continue to play out colonial paradigms or remain locked in postures of futile resistance. Notably, *Chronique des sept misères* examines the implications of drifting in the erotic sphere and on familial relationships as sexual partners meet briefly and move on.

Short-lived, often brutal sexual relations can be seen as part of the legacies of colonialism, which broke apart families under slavery, included incidents of rape, and separated children from their parents. Sorrows ensue for children, parents, and lovers through this drifting social dynamic. In choosing the urban maroon as a protagonist and in exploring the psychic and emotional landscape of the *driveur*, Chamoiseau found a situation (and figure) capable of giving complex expression to the interactions of affective and socioeconomic histories so that the chronicle as a whole fulfils a testimonial function, acting as a drifting witness to Martinican (un)consciousness.

This spirit of mobility is evident in the aesthetics of flux; as noted, the narrators observe that the chronicle can be retold in various ways on different days. At the same time, the voices of the *djobeurs* and the interventions of the ethnographer highlight the need for nostalgia as an ethical and heuristic way to connect, however precariously, fragmented memories in order to cobble together (*bricolage*) a relational history.[37] Notably, the novel's focus on the reclamation and inscription of lost genealogies and the knitting together of lost personal histories recuperates a highly fragmentary account of community. The chronicling of history from below is refracted through the life histories of Martinicans. The stories of public figures (Admiral Robert, de Gaulle, Aimé Césaire, etc.) and significant events in world history (World War II, abolition of slavery, departmentalization, etc.) are embedded in the Martinican drama of everyday life and the quest for survival so that a postcolonial perspective on world and local events emerges. Such events are measured in terms of the ways they impact, for better or for worse, the everyday lives of Martinique's peoples. While the ethnographer's act of narration ensures that the chronicle does not dissipate into oblivion, the *djobeurs'* reference to alternative accounts of history and the ethnographer's inclusion of supplementary materials showcase the unfinished, ongoing activity of narration: the chronicle foregrounds narrative raw materials that have not yet been consumed by the symbolic economies of narrative.[38] Rather than accept the foreclosure of the processes of decolonization, Chamoiseau's ethnographer opens up a space of voices, which resists narrative incorporation and whose presence as an outpost of history points to the need for further reclamation. Footnotes are used to explain certain historical facts, words, and social realities, thus providing the sense that the *djobeurs'* narrative is a performance written for French tourists, including perhaps those Canadian scholars who are described as taking their photo. Various documents are appended to the novel, creating a sense that there is no single, finite version of the tale. The texts include a newspaper article from *France-Antilles* about the reconstruction of the market in Fort-de-France, a note by the ethnographer about the extinction or ethnocide of the *djobeur*, a glossary of cries used by the *djobeurs*, a song in Creole by Kouli, the spoken words of the *djobeurs* (1988 edition), and the notes or outtakes from the novel (1988 edition). The last two texts, prefaced with comments by P.C. (short for Patrick Chamoiseau) initiate a trope that follows in Chamoiseau's novels, whereby he apparently involves the reader in the processes of the fiction-making process. This hybrid discourse mixes together multiple genres of discourse, such as verse, journalism, sociological information, a song, a business card, footnotes, et cetera. These textual maneuvres invoke other versions of the narrative, elicit alternative combinatorial possibilities, and thus leave the reader—like the wheelbarrow driver—to negotiate a way through Martinican space.

Solibo Magnifique

Solibo Magnifique brings together the conventions of the crime novel and Creole storytelling traditions;[39] this detective novel entails an investigation into the suspicious death of a Creole storyteller who appears to have been strangled by the word. The novel's opening citations establish the work's positioning as a metafictional and metaphysical detective story as well as suggest the ways in which the title *Marqueur de paroles* (Word Scratcher) might be understood to bring together processes of inscription and orality. The novel opens with citation from Italo Calvino, who defines writing as a mysterious kind of spiral drawing whose form grows like a crystal:

> Ce qui est au centre de la narration pour moi n'est pas l'explication d'un fait étrange mais *l'ordre* que ce fait étrange développe en soi et autour de soi: le dessin, la symétrie, le réseau d'images qui se déposent autour de lui, comme dans la formation d'un cristal. (*SM*, 11)

> (What is at the center of the narration for me is not the explication of a strange fact but the *order* that this strange fact develops in itself and around itself: the drawing, the symmetry, the network of images which assembles around it, as in the formation of a crystal.) (*StM*, not paginated)

While the citation of Calvino places emphasis on vision and drawing, the quotation of Glissant's remarks on the synthesis of the oral and the written (as a means to participate in the "communal chant") focuses on the oral tradition. Althierry Dorival, a Haitian singer, is cited in Creole: "Mé zanmis ôté nouyé!?" (*SM*, 11), which can be translated loosely as "My friends, where are you!?" Significantly, this troubadour figure is a witness to absence, an act that transforms the situation into one of mourning. The logic of the narrative follows a similar rhetoric. Like the breath that structures *Chronique*, this narrative is broken into "Avant la parole" ("Before the Word") and "Après la parole" ("After the Word"). These titles are ambiguous for the "afterword" is Chamoiseau the narrator's account of the tale that Solibo was telling when he died. The section that takes place before this concerns the investigation into Solibo's death. This achronological approach to narrative is confounded by the fact that both narratives are reconstructive acts of memory. These disjunctive narrative processes reflect the irrational and mysterious workings of memory, orality, and textuality.

The *Marqueur de paroles* (Word Scratcher) marks his presence as a mediator in the relay of events: the composition of a tale in which he is both present as a witness, suspect, and investigator and absent as the author of a fiction that takes place within the real rather than imagined world. Rather than the collective *nous* of narrators, Chamoiseau stages his narrative performance as a kind of *metteur-en-scène* in a novel that is a both a wake for a dead storyteller and a wake for a dying storytelling form. In this mystery of storytelling, it is especially important to distinguish between the imagined and implied narrators. Chamoiseau the *Marqueur* and the *djobeurs* are both imagined narrators: the ones who are supposedly telling the story to the reader. The presence of the investigator-narrator masks the author's role as the agent responsible for the creation of these fictional, multivocal, multigeneric texts. In this case, the mix of genres includes epigraphic citations, dialogues, a police incident report, excerpts from the investigation reports, stories, the wake, translation, interrogations, and a storytelling performance accompanied by drumming, which contains riddles and other genres.

Set in Fort-de-France, Martinique, the novel recounts an investigation into the mysterious death of a Creole storyteller named Solibo Magnificent, who chokes and dies in the midst of his discourse on the Savannah (a local park). Solibo's death foreshadows the fate of Creole culture itself, which is choking to death in modern-day Martinique, but also attests to sociocultural vitality in other ways. For example, Beverley Ormerod notes that the interrogation of the witnesses reveals differing concepts of time in French and Creole worldviews and introduces aspects of Creole popular culture, including magic and the supernatural.[40] Food, sexuality, the market culture, syncretic religious beliefs, and the importance of storytelling in everyday life are recurring themes in the various testimonies. They are not wanted by the police investigators but bear witness through Chamoiseau's narrative. The novel offers a vivid depiction of creolization in the practices of everyday Martinican life.

The poetics of creolization infuse Chamoiseau's approach to the genres and tropes of crime fiction. Chamoiseau came of age during this strong reawakening and circulation of the crime genre across national and linguistic boundaries. From the mid-1940s to the 1970s, Gallimard published numerous novels by Peter Cheyney, Ed McBain, and Chester Himes as part of the famed *Série Noire* and *Carré Noir*, novels that made their way to Martinique and into Chamoiseau's hands. The voyage from France to Martinique is only part of this tale of circulating genre. For just as French critics invented the American film *noir*, they played a significant role in reawakening the literary genre by translating American and British novels and marketing them as *noir*. Moreover, this invented tradition became the source for the French *noir*, which quickly moved from the translation to the creation of texts. The editorial policy of the *Série Noire*, under the direction of Marcel Duhamel, actively encouraged a certain kind of writing. Duhamel provided conventions for would-be authors, notably Himes. Published with distinctive black-and-gold covers, various kinds of crime novels were branded and marketed as a new umbrella genre of French *noir*. In film, a series of Lemmy Caution films appeared in the 1950s, featuring Eddie Constantine in the starring role, which led to the strange versioning of this detective figure in Jean-Luc Godard's *Alphaville, une étrange aventure de Lemmy Caution* (1965). In *Alphaville*, the detective is thrown into a futuristic society where the repression of *language* and emotion are forms of social oppression and domination. Jean-Pierre Melville, Jules Dassin, and Godard are among the directors who revived the *noir* tradition. Films such as *Bob le flambeur* (1955) offered sympathetic views of the working class and the underworld and celebrated the language of the streets, or argot. In some of these works—for example, *Le samourai* (1967), *Le cercle rouge* (1970), and *Un flic* (1972)—the suspect or criminal rather than the detective wins the audience's sympathy, or the narrative offers a critical view of the detective. In *Du Rififi chez les hommes* (1955), the criminal takes on the role of the detective in order to outwit the police as well as the criminals who threaten his life and the life of his colleagues and their families.

In *Écrire en pays dominé*, Chamoiseau expresses admiration for the crime novel: "Je devins un expert en roman policier, un vaillant en affaires d'espionnage" (*EPD*, 45) ("I became an expert in detective novels and courageous in matters of espionage."). He describes a bookseller specializing in detective writing: "Elle semblait avoir misé son existence dans les romans policiers avec Lemmy Caution, Poirot, Carella, Sherlock Holmes, Ed-Cercueil et Fossoyeur" (*EPD*, 45) ("She seemed to have lived her life through detective novels with Lemmy Caution, Poirot, Carella, Sherlock Holmes, Coffin Ed and Gravedigger"). In this passage, Chamoiseau reveals his familiarity with a wide range of crime writers, including Peter Cheyney, Agatha Christie, Evan Hunter / Ed McBain, Arthur Conan Doyle, and Chester Himes. This selection of crime stories covers a number of subgenres including, notably, the classical detective story, the hard-boiled detective, police procedural, thriller, and the African American detective novel. Nor surprisingly, all of these generic influences as well as others are evident in the construction of *Solibo Magnifique*.

In the tradition of the postcolonial detective novel, Chamoiseau mobilizes the crime genre for his own purposes, tweaking its generic conventions in what becomes "a narrative of 'social detection,' to borrow a phrase from Fredric Jameson, a 'vehicle for judgments on society and revelations of its hidden nature.'"[41] Jumbling the well-known patterns of the classical detective genre, the French reawakening of the *noir* tradition introduced existential and metaphysical works of crime fiction with the power to unsettle the reader or viewer: "Instead of reassuring, they disturb. They are not an escape, but an attack."[42] The power to unsettle the reader, the language of the streets, the critique of society, and the idea of the detective as an outsider are all motifs that Chamoiseau appropriates in creating his own detective story. The detective novel offers a protagonist who both embodies and tests law and order; psychologically and symbolically, this figure represents the domains in which the law is carried out or transgressed. Police officers guard the boundaries of the social order, but their actions are also indicative of the extent to which self-policing takes place in Chamoiseau's Martinique. The private detective, particularly in the *noir* tradition, offers an ambivalent, marginalized view of society. In exploring the role of the police, Chamoiseau forges a culturally marginalized detective figure and his own francophone Caribbean genre of investigative fiction. Like San-Antonio, he revels in humor. Where San-Antonio writes in "an untranslatable argot that pushed tough-guy talk to its Rabelaisian limits"[43] and indulges in comically mixed metaphors, polymorphous puns, and malapropisms, Chamoiseau uses French-Creole interfaces for his playful reworking of the genre in a tragic-comic mode. Like San-Antonio, Chamoiseau plays with slippages between his fictional persona and authorial identity because the name of the author and the detective are one and the same.

The role of the police is one example of the tweaking of genre for the purposes of postcolonial investigation. In the characters of the chief investigator, Évariste Pilon, we can see the tradition of the classical detective novel. Pilon favors a rational methodology in order to solve cases. Typically, the classical detective novel is associated with bourgeois attitudes toward society and the assertion of order and reason. Beginning with Edgar Allen Poe's Dupin, this tradition includes Sherlock Holmes, Hercule Poirot, and Maigret. These detectives employ a system or method in order to understand and explain the crime. Maigret bears special consideration, given his already cited influence on Chamoiseau. The detective can be either a policeman or a private individual. At first glance, Maigret seems to be less rational, less prone to rely on forensic evidence, than his counterparts in the classical tradition. However, he does have a method, which is ethnographic or anthropological. In *Maigret's Memoirs*, the detective observes that he has to "know the milieu in which a crime has been committed, to know the way of life, the habits, morals, reactions of the people involved in it, whether victims, criminals or merely witnesses."[44]

Pilon, the middle-class detective, can be said to fit within the tradition of the classical detective story or police procedural, crafting reports written in bureaucratic language, collecting forensic evidence, and employing a "rational" methodology. The narrator observes:

> Pourtant, amateur de mystères policiers, l'inspecteur principal n'appréciait guère le côté irrationnel des «affaires» d'ici-là. Les données de base n'y étaient jamais au fil à plomb, une dose déraisonnable, légèrement maléfique, embrumait le tout, et comme l'inspecteur, malgré son séjour au pays de Descartes, avait levé ici-dans comme nous-mêmes dans la même intelligence de zombies et soucougnans divers, ses efforts scientifiques et de

logique glaciale dérapaient bien souvent. Il s'y tenait au prix d'un arcane mental assez désagréable , et rêvait encore pour ici au jour de la mort de Solibo, d'un mystère trace au compas (et à l'équerre). (*SM*, 117–18)

Though a fan of detective novels, the Chief Inspector never liked the irrational side of "cases" in this country. The initial facts were never reliable, a shadow of unreason, a hint of evil, clouded everything, and despite his long stay in the land of Descartes, since he had been raised in this country like the rest of us with the same knowledge of zombies and various evil soucougnans, the Inspector's scientific efforts and cold logic often skidded. He stuck to it at the price of a rather unpleasant mental exertion, but still dreamed for this country—even on the day of Solibo's death—of a mystery drawn with a compass (and a protractor). (*StM*, 75)

This description presents a satiric view of Pilon's efforts to impose a French worldview on Martinique by employing a rational method that runs counter to the realities of Martinique where simple stories of dirty rum and knife fights prevail (*SM*, 118). This classical approach to detection ultimately fails him. Despite his claims to rationality, unlike Maigret, Pilon does not attempt to understand the milieu or to listen to what the witnesses have to say. Rather, he seeks to force the narrative (as well as all tales of crime in Martinique) to fit within the French narrative pattern for murder and detection.

Ironically, the autopsy confirms the witnesses' attribution of the cause of death: all the symptoms of death by strangulation from the inside, almost to the point of a throat-cutting (*SM*, 215), a view consistent with the idea of having one's throat cut by the word. The European, scientific worldview and the Caribbean, magical worldview are not inconsistent. Inconsistency and irrationality are evident in attempts to rely on a rational French methodology that fails to account for the unique sociocultural contexts of Martinique. In despair, the two detectives, Pilon and Bouaffesse, consult a *quimboiseur* who fails to offer a rational explanation. Instead, this sorcerer figure reinforces the sense of mystery by exploring the connection between the life of the individual and the ability to narrate as a life-sustaining force:

[. . .] sans même réfléchir, à dire qu'il décrivait une pluie habituelle, leur souffla sa connaissance de l'égorgette de la parole. Pilon se la fit répéter une-deux fois mais n'en fut pas plus avancé. Dans le corps, inspectère, avait divulgué le sorcier dans un créole sans âge, il y a l'eau et le souffle, la parole et le souffle, le souffle est la force, la force est l'idée du corps sur la vie, sur sa vie. Maintenant, inspectère, arrête ta pensée [. . .] qu'arrive-t-il si la vie n'est pas ce qu'elle doit être- et si l'idée défaille . . . ? (*SM*, 218–19)

[. . .] without even thinking about it, as if he were describing the rain, whispered what he knew about snicked by the word. Pilon had it repeated to him one or two times but that didn't get him any further. In the body, Inspekder, the sorcerer revealed in his ageless Creole, there's water and there's breath, speech is breath, breath is strength, strength is the body's idea of life, of its life. Now, Inspekder, stop your thinking [. . .] what happens when life isn't what it should be—and when your mind draws a blank? (*StM*, 153)

The detective returns in despair, with more questions and enigmas than answers. The classical detective novel has given way to an unsolvable mystery in which the storyteller's blocked creativity is symptomatic of the loss of narrative.

The inability to provide a coherent narrative marks the transition to the unofficial investigation into who Solibo is and why he is magnificent (*SM*, 219), which is led by the witness-suspect-turned-narrator, namely Chamoiseau. Pilon and Chamoiseau become allies as unofficial detectives who seek to elucidate (even if they cannot explain) the nature of this mysterious death. The novel is represented as the composite narrative outcome of the unofficial and official investigations. Like Maigret, Chamoiseau seeks to understand Solibo's death through an immersion in the cultural milieu. Through the narrator's investigations, the classical detective novel gives way to the metafictional or metaphysical. Jeffrey T. Nealon describes the effects of the metafictional detective story for the reader:

Whether consciously or unconsciously, the genre comments upon the process of sifting through signs, and ultimately upon the possibility of deriving order from the seeming chaos of conflicting clues and motives. The unraveling work of the detective within the story mirrors and assists the work of the reader, as both try to piece together the disparate signs that might eventually solve the mystery. The reader of the detective novel comes metafictionally to identify with the detective, as both the reader and the detective are bound up in the metaphysical or epistemological work of interpretation, the work of reading clues and writing a solution or end.[45]

This unofficial, metafictional detective story reverses the conventions of the classical detective story: for it is the death of the individual that serves to elucidate the dying cultural tradition of oral storytelling. Solibo is the victim who becomes a witness to another death: "Il avait vu mourir les contes, défaillir le créole" (*SM*, 223) ("He had seen the tales die, Creole lose its strength" (*StM*, 157). In narrative terms, the search for the cause of Solibo's death serves as "the pre-text for locating the core of an evanescent, shifting Caribbean identity."[46]

Chamoiseau's reworking of the hard-boiled tradition enables a critique of (post)colonial violence and psychic trauma. Bouaffesse and his assistants, nicknamed Diab-Anba-Feuilles, Nono-Bec-en-Or, and Jambette, typify the kinds of figures found in the hard-boiled tradition. They use unnecessary force, attacking Doudou Ménar, who dies as a result of police beating, and torturing Congo, who defenestrates in order to put an end to suffering. While one might see this use of violence as part of the crime narrative tradition, it reflects also sociopolitical realities. Chamoiseau had already recorded such instances of violence, including the death of the *lycée* student beaten by the police in *Chronique des sept misères*. Chamoiseau the narrator observes that the police "amena les absurdités du pouvoir et de la force: terreur et folie" (*SM*, 27) ("brought together the absurdities of power and might, terror and folly," *StM*, 9). This hard-boiled approach to the novel is reminiscent of Chester Himes. In "Topographies of Violence: Chester Himes's Harlem Domestic Novels," Michael Denning writes that the central character of the novels is Harlem itself, whose topography and character-system they map.[47] Himes "draws his symbolic landscape with detailed but stylised descriptions of food, clothing, and social life."[48] Within this social map, Denning sees the police detectives, Coffin Ed and Grave Digger, as "mediators, between black and white, life and death, law and crime" and as "at once enforcers of the law and figures of violence and death."[49] Not only does Chamoiseau refer to Coffin Ed and Gravedigger in his own writings, there are a number of points of comparison to be considered, including the combination of absurd humor and violence, the idea of Harlem (Martinique) as a marginalized island within the larger society, the role of the black detective, the tensions between the various levels of the police force (with the white superiors representing a kind of colonial order in America), the role of police brutality, the question of legitimate lifestyles, the nicknames for the police, and the array of colorful, street-wise characters. Following the advice of Marcel Duhamel (editor of the *Série Noire*), Himes reinvented the tradition, drawing on the novels of Peter Cheyney, Raymond Chandler, and Dashiell Hammett.

Chamoiseau extends the trope of rewriting by "signifying" upon Himes's own rewriting of the detective novel. Within the narrative, the police function as mediators between the neocolonial present and colonial past. The narrator makes this connection, observing:

> Avec elle, arrivent aussi les chasseurs des bois d'aux jours de l'esclavage, les chiens à marronnage, la milice des alentours d'habitation, les commandeurs des champs, les gendarmes à cheval, les marins de Vichy du temps de l'Admiral, toute une Force qui inscrit dans la mémoire collective l'unique attestation de notre histoire: Po la poliiice! (*SM*, 83)

> With cops the hunting dogs from slavery days return, the maroon-chasing dogs, the militia that watched the plantation, the overseers, the mounted guards, the Vichy marines of the time of the Admiral, all one and the same Force inscribed in the collective memory under the unique attestation of our history: Coppers here come the poliiice! (*StM*, 49)

Bouaffesse seems invincible, having gained the reputation of being a *demi-quimboiseur* (*SM*, 56). He is affiliated with various malevolent aspects of the colonial past and its legacies: he served in the Algerian war and is described in relation to the history of slavery and the Middle Passage. He is intent on gaining power over others within the sociopolitical hierarchy:

> Cet homme, il faut le dire, est du bois des chefs. Sur le bateau négrier c'est lui qui nous aurait baignés à l'eau de mer, désinfecté la cale au vinaigre bouilli, nous aurait frottés d'huile un peu avant la vente. Sur l'habitation, il eût été celui qui donnait la cadence dur travail au champ, puis, plus tard, commandeur. Il était fait pour être chef, mais du côté du manche. Diriger, par exemple, une troupe de nègres-marrons galeux ne l'aurait pas intéressé. (*SM*, 58)

> This man, it must be said, was made of the stuff of chiefs. On the slave ship, he would have been the one to bathe us with seawater, to disinfect the hold with boiling vinegar, and rub us with oil right before the sale. On the plantation, he would have been the one to shout the cadence of the field work until he became overseer. He was made to be a chief but on the win-

ner's side. To lead a group of scabby maroons, for example, wouldn't have interested him. (*StM*, 32)

In an interview about *Solibo Magnifique*, Chamoiseau discussed the Rabelaisian aspects of the humor, the use of the grotesque and caricatures in the text, which have the effect of discrediting the police's rational investigation. According to Chamoiseau, the depictions of police violence are not exaggerated but reflect his personal observations of the violent workings of the Law in Martinique:

[. . .] un personnage comme le brigadier Bouaffesse ou celui qui s'appelle Diab-Anba-Feuilles c'est quelqu'un que j'ai connu. J'ai traîné dans les rue de Fort-de-France lorsque j'avais quatorze ans avec des amis, et on était poursuivi par des policiers qui avaient ce genre de comportement de ces gens-là. C'est à peine exagéré. Le comportement de Diab-Anba-Feuilles je l'ai vu, moi-même j'ai vu des types se mordre avant de dire, je me mords, comme ça j'ai saigné pour toi, je vais te tuer. On a eu ce genre d'attitude dans les forces policères et d'une certaine manière dans tous les quartiers populaires, cette attitude de major. Ceux qui se retrouvaient policiers étaient d'une manière générales des gens assez violents. C'est une caricature mais sans vraiment l'être. C'est vraiment la rencontre entres des êtres qui venaient tout droit de la plantation. La violence plantationnaire qui est la seule nous connaissions. Nous n'avons pas d'exercice démocratique, de concert de tolerance, aux Antilles, nous venons directement de la violence des plantations . . . . La violence était un mode relationnel et elle s'est exprimée de manière terrible des années trente aux années soixante dans les forces policières qui se mettaient en place ici. Ce sont les derniers feux de la violence des plantations, de la violence esclavagiste qui perdurent dans la société en train de se transformer.[50]

[. . .] a character like the Chief Sergeant Bouaffesse or the one named Diab-Anba-Feuilles is like someone I have known. I hung out in the streets of Fort-de-France with my friends when I was 14 years old, and we were pursued by the police who behaved in the same ways as these characters. It is hardly an exaggeration. I have seen behaviour like that of Diab-Anba-Feuilles. I myself have seen guys bite themselves and say, "Since I have bit myself and am bleeding on account of you, I will kill you." One has seen this kind of militant attitude in the police force and to a certain degree in all of the common neighborhoods, this military attitude. Those who became police officers were generally the kind of people who are rather violent. It is a caricature but without really being one. It is really an encounter with those who have descended directly from the plantation [system]. The violence of the plantation is the only one we knew. We do not have the reflex of democracy, the chorus of tolerance; in the Antilles, we come directly from the violence of the plantations . . . . Violence was a way of relating and it expressed itself in a terrible manner by the police who were in force from the 1930s to the sixties. These are the last flames of the violence found on the plantations, of the violence of slavery that was disappearing in a society in the process of being transformed.

Chamoiseau associates violence within culture as the residual influence of the plantation system. Consequently, his hard-boiled genre is underwritten by a satiric critique of postcolonial society.

In his postcolonial crime novel, Chamoiseau appropriates the theme of systemic corruption, which often features in hard-boiled crime novels. Lee Horsley observes that the hard-boiled genre and *noir* "provide insights into the sociopolitical disorders and moral dilemmas of the time in which they are written" and "look critically at the illusions and hypocrisy, the rotten power structures and the brutal injustices of a superficially respectable society."[51] Horsley observes that hard-boiled detective novels are populated by "protagonists living at the margins, outside of respectable society or unable to return to a home that is as they left it"[52] and that the protagonists tend to be "isolated and estranged, existing on the margins of society and, as outsiders, capable of seeing with a satirist's eye."[53] The investigator's ability to strip away pretence and reveal the sources of corruption stems from his marginalization within society. In postcolonial Martinique, both the witnesses and the detective-narrator Chamoiseau present a satirical view of society and the systemic corruption associated with the colonial presence. The detective report about the list of witnesses picked up by the police situates them as marginal figures within an already marginalized society. Among them is Chamoiseau, who like the other witnesses is also a suspect. The questions of name, occupation, and address reveal the marginalization of these persons who refer to themselves by nicknames rather than legal names and hold jobs or perform work that is not officially recognized by the state. These reports inscribe the witnesses as outside mainstream society, while contesting and denouncing their view of their own professions and lives. For instance, Eloi Apollon, nicknamed Sucette, "se disant tambourier de cricracks, en réalité sans profession, sans domicile" (*SM*, 30) ("claims to be a drummer of krickkrack tales, in reality has no occupation or permanent address") (*StM*, 11). Systematically, the police report questions the "claims" of witnesses, implying that they are lying or telling stories about their lives.

Contrary to these claims, Chamoiseau's narrator-investigator presents a different set of interpretive contexts that serve to foreground the misguided, farcical, and sometimes violent ways of thinking that prevail in neocolonial Martinique. In Himes's novels, the detectives act as local interpreters and translators, drawing on their "insider" understanding of the community. Bouaffesse acts as a translator, literally translating French into Creole and Creole into French as an intermediary between Pilon and the witnesses/suspects. Ironically, such translation is not really required for Pilon as he is capable of understanding Creole. In the neocolonial context, then the role of Bouaffesse as interpreter does not so much highlight the differences between "official" white culture and a marginalized Afro-American community. Rather, it highlights the degree to which Martinicans operating within a neocolonial context are compelled to play roles, officially and unofficially operating according to different rules, and deliberately filtering out or blinkering recognition of certain facts, histories, and identities when such information is considered irrelevant or outside of the "proper French" interpretive framework. Both Pilon and Bouaffesse are to some extent satiric figures, the puppets of a power system that compels them to adopt masks, thus fitting within the hard-boiled genre.

As with Himes, Chamoiseau's hard-boiled detective novel operates within a sphere of extreme violence, which is often depicted as absurd or surreal.[54] The fact that the character's throat is cut or "snicked" by the word, from the inside: resulting in a death that is at once marvelous, is at once comic and sad. The violence depicted in the novel, including multiple beatings (one resulting in death), injuries, and a suicide during a hostile police interrogation, stems directly from police violence, a violence which we have already seen is the residual influence of colonialism. More generally, Martinican society is exposed as a communal space in which the borders or territory of the Law and Martinican culture, Creole and French language, metropolitan and Martinican, are a source of underlying tension, prompting the law and the citizens to test and negotiate continuously where exactly those borders are to be situated. For Chamoiseau, the absurdity arises from mistaken identities, ideologies and interpretations, which are tied to socially and culturally construed differences. The weight changes in Solibo's body, from that of several tons to featherweight, and the presence of Guadeloupean ants near the corpse are two inexplicable mysteries. The absurd is also evident in references to cartoons and caricatured descriptions of the detectives as cowboys policing an imagined "Wild West" frontier in the Caribbean (*SM*, 101). Such caricatured elements in *Solibo* resemble the Rabelaisian humor of Tony Delsham and Chamoiseau's comic book, *Le retour de Monsieur Coutcha*, where there is a "Bouafesse" and Monsieur Coutcha is a kind of cowboy. For example, the caricature of Pilon could be a description of a cartoon character: "dans l'ombre de son bakoua, sous des paupières tombantes qui lui donne l'air blasé, Evariste Pilon a les gros yeux d'un crapaud-buffle traquant sous une pluie fine les hannetons des cannes à sucre" (*SM*, 119) ("in the shade of his *bakoua*, under drooping lids which give him a jaded look, Evariste Pilon has the eyes of a bullfrog tracking maybugs in sugar cane during a drizzle") (*StM*, 76). The effect is thus satiric.

While Himes depicts violence as intrinsic to a society where there is a "race problem," Chamoiseau's representation of violence is closely related to the patrolling of the colonial order by the Law and internalized self-policing activities on behalf of many Martinicans. In particular, the figure of Bouaffesse and the police interrogations become the vehicle for analyzing the terrifying effects of colonialism on a number of levels, including the lack of tenderness or love in relationships (*SM*, 63–66), the effects of the Algerian war (*SM*, 55, 121, 147) and World Wars (*SM*, 77, 121) on the colonies, the potentially terrifying effects of the French language (*SM*, 104–5), the sense of marginalization or lack of legitimacy felt by many Martinicans (*SM*, 67), the resentment of the local police toward the metropolitans (*SM*, 104), racism among Martinicans toward one another (*SM*, 173, 204) and the anticolonialist militant movement (*SM*, 188) in the Martinican Progressive Party. Chamoiseau thus appropriates the hard-boiled tradition to examine the residual presence of colonial imperatives and pressures.

The interrogation scenes, particularly that of Congo, offer further evidence of psychic and physical violence within society. Congo is considered a prime suspect because of his prior record as an arsonist who burned a *béké*'s field in 1900 as part of a strike action (*SM*, 201) and became involved in a brawl during another strike in 1935. Absurdly, given the cause of Solibo's death, the fact that Congo sells manioc graters is seen as suspicious because manioc can be used as a poison. Primarily, however, the narrator suggests that Congo is suspect because of his African purity, which seems a defect in the mixed society (*SM*, 204). He is seen as anachronistic because he speaks Creole and suspicious because his use of the language is a reminder of the colonial past (*SM*, 204). The brutal beating Congo receives is symptomatic of violence associated with the colonial past. The description of the beating amplifies the psychological connection to colonial violence; the desk where Congo is beaten is described as looking like "un champ de mulâtre après une battue de gendarmes-à-cheval" (*SM*, 207) ("a mulatto's field after being trampled by a pack of mounted gendarmes") (*StM*, 144). In despair, Congo defenestrates, prompting another suspect, Sucette, to make a similar attempt. Foiled by the police, Sucette fights back and is consequently imprisoned for attacking police officers. None of the police are reprimanded or punished for the beatings and violence that result in the deaths of Doudou Ménar and Congo.

As an investigator, Chamoiseau turns the tables on the police and calls their methods, crimes, and motives into question (*SM*, 169–70). He provides an unofficial report that serves as an alternative to the official police report. Rather than a summary of the crime, he provides a transcription of Solibo's speech at the moment of his death, which ended with a plea for a space free from neocolonial intervention: "où Air France n'a pas d'avions et où les békés pani pièce qualité modèle d'habitation d'usines" (*SM*, 244) ("where Air France got no terminal and where the *békés* ain't got no kind of plantation factory") (*StM*, 172). Solibo chokes on a vision of a world that he cannot change. In this respect, Chamoiseau's narrator-investigator extends the work of the *quimboiseur* by demonstrating that there is an alternative kind of sociocultural logic at work in the Creole world. When the detectives go to the *quimboiseur*, a sorcerer/practitioner of Creole religious and healing practices, they learn that Solibo died of an inner strangulation, a form of cultural asphyxiation. Chamoiseau's narrator-detective takes this strange fact as the basis for his own investigation, which examines various forms of cultural death at work in neocolonial Martinique. From an authorial perspective, the influence of Calvino is evident in the structuring of the novel and the investigator's role, which evolves as a network of interpretations concerning Solibo's death. Rather than explaining the death, the narrative can be seen as an incantory textual field of images, sounds, concepts, and genres that pertain to the idea of cultural asphyxiation and the quest for narrative forms that respond to the needs of contemporary Martinique.

The narrative form radiates from the insights of the *quimboiseur* to the methods of the narrator-detective and infuses the construction of the novel as a whole. The resulting work of fiction serves to creolize investigative genres, methods, and tropes in order to give voice to another kind of investigative fiction that analyzes and expresses the realities of local culture. The intermixing, collision, and transgression of genres invites a collaborative reading process as "both the reader and the detective are bound up in the metaphysical or epistemological work of interpretation, the work of reading clues and writing a solution or end."[55] The double framework of the novel foregrounds two erroneous interpretations of Solibo's death, which are embedded in two competing generic traditions: the first interpretation is the police report with which the narrative begins; the second is the oral narrative with which the novel ends. In the appendix to the novel, Chamoiseau presents a transcript of Solibo's dying words, "Patat' sa." The listeners to the tale, later both witnesses and suspects in the murder investigation, take this exclamation for a narrative cry-response technique, like "cric-crac" or "misticri-misticraa," responding with "Patat' si." *Solibo Magnifique* ends with this call-and-response of "Patat' sa ... Patat' si" (*SM*, 244), a dialogue of incomprehension because the dying man's words are misinterpreted as part of the storytelling performance rather than the end to his (life) narrative. This ironic ending is fitting for a novel in which most of the interchanges and conversations that take place involve mistaken identifications and assumptions about the other. Not only the detective novel but also the generic conventions of the Creole oral storytelling form are subject to subversion. The meaning of "Solibo," a Creole word that can be translated as "chute" in French or "fall" in English, signals the character's fate as well as suggests the potential perils associated with the slipperiness of meaning. Solibo's performance—replete with riddles about Martinique—can be seen as drawing the audience in the hermeneutic enterprise and thereby fostering a sense of mystification about the land.

The storyteller-detective interrogates the mystery surrounding Solibo's strange death without ever providing a final resolution. Like the wandering signifier of the bale of cotton in *Cotton Comes to Harlem* or like the bird statue in *The Maltese Falcon*, the meaning of *Solibo Magnifique* as a man, a magnificent fall, and a novel remains unresolved, open to interpretation, irreducible. In the spirit of Solibo's own riddles, mystifications and interpretations, the detective-narrator's role is to pose puzzles.

From an authorial perspective, Chamoiseau draws on a heteroglossia of detective conventions and genres (hard-boiled, police procedural, classic, forensic evidence, suspense, interrogations), using this multivocal technique to critique the neocolonialism evident in current-day Martinique and to question the ways in which the borders of the community or *communitas* as common sense are established and patrolled. The novel dramatizes the negative impact of this patrolling of the imaginary, while simultaneously opening up an alternative narrative of detection based on the Caribbean performative traditions of call-response dialogues, the wake, oral storytelling, and collective narration. *Solibo Magnifique* appropriates the French-American-English generic conventions of the crime novel, folding them in Antillean genres and social realities, positing the Caribbean mystery as a third consciousness, an irreducible Otherness.

Neocolonial Nostalgia

Chamoiseau has referred to his stay in France as an exile (*EPD*, 91), and it is not surprising that his works from this time express a yearning for home. Nostalgia stems from the etymology of *nostos*, meaning to return home, and *algos*, meaning pain. The painful desire to return home often takes the form of a return to an imagined or idealized past. Linda Hutcheon notes that "nostalgia is less about the past than the present" and observes that it "operates through what Mikhail Bakhtin calls an 'historical inversion': the ideal that is not being lived now is projected into the past."[56] For Homi Bhabha, the borderline work of culture demands an encounter with "'newness'" that is not part of the continuum of the past and present, but functions as an insurgent act of cultural translation whereby the past is refigured as a contingent in-between space that interrupts the performance of the present so that "[t]he 'past present' becomes part of the necessity, not the nostalgia, of living."[57] In response to these observations about the perils of nostalgia, I argue that Chamoiseau engages in a strategic, self-conscious form of nostalgia that distinguishes between modes of regression and the interjection of the new. There are a number of points to be made here: the first concerns the role of creolized vernacular traditions in postcolonial literature, the second speaks to the specificities of the Martinican situation (its ambivalent past-present horizons), and the third touches on the role of the narrative as an attempt to negotiate a viable postcolonial position. As we have seen, the humorously ambiguous *Chronique* and *Solibo* examine the role of folklore and vernacular traditions in colonial, neocolonial, and postcolonial contexts. In a review of *Chronique des sept misères*, Alberto Manguel observes that "Chamoiseau conjures up the stories of the Caribbean without falling into folkloric condescension or obsessive local color, refusing to be either anthropological or exotic"[58] while Beverley Ormerod notes that "Chamoiseau's *Solibo Magnifique* is the only novel to have achieved a plausible balance of realistic and supernatural elements in a contemporary setting."[59] As shown, in both novels, Chamoiseau addresses the risks that folklore can be used to evade contemporary issues or disguise the realities of everyday, contemporary Caribbean life by escaping to an idealized time of anticolonial resistance. The death of Pipi and the death of the storyteller, who chokes on his words, attest to the author's keen awareness of the risks of retreating to a nostalgic folkloric past rather than confront the realities of the contemporary world. *Chronique* and *Solibo* are anti-nostalgic in that they "kill off" the figures, Pipi and Solibo, who fail to adapt to the changing world order because they are caught up in nostalgia for the past. In such cases, nostalgia is shown to be an unproductive form of regression rather than a productive and critical dialogue about the relevance of the past. Through narrative intervention, the presence of the *revenant* (Pipi and Solibo) becomes a means to locate loss, produce alternative chronicles, investigate life in neocolonial Martinique, and confront the spectres of the past that haunt the present.

Chamoiseau's insistence of the resources of Creole culture introduces a reflective form of nostalgia, which discloses unfinished but foreclosed historical trajectories, particularly through decolonization.[60] Chamoiseau's nostalgia for the period following emancipation and leading up to departmentalization can be seen as nostalgic to the extent that he seems to yearn for a return to a historical moment when self-determination and greater autonomy for Martinique had not been foreclosed. In these contexts, the author may be seen as returning to moments of resistance from within or instances when the transition from colonialism to neocolonialism might have been articulated in other forms. In keeping with a point made earlier about the return of history, which appears first as tragedy, then as farce, I see these related temporalities as attempts to construct a relational counternarrative that eludes the Eurocentric emphasis on linear history. While the chronicle discloses hidden histories, the investigative fiction interrogates the porous interfaces of past-present horizons. Whereas the rebel phase of Chamoiseau's writing often tends to recover a heroic past of resistance, in some instances through tales of marooned slaves, *Chronique* and *Solibo* focus on the factors stifling self-determination in modern Martinique. In this respect, Chamoiseau's works can be seen as examples of speculative fiction because they identify points of departure in history as a means to call forth the horizons of an alternative present: the return to this past becomes a quest for moments of historical rupture when postcolonial identities were open to other formulations and when the collective aspired to decolonization.

Finally, the tragic-farcical construction of locality following departmentalization is shown to be the result of a neocolonial quest for home in the metropolitan cultural and economic life. Symptoms of this include the importation of French goods, the turn toward an increasingly consumer-oriented society, the loss of local market traditions, and the erosion of Creole genres of self-expression. From a narrative perspective, Chamoiseau moves beyond a farcical representation of the (mis)uses of the past to interrogate the desire for home: the "nous" of storytellers in *Chronique* stands alongside the ethnographer's account while the multiple investigators of *Solibo* recollect past-present horizons in a variety of ways. Through the collective stories of the *djobeurs*, many characters, and appended materials, the reader is offered multiple ways of linking together the past and present. In *Solibo*, the proliferation of perspectives and voices occurs through interrupted temporalities and narrators, which are brought together through the work of the *Marqueur de paroles*. The stories about the death of *Solibo* are a way of negotiating a new kind of oral narrative and a new kind of relationship between the police and the community. Chamoiseau's nostalgia functions in a reflexive manner as a double critique of past and present: oriented toward a more self-critical present and future. Through representation of individuals who fail to understand their own impulses and actions because they are no longer conscious of how the past informs the present, Chamoiseau discloses the tragic-farcical dimensions of life in Martinique. His self-consciously nostalgic narratives unfold as interrogative forms of economic and sociocultural analysis, which unmask the various masquerades, acts of mimicry, and ideological guises at work in society.

CHAPTER 4

Créolité, Community, and the Word Scratcher

Solibo Magnifique laments the death of the Creole storyteller, but gives birth to *oraliture* or orature, which is produced at the interfaces of the oral and written as well as through the interplay of languages. Similarly, the introduction of the *Marqueur de paroles* represents a new kind of performative writing that self-consciously refers to its own composition. Literary issues are brought into dialogue with ethnographic questions about the role of field research, observation, interviews, data collection, the role of the participant-observer, and so on. For Chamoiseau, the late 1980s and early 1990s were a time of intense analysis and incredible creativity as he articulated his ideas concerning the dynamics of storytelling, creolization, and writing, particularly in *Éloge de la créolité*, *Lettres créoles*, and *Au temps de l'antan*. Many of these ideas found expression in *Texaco*, the novel for which Chamoiseau won the Prix Goncourt. During this period, Chamoiseau also produced the first two of his three narrative accounts of childhood, *Antan d'enfance* (1990) and *Chemin d'école* (1993), which do not so much fulfill as undermine or question the feasibility of realizing the Creolist objectives of recuperating interior vision and discovering an "authentic" voice. With the Word Scratcher, Chamoiseau's efforts to redefine the role of storytelling, narration, and writing become inextricably bound up with his vision of Martinique's past-present culture and perspectives.

Éloge de la créolité / In Praise of Creoleness

In May 1988, Jean Bernabé, Patrick Chamoiseau, and Raphaël Confiant attended the "Festival caraïbe de la Seine-Saint-Denis" where they read the treatise that would be published as *Éloge de la créolité* (1989).

The manifesto opens with the declaration: "Ni Européens, ni Africains, ni Asiatiques, nous nous proclamons Créoles" (*EC*, 13) ("Neither Europeans, nor Africans, nor Asians, we proclaim ourselves Creoles") (*EC*, 75). Beginning with the Martinican situation, the text offers an analysis of creolization in the Caribbean and other regions of the world and ends with the claim that the world is undergoing a process of creolization. Divided into three main sections, "Toward Interior Vision and Self-Acceptance," "Creoleness," and "Constant Dynamics," the work suggests that creolization is essential to decolonization and the protection of diversity in a postcolonial world. "Creoleness" is subdivided into a discussion concerning the role of orality, memory, the "thematics of existence," modernity, and the choice of speech.

The oral presentation met with criticism, particularly on the part of a number of African delegates who objected to the rejection of African identities and the critique of Negritude. Following the publication of the text, a period of intense debate and productive criticism ensued throughout North America, Europe, and the Caribbean. In particular, the publication of the counter-manifesto, *Penser la créolité*, a collection of essays edited by Maryse Condé and Madeleine Cottenet-Hage, articulated a number of key objections concerning the Creolist perspective, citing its masculine (misogynist) perspective, its essentialist vantage point, an overemphasis on the linguistic and a lack of attentiveness to the open cultural process of creolization. The work was faulted for putting forward generalizations about Creole identities, which might have reflected the francophone Caribbean experience, but failed to represent the many experiences of creolization around the world. In retrospect, it may seem somewhat surprising that this short treatise sparked so many debates, particularly as the idea of a Creole society was already well established in the Anglophone Caribbean thanks to the pioneering work of Kamau Brathwaite's *The Development of Creole Society in Jamaica, 1770–1820*. In the francophone Caribbean, academic work on creolization and Creole literature was already quite established by that time. Confiant and others had published works in Creole from the 1970s onward and Chamoiseau had already been "chamoisifying" language (working at the interfaces of French and Creole) since *Chronique des sept misères*. In part, the hyperbolic rhetoric of the treatise is to blame for the criticism it spawned.

Looking back, some of the Creolists' arguments remain contentious. For instance, the authors criticize Negritude as a movement that is seen as having potentially worsened "our identity instability by pointing at the most pertinent syndrome of our morbidities: self-withdrawal, mimeticism, the natural perception of local things abandoned for the fascination of foreign things, etc., all forms of alienation" (*EC*, 82). While one might agree that Negritude fails to reflect the complexities of the creolized Caribbean experience, this argument does an injustice to Negritude as an anticolonial movement. In other instance, the Creolists seem to ignore or be unaware of arguments and debates that have come before them. For instance, the notion of being "fundamentally stricken with exteriority" (*EC*, 76) had already been discussed by W. E. B. Du Bois in the early part of the twentieth century with the idea of "double consciousness." Later, Frantz Fanon would argue for the need for a literature of combat and map out the terrain of decolonization in works such as *Black Skin, White Masks*, and *The Wretched of the Earth*. While the authors go on to acknowledge Fanon's ability to explore "our reality from a cathartic perspective" (*EC*, 83), they fail to acknowledge their debt to thinkers before them. Similarly, their analysis of America as a migrant culture reveals a lack of awareness of American self-reflection concerning creolization, *mestizo* identities and transculturation, debates that had already begun by 1989.

Glissant's *Malemort* and Frankétienne's *Dézafi* are praised for their "interior vision" (*EC*, 84–85). They suggest a way forward for the Creolists who undertake a quest for self-knowledge through vernacular forms and reject French ways of thinking (*EC*, 86). The desire to reject colonial legacies and embrace local culture is at times conflated with a binary view of French as bad (colonial, exteriority) and Creole as good (liberating, interiority). Such an argument runs against the complexity of Creoleness as an identity that includes European and French in its very composition. Nonetheless, the argument concerning the need to recuperate local language, cultural forms, and history is among the most significant contributions of the Creolist movement from the late 1980s onward. The Creolists place emphasis on the importance of the oral tradition, writing, and the recuperation of vernacular culture by turning to history from below. The oral tradition is seen as a cultural resource for the reclamation of what has otherwise been repressed, forgotten, and overlooked. The desire for a literature that would "obey all the demands of modern writing while taking roots in the traditional configurations of our orality" (*EC*, 98) is seen as essential to the ongoing work of decolonization.

Equally, the thematics of existence, the critique of modernity, and the issues related to language are important motifs. The Creolists call attention to the practices of everyday life and the mobilization of these practices through the literary tradition. The idea of the writer as a "detector of existence" whose vocation is "to identify what, in our daily lives, determines the patterns and structure of the imaginary" (*EC*, 100) is a powerful one in terms of postcolonial critique as well as vernacular expressivity. The notion of "permanent questioning, doubt, and ambiguity" (*EC*, 100) not only reflects the postcolonial condition but also provides for self-reflexivity. At the same time that the thematics of existence draw on vernacular resources, the critique of modernity entails a lucid examination of "neocolonized flaws" (*EC*, 103).

The Creolists's strategic reclamation of language and culture is both celebratory and interrogative. They argue that the reclamation of Creole culture marks an important step in moving beyond (neo)colonial discourses (*EC*, 101), which have historically tended to represent Caribbean vernacular idioms, forms, beliefs, and practices as "primitive" and "backward." Here we must recall that the French education system forbade communications in Creole and tended to denigrate local culture. Thus, in terms of decolonization, the reclamation of Creole culture enables the subjects of departmentalization to overcome the stultifying effects of an assimilationist (neo)colonial education as well as to gain a more complete and nuanced view of Martinique's postcolonial identity. Specifically, the investigation of the *djobeurs*, the vegetable markets, folkloric beliefs (such as *dorlis*, *zombis*, and *soukliyan*), sacred beliefs and practices, magic realism, and other manifestations of the vernacular (*EC*, 101) enables a more expansive understanding of communal formation. Presumably, a lucid questioning of neocolonized flaws also recognizes that the processes of creolization have also entailed accommodation as well as resistance and new forms of expressivity. The Creolists argue that they want to "show what, in these [transcultural] practices, bears witness to both Creoleness and the human condition" (*EC*, 101). In so doing, they may seem to speak in the language of liberal humanism with its emphasis on universals and authentic forms of expression, but their account of creolization also suggests that uneven processes of transcultural exchange might be seen as a universal occurring phenomenon. As we have already seen, Chamoiseau's own literary production tends to accentuate this ambivalent yet celebratory view of creolization.

Nonetheless, the treatise teeters between oppositional modes of thinking and a more mediated view of creolization as a dynamic, uneven process of interaction rather than a product of resistant local culture. In terms of oppositional thinking, Creole is presented as the language of resistance and even of inverted conquest: *"We did conquer it, this French language"* (EC, 106). The need for a critical language and a recuperative vision is conflated with the Creole language as the "collective unconscious, of our common genius" (EC, 104) and described as a resource for releasing the repressed. One might infer, as Maryse Condé does in her essay entitled *"Créolité* without Creole Language?" that the Creolists are arguing for literature written exclusively in Creole or an interlectal linguistic space, but this is not the case.[1] The authors state that it "won't necessarily be a Creolized or reinvented French, nor a Frenchized or reinvented Creole, but our own finally recovered and decisive language" (EC, 107–8).

The thesis that the Creole language is a way to release repressed authenticity needs to be understood in its sociopolitical context and from a psychoanalytic perspective. The authors of *Éloge* belong to a generation that experienced corporeal punishment in the school system when speaking the maternal language; they were socialized to mistrust the Creole as a barbarous language. In such cases, reviving the Creole language is an important step in reclaiming personal history and gaining access to memories of events or forms of self-expression that are activated through a return to the Creole language. In reclaiming access to the richness of language, whether in Creole, French, or some other form, the Creolists play(ed) an important role in the decolonization of attitudes toward language. Moreover, the reclamation of a rejected cultural past opened up a terrain of investigation that continues to play an important role in the ongoing work of decolonization. In this respect, the Creolists' stance might be interpreted as an example of "strategic essentialism," to borrow a term from Gayatri Chakravorty Spivak, which enabled them to move beyond colonial discourses of self and eventually adopt a more open, relational attitude toward creolization (at least in the case of Chamoiseau).[2]

The final section of the work on the constant dynamics of creolization is perhaps the least contentious part of the work and the outlines of this argument come closest to the Glissantian idea of creolization as a process rather than a fixed concept of identity. The argument for diversity and the protection of local languages looks forward to debates around globalization and fostering of a sense of locality. This section addresses the connections between creolization and globalization, introduced a theme that comes to play an increasingly significant role in Chamoiseau's work from the 1990s onward. The description of a creolizing world is worth quoting because it helps to clarify the particular kind of lived experience they have in mind:

> A new humanity will gradually emerge which will have the same characteristics as our Creole humanity: all the complexity of Creoleness. The son or daughter of a German and a Haitian, born and living in Peking, will be torn between several languages, several histories, caught in the torrential ambiguity of a mosaic identity. To prevent creative death, one must perceive that identity in all its complexity. *He or she will be in the situation of a Creole.* (EC, 112)

This immersion into Creoleness is depicted as neither wholly communicable nor incommunicable (*EC*, 112–14). Consequently, opacity is seen as a central tenet of communications. The idea of a preserved diversity and the acceptance of constant dynamics sets out the principles of creolization as an orientation toward the changing world (*EC*, 114).

Almost a decade later, an interview with Lucien Taylor, aptly titled "Créolité Bites," offered the theorists a chance to look back and reflect on their ideas as well as some of the critical responses they provoked. Partly in response to this criticism, Chamoiseau refined his articulation of *créolité*, which he now refers to in the plural (though the treatise also emphasized multiple forms of creolization). He defended the specificities of Creole experience within each of the Caribbean islands, an experience that differs from *métissage* because the latter is only one aspect of the creolization process.[3] For him, creolization is a period of chaos and shifts, introducing complexities in identity. The Caribbean experience can be seen as emblematic for the current transformations of identity as the world is now more generally undergoing a process of creolization. While he has never renounced the *Éloge*, it is telling that he says that he thought the treatise was intended to be in praise of Glissant rather than Creoleness, thus signaling a Glissantian emphasis on the ongoing processes of creolization rather than the fixed Creole identities.[4] More recently, in an interview with Maeve McCusker, he stated the *Éloge* reflects in part Confiant's efforts to reformulate "the ancient struggle against colonialism by looking for a language and a culture to oppose those of the colonizer," which he sees as an essentialist approach to Creole language and literature.[5] Following the lead of Glissant, Chamoiseau sees the world as undergoing creolization processes, but he differs in that he stakes out a middle ground that still holds firm to the Creolist stance of a resistant local culture.

The translation of the treatise had a diffuse and influential effect, opening up the doors for renewed forms of Creole storytelling and autobiographical fiction. Even Maryse Condé, who criticized the movement, produced several novels influenced by this work, notably *Traversée de la mangrove* (*Crossing the Mangrove*). In terms of Creole storytelling, the Creolists opened the doors for creolized tales, such as the short stories of Edwidge Danticat and Nalo Hopkinson. Autobiographical fiction and the reclamation of interior vision became an important theme and the 1990s saw the publication of many autobiographical works, including works by Chamoiseau and Confiant. Finally, the Creolist impulse, grounded in sentiment, recognizes the psychological and emotional need to acknowledge and defend a Creole self and the right to the Creole language. In this sense, Chamoiseau's version of *créolité* reflects that of a generation of Martinicans who grew up in a "postcolonial" society where the residual of colonial thinking and educational practices lagged behind the supposed realities of the society's new sociopolitical status. For this generation of Martinican writers, *Créolité* served as a means to connect to aspects of a repressed linguistic and cultural experience in order to acknowledge a richer concept of self-identity. More generally, the productiveness of *Créolité* as a movement can be seen in the ways it has challenged individuals to articulate more clearly their own particular relation to creolization, a movement that resulted in some of the most important works in Caribbean fiction.

Creole Folktales and *Lettres créoles*

In the preface to *Au temps de l'antan* (1988) or *Creole Folktales* as it would be translated in English, Chamoiseau describes folklore and Creole stories as both a resource and a tool during the colonial era: the Creole storyteller "speaks for a people enchained: starving, terrorized, living in the cramped postures of survival" (CF, xii). While acknowledging the ludic function of Creole stories, Chamoiseau emphasizes that these "tales provide a practical education, an apprenticeship in life—a life of survival in a colonized land" (CF, xii). Thus, Chamoiseau argues that folklore is a discourse, shaped by the history of its tellers. For all of its magic, play, and opacity, the tales are engaged, politically and socially, with the situation of reader and storyteller. Chamoiseau's playful ending to the "Preface" defends the "strange words" of these tales (the use of Creole) and asks that they be allowed to work their secret magic, suggesting that these tales shape the consciousness of the teller (*CF*, xiv). Chamoiseau states that he has written the tales with the moon as his sole companion, for fear that he would be changed into a basket without handles, "a fate described by the old storytellers" (xiv). The reader as well is directed to read the tales at night. Thus, the tales speak through the storyteller's voice, shaping the practice of his art as well as the conditions of readership. The narrative performance or retelling of tales produces a new kind of event for the reader of or listener to this "oraliture."

In *Lettres créoles*, Chamoiseau and Confiant define "oraliture" as a means of propagating a collective reading of the world (*LC*, 73). This "oraliture" confronts the values of the colonial system (such as the legitimation of the extinction of the Caribs or the conditions of the slave, etc.) and at the same time diffuses a subterranean counterculture of multiple countervalues. The interaction of this counterculture and the dominant culture gives birth to zones of the Creole culture. "Oraliture," in a mirroring movement, conceals and reveals testimonials of this interaction and creolization (*LC*, 74). Chamoiseau and Confiant place emphasis on the role of the teller in the community, focusing on the pragmatics of the communicative event. Richard Bauman's description of the three elements of storytelling, story, performance, and event is particularly helpful in understanding the Creolists' theory of narrative. That is to say that "narratives are keyed both to the events in which they are told and to the events that they recount, toward narrative events and narrated events."[6]

This narrative model stresses the story's potential for transformation and community building. Bauman takes up Walter Benjamin's discussion of the storyteller as someone who tells tales from experience, whether his/her own or reported by others, and in turn "makes it the experience of those who are listening to his tale."[7] According to Confiant and Chamoiseau, these methods of adaptation occur in several ways. The interactive storytelling performance gives voice to the group, through call-and-response techniques such as the "e kraa" reponse or "kric krac" narrative. The storyteller is the guardian of memories and someone who prepares the listeners for a new way of life. Stories offer distraction, a way of passing the time, laughter. Storytellers verbalize resistance and mobilize the collective. Chamoiseau introduces a metanarrative framework through the presence of the *Marqueur de paroles* (Word Scratcher) who draws on oral storytelling and intervenes in the narrative in order to highlight the relevance of the story for a modern audience of local and metropolitan listeners/readers. In a belated gesture, the Word Scratcher reveals that he is not simply a detached observer; he reveals that he plays a vital role in the narrative process, which is constantly renegotiated through intervention. For Bauman (drawing on the theory of Mikhail Bakhtin), this metanarrative entails two distinct events: the event that is narrated in the work and the event of narration itself. These events take place in different places and times, but are united through the work itself, by the world represented, elicited even, by the text.[8] There is a sense of connection or wholeness and indivisibility as well as a sense of the diversity of elements. Walter Benjamin observes that storytellers "tend to begin their story with a presentation of the circumstances in which they themselves have learned what is to follow."[9] In so doing, they introduce a continuity, one which serves as a source for telling a new kind of tale, a pretext, in the case of Chamoiseau, for an often subversive and disruptive performance.

In *Au temps de l'antan*, Chamoiseau makes ample use of oral storytelling techniques and metafictional references that call attention to the distance between the oral and the written and the space of performance. For instance, between stories four and five, there are several pages with the questions and exclamation: "Are you all asleep? No? Then so far, so good!" (*CF*, 37–41). Such interjections create the illusion that the reader is listening to an oral performance. However, other asides stress the written. For example, in the tale "The person who bled hearts dry," a mysterious figure on a slave ship is mercilessly beaten; the duration of this event is described by the narrator as follows: "he had her whipped, lashed to a gun, flogged for longer than it would take me to write it out ten thousand times" (*CF*, 53). Various temporalities elide: that of the narrative events, that of the time taken to write the tale, and that of the reader who imagines the duration of the possible ten thousand times. This metanarrative technique, which emphasizes the distance of the reader from the time of the events and stresses the fictional processes that separate the reader from the story, also paradoxically creates a sense of immediacy, by emphatically bringing the time of the whipping into the time of the reader. Indeed, throughout the collection, the sense of time is effectively cut-up, disconnected, and fluidly merged into an impossible temporality through the narrator's indeterminate status. For in certain instances, the narrator reflects back on the days of yesteryear from a contemporary perspective (*CF*, 5), but at other times, such as in the tales "Madame Keleman" or "A little matter of marriage," the narrator inhabits a cottage in the distant, supernatural space and time of the narrative world or reports dropping by for a visit. The past-present perspectives continuously converge.

The emphasis on the performance of the story calls attention to the past-present perspective. In the case of the Ti-Jean Horizon story, when the *békés* decide to stuff Ti-Jean in a bag and take him by boat to the horizon and throw the bag overboard, the narrator interjects, "Oh, the story's title is now becoming clear!" (*CF*, 98). The abrupt ending to the collection is worth considering, for it contrasts with the engaged dialogue between reader and "conteur" in the rest of the collection. The tale "Nanie-Rosette the belly-slave" ends with Nanie-Rosette throwing open the doors of a cabin, expecting to see her mother and be given a feast of food, when instead as the reader knows, she will be consumed by a devil. However, the events that ensue are left for the reader to complete, which serves to encourage the reader to participate as an active agent in the performance of the narrative. This call to action serves as an ending to the collection as a whole, suggesting that the call-response mechanism "throws" the reader into the role of the teller of the tales. This ending serves to affiliate the horizons of the folklore world to be narrated with the reader's own present horizon of activities. These rhetorical devices create a sense of engagement with the past and disrupting the boundaries between the world of the reader and the space of the imaginary. As such, these techniques enable an alternative history or the articulation of counter-memory. Specifically, four of the tales, "Rainmaker," "The person who bled hearts dry," "Ye, Master of famine," and "Ti-Jean Horizon" do not symbolically represent or encode power relations (as is often the case with folklore; for instance, if we think of the figure of the "soucagnon" who takes off its skin and demonically tries to suck the life out of others, thus figuratively representing the demonic aspects of those who attempt to deny or escape from their skin color or the *dorlis* which is a rapist, typically the *béké*), but blend the historical and the marvelous timeframes and frameworks of interpretation.

In "Rainmaker," the storyteller starts with a kind of once-upon-a-time beginning for an oral audience, setting up what would appear to be a tall tale: "Listen, in the days of yesteryear, life still blossomed now and again into a kind of dreamworld. Storytellers thus were free to lavish upon their creations liberties that had nothing to do with lies. For instance, they told us of a dismal drought, and of a child who could call down rain" (*CF*, 5). In the course of this marvelous narrative, historical references to the Dominican fathers and detailed descriptions of the *békés* are presented, inviting a socioeconomic critique. Whereas the drought is a complete catastrophe for the folk who attempt to dig up petrified yams or eat stony oranges, the Dominicans discover the effects of the drought only because their good wine had turned into a sludge of vinegar, causing them to fear that the island was cursed. When the community is called together by the Dominicans to pray for a miracle, the wretched condition of the folk is contrasted with the *békés* whose clothing is in disarray and whose houses have been spoiled by the heat and who are now subject to watching their wealth shrivel up in the fields. The narrative event of the drought and the effects of the subsequent rain present the opportunity for highlighting differences in religion, class, race, and social conditions. This omniscient narrative perspective is extended to the ending of the tale in which the narrator notes that this community, Prêcheur, is still hopelessly dry. Thus, the marvelous beginning and the tale of the boy who produces rain are set within a historical framework of interpretation.

The story presents a critique of colonial history and celebrates the possibilities of postcolonial narration. The Dominicans, who call the community together, pray for a miracle, and cry when none is forthcoming, fail to recognize the child as a rainmaker. When offered a big rain or a small one, they jokingly ask for a small rain because they lack faith in his ability to bring about a miracle. When the boy calls forth the rain, it falls in an amount that is sufficient to raise hope but insufficient to solve the drought conditions. Subsequently, the area never receives much rain. At each moment of crisis, the Dominicans are presented in ironic terms: they fail as interpreters, caretakers, and believers. The account is all the more poignant when we consider the African tradition of the rainmaker and the community's loss of collective cultural memory, which leads members of the community to overlook or deny the important role the boy has to play in society. The tale discloses a series of colonial errors and misinterpretations of local contexts and peoples. In addition to the material damage that ensues, these mistakes are amplified and repeated when the Dominicans (mis)record all the events and submit a report to their authorities. In contrast to the official report, the storyteller offers a more comprehensive account that describes the boy's life after this miracle; he is hounded for another miracle for the rest of his life and dies overcome by threats and entreaties. The tale ends with an almost proverbial tone: "For it is indeed true that wherever rank bad luck has taken root, a rainmaker may work his miracle only once and never again" (*CF*, 8). The storyteller's narrative offers a counter-perspective to the Dominican's historic report, which celebrates the marvelous possibility that the community of listeners might, in an imagined future, recognize the marvelous when it presents itself. Historically, folklore provided a tool for recoding and communicating hidden or lost interpretations of colonial events. In retelling these tales, the postcolonial storyteller scratches the surfaces of history, revealing hidden depths and disguised appearances.

Patrick Chamoiseau and Raphaël Confiant's *Lettres créoles* is of considerable interest for the ideas about the role of writing and storytelling in the French Caribbean. This academically oriented literary history presents an anthropological interpretation of Creole writing, which also provides insight into Chamoiseau's own literary contexts and sources of inspiration. This important but often overlooked text is helpful in terms of understanding what writing means for the author. *Lettres créoles* situates literature in terms of the processes of colonization, creolization, and decolonization movements. The authors' anthropological view of literature as part of the "oxygen of life" (*LC*, 12) offers a transcultural history of writing in its broadest sense, including that which is inscribed on the earth, paper, rock, the page, and skin (or bark) and communicated through the spoken word (*LC*, 12). Writing is conceived of as a Babelian, emotional, and ontological experience, expressing a conception of the world, enabling the opacity of each to another (*LC*, 12).

Literature begins with the pre-Columbian form of "la roche écrite" (*LC*, 15) or the written rock (petroglyph) as a double for oral storytelling. Relating Taino, Arawak, and Carib beliefs, they discuss the roles played by Maboya, Shemini, and Yali in culture. Their tales of origin are engraved on the rocks of Martinique, Guadeloupe, Dominica, Saint Lucia, and Saint Vincent (*LC*, 21). Traces of circles, zigzags, stippling, and hash marks (*LC*, 21) attest to the presence of peoples and cultures that were almost completely decimated by the colonial interventions starting in 1625. The musings concerning the intentions of these engravers of rocks remain mysterious, unknowable testaments to the absence of a genesis in this silenced literature (*LC*, 22). The idea of writing the earth and the opacity of the written rock resurfaces in *L'Esclave vieil homme et le molosse* where it symbolizes an epic chorus of voices throughout history so that the silenced rock stands as a witness to history. Moreover, the rock is suggestive of the idea of writing as marking, a form of writing that inspires the *Marqueur de Paroles* as someone whose writing is a graphic double for orality, invoking a space of writing that dates back to pre-Columbian culture.

Colonial presence is configured as part of the creolization of culture and writing. The division of conquest into the periods of settlement (1625–1685) and plantation periods (1685–1950) are seen as distinctive because the former refers to a dynamic time of interracial cohabitation and marriage while the latter, beginning with the imposition of the *Code noir*, introduces slavery and a systemic racial hierarchy through planned colonialism. Colonial writing is seen as a scribal form, used primarily for commercial and juridical purposes (*LC*, 30). These scribal practices are codified and normed; creativity is accidental (*LC*, 30). The emphasis on inventorying the world (descriptions of the New World from geographic, economic, ethnographic, botanic perspectives) means that even the Jesuit and Dominican accounts of the world are situated between scribal practices and writing, which means that they are seen as incapable of giving birth to a creative tradition of writing (*LC*, 31). Aside from the notable exception of Pierre Dessalles (*LC*, 34–36), writing during this period is seen as an enabler of colonization because it is both metropolitan and exogenous (*LC*, 32).

At the same time, the Middle Passage and the plantation are seen as experiences that give birth to new forms of narrative. Ideas about this destructively natal space resurface in the screenplay for *Passage du milieu*, a film adapted into English by Walter Mosley under the title *The Middle Passage*, and sections of *Biblique des derniers gestes*. The description of the Middle Passage provides a kind of cultural metaphysics; this unspeakable moment in the history of holocausts (*LC*, 37) produces both an indistinct cry of protest and revolt (*LC*, 39) and a rupture of silence (*LC*, 40), which are heir to marooning and detours in Caribbean culture and literature. For Confiant and Chamoiseau, the plantation serves as the source of the space of another kind of protest activity embedded in daily life: the birth of the storyteller and the oral tradition in the form of proverbs, songs, and the Creole story (*LC*, 72–73). Historically, the beginning the storyteller is aligned with the African *griot* (musician-storyteller) tradition, but this African diasporic tradition is seen as giving way to creolizing processes (*LC*, 46–47) and practices of detour and survival (*LC*, 51). The authors highlight the importance of transculturation, including the presence of Indian, Chinese, Syrian, and Syro-Lebanese peoples (*LC*, 64). "Oraliture" is the outcome of this history (*LC*, 73), bringing the impulse of imaginative marooning to the plantation (*LC*, 74). While the stories themselves are important, Confiant and Chamoiseau celebrate the processes and methods of the storyteller:

Sa narration se fera tournoyante, rapide, parfois même hypnotique, brisée en longues digressions humoristiques, érotiques, ésotériques. Il va barder la phrase d'un bruitage de ruptures et d'onomatopées, de dialogue incessant avec son auditoire. D'autres emploieront la stratégie d'une *voix pas claire*, à l'articulation déroulante, qui fonctionne plus sur les effets du chant que sur celui de la parole audible. (*LC*, 76)

(His narration will turn itself, rapidly, sometimes even hypnotically, broken into long digressions that are humorous, erotic, esoteric. He will pack a phrase with the sound effects of rupture and onomatopoeia, an incessant dialogue with his listeners. Others employ the strategy of a *voice that is not clear* for an unfolding articulation that functions more like song than that of an audible spoken word.)

The idea of the storytelling process as a kind of rhythmic, song-like performance that unfolds in a digressive and disjunctive pattern, filled with erotic, esoteric, and humorous events, could well be used to describe Marie-Sophie's storytelling performance in *Texaco*. Other traditions are also useful in terms of understanding the total narrative rhetoric. Contradictions and self-derision undermine or contest authorial claims to verisimilitude and mimesis: at the same time that the storyteller claims to hate lying, his discourse takes a delirious turn that reveals him to be fabricating fictions (*LC*, 77). The posture of the storyteller, which suggests he is not who he pretends to be, creates a sense of distance and ambiguity (*LC*, 78). This spirit of storytelling, obscuring and revealing at the same time (*LC*, 79), and the discursive space of contradictoriness it invokes are at the heart of Chamoiseau's fictive processes, including his manipulation of roles, genres, and ambiguous narrative postures.

Other functions of *oraliture* include giving voice to the group (*LC*, 80), acting as the guardian of memories (*LC*, 81), providing distraction (*LC*, 81), verbalizing resistance (*LC*, 81), serving as a source of unspeakable power (*LC*, 82), and fighting against (cultural) death. Notably, the storyteller is likened to the *quimboiseur*, a medical healer and practitioner of Creole spiritual practices (*LC*, 82). Obscurity is a mechanism of resistance (*LC*, 83), but it also holds out the hope of changing the material conditions of life through an undefinable power (*LC*, 82). It involves inhabiting a space of negation, carving out a space of countercultural identity (*LC*, 82). At times, such a contradictory process entails subversion or reversal, such as is the case in certain renditions of Ti-Jean where the protagonist does not win out over the plantation owner (and his father), but dies a terrible death, chewed up by the sugar mill (LC, 83). It is not so much the stories themselves (which are open to transformation) as it is the power of the performance, oriented toward the present horizon, that reveals the creativity and unleashes the power of the oral tradition. In this sense, *oraliture* performs a creative, contradictory act of genesis, which is likened to the sacred, the magical, and perhaps even the quasi-mystical, that strikes out at the material conditions of everyday life.

Following the collapse of the plantation system, the authors see a third eruption of silence, which is comparable to the previous manifestations, including the decimation of the indigenous peoples who produced petroglyphs and the silencing effects of the Middle Passage. Without disappearing, Creole culture enters a period of immobilization (LC, 85) and becomes increasingly susceptible to the global system of capital and consumption (LC, 86) as well as the processes of assimilation to France (LC, 88). Literature bypasses the oral tradition and draws on the French literary tradition (LC, 90). Mimicry of French becomes "not only a sign of distinction but irrefutable proof of one's accession to the rank of humanity" (LC, 94). Gradually, the tide turns as authors move away from *doudousime* and collective bovaryism in order to revive vernacular traditions. They highlight the contributions of the "Acradémiciens" (a creolizing term that mixes together the "academic" and the "akra" (LC, 143), Gilbert Gratiant and Frantz Fanon, the Negritude movement, and post-Negritude authors. Several authors warrant particular mention because their work is the subject of extended analysis: Aimé Césaire, Saint-John Perse, Frankétienne, Simone Schwarz-Bart, and Édouard Glissant.

Writerly Influences: Frankétienne and Glissant

Given the strong influence he has had on Chamoiseau's ideas of writing and literature, it is worth taking a closer look at the discussion of Frankétienne, whom the authors refer to as an avatar of "le Nouveau Roman" (the New Novel). This passage is worth citing in full because this definition of the novel represents the kind of fiction Chamoiseau seeks to produce in works such as *Texaco* and *Biblique des derniers gestes*:

> Mais c'est en 1975 avec la publication du premier roman en créole haïtien, *Dézafi*, que la littérature créolophone, opérant là un retour à soi-même, va trouver ses lettres de noblesse. Son auteur s'appelle Frankétienne. C'est

la révolution. L'écrit en créole accède d'un coup à ce que la littérature possédait à l'époque de plus moderne, de plus audacieux et de plus talentueux, à savoir le Nouveau Roman. Par Nouveau Roman nous n'entendons pas seulement les écarts littératures de Nathalie Sarraute, Robbe-Grillet ou Claude Simon, publiés à partir des années 50, mais aussi la vaste remise en question du roman traditionnel tel qu'il a fleuri au XIXe siècle sous la plume de Balzac, Zola, Thomas Hardy, Dostoïevski ... Ce mouvement va toucher tous les continents et s'épanouir sous une forme spéciale en Amérique latine avec Asturias, Fuentes, Garcia Marquez, Cortázar et bien d'autres. Il s'agit, pour aller vite, d'abandonner l'histoire linéaire et «logique» d'un personnage centrale omniscient-omniprésent, guidé par un narrateur invisible tout aussi présent et omniscient. Au contraire, on bousculera le temps, on déraillera l'espace, le héros prendra une allure collective, évacuant, entre autres, le héros solitaire du roman canonique. (*LC*, 234–35)

(But in 1975 with the publication of the first novel in Haitian Creole, *Dézafi* [meaning Cock Fight], Creole literature, through a return to self, would establish its credibility. The author was named Frankétienne. It was the revolution. Writing in Creole suddenly had access to what was most modern, most audacious and most talented in literature at the time, namely the *Nouveau Roman* [New Novel]. By the *Nouveau Roman* not only do we have in mind the literary misdemeanors of Nathalie Sarraute, Robbe-Grillet or Claude Simon, published from the 50's onwards, but also the vast calling into question of the traditional novel as it flourished in the nineteenth century under the pen of Balzac, Zola, Thomas Hardy, Dostoevsky ... This movement would touch all continents and blossom in a special form in Latin America with Asturias, Fuentes, Garcia Marquez, Cortázar and many others. In short, it deals with abandoning linear history and the "logic" of a central omniscient-omnipresent character, guided by an invisible narrator who is also present everywhere and omniscient. On the contrary, this novel jostles time, derails space; the hero takes on a collective allure, evacuating, among other facets, the solitary hero of the canonical novel.)

This account of the new novel of the Caribbean and the Americas in twentieth-century and contemporary writing highlights the importance of reconceptualizing history and methods of narration.

Specifically, Chamoiseau and Confiant contrast two narrative patterns in Haitian literature: the motif of the messianic hero and the motif of the twins. In contrast to Roumain's *Gouverneurs de la rosée*, which features a hero who plays a messianic role, Frankétienne's novel juxtaposes characters engaged in repetitive tasks (*LC*, 237). The characters play an equal role in this decentered work of fiction. Where Roumain's novel still works according to a linear passage, measured in the times before, during, and after the return of the central character named Manuel (*LC*, 239), Frankétienne's work is constructed according to an isotopic system where personages are coupled. This pairing of characters fits with the *vodou* tradition of the Marasa (twins) (*LC*, 239). According to Confiant and Chamoiseau, the principle of "twinning" belongs to a specifically Haitian semiotic. Even when biological twins are not present, twinning is a common motif. Each person is a kind of twinned figure, himself and other than himself, torturer and victim, guilty and innocent (*LC*, 240). Not only does the idea of twinning differ considerably from the Christian, revolutionary figure of Manuel, it also undermines the idea of the hero as saviour at the center of the novel (*LC*, 240). Such a patterning continues today in contemporary fiction such as in the transformation pairing of the torturer-victim/husband-wife in Edwidge Danticat's *The Dew Breaker*.

Moreover, the tensions between these two novelistic configurations, the messianic figure versus the twins, play a particularly important role in the narrative plots and structural configuration of his two major novels, *Texaco* and *Biblique* (see the readings of these novels for a closer analysis). Another important motif for Chamoiseau, in particular, is the hermetic aspects of Frankétienne's writing, theater, and painting. Each of his novels is seen as a secret invocation to the *loas* of the *vodou* pantheon, to Aida-Wédoh, who makes the rainbow appear, to Erzulie-green-eyes, or Baron Samedi, guardian of the cemeteries (*LC*, 246). The role of the *loas* is worth considering as their presence surfaces in aspects of Chamoiseau's writing, particularly his idea of the novel as a kind of graphical activity, written through textual and oral intersections and movements of intersection and dialogue.

Glissant's role in shaping the idea of the writer as a *Marqueur des échos-monde* (Marker of the echo-world) calls attention to the activity of writing as one beyond either textuality or orality. This tumultuous teller of tales, hagiographer of sites, and delegate of calligraphy (*LC*, 251) is affiliated with the spoken word, ongoing processes of creolization, the opaque, the rhizomic, and a poetics of rupture. The authors explain that the word "marqueur" can be understood in terms of its Creole meaning of writing as well as the solo rhythms of the drum (*LC*, 257), a drumming that is at once solitary and a mark of solidarity. Thus, the idea of writing extends beyond language and communication, evoking the body, the land, and the environment in rhythmic, budding relations. Language and writing are depicted in motion, performance, and gesture, undertaking a detour or imaginary marooning with the result that the narrative discourse takes on an active, embodied, and cognitive set of functions. Textual maneuvres can be likened to the effect of watching the calligrapher draw a sign or the scribing of *vévé* where the drawing in the sand is intended to call forth the *loa*. Less representational than gestural, language becomes an action in the world that simultaneously transforms it. Just as rhythmic writing unifies the activities of speech, action, and inscription, "marking" both represents (depicts in word and image) and calls forth (invokes) a new way of being in the world. *Lettres créoles* remains a key text for the reader who wants to explore Chamoiseau's wider understanding of the power of language to both describe and enact change in the world.

Texaco

Winner of the Goncourt Prize for fiction, *Texaco* (1992) remains Chamoiseau's most popular work of fiction and is often acknowledged as the work that best demonstrates the processes of creolization at work in fictional form. Critics celebrate the novel's linguistic playfulness, narrative complexity, and rewriting of history from a postcolonial perspective.[10] Ostensibly, the novel concerns the French government's decision to raze an insalubrious urban development where individuals are squatting and laying claim to land that belongs to a multinational oil company, named *Texaco*. A city planner (who is referred to as Christ) is sent to examine the quarter and engage in dialogue with the inhabitants. Struck by a rock on his way into this community, he is taken to the leader of these resistant few, a woman by the name of Marie-Sophie Laborieux. She proceeds to tell her life's history and justify claims to the land. Her life's history includes the tale of her parents, grandfather, and the community, beginning with the time of slavery and moving through abolition to the present. This history from below provides a tragic-comic view of events in Martinique, including early attempts to form a community in the hills, the eruption of Mount Pelée, abortion, struggles to survive, war, the visit of General de Gaulle to Martinique, and the perils of life under departmentalization. The chronology that precedes the narrative dates back to 3000 BC, which extends the epic perspective.

Texaco embodies the principles and processes of *oraliture* as well as corresponds to the definition of the new novel as defined in *Lettres créoles*. Structured as a composite of oral storytelling, testimonial accounts, and other textual materials, including reports, archival documents, transcriptions, tape recordings of oral exchanges, this mosaic work offers many points of entry and generic interpretation. With its articulation of concerns about the role of the source (the native informant), transcription, and writing up testimonial accounts, the text foregrounds the crisis of representation and offers a critique of ethnographic methods.[11] The "source" of the novel's main oral account, Marie-Sophie, is a kind of ethnographer who has recorded her father's oral history in a series of journals that have been archived at the Schoelcher Library. Within the framework of the novel, Marie-Sophie's testimonial narrative is represented as a palimpsest, the product of repetition, re-versioning, and intervention. She has recounted the story to Oiseau de Cham, the Urban Planner, and Papa Totone: the source tale set within in the novel is the product of multiple versionings. Furthermore, the novel includes the layers of textual intervention introduced by the Word Scratcher. Marie-Sophie's account is interrupted by various archival documents and voices, creating a multivoiced text that inhabits the borders of storytelling, archive, journal entries, official documents, and reports related to urban development.

Texaco opens with an anthropological chronology of history divided into various periods of "indigenous" housing, including the "Temps de Carbet et d'Ajoupas" ("The Age of Longhouses and Ajoupas"), "Temps de Paille" ("The Age of Straw"), "Temps de Bois-Caisse" ("The Age of Crate-Wood"), "Temps de Fibrociment" ("The Age of Asbestos"), and "Temps de Béton" ("The Age of Concrete"). Alongside this older anthropological approach, the analysis of Texaco within the novel presents a vision of the city as a fluid, contested space where the swirl of modern, globalizing forces exist alongside the older versions of community. Indeed, the city emerges as a *bricolage* of building techniques and concepts of social organization, which takes inspiration from pre-Columbian housing techniques, African diasporic culture, the residual influence of the "inner plantation," the Creole garden commune of "Noutéka," and modern construction materials. In "writing up" the narrative, the Word Scratcher introduces other extra-historical perspectives so that his work goes beyond the mediation of anthropological to offer a vision of an alternative society. Maeve McCusker sees this narrative *bricolage* as a poetic correlative to the narrative's emphasis on the construction of homes. Like the home, which is built from various materials at hand, the novel is "jerry-built from fragments drawn from disparate fictional sources."[12]

Texaco, the novel, offers an alternative vision to the community (of Texaco) it depicts. Just as Marie-Sophie's secret word, "Texaco," magically calls the urban space into existence and transforms the site of a multinational corporation, the novel operates its own magical transformation of sources. Textuality and locality are enmeshed in various flows: the evocation of the spaces of the world and the spaces of writing are inseparable. The production of "Texaco" is continuously contested, situated and resituated through various interpretations, voices, stories, archival materials, journals, and reports. In literary terms, the work is a kind of postcolonial utopia,[13] produced as a critique of existing society, the depiction of a more perfect society, and a plan for reform. Like Thomas More's *Utopia*, the name of the ideal community is contested. It is the name of a society and a text. Whereas Utopia is the product of imperial intervention, Texaco is the site of multinational investment as well as resistance from below. However, "Utopia" and "Texaco" are similar in that both words are subject to interpretation, translation, and rewriting. The mistranslation of "Utopia" via Greek as a source language (when Greek is not the language of Utopia) produces the pun on the "good society" (eutopos) as "no place" (utopos). In Chamoiseau's case, the postcolonial perspective involves bringing the isolated society, cut off from the whole, back together. Texaco both contests the global and reconstructs locality as a kind of anagrammatic reconstruction of the "Noutéka," the name of a self-sufficient, hilltop community whose name can be translated from Creole as the "we that was."

The idea that "utopia" is not to be found in the society that bears its name, but through the process of translation, dialogue, and reworking that bring the meaning of the ideal society into being links the humanist utopia of More and the postcolonial utopia of Chamoiseau. J. Michael Dash observes "writing is intimately related to founding" the town, but observes that the text equally undermines its archival sources through parody.[14] He sees the novel as "giving expression to a world on the edge of the written, saturated in orality, where the spontaneity, playfulness and immediacy of the spoken pervade the entire narrative."[15] Dash sees the novel as ranging promiscuously between the spoken and written: "Texaco raises the possibility of a language that eschews linearity and clarity and that is organically tied to the sensuous experience—that feeds on the corporeal and the actual."[16] This idea is embodied in the circular, repetitive, and more intuitive narrative stylings of Marie-Sophie's story. Furthermore, this circularity, a kind of rippling outward or swirling around stems from the various responses to her tales, fragments that bejewel the narrative discourse.

In many respects, the dynamics of *Texaco* echo the themes and concerns of New Anthropology as represented by James Clifford, Arjun Appadurai, Mary Louise Pratt, and others. New Anthropologists call into question their own position in the field and reject the outmoded paradigm of the insider native informant/outsider anthropological perspective. Fieldwork is seen as a "spatial practice of intensive, interactive research organised around the serious fiction of a 'field.'"[17] Certainly, Chamoiseau's role, like that of the Urban Planner and Marie-Sophie, confirms this disruption for both are neither wholly inside or outside, but take shifting views of their own constructions of locality as well as their relations to the field of "Texaco" as a contested site. This destabilization is a given of the world. Despite the inhabitants yearning for concrete houses and solid community, the dwelling place of the narrative is a fluid, unfinished modernity.

Texaco (the novel) and "Texaco" (the site) unfold as an open contact zone or an ongoing work of creolization, which moves from cultural realities to textual poetics. From the historical processes of transculturation emerges an approach to social development that is grounded in but moves beyond the past. Chamoiseau moves from the history of Creole linguistics and transculturation to the present world as a place to be negotiated through multidirectional processes. His Creole society is attentive to racial hierarchies and the intersections of class, gender, and ethnicities. The Creole society is a contested, collaborative activity, representing an alternative conceptualization of democracy. Society becomes a set of transit points, open to transformation. This approach also infuses the idea of the archive and the role of the Schoelcher Library. The library is not merely a site where documents related to the past are housed. It offers another kind of domestic model where histories speak and vie with one another for a collaborative, open, and shifting account of the past. This colonial building, a historical place, is filled with unreal documents that repopulate the archive until it too appears a contact zone.

The "crisis of representation" is reflected in the composition of the discourse, which purports to include the source tale of Marie-Sophie, but turns out to be multiple accounts, cobbled together from versions presented to different audiences through time. The idea of a "thick narrative," which provides a realist account of the social world from the inside, is called into question by the ending to the narrative in which Chamoiseau calls attention to his manipulative presence. The narrator-ethnographer, far from acting as a conduit, "marks" his presence in the construction of the real. Reflexivity vies with thick description as he describes his dilemma with respect to the use of a tape recorder to create an original transcription, but this activity is undermined by technology that fails to operate perfectly (*T*, 493). The interrupted narrative, the product of belated reproduction, signals the impossibility of recuperating the past perfectly. Chamoiseau's efforts to reconstruct the real are evident in the paratextual references to persons who inspired him, such as Serge Letchimy (an urban planner) and the actual residents of Texaco he interviewed.

The literary critique of ethnography is turned on its head by a fiction that presents itself as an ethnography inflected by the crisis of representation, but which also signals the illusoriness of this self-representation. The idea that writing is central to what anthropologists do and the dilemma about what this activity means, what genres of work it produces, underpins the novel's self-conscious crisis about its own construction. In this sense, the postcolonial attempt to recuperate history is encapsulated within a postmodernist ruse. In *Writing Culture: The Poetics and Politics of Ethnography*, James Clifford argues that culture is "composed of seriously contested codes and representations," that "the poetic and political are inseparable" and "science is, not above, in historical and linguistic processes."[18] These assumptions inform the construction of *Texaco*. The fiction shows itself to be caught up in the invention of Martinique.

New anthropologists examine the ways in which ethnography both describes and participates in the processes of innovation and structuration. Clifford sees ethnography as "actively situated *between* powerful systems of meaning" because it decodes and recodes, telling the grounds of collective order and diversity, inclusion and exclusion."[19] Attentiveness to *Texaco* as a certain kind of meta-ethnographic fiction corresponds to Chamoiseau's view of fiction as oriented toward the complexities and predicaments of culture:

> "I have success as a writer but for the wrong reasons," said Mr. Chamoiseau. "People go back for memories and souvenirs, which isn't what I want to accomplish by writing. Cultural identity is more complex than just a return to sources and roots. I want to show how complex the present cultural identity is."[20]

Chamoiseau's work of interpretive fiction offers an in-between perspective, which is neither insider nor outsider, and situates the return to the past as part of a larger process of cultural anthropology. The new anthropological view of cultural interpretation as an act of fiction-making serves as a useful point of departure for Chamoiseau, whose novel lays claim to the rewriting of culture.

The view of writing as oriented and caught up in processes of description and transformation is helpful in evaluating the complex interplay between the mimetic and diagetic aspects of *Texaco* because the presentation of the storyworld is never unmediated or transparent but always suspended as a work of contested narrative processes. This distinction is crucial to Chamoiseau's efforts to foreground the ethnographic importance of the imaginary and literature in the practices of everyday life. The role of the reader and the activity of reading are scrutinized. Gros-Joseph offers a negative example of the reader as someone who yearns for reality to conform to an ideal canon of literary works: a desire that leads to madness. In opposition to this concept of reading, *Texaco* makes reference to canonical works of French literature and plays in the space between the languages of French and Creole as well as with register of language in French. Critiques of the role of language in literature are used to negotiate poetic and political relations, resituating characters and contexts in networks of meaning that defy the mimetic, chronological unfolding of history. Marie-Sophie reads Rabelais, *Alice in Wonderland*, the fables of Fontaine, and works by Molière. Her oral account is shaped by her understanding of bizarre language, the marvelous, the fabled, and social satire. For her, the literary does not represent reality, but offers an encounter with the Real:

> Chaque livre, pour moi, libérait un parfum, une voix, une époque, un moment, une douleur, une présence; chaque livre m'irradiait ou m'accablait d'une ombre; j'étais comme terrifiée de sentir sous mes doigts ces pétillements de l'âme noués dans une même rumeur. (*T*, 280)
>
> (For me each book released an aroma, a voice, a time, a moment, a pain, a presence; each book cast a light or burdened me with its shadow; I was terrified by these souls, tied up in one hum crackling under my fingers.) (*TX*, 218).

Textual presences are as influential as contact with others and thus contribute to an understanding of a person's life choices.

This fictionalized ethnography documents social, religious, cultural, and sexual practices. One particularly important theme is the tracing of broken genealogies, brutal sexual encounters, and aborted reproductive narratives. Through life narratives, the legacies of colonial violence related to sex and reproduction are seen as passed down from generation to generation. Marie-Sophie, like so many women before her during the time of slavery, resorts to abortion in order to put an end to unwanted pregnancies. Esternome and Marie-Sophie both pass through a string of relationships, which are often cruel affairs. Both female and male perspectives concerning this punitive gender dynamic are examined. Yet, while brutality persists in everyday life as attested to by testimonial narratives, the redemptive effect of the discourse is to offer an alternative voice, an alternative, creolized, cross-gender space of possibility. This intersubjective discourse makes it impossible to separate Marie-Sophie from her father's voice or Chamoiseau's voice from that of the Urban Planner or Marie-Sophie. Together, they construct an overlapping and new account of Martinique.

Intersubjectivity is extended through the literariness of the text, which begins with quotations from Hector Bianciotti and Glissant, both of whose lives reflect the complex dynamics of language and identity that animate the novel. The reference to Bianciotti orients the reader toward the novel's arcane hermeneutics, feminist critique of history, and nascent postcolonial vision:

> Que rappellera ici le scribe qui ne rappelle à travers elle le sévère destin de toutes ces femmes condamnées aux maternités perpétuelles, expertes à déchiffrer les prophéties du vent, des crépuscules ou du halo brumeux qui parfois semble émaner de la lune, pour prévoir le temps de chaque jour et les travaux à entreprendre; ces femmes qui, luttant à l'égal des hommes pour leur subsistance, firent ce qu'on appelle une patrie et que les calendriers réduisent à quelques dates bruyantes, à certaines vanités dont souvent les rues portent le nom? (T, 11)

(What will the scribe recall, who through herself already tells of the stern destiny of all these women forever condemned to pregnancies, who, in order to foresee the day's weather and figure out what labours to take on, are expert at deciphering the prophecies of the wind, of dusk, or of the misty halo which sometimes seems to ooze out of the moon; these women who, while fighting—as much as men—to survive, made what is known as a fatherland, and whom calendars reduce to a few noisy holidays, to a vainglory after which streets are named? [*TX*, unnumbered])

Biancotti's quote attests to the forgotten struggles of women in the history of the nation as well as to the intuitive acts of deciphering associated with a feminine embodiment of history. The reference to the lunar cycles and the mystique of the landscape seems to merge the mysterious feminine presence with the forgotten, nearly indecipherable elements of the landscape, both of which are key figures in the recuperation of community. The motif of the forgotten woman of history, aborted histories, hermeneutics, and nascent perspectives is particularly worth noting in terms of the importance of this network of motifs in *Texaco* as well as in later works such as *Biblique des derniers gestes* and *Un dimanche au cachot* where L'Oubliée (the forgotten feminine presence) comes to play a central role. The second quotation (from Glissant) addresses the black man and refers to the city as the sanctuary of the word, the gesture, and the "geste" of struggle. "Geste" is invoked as a gesture, but it also refers to the "chanson de geste," the name for songs of heroic deeds or the epic poem in French literature. Sometimes these deeds are imagined and other times they refer to historical accounts. As song-poems, they are examples of another kind of *oraliture*, aimed at celebrating combat and heroism. In this context, the story of Esternome and all those who enter into the combat for city takes on an epic proportion. The French literary form is reworked through historic and literary creolization in Texaco, as an urban space as well as *Texaco*, the novel.

Narrative creolization goes beyond the linguistic to incorporate converging genres, genders, times, and places. Like ethnography, *oraliture* confronts issues concerning orality, reporting, transcription, and authorial intention. Chamoiseau as Word Scratcher represents a transposition of the storyteller's ambivalent role-play: he claims to tell the truth, but also signals that he lies. The Word Scratcher's ethnographic posture calls attention to the paradoxical structure of the narrative at the borderlands of ethnography and fiction. This vocal performance, performed by a transgender voice, merges female-male voices through time and place into a composite mosaic. The dynamics of *Texaco* disclose and reflect various systems of meaning contesting the rights to interpret, represent, determine, and narrate locality.

Texaco draws on biblical tropes and figures. The opening chapter of the novel sets forward the idea of the Urban Planner as a Christ figure who is stoned (rather than crucified), and like the Bible this text provides different accounts (gospels) of the Messianic figure. The basic story of the novel, which traces the abolition of slavery and the quest for the Promised Land, echoes the biblical. African presence is a particularly powerful aspect of this novel, which is often overlooked. From the representation of the grandfather as a kind of healer and practitioner of magic to the recurring concern with the figure of the Mentoh, the memory of Africa provides slaves and their children with a powerful embodiment of resistance and emancipation. Notably, four old men appear as the four Mentohs, the four powers: "Simples, bonhommes, d'allure insignifiante, les voir laissait pourtant les vivants ababa. [. . .] ils tournèrent sur eux-mêmes enappliquant au monde des yeux de pénétrance" (*T*, 126) ("Simple, insignificant-looking fellows, yet seeing them nevertheless left the living speechless. [. . .] they turned around setting their penetrating eyes on the world," *TX*, 95). The Mentoh does not communicate in a transparent audible language but through an opaque form that requires an ecstatic form of translation. In colonial Martinique, the Mentoh's power is translated from the mysterious language (possibly African?) into Creole: "Yo di zot libèté pas ponm kannel an bout branch! Fok zot désann raché'y, raché'y raché'y!" (*T*, 128) ("Liberty is not a sugar apple at the end of a branch. You have to wrench it away, wrench it wrench it," *TX*, 96). The Edenic motif of the Apple is reworked in the New World as an indigenous fruit, the sugar apple, which bears little resemblance to the Apple as depicted in the European representations of the Garden of Eden. The repetition of the words "Mentoh" and "raché'y" gives them an incantory force, which is suggestive of Marie-Sophie's powers as a modern-day Mentoh who brings Texaco into being by repeating her secret word in both word and deed. Like her predecessors, she does not wait to be liberated, but makes her own kind of freedom in the world. Like the Mentoh, she too speaks in a "voix-pas-claire" (*T*, 494) or a strange language of un-clarity and "hypnotic enchantment" (*TX*, 388). The quest for voice is shown to be one of self-conquest through "l'inédit créole qu'il nous fallait nommer—en nous-mêmes pour nous-mêmes—jusqu'à notre pleine autorité" (*T*, 498) ("the Creole unsaid which we had to name—in ourselves and for ourselves—until we came into our own") (*TX*, 390).

The power of the Word to create the world in Genesis is reworked through the creolized language of *Texaco*, which in turn draws strength from traces of African diasporic culture. Not only does *Texaco* rework biblical tropes, it also reworks the biblical tradition through creolized spiritual practices and beliefs. As such the creolization at work in Texaco goes beyond dialogues with French and world literatures to include cultural and spiritual practices. In *Lettres créoles*, Chamoiseau and Confiant define the Nouveau Roman as an anti-messianic form in which the role of twinning and the principles of *vodou* serves as sources of inspiration. At the level of plotting, the twins, Adrienne Carmélite Lapidaille and Idoménée, who were separated shortly after their birth by a *béké*, represent a kind of Marasa figuration. The former, accompanied by a rooster on her shoulder, engages in creolized spiritual practices and "black arts." Adrienne Carmélite Lapidaille brings Esternome home in hopes of stealing his vision through supernatural means and then giving his sight to her sister. In another instance, Adrienne Carmélite Lapidaille is represented as one of the evil ones who become flying creatures at night (*T*, 231). The duality of the twins pairs opposing types, the one an active, combative fighter in the world and the other a gentle figure in retreat from the world, and introduces the Marasa motif that is subsequently repeated in the twinning of Deborah and her sister Sarah in *Biblique des derniers gestes*.

The narrative interweaves oral and textual performance to produce a hermetic graphical art that functions as an incantation, a kind of oral-graphic writing like that of the *vévé* (the drawing of a figure in the sand in order to elicit a *lwa*). Textually, the narrative offers not one, but four convergent Christ-like figures: the Urban Planner, Marie-Sophie, Chamoiseau the *Marqueur*, and Esternome. In "The Annunciation," the Urban Planner enters Texaco like a Christ entering Jerusalem, but he is met with a rock to the head rather than palm leaves. The various reports of his coming, which make up "The Annunciation," provide a subversive alternative to the biblical account of the angel who brings the news to the virgin. Marie-Sophie gives a sermon, which is not the Sermon on the Mount but a sermon with rum. She offers the conversion narrative that will transform the penitent Urban Planner into a Saviour. At the same time as she is Christ, she functions as a Marian figure who gives birth to the Saviour through storytelling as the space of re-genesis. The *Marqueur* appears in the section of the text titled "Résurrection" ("Resurrection"), not in Easter's splendor, but in the shameful anxiety of the Word Scratcher, who tries to write life. Finally, Esternome is a double for Christ because he too is a carpenter and man of the people. His concerns with building a house and finding a proper foundation on which to live echo those of Christ. In many ways, Esternome embodies the aspect of Christ as a man of the people. Yet, he gives birth to Mary, one of the saviour's of the community. Thus, the biblical narrative is circuitously reworked in a subversive fashion.

The appearance of four Christ figures, each embodying a particular manifestation of the Saviour in a subversive form continues the Marasa trope of pairing and opposition, but transposes it to the discursive operations of the text. The Urban Planner can be seen as a double for Esternome, someone concerned with the construction of society in its materiality. Chamoiseau can be seen as a double for Marie-Sophie as both are concerned with storytelling as an act of transformation as well as with the idea of recording narratives and passing them along. The intersection of these four voices creates a narrative cross, a repetition of the Christian cross. Like the cross, the text appears as a kind of four-in-one, which merges all of these separate entities together in a cohesive whole. Yet, at the same time, this is not a static symbol of crucifixion and resurrection, but a dynamic process of motion, intersection, and renewal, which functions in a nonlinear, fluid fashion. This narrative motion produces a symbolic cross, much like the *vévé* of Papa Legba, the tricky facilitator of speech and understanding who functions as a link between our world and that of the *loas*. The couplings and convergent narratives represent a crossroads: a speaking-graphic, a kind of prayer that calls forth Papa Legba.[21] This speech reminds the reader that these four contemporary figures coming together participate in the long history of claims to freedom; they echo the powerful, half-forgotten language and presence of the four Mentohs.

This narrative at the crossroads of intersecting voices, approaches, and perspectives suggests that the work of society is a composite one. A Saviour will not come to rescue society and liberate the people, but they should band together in actions and words to revision the world and change its material conditions. In this respect, the Bible for the New World takes the motif of redemption and reworks it as a sacred narrative about self-determination. The miraculous aspects of this text appear in the moments of textual alchemy when the material, spiritual, and linguistic converge to create something new. *Texaco* extends the work of *oraliture*, which seeks to reenact or transpose aspects of the oral performance in the written, and produces a textual drama that invokes the crossroads of communication. Chamoiseau calls attention to the moment when speech crystallizes into action, a concept similar to Hannah Arendt's concept of the power of "space of appearance" as a moment of shared speech, understanding, and action.[22] While Chamoiseau's tendency to play at the interfaces of language can be seen as one form of disclosure, the most manifest form of this work is evident in the sustained allegory of building a society through an alchemical sort of language that serves as the cement of society.

Rather than the idea of the word as the genesis of the world, *Texaco* works through the processes of alchemical linguistics, which are shown at work when language is used to disclose new spaces, herald change, and construct new realities. Language is literally a constructive force in *Texaco*, a means of framing history in order to defend one's foundational right to occupy a home or a way of recognizing the perspective of the "nous" (we) as the speaking voice that is heard in each individual's life. More than simply finding *le mot juste* (the right word or expression), the right words seem to have a magical force. The importance of magic in Chamoiseau's writing is evident in the sorcery of *Manman Dlo*, the conditions for Creole storytelling—where one fears being turned into a basket without handles—and the Creole story itself. The interface of Creole and French becomes a new space of creation where the materials of the past become the building blocks of the future. In "The Annunication," when the Urban Planner enters Fort-de-France, Marie-Clémence alerts the community with a cry, which is described as follows: "Elle disait: La chaux! La chaux! prompte manière d'annoncer une brûlure de la vie" (*T*, 34). Given the context, it is tempting to translate this sentence as follows: "She said, The heat! The heat! A sure way of announcing life burns." However, this would be to misrepresent the meaning of word "chaux" as limestone. In French, the word "chaux" sounds like the word "chaud" (meaning "heat"). By punning on the similar sounds of these words, the semantics of heat and limestone are sonically fused together. This puzzling interplay of sound and meaning becomes clear in the dialogic reconstruction of Marie-Sophie's narrative, when these words resurface and their meanings are shown to be grounded in the history of the body and genealogical history.

Marie-Sophie's narrative includes the tale of her grandfather, a kind of *quimboiseur* who made poisons and medicines as a means of resisting slavery on the plantation. He is one of many who oppose the plantation with its "chaux de douleurs" (*T*, 49) or "heat of suffering." This repetition of the "heat of suffering" as the "burning lime of suffering" reinforces the obscure associations of suffering, solidarity, and resistance as the forces binding the community together. The grandfather helped women to abort children so that they would not be born into slavery and provided medicines to treat yaws. Equally, his words are powerful harbingers of emancipation because he is one of the strong who articulate resistance: *"Pas d'enfants d'esclavage," "Pas de récoltes,"* and *"Plus de forces-l'esclavage"* (*T*, 49–50) ("No children born in chains," "No harvest," and "No strength to slavery") (*TX*, 35). The grandfather is aligned with the African presence in the Caribbean and the existence of *loas*. His ability to heal a snakebite, which remains lethal to this day, is seen as a sign of his special powers. When the *béké* asks him to help locate the source of poisoning on the plantation, he mutters words to himself and refuses to respond. These words are taken as proof of his magical words and he is thrown into the dungeon to be tortured. Later, it turns out that he was fascinated by the birds and his words articulated a muttering wonder about the flight of birds, perhaps as embodying his own desire for flight. This enchantment also gives us a clue about the textual impulses of the Oiseau de Cham as narrator, someone who envisions an alternative field of freedom.

The grandfather who speaks to blackbirds represents a refusal to submit to the conditions of the plantation, which goes beyond the ken of either the plantation manager or the slave community. Like the protagonist of J. M. Coetzee's *The Life and Times of Michael K*, he is more interested in pursuing a certain way of life and his refusal of authority stems from this otherworldly vision of birds freely in flight. He prefigures the quest for libratory politics and true emancipation that begins in slavery and continues through the epic of Martinican history as represented in *Texaco*. He belongs to the species of *homo tantum* or the soul beyond classification as defined by Michael Hardt and Antonio Negri in *Empire*.[23] Like this kind of man, he represents "a kind of social suicide" and indeed he dies a brutal death, but he also clears a space, identifying the need for "a new mode of life and above all a new kind of community," "enriched by the collective intelligence and love of the community."[24]

This striking narrative concerning the magic and opacity of language also serves to unlock the meaning of "chaux" as lime ("les pierres à chaux" means limestone) that provide the mortar for building:

> Dans le sud, Marie-Sophie, les pierres à chaux me donnent mortier. En bord de mer, je grille à la manière des Caraïbes, coquillages et polypiers qui donnent manman-ciment.

Cahier n° 4 de Marie-Sophie Laborieux.
Page 9. 1965 Bibliothèque Schoelcher. (*T*, 50)

In the South, Marie-Sophie, limestone yields me mortar. By the sea, I roast shells and polypary, the Carib way, to make the mama of all cement.
NOTEBOOK NO. 4 OF MARIE-SOPHIE LABORIEUX.
PAGE 9, 1965. SCHOELCHER LIBRARY. (*TX*, 35)

This pre-Columbian method of building blends together shells, polypary, and limestone as the cement for building. The fact that the Urban Planner is hit with a rock, which evokes the cry of "chaux" or "lime," indicates that a call-response mechanism is at work in the construction of the narrative. The cry refers not only to the moment when the urban space of Texaco is under threat, but evokes a longer history of communal memories. The community is bound together through calls to precolonial memory and the long history of resistance to imperialism. In this context, the "chaux de douleur" or "lime of suffering" serves as a kind of mortar. Just as lime burns so does suffering, but both sources of heat prove to be transformative.

The transition from literal building materials to the figurative activity of building a dwelling place and a community is carried out through Esternome's words to his daughter, which are recorded by her in her journals. Chamoiseau the Word Scratcher scatters these instructions throughout the novel, thus creating a dialogic sense of history. Esternome's words interrupt the storytelling event and provide comments in a written equivalent to the kind of call-response technique of oral storytelling. For instance, Esternome's observation concerning the ways in which the Caribs passed on their secrets of construction through the use of indigenous materials interrupts the tale of colonial history. His comment, "Métier c'est belle mémoire" (*T*, 59) ("Craft is good memory"), calls attention to the role of the narrative as a craft that binds together the community in ways comparable to the material construction of the community (*T*, 42). This call-response mechanism also introduces narrative detours, prompting the reader to reflect on past-present relations as well as the processes underlying creolization. For example, Esternome's description of the etymology of words for "l'esclavage" ("slavery") and "travail" ("labor") through French-Creole linguistic exchange takes the form of a detour:

> Ils disaient aves leurs mots: l'esclavage. Pour nous c'était entendre: l'estravaille. Quand ils le surent et dirent à leur tour Lestravaille pour nous parler en proximité, nous avions déjà raccourci l'affaire sur l'idée de travail . . . hi hi hi, la parole sillonnait, Sophie, la parole sillonnait comme une arme . . .
>
> >> Cahier n° 2 de Marie-Sophie Laborieux.
> >> Page 9. 1965 Bibliothèque Schoelcher. (*T*, 65)

> With their words, they would say: *l'esclavage*, slavery. But we would only hear: *l'estravaille*, travail. When they found out and began to say *Lestravaille*, to speak closer to us, we'd already cut the word down to *travail*, the idea of plain toil . . . ha ha ha, Sophie, the word cut across like a weapon . . .
>
> >> NOTEBOOOK NO. 2 OF MARIE-SOPHIE LABORIEUX.
> >> PAGE 9. 1965. SCHOELCHER LIBRARY. (*TX*, 47)

Language emerges as the product of a history of call-and-response dialogues, but it proves to be a tricky process of accommodation and resistance, which is shaped by evasive maneuvers and efforts to maintain opacity. The use of the verb "sillonner" is particularly evocative in this context as it suggests not only the idea of cutting but also that of furrowing the ground so that the work of the plantation ("sillonner" as "to furrow") is reworked as a cutting-like motion in which the word cuts through colonial history as a mode of resistance.

Similarly, the story's call-and-response mechanism is evasive and circuitous. Although Esternome's words appear to be part of an ongoing dialogue, they are the product of textual interventions and roundabout maneuvers. Sourced by Chamoiseau the Word Scratcher from the archive, the words that began as personal memories are brought into the text as official historical documents. The Word Scratcher performs a magic similar to that of the word "Texaco" by appropriating an official site as a space for reconstructing locality. The printed text plays the role of an oral voice: providing the illusion of the father in dialogue with the daughter. This seemingly direct back-and-forth masks an underlying circuitous path because Marie-Sophie's narrative is already based on the stories her father told her and she recorded. Consequently, the father's words circulate and recirculate through the elusive voice of Marie-Sophie, which is also a product of textual intervention. The Urban Planner's words to the Word Scratcher, inspired by Marie-Sophie, speak through her narrative that takes the form of a spiraling response to her question:

Oiseau Cham, existe-t-il une écriture informée de la parole, et des silences, et qui reste vivante, qui bouge en cercle et circule tout le temps, irriguant sans cesse de vie ce qui a été écrit avant, et qui réinvente le cercle à chaque fois comme le font les spirales qui sont à tout moment dans le futur et dans l'avant, l'une modifiant l'autre, sans cesse, sans perdre une unité difficile à nommer? (*T*, 413)

(Oiseau Cham, is there such a thing as writing informed by the word, and by the silences, and which remains a living thing, moving in a circle, and wandering all the time, ceaselessly irrigating with life the things written before, and which reinvents the circle each time like a spiral which at any moment is in the future, ahead, each loop modifying the other, non-stop, without losing a unity difficult to put into words?) (*TX*, 322)

Chamoiseau's narrative puts into practice this idea of a mobile, living language, which serves as a structuring principle for his novel and the concept of community. Marie-Sophie's language transforms him and Texaco (as city) and *Texaco*. Much like the *vodou* practice of being mounted by a *lwa*, this poetic double-voicing functions like an act of spiritual possession that serves to reconfigure intersubjective body-spirit relations.

The patterning of these voices at the crossroads invokes Papa Legba, whose presence is at work in these dynamics of the interplay of four main voices (Esternome, Marie-Sophie, Urban Planner, Word Scratcher) that produce a "concrete" vision of *Texaco*. The Urban Planner discovers that he must live the complex play of forces at work in Texaco (*T*, 401). There is a "coherence to decipher" beneath the disorderly material conditions, a secret meaning that he is meant to decode (*T*, 313). To reinvent the city, the Urban Planner discovers he must think Creole before he even thinks (*T*, 345) and writes to the Word Scratcher, "Quand je dis «l'urbanisme créole», j'invoque: *mutation de l'esprit*" (*T*, 300) ("When I say 'Creole urban planning,' I am invoking: *a mutation of the spirit*") (*TX*, 234). This crossroads "prepares the way" for a new vision of the city in which the rural breathes life into the urban and the urban is envisioned as an ecological system where the shantytown inhabitants serve as a mangrove swamp, breathing life into the system. Such a city mingles two tongues and dreams of all tongues (*T*, 282); it serves as the roots of a new identity that is multilingual, multiracial, and multihistorical, open to the world's diversity (*T*, 282).

Such a claim is best understood with reference to the notion of Texaco as a secret identity of community coming into presence. Like *Texaco*, the novel composed through tricky oral and textual interplay, the word "Texaco" reworks language in a strategically circuitous, meaningful call-and-response manner so that it becomes "The Word" as a source of power. Like "Nouteka," a composite of the Creole words "we" (nou) and "that were" (teka), Texaco is composed of the Creole words "teks" (meaning "text"), "a" (a preposition that indicates the future), and "ko" (meaning "body" come together as "Tex," "a," and "co." This embodied text of the future in an incarnation of the city to come, the mantra of Marie-Sophie, who repeated this magical word to herself in order to bring the city into being. The city, which merges the local and global, the marginalized and the multinational, embodies the people and the people's stories embody the city. These relations of reciprocity form another kind of twinning principle, unifying contradictory ideas about place and time as well as narrative and identity. The name of the novel, *Texaco*, with its discussions about the relations of the city to the world, extends this discursive magic, repeating with the same magical incantation the hope of evoking an alternative future on a grander scale. The local wording becomes a means of transforming the global meaning of "Texaco." In linking the stories of the past community to the embodiment of the future global/local city, the work elicits the horizons of the unfinished work of the postcolonial in the world so that the spiral continues to reverberate beyond the work and the word.

This act of creative translation, the ongoing work of creolization as process rather than a fixed language, offers a utopian moment, situated in the in-between spaces of meaning and discourse. The suspension of meaning, the moment of when dissonance and potential are ambiguously revealed is one of tension, and agonistic potentiality, a kind of reworking of the *chanson de geste* as a literature of combat. This kind of postcoloniality fits with Homi K. Bhabha's observation that "the Utopian moment is not the necessary horizon of hope."[25] In this sense, postcolonial literature with its emphasis on the fractures and the in-between of cultural formation is utopian in the sense that it focuses attention on acts of cultural translation and the remediation of past-present. This redefinition of the utopian moment is particularly relevant in the case of *Texaco*, a novel that remediates temporalities as acts of cultural translation. By calling attention to ambiguous dialogues and the uneven production of meaning, the narrative discloses a community whose fluid construction inverts a top-down approach to regional development and subverts the perilous monolingualism of departmentalization.

Blurring the lines between narrative, history, and ethnography, *Texaco* lays claim to the rewriting of the imagined/real community and the world through extended and ongoing processes of creolization. The ability to mobilize the unspoken and to articulate the unspeakable is brought about through language as gesture and evocation. The idea of the literary as a transposition of spiritual practices embodies a fuller idea of communication, which goes beyond *oraliture* or a playful adaptation of anthropological genres of writing and modes of investigation. Alchemical linguistic processes are part of a writerly strategy that transgresses the linguistic and becomes a means of redrawing, reconnecting, and mobilizing the imaginary. This agonistic activity stems from a disenchanted view of the current horizons and a desire to take an active part in the articulation of the locality as a space of possession in which all of the inhabitants, past and present, speak in harmony with the land. Consequently, the writer plays an active role as a kind of medium or *houngan/mambo* (high priest/priestess in *vodou*) in the reconstruction of locality and the reconfiguration of the dwelling places of the imaginary.

CHAPTER 5

Autoethnographic Fictions of Childhood

Chamoiseau has published three fictional texts on childhood, *Antan d'enfance* (1990), *Chemin-d'école* (1994), and *À bout d'enfance* (2005). Together these three works deal with different stages in the life of the child: pre-school experiences, early school years, and the end of childhood marked by the onset of adolescence. Splitting childhood into distinctive stages, Chamoiseau revives the slow drama of childhood development and recognizes that childhood involves a series of dramatic transformations, and ruptures of consciousness. Despite fictionalizing tendencies, the works are examples of "autoethnographic expression," which Mary Louise Pratt defines as "instances in which colonized subjects undertake to represent themselves in ways that *engage with* the colonizer's own terms."[1] Such texts are constructed in response to (or in dialogue with) metropolitan representations. With reference to Chamoiseau, Pratt's use of the term "colonizer" is somewhat contentious as the author grew up under departmentalization, a state that could be classified as neocolonial rather than colonial. Nonetheless, he confronts colonial legacies in the education system and shows how the child is educated to internalize metropolitan values. At the same time, his work is a form of "autoethnographic expression" that reclaims self-description by making use of the vernacular, particularly through the investigation into the domestic space, the use of the Creole language, and the workings of creolized forms.

The child is situated in a world where the internalization of colonial values persists through the dynamics of family, school, friendship, and other social contexts. Sharon L. Shelley highlights these tensions, observing that the boy in *Chemin-d'école* "struggles to master standard French and to find his voice as a writer; but he refuses to abandon his Creole heritage, or to adopt the racist and colonial values tragically assimilated by his teachers."[2] At the same time, Chamoiseau appropriates Western concepts of childhood and civilization as a means to rewrite these concepts, shifting the viewpoint from the *metropole* to Martinican daily life and its realities. Chamoiseu's work is profoundly engaged in a dialogue with France, but he is equally concerned with the local, the Creole, and the forms that are already formulated through dialogue interaction with France through colonization and creolization. So the processes and layers of autoethnographic formation are inevitably complex.

In the three works, there is a gradual widening of contexts and influences, moving from the domestic space of home to school to the public spaces of Martinique. This is accompanied by the onset of a wider sphere of influences on the local. *Antan d'enfance* records the child's first awareness of the effects of departmentalization as seen through the disappearance of old ways of life. In *Antan*, these effects are recorded and glimpsed by the child, but little is made of their political significance. The author attests to the processes of modernization in the departmental era as water is supplied to the home and the narrator refers to the cleaning up of the canal, previously overrun by rats. Martinique's neocolonial identity is highly visible through the workings of the educational system, described in *Chemin*, and the introduction of French supermarkets, goods, and technologies, described in *À bout*. The third fiction also attests to global media flows as Italian magazines and foreign cinema make their way into the boy's life.

Nonetheless, these texts exceed any narrow definition of authoethnographic expression because Chamoiseau consistently shows the gaps and lapses evident in the neocolonial discourse of childhood. Discrepancies arise through lapses of memory as well as through creolization, which provides another cultural context for the articulation of self and the discourse of childhood. Through the influence of his mother, relations with his friends, and in his engagement to the Creole practices of everyday life, Chamoiseau offers another framework for autoethnographic expression. The child's life is a site of tension whose narrative repeats in a compressed time scale and *en miniature* the collective history of instabilities that have contributed to the cultural psyche of Martinique. These tensions and anxieties are reflected in the events recounted as well as the lexical shifts of the narrative, particularly as the boy in *Chemin* struggles to write for himself rather than the teacher, resulting in a disjunctive effect because the narrative represents a belated response. From a temporal perspective, the boy's lived experiences are already rewritten by his future, suggesting that the autoethnographic narrative's use of the past tense reflects a subjunctive or conditional perspective: the description of events and feelings is impossible (because it did not take place in that way) or improbable (it is doubtful that it was recognized or interpreted in the same way) because is already remediated. The belatedness inherent in self-construction and self-knowledge imbues the shifting poetics of the text as the author switches voices and temporal perspectives. The nostalgic return to childhood is thus thwarted by the impossibility of recuperating the earlier "I" of the boy that once existed. The exile from childhood finds voice in the split subject.

Distanciation is also evident in the literariness of these texts, which can be seen in a number of parodic reworkings of French literary, linguistic, and cultural texts and traditions within a Creole framework. This form of postcolonial autoethnographic expression engages with the (neo)colonizer's own terms, but does so in a way that critiques, reworks, and appropriates the materials of culture as sources for the author's own self-creation. In other words, the autoethnographic engagement with the colonial serves as a point of departure for the postcolonial expression of self. In this sense, the writing of childhood is situated as an activity that is shown in the process of recuperating the nascence of the artistic self. This pre-history separates the child from the man, turning the act of narration into one that continuously suspends the past-present relation as an instance of nostalgia that is less about the past and more about the present.

The instabilities and ruptures of memory, the formation of the Creolist consciousness, the uses of nostalgia, and the nascence of the writer are important themes in Chamoiseau's narratives of childhood.[3] While the texts refer to events in everyday life and pay attention to cultural contexts, these are also highly literate works that might fruitfully be compared to works of childhood and memory by Marcel Proust, Jean-Paul Sartre, Nathalie Sarraute, Saint-John Perse, Joseph Zobel, Raphaël Confiant, Maryse Condé, and Émile Olliver. Mary Gallagher suggests that Chamoiseau views the child and poet as similar in their ability to remain open to the magical aura of the world and its chaotic truths.[4] However, the "gaze of the child survives only in its discontinuities, detours, inventions, and ellipses germane to poetic insight."[5] In this sense, the child represents the poetic capabilities of the adult author. Yet, these are also highly politicized readings of childhood in which the author searches for poetic origins in childhood. The Creolist "avant la lettre" is evident in narrative episodes that bear witness to a disappearing Creole way of life, attest to the effects of neocolonialism in Martinique, and offer a neocolonial critique of the child's formation.

Decolonizing Memory, Rewriting the Self

Chamoiseau personifies memory as a barricaded figure, someone surrounded by fortified walls:

> Mémoire, passons un pacte le temps d'un crayonné, baisse palissades et apaise les farouches, suggère le secret des traces invoquées au bord de tes raziés. Moi, je n'emporte ni sac de rapt ni coutelas de conquête, rien qu'une ivresse et que joie bien docile au gré (coulée du temps) de ta coulée. (*AE*, 12)

> (Memory, let's make a pact that's long enough for a sketch, lower your palisades and pacify the savages, reveal the secret of the traces that lie at the edge of your brushy borders. I bring neither a sack for kidnapping nor knife for conquest, nothing but the intoxication and a mighty docile joy at the rhythm [flow of time] of your flow.) (*CH*, 4)

Given the imperialistic images associated with memory, it is not surprising that the first memories make use of Western definitions of time relating to the infancy of civilization: the ages of mankind, such as the age of fire and tools, references to the floods, and the idea of the child as a conqueror and torturer, invoke Eurocentric discourses of civilization that are seen as affiliated with the narcissism of the violent child conqueror of nature.

The child's desire to conquer the world around him is described as an imperialistic tendency. *Antan* begins with the phases of mankind, representing the infancy of man in the desire to kill and conquer:

> Son seul génie fut d'être un tueur. Il fut sacré roi (par lui-même) des araignées et des fourmis, des libellules et vers de terre victimes pourtant de ses massacres. Il fut l'Attila des blattes rouges et des gros ravets sombres

que l'on criait klaclac. Et il mena campagne contre une colonie de rats impossible à ruiner. Ce tueur a une histoire—la voilà—il est douteux qu'il en soit fier. (*AE*, 14–15)

(His only genius was as a killer. He was anointed [by himself] king of the spiders and ants, of the dragonflies and earthworms, victims, nonetheless, of his massacres. He was Attila of the red beetles and of the big dark cockroaches called *klacclac*. And he waged a campaign against a colony of rats that was impossible to destroy. This killer has a history—and here it is. It's doubtful he is proud of it.) (*CH*, 5–6)

However, the young boy soon finds a worthy adversary in the form of a wily, older rat. His failure to conquer this rat leads to a certain kind of respect and also seems to mark the boy's waning interest in destruction. Instead, the narrative turns to the boy's sense of wonder about the world he inhabits, a transition that is of particular importance for Chamoiseau the writer whose works often replay the turn from battling the world to more pacific and poetic ways of staking a claim in history.

Nonetheless, even the turn toward poetics marks a self-conscious, politicized use of intertextual allusions for subversive purposes. Chamoiseau parodies the Proustian trope of involuntary memory, which is evoked through an appeal to the senses, most notably in the episode of the Madeleine. *Antan* begins with a section titled "Sentir," a verb that can be translated as "to smell," "to taste," and "to feel." The synesthesia implicit in the related meanings of this verb belongs to a French literary tradition (including French Symbolism and decadence of Baudelaire) to which Proust is heir. Chamoiseau reworks this tradition through appeals to the creolization of the senses, meaning that the senses are intermixed and related to the Creole world with its heat, plants, colors, and sounds. For instance, Chamoiseau describes the paper flowers, which his mother makes and sells as home decorations, but which she does not display in her own home because she prefers real flowers. The narrator observes that without a word she taught the boy that a flower is mainly a perfumed scent (*AE*, 75). The artifice evokes the sensory real, which reverses the expansiveness of the Proustian memory that moves from the sensory trigger of memory to the world of the past.

Instead, memory functions as a deconstructive gesture in which the memory of sensations is inextricably bound up and released through language. An example of this occurs in Chamoiseau's reworking of the

Proustian scene of the Madeleine. Rather than the child's delight at eating this purchased commodity, which evokes the entire rush of memories and the production of the novel, Chamoiseau returns to production and consumption of the sweet and the discourse. The memories stem from his mother as the producer of Creole sweets to be sold to wealthier ladies, but this is an event in which the child also participates and profits:

> Les jours du sucre étaient bénédiction[.] Man Ninotte savait tout faire, les gâteaux, les sikdôj, les filibos, les torsades colorées fondantes sur la langue, les macawon, les lotchios câpresses, les la-colle-pistaches. Des madames de bonne famille lui passaient des commandes, et elle piétait durant des heures au bord du four en compagnie de la Baronne. Mesurer la farine, casser les œufs, brasser le tout, lever les blancs. (*AE*, 75)

> (Sugar days were a blessing. Ma Ninotte knew how to make everything: cakes, *sikdoj*, *filibos*, twists of color that melted on your tongue, *macawon*, *lotchios*, *câpresses*, *la-colle-pistaches*. Ladies from good families would send her orders, and she'd stand for hours by the oven in the company of the Baroness, measuring the flour, breaking the eggs, stirring it all up, whipping the whites.) (*CH*, 50)

The boy omnivorously tests, tastes, measures, and licks up these sugary texts under production, a greediness that prefigures his democratic tastes for all kinds of texts and stories (*AE*, 75–76). The catalog of sweets described by their Creole names evokes a world that may not be familiar to many French readers, but the tantalizing descriptions of twists of color that melt in your mouth evokes the familiar but impossible to recall past-present of Martinican otherness. At the same time, through Creole language, the distant memories of the past call upon the shared memories and experiences of Martinicans. Rather than a delicate Proustian bite into the past, releasing the flow of memories, Chamoiseau evokes the past-present dynamics of French-Martinican relations through the rewriting of the Proustian in a local context.

The production and consumption of cakes functions as an allegory on the rituals and orthodoxies of race and language through the description of the scene of production, which begins in a vaguely religious context with the boy's eating of the "les dentelles figées de la benediction" (*AE*, 76) ("stiffened lace of benediction") (*CH*, 51) from the pan to the more specific context of an "atmosphère de baptême irréel" (*AE*, 77) ("unreal baptismal atmosphere") (*CH*, 51). Orthodoxies of color are invoked as some of the overly blackened cookies require a knife to achieve the normative shade of light brown. Cookies are decorated, sculpted with white swirls. This ritual around the production of whiteness can be seen as an ironic gesture concerning the artifices involved on the part of some upwardly mobile Martinicans who undergo comparable processes for concealing their underlying identities. To top off the icing on the cake, the Baroness sometimes inscribes words and names for special occasions; these words are indecipherable to the illiterate child, but he learns to love the taste of language. The semiotics of adult pleasure in linguistic production and consumption are initiated in the child's early and indiscriminate consumption of language itself:

> Écrire avec du sucre et dévorer l'écrit. Cela fleurit bellement son enfance: le mystère de l'écrire et la joie du manger. Quand Anastasie se trompait, elle lui décollait une lettre, un mot. Il les engloutissait en confiant au plaisir de ses papilles le soin du décodage. (*AE*, 76–77)

> (To write with sugar and devour the writing. This flowered his childhood beautifully: the mystery of writing and the joy of eating. When Anastasia made a mistake, she'd peel off a letter or a word for him. He wolfed them down, entrusting his taste buds with the pleasure of decoding.) (*CH*, 51)

The baptism into language as hermeneutics is repeated through the ritual of making the First Communion bread, which effectively displaces communion with God and initiates an awareness of incertitude and possibility rather than faith (*AE*, 78–79). Making bread becomes a metaphor for the production of selfhood. The outer crust of the bread contains still within it the more dextrous substance from which it arose under the incredible heat of the oven's fire with its dragon's breath and dormant volcanic waves (*AE*, 77–78). In *Chemin*, this cycle continues with the age of petrogylphs, a humorous name that the author uses to describe the child's scribblings on the walls of the home. This pre-Columbian form of writing symbolizes a desire for a form of self-expression that evades colonial memory by operating beyond its perimeters. In *À bout d'enfance*, the image of the fortified self is reworked through neo-medieval parody in the form of the adolescent's encounter with a modern-day case of medieval lovesickness and his accompanying quest challenges as a member of the Round Table. As with the Proustian echo, this later intertexual allusion to French literature in a Creole context provides a parodic space of otherness in which to commemorate and inscribe the emergent sense of self.

This is not to say that *Antan* lacks a political dimension, but rather that politics radiates through the practices of everyday life so that the domestic, insular life of the young child is shown to be infused by the postcolonial. The work begins with references to imperial impulses, which are mediated through historic and literary references to European culture, but gradually slips into the dramas of everyday Creole life. Unwittingly, the child is witness to an already disappearing way of life. Creole medical practices and skilled craftsmen are no longer needed in a world where French medicine and imported goods are readily available. Nonetheless, the references to the markets, the role of the Major in each local neighborhood, and the space for entrepreneurs suggest that the Creole economy still survived in the early years of Chamoiseau's childhood. These details are noteworthy, particularly when we compare the streets and markets of early childhood to those described in *À bout d'enfance* where French-owned supermarkets and imported commodities are prevalent.

Women play a particularly important role in the evocation of the Creole world. Jeanne-Yvette, a girl from the countryside, enters the post-cycle world of the young boy as a Creole storyteller. Not only the content but also the form of the narrative are imprinted on his memory; he learns that a real storyteller possesses "une mémoire impossible et une cruauté sans égale" (*AE*, 108) ("unfathomable in memory and unbeatably cruel") (*CH*, 75). She teaches him about many of the figures who will later populate his fictions, such as Manman Dlo, and serves as a source of knowledge about *quimbois*. Her opaque methods give the boy a sense of the impenetrable strategy of strength of Ma Ninotte and the other mamas of the city (*AE*, 110). These strategies of craft and wile are particularly in evidence in the section of the narrative called "Sortir," which contains a hilarious dialogue between Ma Ninotte and a vendor as she negotiates for the best price on local produce.

Given this domestication of history, it is not surprising that *Antan* ends with the substitution of a Creole house of memory for the fortress. Unlike the heavily fortified walls, the Creole house is a dusty, dissolute archive of memories, kept and cared for by Ma Ninotte, who cultivates memory as "une jungle créole" ("a Creole jungle") (*AE*, 164). Instead of an apostrophe to memory, the tale ends with a speech directed to "my brothers." This fraternal address echoes the rhetorical techniques of French

Revolutionary speeches. Chamoiseau's extratextual allusion can be seen as an alternative to the Haitian appropriation of the Revolution as well as the conventional understanding of the motto "Liberté, Égalité, Fraternité." The ideas of liberty, equality, and fraternity have yet to be fulfilled in a postcolonial France. Through his narrative, Chamoiseau reworks communal memory, invoking a more inclusive French-Creole history that pays attention to the stories of the past told by those now departmentalized subjects that form part of its own diversity.

The (Mis)education of Patrick Chamoiseau

The themes of inclusivity and accommodation to diversity are made explicit in the second work of childhood, *Chemin-d'école*, which picks up from where *Antan* left off. The dedication of the work is worth citing in full for it clarifies the kind of solidarities that Chamoiseau's revolutionary address evokes:

Petites-personnes,
des Antilles, de la Guyane, de Nouvelle-Calédonie, de la Réunion, de l'île Maurice, de Rodrigues et autres Mascareignes, de Corse, de Bretagne, de Normandie, d'Alsace, du Pays basque, de Provence, d'Afrique, des quatre coins de l'Orient, de toutes terreurs nationales, de tous confins étatiques, de toutes périphéries d'empires ou de fédérations, qui avez dû affronter une école coloniale, oui vous qui aujourd'hui en d'autres manières l'affrontez encore, et vous qui demain l'affronterez autrement, cette parole de rire amer contre l'Unique et le Même, riche de son propre centre et contestant tout centre, hors de toutes métropoles, et tranquillement diverselle contre l'universel, est dite en votre nom. (*CE*, 13)

(Youngsters,
of the West Indies, of French Guyana, of New Caledonia, of Reunion, of Mauritius, of Rodriguez, and other Mascarenes, of Corsica, of Brittany, of Normandy, of Alsace, of the Basque country, of Provence, of Africa, of the four corners of the Orient, of all national territories, of all far-flung dominions, of all outlying posts of empires or federations, you who have had to face a colonial school, yes, you who in other ways are still confronting one today, and you who will face this challenge tomorrow in some other guise: This voice of bitter laughter at the One and Only—a firmly centered voice

challenging all centers, a voice beyond all home countries and peacefully diversal in opposition to the universal—is raised in your name.) (*SD*, 7)

The first page of the fictional text addresses brothers and sisters, thus extending the Revolutionary claims to an extended family of those undergoing the processes of decolonization.

The extent to which these narratives consider the social and political construction of the child helps to pinpoint these as autoethnographic texts. Critics have applied Pratt's description of autoethnographic expression to life-writing as a genre that is poised between "the authorized discourses of autobiography and ethnography."[6] James Buzard comments on the difficulties inherent in this practice:

> Autoethnography is characterized as a mode of practicing the "defining of one's subjectivity ethnicity," this mystifying dyad "subjective ethnicity" leaving tantalizingly open such usual questions of cultural or racial determinism as how much the defining of one's ethnicity lies in one's power. But can we have autoethnography without invoking *as if real* the idea of culture that is truly and/or originally ours, and that authorities outside the self impose upon it [. . .]?[7]

Autoethnography deals with the thorny issue of self-definition when there is no essential cultural identity left to recover. The extent to which the self can clear a space for self-articulation remains one of the most problematic and perplexing questions of this genre.

Chamoiseau's multivocal poetics of self-negotiation reflect the impossibility of fulfilling the autobiographical pact, which Philippe Lejeune defines as the pact between the "je" (I) and the "moi" (me) or the promise of sincerity.[8] Instead of a pact with self, Chamoiseau makes a pact with memory and the result is a text that both represents and renegotiates the decentered perspective of the postcolonial subject. The man and the child remain separate selves, unable to be reconciled into a single unified entity that is both "je" and "moi." For Maeve McCusker, memory is "a locus of struggle, due to the dialectical relationship between experience and narrative, between narrated and narrating self."[9] Through its associations with colonial modes of power, memory plays the role of an uneasy ally, one prone to shutting out the postcolonial subject. The pact with memory introduces the dialogic structure of the narrative, intensifying dramatic tensions because each revelation or narrative episode appears to have been wrested or tricked from memory. Memory remains entangled in the "post/colonial" condition, a neologism that Chris Bongie coined to describe the liminality of the contemporary position which is neither colonial nor postcolonial but somewhere betwixt and between.[10] Consequently, the pact with memory entails a constant detouring of self in order to negotiate the liminal space and work toward a postcolonial horizon of transculturation.

This ambiguity haunts the "we" or "nous" of the text in which the term is used to refer both to the Martinican community and the pact that joins memory and Chamoiseau. Presumably, the man and boy come together in this uneasy alliance of "we" where two overlapping communities mingle together. The ambiguous rendering of this subject position is particularly evident in the Creole position, which is shown to be compromised and incomplete in its aspirations toward the transcultural horizons. For example, in *Antan d'enfance*, the discussion of the presence of the Syrian shopkeepers suggests that the experience of creolization is not without prejudices toward the non-Creole. Migrants to Martinique, the Syrian shopkeepers, are depicted as wily outsiders who take advantage of local yearnings for metropolitan fashions, pulling out wares that are described as the latest in French fashion (*AE*, 118). Shut out of the "we" of the narrative, the exclusion of the shopkeepers represents the limited realization of the post/colonial ideal of transculturation.

The interactions of writing and identity come to play an increasingly important role in *Chemin* and *À bout d'enfance*. In *Chemin*, the inscription of self begins in the age of petroglyphs when Jojo "captures" the boy in a chalk mark (*CE*, 31). Afraid of being erased from the world, the boy copies out his name numerous times (*CE*, 31). The relationship to chalk is important because it prefigures the idea of writing as marking, gesturing, combat, and action. He holds the chalk like a dagger before learning to hold it in a pen-like fashion (*CE*, 31). Jojo draws the sign of infinity (*CE*, 32), which comes to symbolize the endless possibilities for capturing the world through inscription in its widest potential: drawings, equations, notations, scribblings, and words. The notion of inscription or the writing of the self as a drawing, a motion, looks forward to the activities of the writer as a Word Scratcher, someone who works at the interfaces of writing and orality.

The Creole storytelling conventions of call-and-response offer another way of negotiating subject positions. In *Chemin*, a chorus of respondents provide a kind of Greek chorus to the narrative, amplifying and undermining the events of the narrative through interjections. These respondents put forward a new concept of forgetting and remembering:

Répondeurs:
L'oubli
parfois
fait souvenir
C'est émotion
pile-exacte
c'est sensation
Intacte

L'oubli
parfois
fait mélancolie douce
C'est mémoire
hors mémoire

L'oubli
parfois
fait l'oubli
C'est seuil de souvenir
à l'orée de l'absence

Mémoire
tu te façonnes
à petites touches
d'oublis
et
chaque oubli
consolide ce qui reste . . . (*CE*, 158)

(*Répondeurs*:
Forgetting
sometimes
creates remembrance
it's emotion
exact

it's feeling
intact

Forgetting
sometimes
brings
sweet sadness
it's memory
beyond memory

Forgetting
sometimes vanishes into oblivion
it's the threshold of recollection
on the edge
of absence

Memory
you fashion yourself
with dabs
of oblivion
and each one
strengthens what remains . . .)
(*SD*, 112–13)

This mirroring device is refracted in other ways, such as Chamoiseau's reference to himself as the "tu" ("you") who wanders through the city and the world of inner reflection on his way home: "Le détour s'effectue en silence, retiré en toi-même" (*CE*, 135) ("You make detours in silence, withdrawn into yourself") (*SD*, 96). These detours of introspection are forms of self-reliance, alternatives to the French-Negritude-Creole positions represented by the teacher, the supply teacher, and Gros-Lombric (Big Bellybutton), respectively.

The fractured narrative subject reflects the fracturing of consciousness that takes place through the education system. While the child struggles to adapt to a French-language environment, the narrative of childhood articulates the suppression of the creolized self. What is experienced as a split consciousness, a Creole private self and a French public self, is pulled apart and knit together through the fictions of memory and the art of storytelling. In repeating the stories of the initial failures to master French, Chamoiseau teaches the reader about the language and initiates him or her into the emotional terrain associated with the language acquisition experience. The narrative handling of these episodes is significant at an autoethnographic level because it bears witness to the second language acquisition process carried out through neocolonial pedagogical practices. Chamoiseau observes that the teacher had reduced him to a silence that only deepened each time he heard the now constant lament: "*Ô cette engeance crréole n'a rrien à dirre!* . . ." (*CE*, 91) ("Oh, this Creole brood has nothing to say!") (*SD*, 65). Consequently, speech becomes a heroic feat and his inner voice grew ashamed (*CE*, 92). Through corporal punishment, constant chastisement, and reminders to speak civilized French, the child's maternal language is silenced and the child learns to internalize the lesson that French is civilized and Creole is barbaric.

At the same time, the literariness of Chamoiseau's parodic retelling of these neocolonial events transforms a story of oppression and loss into a narrative of creative potential, the origins of which the child discovers by the end of this tale. Much of the bittersweet comedy of the narrative derives from this double-voiced view of the narrative, which is attentive to the effects on the child, but expresses the adult's Creolist perspective regarding the poetic and political possibilities of language. While Chamoiseau's name turns out to be a hermeneutic puzzle, containing within it words like "chat" ("cat"), "chameau" ("camel"), "oiseau" ("bird"), and "os" ("bone") (*CE*, 54), Gros Lombric or Big Belly Button does not recognize a French name as his own, but holds onto his Creole nickname. When the teacher castigates the child for his ignorance and hauls him to the principal's office, Chamoiseau's respondents subvert the teacher's authority with a footnote in Creole: "Non Bwa-mitan / Non Savann / Non negsoubawaou / Non Kongo!" (*CE*, 55) ("Backwoods name, Savanna name, Field-nigger name, Darky name!") (*SD*, 38). This oppositional chant calls attention to the colonial acts of naming and the ways in which the present remains haunted by the legacies of the power to name and define the other. The repetition of the word "Non" for the word "name" also could be interpreted as resonating with the French "non" meaning "no" so that this repetition takes on a dub-like power to resist the imposition of meaning.

The transformation of space associated with linguistic spheres is also powerful as Creole is consigned to the domestic sphere and the playground while French becomes the language of the public space. Within the teacher's system, the ability to speak Creole fluently becomes a marker of the uncivilized, the backward, the colonized, and blackness while the ability to speak French fluently brings the individual closer to the "civilized" metropolitan of French whiteness. The remapping and migration of French onto Martinique has disorienting and humorous consequence as French world references emerge as *non sequiturs*. In a lesson about the ethics, the teacher tells the story of a peasant who grows and sells apples as a means of making a living to support himself and his family. One day the apples are missing. He asks the children what might have happened. When one of the students suggests that the apples were stolen by a thief, using the Creole word for a pilferer, which is "chicken thief," the teacher instructs them that this is an apple thief and that the Creole word does not apply. That night the boy repeats the lesson, "I will not pick apples that do not belong to me," to his family and receives another form of instruction when his father wonders aloud where the boy thinks he could pick apples as they all have to be imported to the island by boat in closed crates and arrive half rotten (*CE*, 80). Unfazed, the boy proceeds to draw a picture of their Creole home with apples and police with truncheons and produce pictures of tall, pointy castles, a church steeple, and a wolf. Symbolically, these drawings attest to another kind of violence as the self learns to assimilate to an imagined community that has little bearing on the realities of the world in which he lives. The following day, when the teacher recapitulates the moral lesson about the evils of thievery, he discovers that *Gros Lombric* believes that the French verb "to steal" is linked to apples and therefore sees nothing wrong with stealing other items (*CE*, 84), such as mangoes. This comic reworking of French via detours into Creole expressions serves to undermine and evade the rationalism of French legal thought.

Language is associated with detours and displacements as French and Creole never map together into a harmonious whole, but remain in a relationship of constant tensions of undigested meaning and excesses that cannot be entirely assimilated. There are bewildering reversals as the students learn that the word for "pineapple" in French does not start with a "z" (the Creole for pineapple is "zannana") but with an "a" (the French word for "pineapple" is "ananas") (*CE*, 85). The discrepancies between oral and written language come to the foreground through Creole presence, which subverts the meaning of French words through Creole pronunciation practices as well as the subsequent over corrections introduced by students who are overly eager to apply the new rules they have learned. For instance, the "r" tends to be dropped or pronounced more like a "w" sound in Creole: the word "force" becomes "fôce" (*CE*, 86) and "Présent" becomes "Pouézon" (*CE*, 52). Overcorrecting, the children turn the word "fumer" into "furmer" (*CE*, 90). The children continue to speak through images and meanings from Creole in French so that the language is constantly mediated and displaced. Language becomes carnivalesque. The techniques of *oraliture*, which characterize so much of Chamoiseau's work as the Word Scratcher find their origins in this childhood experience of learning to suppress the space of translation, a space that ultimately becomes the home of the writer.

Masquerade and the Ludic Self

Published in 2005, *À bout d'enfance* takes up the writing of childhood more than a decade after the publication of *Chemin*. In the intervening years, Chamoiseau published *L'Esclave vieil homme et le molosse*, *Écrire en pays dominé*, *Émerveilles*, and *Biblique des derniers gestes*. During this decade, Chamoiseau rose to international fame (following the *Prix Goncourt* for *Texaco*) and suffered the loss of his mother, an event that prompted him to reflect once more on the abyss separating him from his early life. While the first two works of childhood, *Antan* and *Chemin*, can be associated with the Creolist project of recuperating interior vision through memory and forays into the repressed articulations of the Creole self, the latter work is characterized by a literariness that belies any sense of glimpsing the "authentic self" in a nascent state. While it is tempting to ascribe this distancing to the loss of parents as those who are guardians of memory and childhood, the literary qualities of the text have more to do with changes in Chamoiseau's writing in the intervening years. The interest in how to write in a dominated land, the introduction of the *émerveille* (the marvel), and the interest in epic are aspects that situate *À bout d'enfance* in this later phase of writing.

This task of writing invokes a time of transition as the boy passes from childhood into early adolescence. Mary Gallagher remarks that Chamoiseau's concept of "childhood is less a state of grace in which the true nature of reality is perceived 'unmediated' than a time of transition, in which a shell is progressively secreted around the self."[11] If so, then the end of childhood marks a period of time in which secretions around the self are becoming increasingly difficult to pierce. Chamoiseau figures this encapsulation around the self through two general movements: the lament and the ludic. The first two sections of the narrative, entitled "Order and Disorder of the World" and "Oppositions and Antagonisms," function as a pre-history to the "the discovery" of the penis, the growing interest in young girls, and the quest narrative. This initial movement moves from the ludic to the lament, a tendency that is reversed in the second part of the narrative, which moves from lament and mourning to a ludic celebration of Creole youth. The tale begins with a series of negations and oppositions, including a list of interdictions imposed on the child, which are reduced to the emphatic negation of "Non" (the no). *La Baronne* functions as an intermediary for parental law and her presence calls attention to the lack of direct parental care given to him. While the mother is preoccupied with finances and running the household, the father is depicted in a slow decline toward death. In this context, the initial part of the narrative operates on a lament on several levels, mourning the end of childhood, the absence of the father, the decline into old age, and the adult's sense of a lost opportunity in his life.

In terms of oppositions and antagonisms, the child is depicted as opposing the colonizing tendencies of the elders who seek to order the disorderly world of childhood (*BE*, 29). Literature becomes a refuge, opening up the possibilities of imagining rather than seeking to dominate the world (*BE*, 31), particularly as he begins to explore the interfaces of European literary and Creole storytelling traditions (*BE*, 33). At the same time, the father extends the opposition to the colonial when he states his reasons for refusing to migrate to France:

> Un jour, avant de se murer dans un silence définitif, il finit par déclarer que ces pays d'Europe avaient engendré les guerres apocalyptiques, les tranchées, les gaz, Hitler, Mussolini, les camp de concentration, les massacres coloniaux, la bombe, le twist, Jack l'éventreur..., donc que ces lieux n'étaient de toute évidence pas complètement civilisés. (*BE*, 69)

> (One day, before retreating into a definitive silence, he ended up declaring that the countries of Europe engendered apocalyptic wars, trenches, gassings, Hitler, Mussolini, concentration camps, colonial massacres, the bomb, the twist, Jack the Ripper..., all of which bears evidence to the fact that these places were not completely civilized.)

Aside from this memory and the image of the father in the hospital as a man lost among the "zombies" (the other patients), memories of the father are recounted in an indirect fashion or as the result of the criss-crossing of his siblings' memories and accounts of the father. In this respect, the father's narrative takes the form of a marvel or *émerveille* where multiple stories and accounts converge in a single story.

The father signifies an absence, a failed quest; he remains a mysterious presence whom the boy and the man never fully fathom. Instead of "authentic" memories of the father-son relationship, Chamoiseau figures the adult-child relationship as a sense of forgotten powerlessness (*BE*, 77). Describing the day on which he received news of his father's death, when he was living in France, the "land of exile," he speaks of his failure to locate the other. Mourning is initially perceived in narcissistic terms as the man searches for the boy he once was and discovers the extent to which the child is absent, effaced in the process of giving way to adulthood (*BE*, 77). This gives way to self-recrimination for having failed to engage with the father, which is transposed into a censored poem scribbled on the telegram giving news of his death. The relationship to the father is once more distanced from the self through the anecdote of the Baroness who looks into the eyes of her father in his final moment before death. Mourning is diffracted, reflecting once more the obstacles presented by the boy's belated entry into his father's life, his lowly role in the family hierarchy, and his sense of exile. Exiled in France, seeking to mourn his father's death, the sense of exile opens up a metonymic series of moments of forgotten loss. Once more, the ideal parent-child relationship takes place in the shared gaze of the Baroness and the father (*BE*, 78).

Emotively affective, the initial part of the narrative can be seen as establishing the importance of creolized literary forms as well as foregrounding the theme of the detoured, failed quest. The ludic lament that follows does not attempt to provide access to authentic memories of childhood, but takes inspiration from the ludic, playful impulses and activities of boyhood games and other forms of amusement. Inaccessible memories are rerouted through literary game-playing and parodic reworkings of the self. The initial antagonisms and oppositions of the neocolonial and French imaginaries give way to a discursive reconciliation of these vying tendencies. This hybrid parody of quest literature offers a satiric reconciliation of the lament and the ludic, the neocolonial and the Creole.

In French literature, the rich tradition of quest literature is well represented by the *chanson de geste*, such as the heroic epic of *La chanson de Roland*, as well as the medieval romance works of Chrétien de Troyes and Guillame de Lorris and Jean de Meun's *Roman de la rose*. In these works, the *merveille* can refer to a wonder or mystery as well as the ultimate secret and marvel: love. The quest involves confrontations with marvels, but it is the marvel of love that typically serves as a driving force. Often, love proves to be conflicted as courtly love and chivalric duty (love of king and God) come into conflict. Chamoiseau's narrative takes these motifs as the sources for its own marvels or *émerveilles*, a noun that Chamoiseau coined from the French verb *émerveiller*, meaning "to marvel," in order to reflect the active principle involved in his poetics of the marvelous, which entails cross-cutting and intersections. Chamoiseau's concept of the marvelous is defined in the afterword to *Émerveilles* as a principle of disruption and activity that entails a strategic rewriting and cross-cutting of many kinds of materials. The *émerveille* mixes together legends, myths, miracles, inexplicable events, uncertain beings, and marvels. This strange, disruptive, and multivocal admixture of perspectives and sources differentiates it from magical realism. Chamoiseau states that the *émerveille* introduces a readiness for the unknown and change in the world, initiating a consciousness of the creolization of the world, a phenomenon that Glissant refers to as the "*Tout-monde*" (*E*, 126).

One method of cross-cutting the marvel involves the use of split narrative perspectives, introducing multiple viewpoints and sibling memories. The split adult-youth perspective works well because the narrative ably captures the immediacy of youthful enthusiasm for quest literature and popular genres while the narrator's ironic voice serves to highlight parodic aspects of their unintentionally humorous reworking of the quest tradition. The work opens with a tantalizing foreshadowing of the quest motif, which is prefigured in the discovery of the opposite sex: "Un jour, bien des années avant l'épreuve du mabouya, le négrillon s'aperçut que les êtres humains n'étaient pas seuls au monde: il existait aussi les petites-filles" (*BE*, 13) ("One day, many years before the test of the mabouya [a lizard], the black boy perceived that human beings were not alone in the world: there also existed little-girls"). The youth's understanding of girls is mediated by folklore and fairytales, both of which reinforce gender stereotypes. The boy provides a biological reading of this passivity, suggesting that the loss of the penis accounts for the loss of humanity and character as well as intelligence, initiative, strength, courage, resourcefulness, and the capacity for survival (*BE*, 141, 143). Equally elaborate theories are developed to account for pregnancy and the birth of babies, particularly as the boy puzzles over the lack of storks in Martinique and reasons that the kiss must lead to pregnancy, following the logic of cinematic editing where the scene cuts from the kiss to the next scene with the mother holding the child (BE, 179).

Similarly, masculinity is constructed through literature and the media. The examples of Hercules, Maciste, Lancelot, Django, Lemmy Caution, and D'Artagnan of the Three Musketeers are cited as influences (BE, 180). The reworking of popular culture and high literary forms inspires the boys to form their own Round Table, called "Le Conseil de la Table-bobine," which includes the usual characters, Lancelot, Merlin, Perceval, and Arthur, as well as cowboys such as Kit Carson and Jesse James and other heroic figures like d'Artagnan. This parodic version of the Round Table functions as pastiche and evidence of the cultural globalization already at work in Martinique during Chamoiseau's youth.

Chamoiseau situates his adolescence as a parodic reworking of chivalric literature in which the questing knight faces the conflicting claims of love and duty. Like Dante, Chamoiseau reworks the theme of the lovesick writer who is led by love to literature. Chamoiseau's young boy begins by writing love letters, which are addressed at first to no one in particular, and later formulates his first poems (BE, 261). In French romances, love, death, and fantasy (*l'irréel*) are three themes connected by the idea that love and death operate in a zone apart from the everyday world. For Chamoiseau, Gabine is the *Irréelle*, and the narrative about her brings him into contact with fantasy as a literary mode. Chamoiseau's muse is a *chabine* named Gabine (sometimes called "Gabine la lune") and the lovestruck youth finds himself unable to focus on his regular sport and duels on account of his great melancholy (BE, 230). His lack of interest in chivalric pursuits is duly noted and the council comes together to judge his fate. His profound knowledge of Arthurian literature does not suffice as proof of his loyalty so he is assigned a test as proof of his manly loyalties: the sticking of the *mabouya*. The *mabouya* is a type of lizard who serves as a parodic double for the dragon of quest literature. According to the Creole legend of Gros-Lombric, the *mabouya* has sticky feet and once it adheres to the body, it is impossible to remove it without cutting it apart, which could result in the feet adhering to the body of anyone foolish enough to let this lizard walk on his body (BE, 246). Tony (presumably Delsham) is assigned to locate a mabouya in order to put the young Chamoiseau to this test.

As the tale progresses, the language and descriptions of the narrative conform increasingly to the language of the quest narrative. This remapping of the Creole adolescence in Martinique as a neo-medieval space is reflected in the use of the literary past tense and the appropriation of the Arthurian motif of a world falling into disorder: "Cette ère nouvelle troubla le monde des chevaliers. Le roi devint soucieux." (*BE*, 253) ("This new era troubled the world of the knights. The king became worried."). Increasing tensions in the kingdom are accompanied by anxieties as word that "l'Irréelle" wants to arrange a *rendezvous* reaches him (*BE*, 262). Rather than face her, the boy averts disaster by choosing to enter into the encounter with the lizard. She sends him a cutting of her hair, which he carries on him when he enters into the encounter with the lizard. The episode ends humorously as the lizard walks along his chest and springs from his body into the air. The other youths flee the scene, leaving Chamoiseau the boy behind to reflect on the cold, viscous touch of the *mabouya*.

What emerges from this quest is a portrait of the melancholy contradictoriness. The boy, like the man, seeks solitude but suffers from a horror of isolation (*BE*, 271). The beloved provides a pretext for indulging his dreamy nature and the fascination that the city exercises over him (*BE*, 276). Rather than the girl, he falls in love with the symbolic order of the Unreal. His love for her becomes an initiation (*BE*, 278) as the Unreal establishes its presence in him. In the end, the waning of childhood reflects the author's interest in the transitory phases in the stages of life. The dialogic text serves as a lament for the disappearance of childhood as a time of marvels, the death of his parents, and the disappearance of the creolized world of Fort-de-France during his youth. By invoking the Arthurian world, the lament for a changing world order, whether it be departmentalization or the transformations associated with adolescence, and the nostalgia for an ideal age find a literary correlative in creolized parody of French literature.

Bricolage and the Space of Memory

Considered as a trilogy, these narratives show signs of coherence as well as shifts in style that reflect Chamoiseau's own changing poetics. Thematically, the works explore the nascence of the writer and the role of memory and trace the disappearance of the creolized world under the pressures of departmentalization. Stylistically, the texts are narrated in a similar style that employs a first-person adult perspective, a third-person perspective on the boy of the past and a second-person address to others who are implicated in the narrative. While there are striking differences, I would like to conclude this chapter by examining the role of memory as both the unreliable source and interlocutor of these narratives. Moreover, the personification and projection of memory changes in the three works. *À bout d'enfance* marks a stylistic departure in the handling of childhood memory as the narrator is less concerned with recuperating an authentic past and more engaged with the liberating poetics of the memory as a marvel. In *Chemin* and *Antan*, the anxieties related to the recuperation of childhood memory are in many ways similar to the troubling aspects of Black Atlantic memory and the cultural amnesia of the Middle Passage. Similarly, childhood is depicted as a problematic space of memory, particularly through the processes of socialization, which threaten to extinguish or repress the Creole. Chamoiseau views the past as irrecoverable but as full of imaginative possibilities.

Nostalgia is an important theme in the Black Atlantic, particularly for those who long to return to an imagined African homeland. In this respect, one might argue that Chamoiseau sees the nostalgia for childhood as comparable to diasporic yearnings for home, particularly as the world of childhood represents a time and a place from which all adults are exiled. This feeling of loss is all the more powerful for Chamoiseau because the world he looks back to is one when there was still a great deal more hope concerning the possibilities for autonomy and agency in Martinique. For Martinique, there can be no return to the creolized world of the past. In this sense, the tales of childhood function as a reconciliation to the passage of time and transformations in the social order.

Precisely for these reasons, the idea of memory as a creative activity becomes a powerful tool for reorienting oneself toward a new understanding of history and narrative. Memory is allied to creativity as the fragments of the past can be reworked with imagined events to construct new possibilities for the articulation of self. In *Chemin*, Chamoiseau observes that "on ne mente que quand on raconte mal" (*CE*, 149) ("a story is only a lie if you tell it badly") (*SD*, 106). *À bout d'enfance* takes this logic to the extreme as the author raises questions concerning the truth of the events he recounts: "Qu'y a-t-il de vrai dans tout cela, en dehors du mouvement général? / Rien et tout, mais juste ce qu'en fait cet écrire" (*BE*, 283) ("What is true of any of this aside from the general movement? / Nothing and everything, but simply that which makes up this [act of] writing"). When memory cannot be recuperated, Chamoiseau stages encounters with "false memories." While he seems to suggest that this is not an ethically compromised means of life writing, it is worth considering his position on memory in other texts. In *Chronique des sept misères*, Pipi's regression to fantasy is depicted as a fatal retreat from the realities and struggles of self-determination in everyday life. In *Texaco*, Esternome provides contradictory accounts of Ninon's departure, which differ and contradict one another because he cannot remember all of the versions he tells. The narrator observes that "lies don't become part of memory" (*TX* 146), but this perspective is contradicted by the narrator's viewpoint in *Un dimanche au cachot* when it turns out that the story Chamoiseau has recounted about a dungeon cannot be true of that particular site because it never was a dungeon. In this instance, Chamoiseau takes a similarly laissez-faire attitude toward the actual events of history (*UDC*, 319). In *Écrire en pays dominé*, the imagined encounter with a warrior figure is an event that brings about a transformation of self. In this sense, the relationship between the imagination and memory is a complex one in which false memories are be mistrusted while imagined truths can be incorporated in memory as "lived" events.

The narrator experiences difficulty when attempting to negotiate the truths and falsehoods of childhood. The construction of the autobiographical self is fraught with anxieties about the intersections of various kinds of narratives and narrative sources. Yet, these intersections are also seen as a source for the marvelous. Instead of the chorus of *Chemin* or the pact with memory in *Antan*, *À bout d'enfance* takes up the question of childhood as a time of marvels: "*Enfance, émerveille et douleur, où es-tu?*" (*BE*, 14) ("Childhood, marvel and pain, where are you?"). The space of childhood, with its wonder and suffering in the world, becomes the object of the quest as the narrator attempts to recover the diffuse point at which childhood was effaced and to reconstitute it for always in this slow waning away (*BE*, 42). He addresses his former self, the black boy, noting that it takes multiple memories to found one and multiple fictions for the single to gain a strong foothold (*BE*, 56). Chamoiseau, the author, disgorges his former self (*BE*, 73), demonstrating that the child contains the man and the man contains the child.

While the question of authenticity is a primary one for Creolists whose *Éloge de la créolité* sets out a plan for recuperating interior vision and memory, Chamoiseau's efforts to retrieve memory in his autobiographical fictions do not focus on the recuperation of an essential self, but the discovery of a poetics through which the self might be negotiated and imaginatively reconstructed. Chamoiseu evokes an uneasy set of relations among various subjective ethnicities that vie for the child's autoethnographic definition: a Creole identity that stems from the long history of transculturation, a metropolitan French identity and an in-between of ongoing creolization in the interactions and dynamics of French-Creole identities. Autoethnographic performance not only situates the exiled adult in relation to childhood and the mysteries of the child as other, but opens up a space of resistance between the individual (*auto-*) and the collective (*-ethno*) where writing (*-graphy*) becomes a process for rewriting given affiliations and relations. Through carnivalesque and deconstructionist maneuvers, the author simultaneously appeals to and debunks cultural traditions. Parody plays a particularly useful role as a trope that introduces the possibility of critical difference and with difference the possibilities for an alternative kind of autoethnographic expression. By bringing autoethnographic expression into contact with satire and parodic revisioning, Chamoiseau evokes a narrative space of tension where epistemological and ontological anxieties are freely reworked in creative ways. The self and the community are open to rewriting, and autoethnographic expression serves as a source for world-making.

Questions of the fictive and the real trouble the situation of the self in lived and imagined communities, past and present. Reminiscent of the themes presented in Glissant's *Pays rêvé, pay réel*, Chamoiseau looks back to a forgotten place as well as ones that change through imagined transformations through time, reflecting changing poetic and political conceptions. The mimetic aspects of place and time are therefore unstable subjects of meta-autoethnographic reflection. Childhood is "le pays d'avant," a place that cannot be recovered, but whose reconstitution is essential to situating the self as articulated and extended through multiple, shifting relations. The dissection and cross-cutting of Creole childhood seems to oscillate between nostalgic yearning for authenticity and a cleverly contrived play of fictions in which the discourses provide a fragmented mirror for that which is irrecoverable but can only be partially reflected as the mosaic of self. Between these polarities, Chamoiseau elicits the space between ethnography and fiction, between the world and the word, as the site of self-generation.

CHAPTER 6

Initiating the Warrior of the Imaginary

Following *Texaco*, Chamoiseau embarks on a highly experimental phase of writing during which he articulates his theory of the *émerveille* ("marvel") and introduces a new figure, the Warrior of the Imaginary.[1] Through innovative poetic forms and narrative figures, he creates a poetic vocabulary that shapes his writing through much of the 1990s and up to the present. During this period, he also addresses the ways in which the Martinican experience of domination and creolization shed light on the processes of globalization. The narrative processes of intersection and dialogic construction already present in *Texaco* take on an increasing complexity as his examination of the construction of locality deepens its inwardly and outwardly directed trajectories of analysis. Increasingly, he expresses interest in the psychic dimensions and psychological effects of departmentalization and manifestations of imperialism. Examining past-present horizons, he perceives both threats and opportunities, which necessitate increased vigilance and imagination of an interrelated world where criss-crossings of local histories, peoples, and transcultural flows take place continuously.

Frequently, his writing takes the form of a conversion narrative in which a central figure is represented as undergoing a transformation of consciousness. The individual enters into an initiation through a vague impulse toward resistance, the desire to flee, or an insurgent attitude of rebelliousness. These rebellious instincts develop into a more profound, reflective, and strategic consciousness of the imaginary. Typically, this conversion scenario depends on the work of two new figures, the rebel and the Warrior of the Imaginary. Given Chamoiseau's early interests in figures of resistance, such as maroons and rebels, the introduction of a warrior figure is not surprising. However, his approach to questions of resistance and domination differs considerably from the 1990s onward as he takes into account a longer history of imperialism, which includes colonization, departmentalization, and the long history of globalization. Moreover, the warrior figure cannot be understood in isolation because he functions as a pivotal figure of transformation in Chamoiseau's conversion narrative, which aims to function through a kind of radiating poetics that moves from the fictional situation through a metafictional frame to the reader. In many ways, the question with which *Écrire en pays dominé* begins becomes the central preoccupation of his work:

> Comment écrire alors que ton imaginaire s'abreuve, du matin jusqu'aux rêves, à des images, des pensées, des valeurs qui ne sont pas les tiennes?
> Comment écrire quand ce que tu es végète en dehors des élans qui déterminent ta vie?
> Comment écrire dominé? (EPD, 17)

> (How can you write when, from the break of day to dreams at night, your imaginary drinks in images, thoughts and values that are not your own?
> How do you write when what you are grows outside of the impulses that determine your life?
> How can you write dominated?)

The narrator goes on to explain that by domination he is referring to the contemporary age where stealthy forms of domination exist through neocolonial presence and globalization. Unlike earlier forms of domination, which were clearly visible and open to attack, Chamoiseau argues that we live in an age when it is often difficult to identify the obscure sources of oppression. The quest for nourishment and self-expression in this situation of domination becomes the subject of his self-reflective writing processes in *Écrire* as well as throughout his oeuvre during the 1990s.

Locating the Warrior of the Imaginary

The first tale to take this form is not a novel but the screenplay Chamoiseau writes for Guy Deslaurier's *L'Exil du roi Béhanzin*. The film tells the story of the deposed African king and his exile in Martinique. Chamoiseau invents a Creole mistress and creates a fantastical narrative about the king who comes to understand the role of creolization. The film won several awards,[2] but was also criticized for its historical inaccuracies and anachronisms.[3] In retrospect, it is perhaps most usefully considered as an important testing ground for Chamoiseau's evolving poetics about the warrior, the depiction of the role of the journalist, and the workings of erotically charged political transmutations. Jean Bernabé forwards a poetic interpretation of the film's events when he situates the representation of Béhanzin in literary history, beginning with Aimé Césaire's myth of a *nègre-roi*.[4] Chamoiseau's script offers an alternative poetic interpretation of this figure because he represents the king as able to reconcile Negritude (which he intuits before it existed as a theory) with a Creole identity that is already emergent through the processes of an irreversible modernity.[5] Instead of a figure of exile, who desperately wanted to return to Africa, the film presents the king as an early representative of postmodern subjectivity as defined by Stuart Hall when he asserts that "migration has turned out to be *the* world-historical event of late modernity, the classic postmodern experience turns out to be the diasporic experience."[6] Consequently, Bernabé views *L'Exil* as prophetic in its representation of contemporary issues of migration, diasporic identities, and creolization.[7] More generally, the film introduces archetypes and dynamics that play a prominent role in Chamoiseau's fiction following *Texaco*. The African warrior figures in *Écrire* as the one who initiates Chamoiseau as a warrior of the imaginary. The film offers an early embodiment of this scenario in showing how the African warrior undergoes an initiation process. As well, the film features an exchange between the warrior figure and his son, the journalist, Ouanilo. This scenario prefigures the initiation of the journalist by the warrior Balthazar in *Biblique*. Finally, the message emblazoned across the screen at the ending of the film serves as a kind of motto for Chamoiseau's fictions to come: "Le monde n'est plus à conquérir. Il est à habiter" ("The world is no longer to be conquered. It is to be inhabited").

Following *Texaco*, Chamoiseau began writing a semi-regular column that appeared in *Antilla* from 1993 to 1996. Initially titled "Une semaine en pays dépendant," the column was very soon after retitled "Une semaine en pays dominé"; it took the form of visceral attacks on other writers, scholars, and local politicians as well as discusses events in the news. These columns reveal an entirely different side to the author's Word Scratcher. Often irascible, this Chamoiseau hits "below the belt" in attacks on others.[8] Perhaps a more accurate metaphor for this kind of writing is that of *laghia* as the *guerrier* takes on his enemies and delivers symbolic blows to his opponents. As a columnist, Chamoiseau takes the opportunity to articulate the opinions and express the ideas that are central to the Warrior of the Imaginary. In a column from 1995, Chamoiseau turns a discussion of banking into a tirade against departmentalization as responsible for the suppression of fundamental resistance in Martinique.[9] In another instance, Chamoiseau observes, as he would again in Écrire, that domination is all the more effective because it is invisible and its effects are interiorized: "La domination-répression est invisible et ses effets, mille fois plus efficaces de ce fait, sont intériorisés"[10] ("Domination-repression is invisible and its effects, a thousand times more efficacious as a result, are interiorized"). In a column on archaeological excavations, he discusses the discovery of bones in terms that looked forward to the trepidation felt when the narrator in L'Esclave vieil homme et le molosse touches history itself when he comes into contact with the bones of the escaped slave.[11] Chamoiseau's "Contre la Départmentalisation: autopsie d'un désastre" provides an account of the factors that led to departmentalization and reliance on France as a maternal figure.[12] Parts of this argument (pages 5–6) are later incorporated almost word for word in Écrire en pays dominé (pages 247–51), but in the case of the latter he interrupts and breaks the flow of his discourse with the warrior's comments. In these works, he takes a cynical view of the collective zombification brought about during the 1970s. Speaking of Martinicans as "rebelles, oubliés par la vague décolonisatrice" ("rebels forgotten by the wave of decolonization"), he accounts for the failure to rebel as a failure of the imagination due to an inability to identify who was in need of liberation.[13] In the 1980s and 1990s, he traces the entry of militant anticolonialists into politics, which brings about the illusion of local power at work for the country.[14] War veterans failed to change the situation because they either lived off a heroic past (such as the description of a legendary desertion during the Algerian war) or created the impression they were actively preparing for a revolution, which never came about.[15] Intellectuals deserted their revolutionary potential and contented themselves with the benefits of a consumer-oriented culture, all the while listening to belligerent speeches every now and again.[16] This article reflecting back on fifty years of departmentalization in Martinique articulated themes central to Écrire and Biblique: the desire for a Creole maternity as opposed to a maternal France, the zombification of Martinique, the failures of academics and intellectuals, and the figure of rebel who fails to realize his aspirations toward liberation.

Issues of domination are not only historical but inevitably tied to the intersections of place and space or the ways in which locality is constructed. Chamoiseau's theories of place and a new genre of fiction, which he calls the *émerveille*, serve to show how the artist and the individual can rework external forces in order to achieve vernacular and personal forms of self-expression that are neither dominated nor isolated but exist in open relation to the various flows and forces of the world. In "Contre la mémoire et l'histoire" ("Against memory and history"), Chamoiseau refers to the need to recuperate places of memory:[17]

> Le Lieu est traversé de racines multiples, qui s'étendent, qui s'étalent; le Territoire est arc-bouté sur une racine unique.
> Le Lieu vit en réseau; le Territoire dispose d'un centre et de périphéries.
> Le Lieu vit de la poétique de la diversité; le Territoire s'arme de la pensée de l'Unique.
> Le Lieu participe à la Diversalité; le Territoire invoque l'Universalité.
> Le Lieu a des histoires, le Territoire a une Histoire.
> Le Lieu a des mémoires, le territoire a une Mémoire . . .[18]

> (Place is traversed by multiple roots, which extend, which spread out; Territory is the sprouting arch of a single root.
> Place lives in a network; Territory is composed of a center and peripheries.
> Place lives on the poetics of diversity; Territory arms itself with the thought of the Unique.
> Place participates in Diversality, Territory invokes Universality.
> Place has stories, Territory has one History.
> Place has memories, Territory has one Memory.)

Inspired by Glissant, this utopian concept of place is represented as giving voice to the poetics of diversity, a multiplicity of memories and multiple roots, which in turn leads to solidarity. He sees this interpretation of place as relevant not only to neocolonial Martinique but also to the contemporary world of interdependencies: "Nous avons le sentiment d'être sur le même bateau. Que le destin de l'un est lié à celui de l'autre"[19] ("We have the feeling that we are in the same boat. That the destiny of one person is linked to that of the other"). Chamoiseau argues that this concept of "place" could help Martinicans to constitute themselves in transnational networks of solidarity, of cultural relations and exchanges, and enable them to move beyond the "detestable idea" that Martinique plays a peripheral role in the world.[20]

The Marvel and the Relational Self

In poetic form, the *émerveille* becomes a means to express this new poetics of place and time. *Émerveilles* (1998) warrants attention because it offers a definition of the genre as well as many examples of the genre that comes to function as a building block in his fiction from 1997 onward. As Stephen Greenblatt's *Marvellous Possessions: The Wonder of the New World* demonstrates, the marvel played an important role in colonial and travel writings about the explored worlds.[21] Chamoiseau's collection of tales for children, entitled *Émerveilles*, reworks this genre in name and spirit. His *émerveille* is distinctly different from the colonial marvel for it does not place emphasis on a single self viewing the landscape, but situates the reader in a world of unpredictable, multiple, and shifting marvels that cannot be contained by a single historical metanarrative. This marvelous activity is redescribed in the afterword to the tales where Chamoiseau defines the *émerveille* as a principle of disruption that mixes together legends, myth, fables, inexplicable events, and stories in a strange and fantastical manner (E, 126). The very word "*émerveille*" suggests an active poetics that seeks to transform the imaginary of the reader: this neologism or "Chamoisification" entails a transformation of the verb "*s'émerveiller*" into the substantive "*émerveille*," a noun that does not exist in so-called proper French.

This strange, disruptive, and multivocal admixture of perspectives and sources introduces a readiness for the unknown and change in the world, initiating a consciousness of the creolization of the world, a phenomenon that Glissant refers as the "*Tout-monde*." With such a poetics of childhood, Chamoiseau affirms his desire to foster an imaginary that permits one to fight against racism, ethnic purification, and the barbarism of nationalisms (E, 126). More recently, in a discussion of *Biblique des derniers gestes*, Chamoiseau described the importance of "le grand merveilleux" in terms similar to that of the *émerveille*. Differentiating his concept from the marvelous realism of Gabriel Garcia Marquez (which remains affiliated with realism), Chamoiseau stated:

> Donc, il y a le réalisme merveilleux; on connaît le fantastique, on connaît l'étrange, on connaît les procédures du conte, on connaît les modalités des légendes, des mythes, des miracles, on connaît les événements inexplicables, on connaît la merveille enfantine, et tout ça aujourd'hui doit se mobiliser. On ne peut pas simplement pratiquer une merveille de conte ou une merveille de légende, mais on devrait pratiquer le grand merveilleux, parce que c'est le grand merveilleux qui nous rapproche plus de la grande complexité indéchiffrable de la totalité-monde.[22]

> (Thus, there is marvelous realism; one knows the fantastic; one knows the strange, one knows the procedures of the story; one knows the modalities of legends, myths, and miracles; one is familiar with inexplicable events; one is acquainted with childhood marvel, and all of this ought to be mobilized today. One cannot simply practice the marvel of the story or marvel of the legend, but one should put into practice the grand marvelous because it is the grand marvelous that brings us closer to the great indecipherable complexity of the *totalité-monde* [totality-world].)

Chamoiseau goes on to say that for him this means mobilizing the space of orality, *oraliture*, the literary, the Creole language, the Creole imaginary, and the French language.

Although Chamoiseau does not explicitly refer to the essays by Alejo Carpentier in either of these discussions, Chamoiseau's definition of the *émerveille*, with its principles of admixture is a response in part to the tradition of the marvelous or magical realism as it is traditionally defined. Carpentier sees magical realism as a European form, "where real forms are combined in a way that does not conform to daily reality."[23] We might also refer to Jacques-Stéphen Alexis's notion of the marvelous or *le merveilleux*, which situates the terms in reference to creolization as "globalized cultural interpenetration."[24] Similarly, the marvelous of surrealism is a "manufactured mystery,"[25] a kind of deliberate mystification. By contrast, Carpentier sees marvelous realism as omnipresent in Latin America, the result of actual sociohistorical and cultural conditions and events.[26] Marvelous realism is "an amplification of perceived reality required by and inherent in Latin American nature and culture."[27] Intersecting with the marvelous real is the baroque spirit, fostered by the symbiosis of *mestizaje* or *metissage*:[28] "the *Criollo* spirit is itself a baroque spirit."[29] This raises the question of whether or not Chamoiseau's *émerveille* is simply an extension of his Creoleness, an example of the baroque spirit with its "series of proliferating foci,"[30] so characteristic of *Texaco, Solibo Magnifique,* or *Chronique des sept misères*.[31] While the *émerveille* shares this baroque spirit, it takes its logic to the extreme, consciously and deliberately mixing forms and voices in a self-conscious, strategic manner. As with magical realism, the *émerveille* entails deliberate intermixtures, but these entail an added political dimension because the *émerveille* is meant to not merely express but also to transform the understanding of a world order where creolization is seen as an ongoing process.

The introduction of a map of Martinique, with numbers designating the sites of various marvels on the island, prompts an interactive, achronological reading of the work. The notion of the *émerveille* as an activity is reflected in Chamoiseau's description of how the stories were collected by Maure, the illustrator, who went into the landscape with her "bakoua" (a traditional hat), a cutlass, her paintings, and a sack to collect the marvels contained within the book. The act of storytelling is grounded in the physical landscape as a literal source of tales, involving the performative event of collecting tales. A map of the literal and imaginative landscape of Martinique is included in the book, prompting the child to traverse the landscape of marvels, following in the footsteps of Maure. This map of the marvels of Martinique associates the tales with actual places. Thus, while learning something about the geography of the island, the child is invited to explore alternative mappings of place. From the perspective of the child as reader, this also invites an alternative reading of the book. Whereas the table of contents presents the narratives in their chronological order in the book, the map of tales invites the child to take different routes through the book. The textual landscape thus unfolds in any direction that the child chooses to follow.

The twenty stories contained within this collection refer both to events within the history of Martinique, such as the fishing communities that evolved after the abolition of slavery, as well as to contemporary references to the predominance of television, access to computers, mobility through migrations between Paris and Martinique, single parent households, and tourism. The narratives celebrate hybrid identities, dreamers, strange alliances between very different selves, strange Others, alternative lifestyles, unexpected encounters, and the metamorphosis of self. For example, "Mabouc l'âne-chien" ("Mabouc, the Donkey-Dog") tells the story of a dog named Mabouc who learns to live a double-life and take on a plural identity as a dog and as a donkey. "Le baiser-étonné du chien au chat" ("The Surprising Kiss of the Dog and Cat") tells about the surprising kiss that takes place between natural enemies, the dog and cat. The coexistence of past and present marvels demonstrates that the folklore tradition serves as a source and tool, not only for critiquing the past but for orienting the self in an increasingly mobile world.

The marvel is intended to evoke a theory of relations and one can see this principle at work in stories that explore the parent-child relationship: fostering dialogues between children and parents while also inviting parents to reflect on the politics of parenting. The last story in the book, entitled "Ingénu porteur du soleil et du croissant de lune" ("Ingénu, Bearer of the Sun and the Crescent Moon"), concludes with the observation that one can gain ancient wisdom in the great open book of the eyes of our children (E, 124). Whereas the child is encouraged to gather (*ramasser*) marvels (like picking flowers or plants), the parent is prompted to pluck and gather (*cueillir*, a verb used for picking flowers) wisdom by reading, and learning from, his or her child. Some stories demonstrate that the child can teach the parent to gain a fuller understanding of life. For example, "Kosto et ses deux enfants" ("Kosto and His Two Children") is an account of a father who learns to raise his children as a single parent when his wife leaves him and the children. The account makes it clear that he has had little to do with raising the children up to this point. He learns what it is to take care of a child from morning to night. After one week of running in all directions, he is exhausted (E, 104). The narrator observes that Kosto discovers that all that his wife did on a daily basis, with a smile on her face, is an impossible task for him (E, 104). He attempts to take on the role of the man, father, master, and chief (E, 104), but finds that he is locked in a solitude. He realizes that something needs to change and begins to reflect on what his wife's life must have been like and realizes the incredible pressures placed on women who are expected to be perfect mothers. Finally, after weeks of raging, he learns to coexist with his children. He enters into the drama of their lives in an alliance based on love and respect (E, 106). The narrator observes that he no longer interprets a role, but invents, day after day, a new life (E, 106). The story ends with the observation that in learning to live harmoniously with his children Kosto has learned to be the most fantastic being that a man, a father, a woman, a mother could ever aspire to become. The story thus tells a tale about parent-child relations as well as gender roles, instructing both adult and child through the story of how a wondrous new kind of person is "born" and "nurtured" through a deeper, more real interaction with his children.

One of the oddest, most compelling tales in the collection, "Bleu et l'oreiller plein de sommeil" ("Blue and the Pillow Full of Sleep"), explores the role of wishing and dreaming. This marvel is a story about a family with two girls. The parents long for a son and do all they can to magically influence the mother's pregnancy, including painting their entire house blue. A son is born and nicknamed Ti-Bleu ("Little Blue"). Seemingly healthy, when Ti-Bleu comes home, he gradually turns blue. With his eyes the color of the sky, he begins to sleep and dream, and at the same time his pillow begins to grow larger and larger with each passing day of reverie. Faced with this sleeping son, the family becomes increasingly despondent until one day a riddle-telling monster shows up at their home and moves in. This creature proves to have an omnivorous appetite, not just for food but also for life; he speaks many languages, seems to know everything, and has traveled all over the world. With all that he has learned, he has become crazy and accepts only one unique truth: his own (*E*, 20).

Formulating a universal law of truth, the monster is presented as bad, hostile, and detestable (*E*, 21). This despot forces the family to listen to his tales of despair, misfortune, military raids, conquests, villages under siege, ethnic cleansings, and of a god and a language that wipe out others in the name of the Universal (*E*, 21). Eventually, the monster starts to consume the members of the family, until only the mother and Ti-Bleu are left. The mother diverts the monster with the blue colors of the home, which hypnotizes him as he seeks to compare and order this marvelous experience. Ti-Bleu interrupts the monster in this state of reflection, offering to give him his enormous pillow. Both the monster and the mother realize that the child has grown and explored the world as a voyager through his dreams (*E*, 21).

Contrary to the monster, the child has seen many truths and his wanderings have opened him up to the world. The stupefied monster demands that Ti-Bleu reveal the secret source of his learning. The child responds that the pillow is his secret (*E*, 21). Seizing the pillow, the monster starts to dream, which allows the mother the chance to free the other family members. The monster is imprisoned and spends the rest of his existence dreaming. The reunited family learns to accept this son who is a dreamer, someone who sees the sky as a place that is completely empty and completely full (*E*, 22). The narrator ends the tale by reflecting on the life of this boy who spent his existence in the "open wandering" (*errance* ouverte) of the life of dreams (*E*, 22). This tale, which celebrates the life of the dreamer and castigates the desire to impose one's dreams on others, can be seen as an allegory about the monstrous desires of parents and families who seek to predestine and control the lives of their children. It is also a tale about a child who asserts his own identity and rescues his family from the grip of the desire for a universal truth. Thus, the politics of the family narrative also prove to be linked to the political philosophies of the world. This tale for and about childhood is surely also one that is for and about adulthood. Dreaming is depicted as a form of imaginative wandering in the world, and thus as a form of agency for both child and adult alike.

Initiatory Poetics in *Écrire en pays dominé* and *L'Esclave vieil homme et le molosse*

At first glance, it may seem that *Écrire en pays dominé*, a partly autobiographical, partly theoretical text about the neocolonial present, has little in common with *L'Esclave*, a novella concerning the escape and pursuit of a slave in the colonial past. Yet, the works are linked together by repeating and cross-referencing paratexts, intertexts, themes, figures, objects, and characters. These points of linkage, echoing, connection, and intersection encourage the reader to consider more deeply the relationship that each bears to the other. The works share the same echoing question: "Le monde a-t-il une intention?" ("The world, does it have an intention?"). It is as if the texts intersect when they run into this question; implicitly, the works spill into one another as they pass through the shared discursive space between them. The fraternal relationship of these texts is further suggested by the presence of Chamoiseau's brother, Miguel Chamoiseau, and Glissant in both narratives. The "remerciements" at the end of *Écrire en pays dominé* are addressed to both Édouard Glissant and Miguel Chamoiseau. The opening to *L'Esclave vieil homme et le molosse* is subtitled "Avec un entre-dire d'Édouard Glissant" (With interjections from Édouard Glissant) and is dedicated to Miguel Chamoiseau with a playful remark that he perhaps knows where the stone is to be found. These linked paratexts lead the reader from the end of one text and to the beginning of another, suggesting that the activity of reading and deciphering meaning occurs in a commonly apprehended aporia. Intertextual tropes and figures in both works suggest points of comparison and invite deeper readings of these mutually entangled narratives.

Together the tale of the colonial past (*L'Esclave*) and the tale of the neocolonial present (*Écrire*) invoke a common figure, the Warrior of the Imaginary, through the shared poetics of the *émerveille*. Both of these initiatory works are structured as "un exercice de connaissance" (exercise of knowledge or consciousness), which takes place through a marooning of consciousness.[32] Victor Turner's definition of the initiation as a three-stage process characterized by separation, margin or liminality, and aggregation or reincorporation is particularly helpful in terms of understanding how this transformative process works. During the first phase of separation, the individual is stripped symbolically of social status, insignia, and other identifiers of rank. Often this separation is physical, which leads to a liminal stage during which a symbolic death occurs. In the final stage, the initiate is reintegrated in the social order and acquires a sense of *communitas*.[33] For Chamoiseau, this initiatory process is effectively redoubled through an interrupted network of textual relations or the poetics of the *émerveille*; these self-reflexive tales are presented as a means to bring the characters in the narrative (as well as the reader) to recognize and embrace a new theory of history, community, and identity in which all three are revealed and constituted through a proliferation of voices, modes, and identities. In this way, the initiation is but the beginning of an initiatory journey without end and comes closer to a creolized spiritual initiation (such as performed in *vodou*) where the rites of initiation mark the entry into a new apprehension of the world and one's role in this cosmic order.

The impossibility of recuperating origins within the Caribbean becomes a self-conscious vehicle for a poetico-political process of writing that is no longer rooted in a fixed, certain identity. In *Écrire en pays dominé*, Chamoiseau dreams of the *lieu* as an open, multilingual space of diversity (*EPD*, 226) and as continuously taking place, what he calls the "place that is becoming" or the "*Lieu-en-devenir*" (*EPD*, 341). This concept of space is dialogic and fluid, rather than fixed and closed. The *émerveille* bears witness to the existence of this *lieu*. To draw on Mikhail Bakhtin's terminology, *émerveille* is a heteroglossic form through which multiple genres or voices intermix. The *émerveille* serves Chamoiseau's larger poetic and utopian aim of fostering an imaginary that lives in the consciousness of the "Tout-monde" (*E*, 126): that does not seek to dominate or conquer the world, but to inhabit it. The *émerveille* initiates the reader into a new state of consciousness by inducing a state of imaginative marooning and a propensity for marveling at the world.

These initiatory tales involve transformational encounters with the Martinican landscape. Through an imaginative marooning of consciousness, these narratives disclose that the "champ de bataille est celui de l'imaginaire"[34] ("the field of battle is that of the imaginary"). Like the Martinican landscape, the figure of the maroon is reworked through textual intervention. In the case of *L'Esclave*, the maroon slave, literally present in the narrative of the slave who flees, serves as a double for Chamoiseau the narrator's marooning of consciousness. In *Écrire*, the narrator engages in a textual poetics of marooning of consciousness through an exploration of Martinique's topographic and historical landscapes. Some might view this recuperation of the maroon as a departure for the Creolist who showed a preference for the storyteller on the plantation in *Lettres créoles*. However, in many ways, this revival of the maroon figure in his writing marks a return to early theater and comic book works where the maroon is depicted in acts of heroic resistance. However, Chamoiseau clearly distinguishes between the historic figure of the maroon and his poetic reinterpretation of this figure.[35] The desire for freedom marked by the maroon's "décharge" ("discharge") and "lieu du passage à l'acte" ("process that leads to the act of flight") are significant.[36] To the extent that the maroon impulsively flees from a subordinate understanding ("mise-sous-relation") to gain a relational identity ("mise-en-relation"), he/she prefigures the Chamoiseau's Warrior of the Imaginary. The latter transforms the obscure maroon impulse into an inwardly directed struggle for liberation (*EPD*, 307): "Le Guerrier n'a pas d'ennemi, la guerre qu'il mène, c'est avec lui-même, par la beauté de son existence, de ses postures" ("The Warrior does not have any enemies, the war that he leads is with himself, in the beauty of his existence and postures").[37] This "exercice de connaissance" ("exercise of knowledge," but it is more like an exercise of consciousness) as he terms it is described as "[u]ne onde mentale qui éclabousse l'imaginé de la totalisation du monde avec les forces d'un Lieu" ("thought wave that splatters the totalized imagination of the world with the force of the local").[38] The Warrior of the Imaginary discovers a more complex way of relating to the world through his encounter with the *émerveille*. He learns that he must draw on investigative, ethnographic, historical, and poetic perspectives (*EPD*, 307–8). Various methods of analysis and modes of study converge.

Chamoiseau's ravine of the marvel ("ravine d'émerveille") in is a *lieu* of place that embodies the poetico-political principles of *émerveille* because it serves as a place and space of encounters. The ravine is quite literally a place of encounter for the fleeing slave in the world (mimesis) as well as a place of vision (diegesis), but it is also depicted as a space of storytelling (extradiegesis) that can only be disclosed through multiple, criss-crossing tales (metadiegesis). The discovery of the magic Carib stone serves as an initiatory experience because it also represents the contested site (*lieu*) where multiple stories and histories converge. Two tales, a tale of an escaping slave (set in the space and time of the novella storyworld) and an aporic, impossible metanarrative of origins (in the space and time of Chamoiseau's text as discourse), converge in this shared ravine where a magical stone is apparently located. This stone is an object of wonder, both the ending and the beginning of these three narratives of initiation:

1. The first tale of initiation involves the literal story: the triangulated narrative of what happens to the slave, *molosse*, and *béké*.
2. The second tale of initiation involves the triangulated tale of the discovery of the ravine, apparently located by the old man or Chamoiseau or his brother.
3. The third tale of initiation involves the triangulated metanarrative structure, consisting of the three "je" of the narrative, namely Chamoiseau as narrator, Édouard Glissant as interlocutor, and the imagined warrior or escaped slave as an emergent self.

The marvelous ravine is the literal and figurative space where multiple narrative trajectories converge, intersect, and cross, including each of the three triangulated tales listed above. This fantastic, uncertain, and marvelous *lieu* serves as the source for the initiatory consciousness, not only of the slave as imagined warrior but also for the reader as a potential warrior of the imaginary.

Described by Chamoiseau as a "conte fondateur,"[39] *L'Esclave vieil homme et le molosse* presents the archetypal New World tale of a fugitive slave who escapes from the plantation and is pursued by a *molosse* and a *béké*.[40] Chamoiseau and several of his critics have noted that this flight functions as a rehumanizing experience for the slave who undergoes a personal liberation,[41] which has been described as an "allegory of individuation"[42] and a "journey to the centre of his self, which he is at last able to assert fully."[43] This flight proves to be a tale of initiation for all three figures—slave, *béké*, and *molosse*—as the literal pursuit of the slave becomes a symbolic pursuit in which each of the figures confronts memories, impulses, and visions that challenge the known certitudes about the system of slavery and the roles it entails. The initiation begins with the physical separation from the plantation system and the entry into the forest. Traversing the woods, the mysterious space of initiation, each undergoes a liminal phase in which the sense of time and place is suspended. Subject to the challenges of renewed memory and imagination, each undergoes a rebirth of consciousness. The amnesiac effects of the forest unleash various memories and visions of the Middle Passage for the slave and *molosse*. For the *béké*, this liminal phase involves an inner confrontation as he realizes that he had never understood the slave's resistance. Indeed, one might say that the *béké* undergoes an imaginary *marronnage* of consciousness as he comes to recognize that this slave always pursued his own course and always refused to accept a place in the system of slavery. However, for each of these three, the final stage of reintegration proves problematic for none can return to society as he knew it.

Entering the "ravine d'émerveille" (*EV*, 124) ("ravine of the marvel") he discovers a magical stone and undergoes the final phase of reintegration. Clasping the stone, he experiences its dream and speaks to it. The stone is engraved, with points and interlaced lines, spirals, double crosses, triangles, and hatch marks. Marked by animals and peoples through different epochs, it's an "ouélélé" of myths and geneses (*EV*, 128). This final resting place of the slave opens up a vision of a chaos of millions of souls, content, singing, and laughing (*EV*, 130). This flight, with its multiple challenges, encounters with and visions of the Creole world, transforms the fleeing slave into a "guerrier" figure (*EV*, 79) and integrates this warrior into a new kind of community. This initiation contrasts with that of the molosse and *béké* who return home changed, but who are no longer able to reintegrate into the known world order. The dog's ferocity dissipates in face of this marvelous rock and he is not able to recover. The once ferocious monster is described as coming toward this mystery like a shepherd dog, and finally as licking the slave. The dog is no longer a monster and the *béké*, after drying his eyes, returns home, not with the sense that he has lost a slave or been mocked by an "ungrateful" maroon slave (*EV*, 137). Instead, he returns charged by something that he cannot name, no longer tired, ashamed, or afraid (*EV*, 137). The *béké* is described as shaking with the awareness of other spaces; he may never pursue the implications of this revelatory experience, but his subtle transformation of consciousness may nonetheless affect future generations. The *émerveille* leaves him in a state of irresolution. Thus, the experiences of the molosse and *béké* disclose a set of unresolved tensions, the inability of the closed *territoire* of the plantation system to adapt or transform itself in the face of new identities or experiences.

The space of the narrative discourse provides a collective initiation and projects a vision of *communitas*. Related experiences of initiation are collected in the shared space of the landscape and the narrative. Through strategies of linkage and affiliation, the narrator discloses a network of relations in which the slave and the *molosse* are seen as the suffering doubles of the slave system (*EV*, 51). Both undergo a Middle Passage, a liminal experience that precedes their forced integration into the plantation system. However, in both instances, neither fully emerges from the liminal state. The slave does not remember the Middle Passage (at least, not in a coherent way) and for this reason remains in the "cale du bateau" ("ship's hold"), haunted by fragmentary memories (51). The situation of the *molosse* is similar, but his instincts and the master's punishment serve to mobilize him, enabling him to act out his role as the keeper of the slave. For both the slave and *molosse*, the journey through the forest is a return to the unresolved liminal phase of the Middle Passage, thus reopening the rites of passage. For the *béké*, the flight of the slave and the transformation of the *molosse* are events that introduce a failure of signification, disrupting slavery as a hierarchical system. His also becomes an initiation into something new, even if he cannot find his place in this new domain. Thus, the narrative opens up dialogues, a new network of relations, and discloses a *lieu*, a site where the failures of the slave system are collectively recognized. Similarly, this initiation discloses a New World, a space of multiple origins and mystery, a space, unlike slavery, which is not subject to systemic thinking.

The narrative of the ravine, the space where the escaped slave imagines that his own bones will be found, is the site of multiple narratives of origin, the tales recounted by Chamoiseau in the final chapter of the novella (*EV*, 135). The first is a metanarrative tale of origins, the kind normally told by the *Marqueur de paroles*, leading the reader into the story by introducing the various narrators through whom the story is passed on. In this case, Chamoiseau describes meeting an old man who has discovered a magical Carib stone that he offers to show Chamoiseau, who is known to the reader as the Word Scratcher or the *Marqueur de paroles*. Chamoiseau describes his response to this offer, stating that he refused the offer or that he went and the rock could not be found or that one of his brothers went instead or that no one saw it except this old man, unless of course it was his brother. However, instead of a description of the rock that Chamoiseau might have seen, the reader is presented with a description of another rock covered in Amerindian signs from various epochs. Using evasive language, mediated reports of events and negative descriptions (of what he did not do or see), Chamoiseau suggests that this rock is doubtlessly not comparable to the one that seemed to be in a deep ravine in a ceremonial location as evoked by the old man, and if not by the old man then by someone else whom Chamoiseau cannot identify. This uncertain narrative makes both the location of the ravine and the rock impossible to ascertain. Consequently, the entire narrative account is figured as an aporia; it is impossible to know with certainty what took place or how the narrative originated.

Symbolically, this textual aporia reflects the cultural realities of the Caribbean where the indigenous past is irrecoverable and identities are intermixed. Chamoiseau persists in the narrative of discovering the rock and the bones of a human body, an action both taken and not taken to discover artifacts that remain irrecoverable. Chamoiseau describes seeing and touching the bones, despite a warning that he should not do this. Yet, the "reality" of this discovery is flouted by Chamoiseau's assertion that he might not have gone to the site where the stone and the bones lay. Upon touching the bones Chamoiseau observes "mes songes sont marronneurs" (*EV*, 144) ("my dreams are maroons"), which seems to call into question the reality of this contact. Alternatively, the moment of contact is of less consequence than the imagined marooning it prompts. The tale of the marooned slave is a dream that signals the narrator's own drifting of consciousness through the (im)possible and the (un)known. As the origins of the tale cannot be situated in either the real or the imaginary, it produces a kind of radical, irresolvable doubt. Confronted with this fantastic otherness, the reader hesitates to interpret the truth about the narrative; this uncertainty principle, a characteristic element of the fantastic,[44] provides the basis for a new kind of hermeneutics.

The Otherness of the tale reflects anxieties about identity in the Caribbean. There is no particular reason for imagining that the bones discovered are those of a maroon slave. Indeed, these might well be the bones of an Amerindian, a black person, a *béké*, a "coulis" (someone of Indian descent), or an Asian person (*EV*, 144). Chamoiseau describes his brother's outraged reaction when he learns that the tale of an escaped slave should be told for he had imagined the tale of a Carib might be told instead. When Chamoiseau suggests that his brother might write this alternative story, the brother, presumably Miguel Chamoiseau, states that writing is "raide." Whether he means it is difficult or far-fetched or both one cannot be sure, but in any case Chamoiseau states that he agrees with this opinion. Chamoiseau's brother, a double for the narrator, is presented as a source for an alternative story that might have otherwise been told. Indeed, the novella is dedicated to Miguel Chamoiseau as the one who might know where the rock is, thus situating the brother as the possible true source for the tale. Thus, Chamoiseau reinforces the idea that the origins of Creole culture remain opaque.

Chamoiseau the narrator suggests an allegorical reading of the tale as a kind of moral fable. Chamoiseau the narrator writes: "Nous sommes tous, comme mon vieux-bougre en fuite, poursuivis par un monstre" (*EV*, 146) ("We are all, like my old fellow, fleeing, pursued by a monster"). This monster is no longer the *molosse*, but rather the old certitudes, systemic thinking, and our sumptuous truths. Thus, even the meaning of the bones is open to interpretation. Chamoiseau's brother is reported as saying that the bones, the artifacts of this tale, are those of the warrior without fear of conquest or domination. In reply, Chamoiseau suggests that perhaps this man simply ran. The novella ends with Chamoiseau's impulse to touch the bones of the slave, not a dream, not a delirium, not a chimerical fiction, but an immense detour to return to the combats of one's own age with a new poetry (*EV*, 147). Chamoiseau is represented as undergoing his own imaginary marooning of consciousness and initiation as imaginary warrior. As such, this final scene calls attention to the *mise-en-abîme* structure of the narrative. Unlike the cultural abyss of the colonial encounter and its legacies, this postcolonial abyss provides a new orientation to the past. In proposing a tale of origins that undermines its own interpretive framework, Chamoiseau destabilizes the framework of interpretation. This historical fiction calls into question the fictions of history. The opening to the story is no longer registered as a historical setting, but as the "once-upon-a-time" phrase that opens a fairytale: "Du temps de l'esclavage dans les isles-à-sucre, il y eut" (*EV*, 17) ("In the time of slavery in the sugar islands, there was").

Consistent with the reading of the narrative as *mise-en-abîme* and as allegory is Chamoiseau's suggestion that *L'Esclave vieil homme* is a *conte fondateur*, dealing with a primordial scene of the imaginary, involving three archetypal figures: the slave who flees, the dog, and the master who goes looking for him. By introducing Glissant as an interlocutor, Chamoiseau links his narrative to alternative tales and interpretations of marooning, running counter or parallel to his own, in pursuit, flight, interlocution, or subversion. Chamoiseau names two sources for the *entre-dire* from Glissant, one is an unpublished work, titled *La folie Célat*[45] and the other is *L'Intention poétique* (1969). Dawn Fulton argues that madness of Celat also serves as the thematic underpinning of *La case du Commandeur*. Fulton views this intertextuality as a way of rethinking not only the authoritative "we" but also the literary "we" by positioning the question of collectivity in a wider field of narrative perspectives.[46]

The quotations from *L'Intention poétique* suggest the complex interrelations (*mise-en-relation*) that underpin identities. Certain sections of *L'Esclave vieil homme et le molosse* ("Matière," "Vivant," and "Les os") are preceded by quotations from the first section of Glissant's *L'Intention poétique*, which is titled "Histoires." By introducing these quotes, Chamoiseau affiliates his story with the tale of the old slave in Glissant. Glissant's text presents a fable, beginning with a fugitive who maroons and pursues his own history, which runs parallel to that of the *béké* and his dog. Glissant suggests that these two separate histories are unified, reduced to a single unity. Glissant asks: "Qui revient pourtant sur la déclive du morne, et fouille?" ("Who returns yet to the edge of the hill and searches?")[47] Seemingly, in answer to this rhetorical question, he describes an old man who has the pure and restive power of a root within these two histories, a figure who looks out searching for "l'espace du monde" ("the space of the world").[48]

By cutting up this quote and rearranging the order of these quotations in his own narrative, Chamoiseau effectively offers alternative answers to Glissant's question concerning marooning. In Chamoiseau's work, the question "Who returns to the edge of the hill [. . .]?" follows the answer. Glissant's answer to the question is cited in "Matière" the first section, while the question is placed at the beginning of "Les os," the final section of the novella. Thus, the answer and question frame the novella as it were, only the terms of this dialogue are split and reversed by Chamoiseau's own narrative intertext. In "Matière," Chamoiseau's use of the Glissantian intertext introduces a multiply constructed self, as the "je" of the narrative telling the tale is displaced and transformed. The first occurrence of "je" occurs in the citation of Glissant: "J'ai vu ses yeux, j'ai vu ses yeux égarés chercher l'espace du monde" (*EV*, 16) ("I have seen his eyes, I have seen his distraught eyes, looking for the space of the world"). Here the "je" is the voice of the Glissantian narrator and the third-person "his eyes" ("ses yeux") to the eyes of Chamoiseau's slave who is about to take flight and/or Glissant's old man. However, the continuation of the narrative as reported by various sources (including "one"/"on" and "we"/"nous") comes to another me ("moi") or "I" ("je"), presumably Chamoiseau as narrator who says: ""Ainsi, m'est parvenue l'histoire de cet esclave vieil homme" (*EV*, 18) ("In this way, the story of the old slave man reached me"). Glissant's *entre-dire* enters into the "I" of the narrator telling the story, providing a double narrative, not only for the "matière" or content of the tale, but also for the storyteller. This "je" is eventually joined by a third, that of the old slave himself, when he emerges from the source and his metaphorical return to the abyss of the Middle Passage. Thus, a triple metalepsis occurs, as the voices of narrators include Glissant's narrative voice, Chamoiseau's, and that of the maroon slave, a figure imagined and brought to life through the *entre-dire* of Glissant and Chamoiseau. This metaleptic structure underscores the workings of the text as an "exercice de connaissance," a kind of textual initiation through a mise-en-relation of the "je." These textual *jeux* or games produce a marvelous self, an *émerveille* of identity or self-consciousness.

Chamoiseau's poetics of the *émerveille* are used to release the electrifying discharge energies associated with marooning in order to initiate the warrior of the imaginary. In the context of *L'Esclave vieil homme et le molosse*, Chamoiseau is at pains to emphasize the difference between the literal and figurative activities of marooning.[49] When the slave flees, the commanders cry "*Marronnage* ! . . ." (*EV*, 42) ("marooned slave"), but this is mistaken as the narrator observes: "Il décide donc de s'en aller, non pas de marronner, mais *d'aller*" (*EV*, 54) ("He decides then to leave, not to maroon, but *to go*"). Nonetheless, Chamoiseau does not reject marooning as a figurative term indicating a pursuit of consciousness. Contemplating the marvelous rock, he writes "mes songes sont marroneurs" (*EV*, 144) ("my dreams are maroons"). The distinction between the maroon as a historic figure and marooning as an activity of the self-liberating consciousness is essential to Chamoiseau's concept of the Warrior of the Imaginary. For the Warrior of the Imaginary, this instinct or impulse is a first step, a necessary step toward a fullness of consciousness: a deliberate, articulate, openness to new forms of life and self-creation. It is not the literal flight, but the imagined departure from the known that makes for a positive form of *marronnage*.

Unlike the conventional pattern of initiation, which results in reintegration, this process leads to an initiatory vision of the world as well as the subject's place in it. This criss-crossed narrative structure, a manifestation of the poetics of the *émerveille*, presents a thought experiment:

a narrative whose origins are impossible to determine, a place in which the origins of a new kind of consciousness is possible. In *L'Esclave vieil homme et le molosse*, Chamoiseau provides various narrative starting points. The tale begins with the effects of the *paroles* of the *conteur* on the plantation, whose words prompt the slave to take flight. In response to the storytelling event, the slave undergoes a transformation: he experiences a "chant génésique au-dessus de son ventre" (*EV*, 48) ("a Genesis song in his belly"). This cry of consciousness is experienced as a moment of *décharge*, born by the sense that he has become a "pierre brulante" or "burning stone" (*EV*, 49). During his flight, the slave's memories return to the past, including recollections of the Middle Passage and fragmented memories of Africa (*EV*, 101). The narrative path takes the reader back into Caribbean cultural history for it brings the slave into contact with a stone engraved by the Caribs, which offers a visionary story.

This petroglyph with its various inscriptions is described by Confiant and Chamoiseau as follows: "Nos pays ont inscrit dans leur terre ces paroles brisées, éparses, partielles, qui remontent la tracée infinie d'une absence de Genèse: cette silencieuse littérature" (*LC*, 23) ("Our countries have inscribed in their earth these broken words, scattered and partial, which bear the infinite trace of an absence of a Genesis: this silent literature"). However, the rock that the slave confronts is not a silent absence of a genesis, but rather a communal outpouring. The rock dreams, signs, and communicates with him, revealing a vision of the land and the people as one. Thus, the narrative returns to the origins of plenitude. The Warrior of the Imaginary undergoes the birth of the "je" by recovering an inner space of memory and imagination, by recognizing a narrative of self in the shifting fragments of the past. This enables the fleeing slave to declare "Je me sentais guerrier" (*EV*, 101) ("I felt like a warrior"). This transformation of the imaginary is what distinguishes Chamoiseau's slave from the maroon: the maroon embodies an impulse of resistance and flight from domination, but does not necessarily have the imaginative power or inner freedom to pursue a new reality. A decade later, Chamoiseau takes this subject as a point of departure in *Un dimanche au cachot* where he continues the narrative and shows how the escaping slave's radiating influence transforms all of those with whom he comes into contact.

In *L'Esclave*, Chamoiseau prompts the reader to take an active role in negotiating this discursive world of intersecting narratives, varying perspectives, and points of intertextual affiliation. Consequently, the "ravine d'émerveille" ("ravine of the marvel") is invoked as a shared site of reflective consciousness. The literal *roche-écrite* discovered by the slave serves as a double for the poetics of the text, which is marked by multiple inscriptions and voiced through multiple presences. As a result, the literal landscape of the narrative is disclosed as the imaginative space of a shared consciousness and multiple initiations. The imagined warrior, this "I," is a double for not only the fleeing slave, Chamoiseau, and Glissant, but also for the reader as a potential warrior of the imaginary, pursued by the "monster" of absolute certainties. This imagined space is presented as a site of multiple origins and renewals of the self as "je" (I) and as "nous" (we) of community. The literal stone discovered during this archetypal tale of the escaped slave serves as the origins of an opaque tale about the aporia of being in the world. The Caribbean stone is a marvelous textual fragment, disclosing a world inhabited by a multiplicity of voices throughout Caribbean history as well as a more fluid, transformative space of dialogue. This vision of the world as through the marvelous stone corresponds to the vision of Pierre-Monde as described in *Écrire en pays dominé* where it refers to an apprehension of the world energized by the alchemical processes of transformation underlying creolization (*EPD*, 326) and promotes the acceptance of incertitude.[50] Speaking of the idea of the philosopher's stone as a metaphor for the search for a new kind of alchemical world order, Chamoiseau writes:

> Il nous faut considérer le monde non pas comme une table lisible, mais comme une entité aussi opaque et imprévisible (mais potentiellement porteuse de plénitude) que l'ancienne pierre philosophale des alchimistes. Apprendre à vivre dans l'énigme du monde, ce que j'appelle: *la Pierre-Monde*.[51]

> (We need to regard the world not as a tablet on which we read a message, but as an entity as opaque and unpredictable [though potentially fruitful] as the old philosopher's stone of the alchemists. To learn to live in the enigma of the world, which I call: the *Pierre-Monde*.)

Through the poetics of the *émerveille*, Chamoiseau extends the processes of initiation to the reader as a potential warrior of the imaginary who works to decipher this complex textual hermeneutics.[52]

The initiatory structure of *Écrire en pays dominé* is evident in the titles of three cadences, "Anagogie," "Anabase," and "Anabiose." "Anagogy" is a special form of allegorical interpretation, a genre particularly associated with medieval thinking and literature, which relates to the ultimate destiny of humanity and reveals a higher spiritual meaning behind the literal meaning of the text. "Anabase" is a term originating with Saint-John Perse, referring to the visionary force of language, which Chamoiseau specifically interprets as "ce voyage intérieur" ("this interior voyage") through imagined landscapes (108). "Anabiose" is a botanical term referring to the revival of a plant after a long period of dormancy or more generally to a revival after an apparent death. With this ecological reference, Chamoiseau likens the activity of imaginary wandering through an internal landscape to an organic revival of the self in the world.

"Anagogie par les livres endormis" begins with the dominated self, asking the question: "Comment écrire dominé?" (*EPD*, 17). The literary landscape is seen as a suffocating space or sedimentation of colonial thinking: "Qu'ont-elles sédimenté au fil du temps pour toi qui suffoques sous cette modernité coloniale?" (*EPD*, 17). The use of the second person singular "tu" suggests the separation of self from the "je" and also serves to generalize Chamoiseau's individual dilemma as one that also belongs to an implied reader, someone also living with a colonized imaginary. In a sense then, the work begins with the fundamental separation of the self split from the imaginary. Domination stems from the residual influence of the colonial past in postcolonial society as well as the sources of domination present in contemporary Martinique, both from the metropolitan center of France and from the increasing influence of globalization at the local level.

Richard Watts notes that for Chamoiseau departmentalization is primarily experienced through the domination of television and the supermarket.[53] Subsequently, "[s]ites of exchange were transformed into sites of distribution and sites of participation were replaced by sites of passive consumption."[54] Chamoiseau the narrator begins with a critical view of Martinique as a place of "colonial modernity" (*EPD*, 17). Addressing himself in the second person, he adopts a retrospective view of the writerly self in the history of literary protest:

> Tu n'es pas de ceux qui peuvent dresser des cartes de goulags, ou mener discours sur les génocides, les massacres, les dictateurs féroces. Tu ne peux pas décrire des errances de pouvoir dans des palais stupéfiés, ni tenir mémoire des horreurs d'une solution finale. Autour de ta plume, aucun spectre de censure ni de fil barbelé. (*EPD*, 17)

(You are not among those who can draw up a map of gulags or lead a discourse on genocide, massacres, or fierce dictators. You cannot describe the wandering course of power in stupefying palaces, or recall memories of the horrors of a final solution. Surrounding your pen, there is neither a specter of censorship nor of barbed wire.)

In an almost nostalgic tone, Chamoiseau laments the lack of clearly identifiable evil forces against which to pit his writerly energies. Instead, he suggests that the contemporary Martinican writer confronts more insidious forms of domination (*EPD*, 18).

Chamoiseau's challenge to the dominant imaginary takes the form of an imaginative detour as he envisions an encounter with a warrior figure. Described as coming from all ages, from all wars, from all acts of resistance and also from all dreams of nourishing dominated peoples (*EPD*, 21–22), the warrior initiates Chamoiseau the narrator into a new apprehension of the world. This trans-Caribbean warrior figure confirms Chamoiseau's suspicions that his liberty is only apparent and that he must seek true liberty through an art of resistance and take comfort in this marooning of thought from the dominant (*EPD*, 23). In the sustained dialogue that follows, the narrator unleashes a critique of the global imaginary that finds its force in a history of vernacular modernities and an analysis of various forms of domination. Chamoiseau's engagement with the local recognizes the complexities of vernacular modernities. Discovering place is an act that requires multiple trajectories of engagement, critique, and remembering. Chamoiseau unveils the need to explore critically one's place in the world and to embrace a trans-local perspective as a mode of resistance.

Chamoiseau's critique of neocolonial modernization in Martinique demonstrates the importance of the local in disrupting master narratives and initiating a vision of a more democratic world order. In pursuing this argument, he makes the vernacular form the subject of his discourse. Thus, the text that we are reading is already an answer to the problem he poses. Eventually, he discloses the metafictional frame of the narrative: this story about the writing of a story deals with the potential dangers of global flows as well as with the risks entailed by accounts of modernity that fail to take into account the vernacular. To tell this story then entails a disruptive narrative form that rewrites history as it has come to be known in Martinique by retelling it through the mediating effects of personal memory and dreams. In effect, the narrative achieves the aim of articulating a way to free itself from domination through the act of narration. In this sense, we can see the narrative as inhabiting multiple perspectives both in time and place, shifting among them in a way that reflects the uneven account of vernacular modernities in Martinique and as a model for the trans-Caribbean experience in the face of globalization.

The tripartite structure of *Écrire en pays dominé* with its "Anagogie par les livres endormis," "Anabase en digenèses selon Glissant," and "Anabiose sur la Pierre-Monde" functions as a critique of master narratives, a demonstration of the importance of the local and an argument for a vision of a new kind of democracy. In the *Anagogie*, Chamoiseau's critique of hegemonic ways of thinking includes an analysis (along the lines of Foucault) of institutions, examining the ways in which religion, education, and healthcare function as modes of dominating body and spirit by ignoring the local. Thus, the underlying ideoscapes of colonization, relying on Enlightenment rationalization, are subject to attack. The warrior is a witness to the devastating effects of colonial education in Vietnam, India, Algeria, Senegal, Cambodia, the Congo, the Antilles, and other places (*EPD*, 49). Chamoiseau offers a transnational critique of domination, which situates the Caribbean in relation to other sites of colonization. Simultaneously, Chamoiseau provides an account of his own childhood and adolescent reading habits, suggesting how reading served to help him release his imaginary from the prison of French thinking. In a gesture typical of this text, which plays with the relations among various registers and sites of meaning, he extends the signification of his literal experience working in the French penitentiary system to the symbolic level.

The *Anabase* (an introspective journey) maps "the landscape of persons who constitute the shifting world in which we live."[55] Chamoiseau's analysis of the modern world of flows resembles Arjun Appadurai's analysis of ethnoscapes: that "tourists, immigrants, refugees, exiles, guest workers, and other moving groups and individuals constitute an essential feature of the world and appear to affect the politics of (and between) nations to a hitherto unprecendented degree."[56] Appadurai argues that the warp of stable communities and networks is "everywhere shot through with the woof of human motion"[57] with the result that "moving groups cannot afford to let their imaginations rest too long, even if they wish to."[58] For Chamoiseau, self-identification is inseparable from the history of migrating peoples who make up the trans-Caribbean self. If, for some, migration produces a fluid, restless imaginary, perhaps even a sense of drifting, Chamoiseau proposes another alternative. In response to this discourse of domination, he turns to the task of dreaming the land (*rêver-pays*) as a means to undo the colonial chains that place constraints on everyday realities (*EPD*, 106).

Following Perse's lead in *Anabase*, Chamoiseau's *anabase* begins with an interior voyage where he catalogs vernacular culture with its stories, proverbs, marvels, Creole language, and local traditional objects, such as the *yole* or boat (*EPD*, 108). He envisions the "landscape of persons who constitute the shifting world in which we live" as an "anthropological magma" or as a diagenetic model of self (*EPD*, 110). Indebted to Glissant,[59] Chamoiseau takes up the concept of diagenesis, the process by which sediments of rock become fused as sedimentary rock. Transported and deposited, the rock undergoes a process of compaction as the grains are forced together and then cemented into one. The mode of transport and deposition leaves visible signs or clues in the sedimentary rock. Chamoiseau applies this model to creolization, which also entails a process of transport, compaction, and transformation. Tracing the accumulation of migratory groups to Martinique as the sedimentary layers of himself, he creates his own cultural geology: describing how these fluid layers, subject to the pressures of the New World, are transformed into a sedimentary, solid yet fluid, rock-like identity. The result is a diagenetic self, including the *moi-colons*, *moi-amérindiens*, *moi-africains*, *moi-indiens*, *moi-chinois*, *moi-syro-libinais*, and *moi-créole* (colonial-me, Amerindian-me, African-me, Indian-me, Chinese-me, Syro-Lebanese-me, and Creole-me). Creolization is envisioned as a diagenetic process where each identity traverses the other, producing a composite yet distinctive self (*EPD*, 233). This vernacular experience of modernity, formulated as a fluid geology of selfhood and communal identities, has implications for the trans-Caribbean imaginary.

In his third movement, titled *Anabiose*, Chamoiseau's critique of technology plays a particularly influential role in describing the trans-Caribbean imaginary. Chamoiseau describes the influx of communications technologies in Martinique and elsewhere, noting the rapid-flash communications of cable, satellite, Minitel, fax, fibre optics, modem, telephones, and so on (*EPD*, 238). The *guerrier* observes: "Les circuits de communications s'étaient agrégés en réseaux, les réseaux en mégaréseaux, les mégaréseaux en un rhizome technotronique qui couvrait l'ensemble de la terre, et me plongeait, à chaque instant de ma vie" (*EPD*, 238) ("Circuits of communication were integrated into networks, networks into mega-networks, and mega-networks into a technotronic rhizome that covered the entire world, and engulfed me, at each moment of my life"). Chamoiseau expresses an ambivalent view of technology: for at the same time that technology enables the sharing of local knowledge, it also functions as a diffuse system of domination (*EPD*, 261–62). Chamoiseau's warrior notes that technology is not equally accessible and is even sometimes subject to abuse, often mirroring and even promulgating existing systemic inequities (*EPD*, 290–91, 295–96). For Chamoiseau, the center / periphery problem with its unequal balance of forces manifests itself in new ways.

Through references to cyberspace, Chamoiseau reworks the Glissantian understanding of the rhizome. Gilles Deleuze and Félix Guattari first introduced the term rhizome in order to articulate a poststructuralist idea that there is not simply one root or origin but multiple, reproducing roots that exist in a proliferating networked system. This notion has been applied to the Internet or "world wide web" as a model of decentralized, circulating flows of information. It has also been taken up by Glissant as a model for the Poetics of Relation, in which "each and every identity is extended through a relationship with the Other."[60] For Chamoiseau, the rhizome is a neutral concept, capable of being experienced in both negative and positive ways. A rhizome can also be experienced at the local level as a mode of domination as is the case for a globalization driven by the logic and energy of the "jungle" of Western centers, where media powers, political powers, economic powers, financial powers, and cultural powers overlap with and constrain one another (*EPD*, 280).

Eventually, the Warrior's peripheral comments about the decentered network of power relations and global circulations flow into the main discourse and transform Chamoiseau's narrative as he begins to react to and acknowledge the force of these supra-narrative strands. Chamoiseau's narrator documents the stultifying effects of departmentalization on the collective imaginary. He notes that departmentalization has led to a profound self-alienation, observing that an ejection from oneself, from one's biological, geographic, cultural, and mental realities, began with this change (*EPD*, 247). Simultaneously, the Warrior interjects remarks concerning the dangers of technological flows. These two separate narrative threads, one a critique of colonial modernity and the other a critique of homogenizing global forces, converge in the figure of the sea, the marooned slave, and cyberspace. Despite his admiration for Perse, Chamoiseau observes that the poet's construct of the sea, which is seen as an element of power and a source of knowledge, is indicative of the Western imaginary at work (*EPD*, 263). By contrast to the presumptuous spirit of the Westernized imaginary, Chamoiseau admires the imaginary as represented by the marooned slave: this is a figure who is arrested by the sea as the great unknown (*EPD*, 264). Several pages later, Chamoiseau's Warrior reconstructs the marooned slave as a hacker who circulates in this rhizomatic space as a rebel figure (*EPD*, 286). Thus, he retroactively imagines the marooned slave as a hacker. This hybrid figure is a product of various temporal and spatial flows, including local cultural memory and the flows of the Internet. The local and global flows of the imaginary, past and present, merge to create a new figure of resistance. The "Négre-marron du rhizome-de-réseaux" or "Negro-maroon of the rhizome of networks" (*EPD*, 286) follows an impulse to confront the unknown and to seize on the imaginary as a virtual space of wandering. This glocalized figure is an example of the inter-retro-active imaginary at work. This rebel and warrior is imagined through a self-conscious dialogue with local and global impulses, past and present (*EPD*, 286).

Cyberspace and virtual identities are invoked as aspects of Chamoiseau's virtual hero, the Warrior of the Imaginary, and imagined reality in the spaces/places of the *Pierre-Monde*. Linguistically, the *Pierre-Monde* can be seen as an alternative to the Glissantian notion of the *Chaos-Monde*, but the concept also has other roots. The *Pierre-Monde* finds its etymology in the alchemical idea of the Philosopher's Stone, the result of turning base metals into gold. In this sense, the *Pierre-Monde* is a way of reconceptualizing the diagenetic model of creolization whereby multiple cultures (base metals) undergo a cultural alchemical process of transformation. The Caribbean experience of creolization is a precursor to the discovery of the *Pierre-Monde*, an imagined world grounded in a relational concept of identities. The self as warrior of the imaginary embraces a relational mode of being. The warrior puts forward a view of democracy that fosters relations of diversity and allows for equilibrated communions between modernity and tradition (*EPD*, 334). The trans-Caribbean vision of the *Pierre-Monde* is a way of reconceptualizing vernacular modernities as a model for a rhizomatic approach to globalization. Chamoiseau sees an attachment to place as a necessary precursor to entering the *Pierre-Monde* (*EPD*, 337). The vision of the *Pierre-Monde* enables the writer to find a virtual niche: a space that unifies the imaginary of places and instructs one about the proliferation of roots (*EPD*, 339). The circulating discourse forms an open textual landscape that traverses multiple genres and languages in order to embrace a "transversal fluid" form (*EPD*, 340–41). Stylistically, the text thematizes its own multiplicity of sources through the cross-cutting of literary citations, which serve to disrupt the chronological flow of the text. These interruptions are inter-retro-active because the unfolding narrative about the initiation of the warrior of the imaginary contains insights that are accumulated in the process of writing the text. Thus, through authorial interventions, the discourse proves to be a self-reflexive, inter-retro-active construction.

Furthermore, the sense of wandering through a virtual space is fostered by the structuring of the text into three sections, each of which functions as a kind of niche or virtual reality: *Anagogie*, *Anabase*, and *Anabiose*. Within these niches, the reader can meander through the text, following its textual flows in achronological and atopical ways, all the while traversing through narrative fragments that nonetheless offer analyses of "real" histories and places. In these sections, as we have seen, the writer pursues an internal voyage, one that includes chronological and topographical and analyses of the self as a site of plural identities, shaped by experiences past and present as well as local and global. Thus, the text functions to recreate for the reader an experience that has already transpired and has yet to take place: the readerly experience is both situated and dislocated.

These metatextual cues prompt the reader to circulate through the text, exploring a dialogic narrative that exposes uneven chronologies and shifting topographies. *Écrire en pays dominé* is a compelling example of inter-retro-active imaginary at work; whereby that which was effaced from the history of modernity resurfaces and transforms the perception of global flows. Fostering a deeper sense of place is a positive mode of adapting to the effects of globalization, where increasingly we are witnesses to the fact that (in an echo of the Middle Passage): "Nous avons le sentiment d'être sur le même bateau. Que le destin de l'un est lié à celui de l'autre"[61] ("We have the feeling that we are on the same boat. That the destiny of one person is linked to that of the other"). This fits with his earlier definition of *Lieu* or place as that which enables Martinicans to constitute themselves in networks of solidarity, of cultures, of exchanges, that traverse nations and territories, and to get rid of the "detestable idea that we are on the periphery of the world."[62] He insists on the importance of narrating Martinique through stories as a means to preserve interior diversity and to better live in the diversity of the world.[63] Chamoiseau's concept of place entails an open relation between local and global flows. He argues for a "Place-centred perception of the world, its changes and exchanges (*the world must have a shimmering fabric of Places undergoing inter- and retro-action*)."[64] This requires an ability to balance the interaction and retro-action of global and local flows, an ability that demands reconfiguring place in time and history in a fluid yet concrete way. This inter-retro-active view is both rooted and rhizomatic: "We reject this kind of evanescent world citizenship which is a desertion of Place. [. . .] *True world citizenship is multi-citizenship in a multiplicity of Places*."[65] This is not a Kantian notion of citizenship, but rather a notion of the citizen as someone who participates in a multiplicity of real and imagined communities. Citizenship is understood as an active effort of imagination and memory that seeks to relate and reconstitute one's own local conditions in dialogue with those of others.

Écrire raises the question of how Chamoiseau perceives the connection between creolization and globalization. In what ways does the local Martinican experience become useful as a mode of analysis for the global imaginary? Like Stuart Hall, who views cultural hybridity as an agonistic, ongoing, and undecidable process, Chamoiseau argues that creolization, a process taking place around the world, is accompanied by dynamic diversity and flux.[66] Chamoiseau notes the world today is experienced as "a complexity in which contrarieties and antagonisms are balanced in a constantly renegotiated dynamic."[67] What is required is not a fixed position on modernity or domination but a "capacity to relate to others" as a mode of self-definition.[68] A new concept of identity is required: identities "will no longer be stable but at the same time fluid and permanent—like a river which is in a constant state of flux while remaining itself in an irresistible process of transformation."[69] As the Caribbean experience has shown, the process of creolization brings with it changes and challenges in terms of conceptualizing one's place in the world. Describing the Philosopher's Stone World or the *Pierre-Monde* as he calls it in French, he argues:

> We need to regard the world not as a tablet on which we read a message, but as an entity as opaque and unpredictable (though potentially fruitful) as the old philosopher's stone of the alchemists. We are learning to live in the enigma of the world—what I call "the Philosopher's-Stone World."[70]

The principles of place and the harmonious relating of preserved diversities are essential aspects of the *Pierre-Monde*, which provides a model of vernacular modernity in Martinique as well as for a trans-Caribbean articulation of relations to global flows.

Attachment to the local as a place of imaginary battle serves to prepare the writer for the global struggles to affirm solidarity through a shared commitment to defending the specificities of place, memory, and culture. Chamoiseau's global imaginary affiliates distinctive local struggles to defend the vernacular in face of various forms of domination. This point is exemplified by Chamoiseau's written response to political unrest in Corsica. In the article subtitled "Enrayer la violence en Corse" ("Checking violence in Corsica"), he defends a radical concept of democracy as a mode of government that risks chaos in order to defend freedom of speech. He observes that democracy is an ocean of contrary forces, all the more sane because it boils at a temperature close to its dissolution. The cross-cutting of imagined landscapes through the use of the *émerveille* serves to express a vision of citizenship in a world that celebrates the solidarities of agitated places of democratic struggle. Chamoiseau invokes a transcultural space where the landscapes of Corsica and Martinique converge.[71] Violence in Corsica is reenvisioned through the haunting imagery of the terror, destruction, and rebirth that followed the eruption of the volcano, Mount Pelée. Eruptive energies, of lava and waves, past and present, converge in apocalyptic geneses that also function as an ecological, organic model of community. Chamoiseau affirms that he is a Corsican because he is an Antillean. In this renewed space of the trans-Caribbean imaginary, grounded in vernacular solidarities, where various places are interrelated in the global imaginary, Chamoiseau argues for a vision of the world where each person is transformed into a Warrior of the Imaginary battling for the preservation of diversity. Through an imaginative extension of his own local Martinican experience, Chamoiseau negotiates the seascapes of the Caribbean. These waters prove to be salient beyond the region as this vernacular washes up on other shores, disrupting the notion of insular identities through acts of elective affinities.

CHAPTER 7

Visual Texts and the Revolutionary Epic

During the 1990s and first decade of the twenty-first century, Chamoiseau's interest in issues of representation has been evidenced through the author's numerous contributions to visual texts in the form of screenplays, books of photography, children's literature, and art criticism. Following *L'Exil du roi*, Chamoiseau's screenplays include *Passage du milieu* (2000), *Biguine* (2002), *Nord-Plage* (2003), and *Aliker* (2009). He has also collaborated with photographer Jean-Luc de Laguarigue to produce *Elmire des sept bonheurs: confidences d'un vieux travailleur de la distillerie Saint-Etienne* (1998), *Métiers créoles* (1999), and *Cases en Pays-Mêlés* (2000) to produce works that reflect on everyday life in Martinique and the Caribbean as manifest through rum production, Creole trades, and domestic spaces. Two of Chamoiseau's short stories were republished for children in *Le commandeur d'une pluie suivi de L'Accra de la richesse* (2002) with accompanying illustrations by William Wilson. Chamoiseau has written the text for *Encyclomerveille* (2009), the first in a proposed series of comic books for children and adolescents, which includes Thierry Ségur's richly detailed, beautifully colored illustrations in a fantasy mode.

Meanwhile Chamoiseau's novelistic style in the first decade of the twenty-first century tends toward the nonrepresentational as he explores the multifarious flows and dynamic forces that beset and give voice to the construction of locality. In works such as *Biblique des derniers gestes* (2002), *Un dimanche au cachot* (2007), and *Les neuf consciences du Malifini* (2009), the narrative often takes the form of wandering (often in a circling or spiral pattern) through spaces of the Caribbean imaginary, such as the rain forest. Spasms of embodied knowledge, such as pregnancy, hiccups, or flight patterns, come to embody the ambivalent forces of chaos and vying forces of regression and progression inherent in world transformation. Premonition, telepathic moments of collective intuition, and poetic clairvoyance are motifs that resurface in these works that attest to the power of the imaginary as a means for rearticulating the places, spaces, and temporalities that make up an enriched and relational vision of the world. In short, the poetics of the *émerveille* take on a socio-psychological dimension and often introduce eco-poetical perspectives through the criss-crossings of intersubjectively related perspectives and intuitions about the landscape and its inhabitants.

A Vision of Martinique in the World

Chamoiseau's writings about the *bricolage* aesthetics of the Caribbean shed light on his own textual strategies of intermixture. In *Les bois sacrés d'Hélénon*, he pays tribute to the *bricolage* artist, Serge Hélénon, who creates assemblages composed of fragments of wood and other materials that evoke the Middle Passage. In "L'Éclaboussure Afrique" (2002) ("The Splatter of Africa"), he suggests that the African diaspora represents a beautiful enigma of surges (9), resulting from a rupture of consciousness, language, and culture (10). He celebrates "*La vision qui assemble ses éclats dans l'obscur et le geste fondateur bien affairé aux océans de la diversité*" (11) ("*The vision that assembles its splinters in the dark and the founding gesture that bustles with the oceans of diversity*"). The works combine the blistering specificities of history with a fluid sensibility and as such offer a key to interpreting Chamoiseau's poetic strategies during this period. Similarly, in *Laouchez* (1997), Chamoiseau observes that Louis Laouchez's fluid, abstract works (inspired by post-expressionism) produce the effect of the spoken word traversing the forest, calling forth the response of "une digènese in-commencée" or "a non-commenced yet initiatory diagenesis." This striking phrase also applies to Chamoiseau's writing from *L'Esclave vieil homme et le molosse* onward with its focus on the errant figure or poetic gesture as the source of an initiation of consciousness. His abstract prose style evokes the genesis of a new perspective, which functions as a textual response to the Laouchez's visual art. In terms of landscape representation, *Martinique vue du ciel* (2007), produced in collaboration with Anne Chopin, offers stunning aerial views of the island accompanied by poetic texts in which Chamoiseau describes the poetical significance of various sites. This bird's eye perspective is taken up again in *Malfini*, which offers an eco-poetical sense of the Martinican landscape.

Chamoiseau's travel guide, *Martinique* (1995), offers a sociohistorical and semi-autobiographical account of the island's places and histories.

As a screenwriter, member of the jury at the Cannes film festival, and active participant in film production, Chamoiseau's contribution to the francophone Caribbean film industry is an important one. In collaboration with Guy Deslauriers and José Hayot, Chamoiseau has helped to foster local film production. These films have been produced on modest budgets, often with financial assistance from the French government; they tend to fall within the category of heritage films with the drawbacks that this genre typically implies. Nonetheless, local film production plays an essential role in developing skills and building an industry that will eventually (one hopes) be self-sustaining and more daring in its productions. Chamoiseau's scripts often take the form of a reverie or a transposition of an oral narrative to cinema, which has resulted in a somewhat plodding cinematic experience. In particular, the films directed by Deslauriers lack the experimental qualities of Chamoiseau's prose style with its antirepresentational, fragmentary poetics, shifting perspectives and multivocal narration. One of the most intriguing aspects of Deslauriers's work is his reworking of ethnographic visual materials and archival sources. At times, the films present successfully a critique of the colonial gaze and rework archival images from new points of view, but at other times this daring strategy runs the risk of repeating a colonial and/or *doudouiste* vision of the Caribbean.

In the 1990s, Chamoiseau began collaborating with Guy Deslauriers, beginning with his screenplay for *L'Exil du roi*. Importantly, this collaboration marked a decisive moment in the careers of both artists who have worked together on numerous films since then. By the early 1990s, Deslauriers had already established a reputation through his work with Euzhan Palcy on the cinematic adaptation of Joseph Zobel's *Rue case nègres* as well as his own short film, *Quiproquo* (1988). The collaboration with Chamoiseau was a natural one given the affinity the men felt for one another as well as Chamoiseau's desire to give full audio-visual expression to his creations. Indeed, in 1992, he seems to hint at the films to come when the Word Scratcher in *Texaco* remarks, "J'eus un instant envie de la filmer car il m'était de plus en plus sensible que l'audio-visuel offrait de nouvelles chances à l'oraliture, et permettait d'envisager une civilisation articulée sur l'écriture et la parole" (*T*, 496) ("The desire to film her came over me for a second, for it seemed more and more to me that audio-visuals offered new opportunities for oraliture and permitted me to envision a civilization articulated by writing and word") (*TX*, 389).

In the anglophone world, *Passage du Milieu* is probably the best known of the films as it was translated and adapted for the American audience by Walter Mosley as *The Middle Passage*. This psychic drama recounts the horrors of the Middle Passage in a kind of poetic rumination and ends with the suicide of the protagonist who would rather die than be sold into slavery. While the concept for the film is intriguing, this film (like many others on the Middle Passage or the holocaust) fails to rise to the challenge of depicting events that have become part of the collective trauma of history. The film's plodding pace and strangely pacific tone are at odds with the representation of the horrors and violence of enslavement. The attempt to render an impressionistic account of the past and convey the physical suffering of the transported Africans is undermined rather than intensified by the use of voice-over narrative (Djimon Hounsou). The meditative reverie, a mode that works well in Chamoiseau's prose, does not translate successfully to the screen, particularly as it tends to create a distancing effect. Despite the lack of dramatic tension and a clearly articulated narrative arc, the film has pedagogical merits and can be used for teaching the history of the Middle Passage.

By comparison, Deslauriers's *Biguine* is a more successful cinematic venture, which merits attention for its intriguing storyline, fine acting, and outstanding musical performances. Deslauriers very successfully adapts Chamoiseau's screenplay, capturing the whimsy, incantory power, and humor of his writing. Readily available on DVD with English subtitles, the extras include photos, archival images, and a "making of" documentary, which includes interviews with Chamoiseau and Deslauriers. Chamoiseau comments on the importance of music, which he argues is not only a form of cultural expression but also a tool of survival, existence, and resistance. He sees the story as an example of the kind of tales of everyday heroism forgotten by history. As a possible myth of origins for the mixed musical and cultural origins of the beguine (an English sailor yells "begin" to the musicians), the film provides a dramatic example of creolization at work. *Biguine* does justice to Chamoiseau's historiographic approach to storytelling and is well worth viewing as a cinematic versioning of the author's work.

The film offers a compelling look at what Saint-Pierre may have looked like prior to the devastating volcanic eruption of 1902. From the outset, the film introduces the voice-over narrative to good effect as a contemporary radio announcer tells the story of her grandparents, migrant musicians who came to Saint-Pierre from the hills in 1873 and lived there in the years preceding the eruption of Mount Pelée. This genealogical framing device lends a credible sentimentality to the film and serves to diminish the overtly nostalgic and/or pedagogical sensibilities often associated with the "heritage film." The fine musical performances, which make up the film, help to tell the story in a dramatic fashion and show how various forms of music intermix, including popular songs, classical music, African-descended rhythms, and so on. Critics of Chamoiseau's prose will be intrigued by the introduction of themes that play a more fully developed and significant role in *Biblique des derniers gestes* and *Un dimanche au cachot*: motifs of premonitory consciousness, the relation of pregnancy to the collective unconscious, the role of stones as witnesses and participants in the composition of St. Pierre's history of colonial violence, and the flowing, destabilizing energies of destruction (volcanic) allied with creation (music).

Directed by Hayot, *Nord-Plage*[1] proved to be a controversial choice for Chamoiseau because some criticized his decision to collaborate with a *béké*. This experimental film includes the respondent voices of Glissant and Linton Kwesi Johnson (in the form of works entitled *Street 66* and *More Time*) and also features Marianne in a minor role. The film explores the fate of a small town named Macouba, situated at the edge of the sea, which is on the verge of extinction as people migrate elsewhere and the remaining inhabitants fall victim to passive consumption under departmentalization in Martinique.[2] The mayor (Pascal Légitimus) attempts to convince the members of the community to enter into low-rent council flats (referred to as HLM or Habitat à Loyer Modéré), but the people refuse to do so. A young orphan, Anastasie, remains in communication with the tradition of the marvelous in Martinique and engages in dialogues with the statue of the Virgin Mary in the town. Thanks to this Marian dialogue, she knows how to re-enchant the town, but due to her isolation finds it difficult to share this vision. Two new members of the community, Osélia (Viktor Lazlo) and her troubled son Jacquot, change the situation when the young girl and boy become friends. Osélia, a singer in France, returns to the village to reconcile with her mother, but it is too late because she arrives on the day of her mother's funeral.

Her grief echoes that of others in the village, all of whom are suffering and have retreated to morbid fantasy lives. The shoemaker, who lost his legs in the war, passes his time polishing his boots and waiting for the day when he can wear them once more. The hairdresser is fixated on Marilyn Monroe. The barman is an amateur boxer involved in cockfighting and a fan of African American leaders; he spends his time watching television and waiting to see Mohammed Ali in a fight. There is a raving madman, a fisherman, who refuses to accept that there are no more fish to catch. Nonetheless, Elmire, the guardian of memories remains as a figure of hopeful connection to the past. The children discover a secret grotto with a "Chouval-bwa" (merry-go-round) and decide to make it operational once more. This work of reconstruction involves the entire community. The merry-go-round plays a symbolic role because its repair enables Osélia and the community to work through their grief. According to Chamoiseau and Hayot, the film presents a symbolic contraction of events that took place during the 1960s and 1970s under departmentalization. The reconstruction of the merry-go-round brings the community together, but it does not save the community or prevent Osélia from leaving once more. As with many works during this period, Chamoiseau aims to show the extent to which a simple dream or moment of clairvoyance serves to introduce new perspectives and redirect human lives for the better through an enriched imaginary.

Deslauriers's *Aliker* deals with events from the life of André Aliker (1894–1934), a militant communist and journalist whose life ended in assassination. This is not the first work to deal with this figure: the discovery of his drowned body (with his arms tied behind him) is briefly mentioned in André Breton's *Martinique charmeuse de serpents* and Vincent Placoly wrote a play on the subject, entitled *Mort douloureuse et tragique d'André Aliker* (1969). Aliker came of age during a time when the plantocracy's control over the island extended beyond economic affairs to judiciary and electoral matters. The story details the *békés*' efforts to hold onto their power and shows the powerful role played by the communists who sought to defend the rights of the working class. Aliker's journalistic investigation into the life of Aubéry, a man married to the daughter of Gabriel Hayot (the richest member of the *béké* oligarchy), threatened to expose fraudulent business activities in *Justice*, the journal of the Communist Party. For Chamoiseau, the story is of interest because it calls attention to the nascence of a political consciousness in Martinique, however short-lived, as well as to the role of the Communist Party.[3] With its emphasis on the potential for solidarity, the film might be compared to *Biblique des derniers gestes* in its focus on the potential of a revolutionary imaginary.

Finally, *Encyclomerveille* (2009) is the first in a proposed series of comic books for children and adolescents. Ségur's richly detailed and beautifully coloured illustrations are wonderful examples of visual storytelling in the fantasy mode. The illustrator was born in Martinique, but moved to Paris at an early age where he studied fine arts. He has contributed works to *Casus Belli*, a magazine that specializes in role playing games and simulation. He is perhaps best known for his work with Bruno Chevalier with whom he completed a three-volume heroic fantasy series, entitled *Les légendes des contrées oubliées* (The legends of forgotten lands). In 1997, Ségur published *Le Roi des Méduses* (The King of the Jelly Fish) with writer Igor Szalewa, based on a novel by Pierre Bettencourt. Chamoiseau's and Ségur's first collaborative work, subtitled "L'orphelin de Cocoyer Grands-Bois" ("The Orphan of Cocoyer Grands-Bois"), takes the form of framed narrative told by a scribe about an orphaned child whose parents have been killed by a monster. This tale takes up a number of familiar themes and topics for readers of Chamoiseau's oeuvre. The motif of the threatened orphan who undergoes an initiation and becomes a warrior figure is reminiscent of *Biblique des derniers gestes* and to a lesser extent *Un dimanche au cachot*. However, in the case of *Encyclomerveille*, the young boy is raised by a gravedigger who acts as a mentor to the boy as he confronts various threatening forces via a portal to the underworld of Caribbean history and supernatural folklore. In this respect, the story might be affiliated with *Chronique des sept misères*, which begins in a cemetery, includes dialogues with the dead, and unearths tales of Martinican history when Pipi searches for buried treasure.

The relations between life and death in Caribbean culture are revived and brought to the foreground through the figure of the gravedigger, who is also a "conteur clairvoyant" or a "clairvoyant storyteller" and guide to the underworld of Caribbean folkloric traditions (*Encylo*, 10). This graphic, Caribbean *Bildungsroman* places emphasis on alternative pathways to enlightenment through a tale of initiation that dramatizes the need to confront the nightmares and terrors of personal and collective history. The titular reference to an "enyclomarvel" signals that the reader will gain entry to a world that challenges Enlightenment conceptions of attaining knowledge through a rationalized structure, such as represented by the work of Denis Diderot and D'Alembert. The marvel confounds reason, suggesting an alternative pathway to knowledge. This point is made clear when the clairvoyant gravedigger tells his young apprentice:

> Tu as enfin l'âge d'apprendre certaines choses . . . il existe trios sortes de personnes: les jean sotte qui ne voient que le réel, les jean fol qui ne voient que la merveille, et les initiés qui peuvent atteindre les deux . . .
> Alors sache qu'un bon fossoyeur est toujours un initié, grand ou petit . . .
> (*Encyclo*, 11).

> (You have reached the age to learn certain things . . . there are three kinds of people: the foolish who only see the real, the crazy who only see the marvel, and the initiates who can attain both states . . .
> It's important to know that a good gravedigger is always an initiate, great or small . . .)

The ability to apprehend the real and marvelous is celebrated as the condition of the initiate. While Chamoiseau's story may attempt to do both by using the fantasy genre to interrogate the realities of Martinique, he does so, for the most part, in a poetic way, which suggests that the tale does not fully (at least in this first book) live up to its initiatory claims. The inclusion of Creole language, mobile phones, and village life contribute to the sense of everyday reality on the island. Yet, through its reference to chaos in the world, rifts in time and space, and the creolization of spiritual practices and beliefs, the narrative discloses the continuities of Martinican history through a disruptive spatiotemporal chronicle presented from an otherworldly, visionary perspective. This initiatory tale for children may be seen as a correlative to Chamoiseau's recent novels, *Biblique*, *Un dimanche*, and *Malfini*, all of which focus on alternative pathways to enlightenment.

Biblique des derniers gestes

Richard Watts describes *Biblique des derniers* gestes as a "sprawling novel" that evinces a wide range of concerns and presents a "a cultural history of Martinique, a reflection of gender roles and sexual dimorphism, an impassioned rant against ecological degradation, a treatise on violence, a meditation on memory and its transcription" and an analysis of the malevolent side-effects of departmentalization.[4] This encyclopedic novel traces its history back to the origins of earth with the creative energies of chaos, which serve as the sources for the impulses driving its genesiac course. Epic in scope, the work recounts episodes from the Middle Passage, colonization, anticolonial struggle, and the history of ongoing efforts to decolonize land, bodies, people, and the imaginary. The novel's cosmic protagonist, anticolonial rebel, and warrior, Balthazar Boldule-Jules, appears 15 billion years ago in the cosmos and is twice reborn: first, during the Middle Passage and, second, in colonial times as the son of Manotte (an enslaved woman) and Limorelle Bodule-Jules (a man living in the woods). Pursued by a diabolic sorceress, Yvonette Cléoste, who personifies the all-consuming evil forces associated with imperialism, the hero passes his childhood in the care of Man l'Oubliée, a figure who retreats from history to the world of nature. As an adolescent, he lives with a transgender hero/ine, Déborah-Nicol, and Sarah-Anaïs-Alicia, who teach him about armed struggle and poetry by way of preparation for his adult struggles as a rebel and warrior.

From its farcical opening, which offers a Felliniesque reading of the role of the media and neocolonial flows through Martinique, to the methods of the narrators, which are intuitive and telepathic, the discourse also subverts the very fabric of the narrative. The lives of characters, events, and plotting are intuited, reported, witnessed, and cobbled together in a highly uncertain fashion. In this sense, the novel is very much about the power of the imaginary as a source for revisioning history, places, and solidarities. The gestural work of the novel unfolds through the errant pathways of the narrative that tend to link up history in a rhizomatic fashion that runs counter to the hyperreal versioning of Martinique with which the novel begins. For instance, Balthazar participates in various Third World struggles for liberation. Accounts of these struggles interrupt the tale of his childhood, which is spent in flight from the pursuing evil forces of the sorceress who seeks to destroy him. How the hero travels to these places is never described. Rather, the space of Martinique fades away to the spaces of Third World struggles. These cinematic techniques of cross-cutting and fades serve to associate visually the Martinican rainforest with other sites of anticolonial struggle around the world. In poetic terms, this could be seen as a kind of Poetics of Relation or rain forest rhizomatics, as Lorna Milne has suggested in her reading of the role of the forest in *L'Esclave vieil homme et le molosse*,[5] which prompts the reader to consider the past-present work of solidarity. The rhizomatic outcroppings of anticolonialism are linked through the land:

> Les paysage de l'Indochine rejoignaient ceux de son enfance: arbres à pain, cannes à sucres, manguiers, feuilles à choux, féeries des fougères, lianes, citronniers, mangroves, trombes de rivière, rumeurs de mer, case en paille,

volailles et cochons planches se nouaient sans qu'il s'en aperçoive par-dessus la distance. (*BDG*, 161)

(The landscape of Indochina were similar to those of his childhood, breadfruit trees, sugar cane, mango trees, leaves of cabbage, fairylands of ferns, creepers, lemon trees, mangroves, outpourings of the river, rumors of the sea, straw huts, poultry, and a local species of pigs blended together into the distance.)

Descriptions of anticolonial struggles tend to reinforce the poetics of relation because the narrative deals with the material conditions of struggle in superficial ways and the narrator opts instead to focus on erotic interludes, healing encounters, moments of connection, and spurts of heroism. The focus on the intersubjective encounter and moments of intimacy calls attention to these battles and struggles as momentous events in the history of the collective global imaginary.

Biblique shares thematic and stylistic concerns with *Livret des villes du deuxième monde* (2002). Not only does this short text offer an expanded explanation of the principles of the imaginary outlined in *Biblique* but it also demonstrates *en miniature* the dynamics of the novel. With its tale of a found manuscript, descriptions of imagined cities, and metatextual playfulness, this short text has the kind of mystical effect of a work by Jorge Borges and bears a certain resemblance to Italo Calvino's *Invisible Cities*. Chamoiseau's *Livret* consists of an "Envoi" in which the narrator presents the tale of a found manuscript, followed by the "Livret" proper. The latter is subdivided into sections called "Circulations," which evoke diurnal, resurrective, and cosmic cycles: "Circulations 1—Solaires," "Circulations 2—Nocturne," "Ciculations 3—Néant," and "Circulations 4—Recommencements." The motif of wandering and circulation is evident in the opening line of the text: "Ce livret a été retrouvé dans les affaires d'un errant. Qui était-il? Nul ne peut le dire. D'où provenait-il et où s'en allait-il? Personne ne peut en raison le savoir" (*LDM*, 13) ("This logbook was discovered among the affairs of a wanderer. Who was he? No one can say. Where did he come from and where was he going? No one can really know"). The uncertain origins and course of the wanderer raise questions that extend beyond the exploration of places to concerns about temporality.

This bible of cities the voyager traversed (*LDM*, 14) follows its own migration course throughout the world. Initially, it is found in a port in

Bangkok alongside a worn pair of boots, weapons, a broken-down gun, an old map of the world, books of poetry, and fetid rags that attest to the sweat of incessant wandering. Passing through the hands of several others, the narrator inherits the book, which he discovers in a trunk alongside an Armenian bible and photos. The *Livret* is presented as the result of the narrator's transcription of the original, which is a *bris-collage* of skins, pieces of cardboard, pulverized rock, bits of tires, small fibers of old vegetation, and tiny strips of plastic. This mixture of natural and man-made objects constitutes a "bible of the cities" he traversed, glimpsed, or believed himself to see (*LDM*, 14). The book was written using monastic ink and when that failed turning to concoctions of asphalt, ketchup, oil, and multicolored powders from posters (*LDM*, 14). As described, the original text, which might be confused for a work of art, resembles the assemblage work of Serge Hélénon.

The translator's work and the wanderer's quest for a *deuxième monde* or "second world" underscore the importance of the imaginary. For the translator, the work is one of transposing the materiality of the work as well as its transgressive energies into something readable. According to the translator, the writing reflects the voyager's experience of the turmoil of time when the past pours into the future or the future returns to the past (*LDM*, 15). The slow recursions of time are experienced as an ending that opens up a recommencement so that a spiraling dynamic takes place. Cities become points of focalization for this sense of time as between all possible pasts and futures, all the orders and disorders of the mutating world (*LDM*, 16). The physicality of wandering and the motions of the text are doubles for an apprehension of the mutability of time and the world. Consequently, the errant figure and author of the notebook is depicted as a kind of poet-soothsayer or augurer without a successor (*LDM*, 13).

The pattern of illumination, darkness, void, and recommencement suggests the passing of two days and the possibility of a kind of resurrection on the third as the second world recovers a vital connection to the earth. Whereas the circulations of "Solaire" and "Recommencement" explore these vital connections, circulations in "Nocturne" and "Néant" ("Void") present the dark side of the city and offer examples of the pursuant forces that threaten to destroy human communities in ways far more mundane than the events chronicled in histories of colonization and imperialism. The banality of evil is manifest in misery, regression, the loss of the sacred, the selfish pursuit of bodily pleasures, and the solitariness and solipsism of cities that promote a superficial view of living together. These cities without oxygen (*LDM*, 43) have forgotten the connection to the earth (*LDM*, 45). If the nocturne is marked by an absence, the void is present in the dead city, which is forgotten or abandoned (*LDM*, 46). Such cities offer little in the way of community or the ideal of the agora as a space of communication (*LDM*, 48). Drugs, violence, ghettos, and other symptoms of the malign are evident in these deadened places. Interestingly, such cities also seem to be the result of a world where imperialism is latent or manifest in the opposition of two extremes: forces of centralization and marginalization (the rejection of the world and the acceptance of the periphery) acting in opposition toward one another (*LDM*, 56).

By contrast, the second world offers a regenerative perspective through relational modes of interaction, which is associated with the genesiac principle evident in the idea of the city as a space of encounters, contacts, and exchanges (*LDM*, 24). The second world is not necessarily an urban space, but it can be seen in the idea of a social organism in flux, responsive to flows and times (*LDM*, 17, 24). The description of cities as representing a new kind of vital body or social organization warrants particular attention because of its relevance to the organizing principles at work in *Biblique*'s depiction of social relations:

> Ces villes n'étaient pas des territoires. C'étaient des sociétés. Elles inscrivaient le mouvement même du monde dans la chair même des hommes, jusqu'à en souligner un sens renouvelé. Mais elles projetaient aussi dans le monde leurs désirs et leurs rêves: imaginaires retravaillés des hommes. C'est pourquoi toute ville accueille le souffle du monde, et que toute ville souffle sur le monde. (*LDM*, 34)

> (These cities were not territories. They were societies. They inscribed the very movement of the world in the very flesh of men, foregrounding a renewed sense of both. But they also project their desires and their dreams into the world: reworked imaginaries of men. This is why every city receives the breath of the world and every city breathes out into the world.)

Chamoiseau's rain forest in *Biblique* plays a similar role and the ecological function of the rain forest as the lungs of the island tends to underscore this respiratory role in the local and global imaginary. The notion that the city should live with the earth ("*vivre-avec-la terre*") is further amplified through the rain forest as a space that is constituted at the interfaces of society and nature in *Biblique* (*LDM*, 34). In "Recommencements," the Poetics of Relation are affirmed as the basis for an ideal city, the metacity that is confronted with the kinds of flows and circulations associated with globalization (*LDM*, 68). By placing emphasis on the exchange of peoples and cultures rather than the economic and market flows, Chamoiseau evokes a second world order in which the global presents not only risks but also opportunities for the enrichment of the collective imaginary.

Chamoiseau takes a geo-poetical perspective, which seeks to renew the city and society through a connection to the earth and its history. This organic approach, attentive to the earth as an ecosystem, represents an alternative to the free-market model for social organization. This alternative is represented in the alternative opening to the real-world situation of Martinique where the biblical flooding of the world is no longer represented as a divine intervention or natural disaster but as the *deus ex machina*(tions) of departmental interventions on the island. In *Biblique*, Chamoiseau rewrites the genesis of the world through a return to chaos as the space-time continuum that initiates a new world vision. The beginning of the novel with its multiple genesis stories calls attention to the global concerns of the novel. By invoking creation, the narrative undermines the logic whereby nature is socially and culturally constructed and calls attention to the nonhuman environment as a framing device and witness to culture.

To date, the most compelling readings of *Biblique* call attention to the ecocritical context, particularly with respect to the role of water and orchids as exemplary of the structuring logic of the narrative. Watts argues for the fluidity of the text in its "water poetics" that blend the historical record and authorial intervention.[6] His interpretation of the orchids as "figures for an intermediate point between root and rhizome or between complete immobility and total dissemination"[7] is particularly well argued in the context of Chamoiseau's concerns with the flows between local culture and global solidarities. Heidi Bjosen argues that the "narrator's rapport with orchids becomes an emblem of co-existence with Nature as an Other whom you may not fathom, but with whom you can still communicate."[8] Similarly, Michael Niblett argues that *Biblique* dramatizes "the inseparability of the political and the ecological"[9] and suggests that the land is a "crucial repository of collective memory."[10] Niblett's analysis of the imbrication of Balthazar's body with the natural world as a reorientation toward the landscape is particularly compelling. He notes connections to creolized spiritual practices, such as *vodou*, that entail degradation followed by integration into the community and sees the grotesque, libidinal bodily processes of initiation into the community as a parallel to the forest section's evocation of a mythic worldview.[11] Together, these ecocritical readings underscore the initiatory aspects of the novel as well as the geo-poetics at work in the text.

Ecocritical perspectives call attention to the ethical dimensions of the narrative and the ways in which relations to the earth suggest new dimensions for human relations, whether in the form of "amour-grand," anti-imperial affiliations around the world, or a renewed participation in the local community. In "Distancing, Determining," Glissant emphasizes the need for ecological visions of Relation that foreground the interrelations and interdependence of "all lands, of the whole earth."[12] This global perspective suggests metonymic relations, and we can see Balthazar's connection to the rain forest in various nations and his ability to absorb himself into the trees as instances of his global perspective, which is grounded in an awareness of what Jana Evans Braziel refers to as a "poetics of (eco-)relation" as a way of rethinking ecocritical relations of nature and culture, land and sea, and among mineral, vegetal, animal, and human.[13]

Among the ways to account for this initiatory patterning and its operations throughout the narrative, the role of guerrilla poetics, creolized spiritual practices, and epic are particularly important as trajectories entangled in the criss-crossing processes of the discourse. In this respect, the novel operates according to the principles of the *émerveille*, but moves beyond the interaction of Creole storytelling and European fairytales to invoke a more complex textual ground of marvelous encounters. The novel unfolds through "guerrilla poetics" or sieges on history as various incidents in the history of Third World struggles for liberation are brought together through the presence of Balthazar, the global freedom fighter. Balthazar's role is very much like that of the Warrior of the Imaginary present in *Écrire* whose initiatory presence serves to evoke a new field of combat for the narrator. However, in this case, the narrator's initiation follows the story of Balthazar's conversion from rebel to warrior. Initially, Balthazar is presented as an antimodern, irrelevant figure:

> le grand indépendantiste n'était même plus notre mauvaise conscience: nous n'avions plus besoin du juvénile de sa révolte ni même d'illusions (confirmées sans issue) de sa lucidité. (*BDG*, 27)

> (the great independent was no longer even our bad conscience: we no longer had need of either his juvenile revolt or even illusions [confirmed dead-ends] of his lucidity.)

Nonetheless, for some he becomes a figure for reflection and discussion, a "vague silencieuse" (*BDG*, 28) or a silent wave of underground consciousness and an antenna receptor for the collective shadow (*BDG*, 29). Balthazar is associated with that which surges underneath official indifference in the form of the voice of the conch shell that resounds on its own (*BDG*, 46).

Intrigued by the story of the dying hero, the journalist joins those who attend the warrior in his final days. Gazing at this figure, the reporter recounts the epic life of the hero from the chaos of the world to the present. The story of this hero is intuited from his gestures by a narrator who gives him life. Although the narrator claims to have done research and report tales told by others, this meditation is consciously grounded as an act of the imagination, a kind of *marronage*. The narrator observes:

> Plus qu'à un homme, j'étais confronté à un système ouvert. Une interaction de faits, d'événements, de sensations, de paroles, de gestes, dont l'architecture était mouvante, incertaine, modifiable par l'irruption d'un élément nouveau qui mettait en relief une composante ancienne. (*BDG*, 692)

> (I was confronted with an open system rather than a man. An interaction of facts, events, sensations, spoken words, gestures, the architecture of which was in motion, uncertain, modified by the eruption of a new element that called attention to an ancient composition.)

With this epiphany, the narrator is described as becoming a combatant in the adventure. He is no longer the *Marqueur de paroles*, but a *guerrier* or Warrior in the field of battle where the overall perspective is nonexistent and the end improbable (*BDG*, 692). The narrative is represented as a clairvoyant apprehension of multiple, entangled voices. Events records are the uncertain product of reports, sympathetic intuition, and witnessing. The warrior's adventures become the basis for locating an alternative vision of the global imaginary, which is grounded in an alternative recounting of historical flows through the island. Faith and certainty are replaced by incertitude and moments of poetic clairvoyance.

This epic counternarrative returns to chaos and traces events up to the twenty-first century. The reporter recounts the warrior's numerous struggles for liberation in the Third World, using the hero's childhood wanderings in the rain forest of Martinique as the point of departure for a series of narrative flashbacks or raids on revolutionary history. With its celebration of heroic figures, such as Frantz Fanon, Malcolm X, Che Guevara, Patrick Lumumba, Ho Chi Minh, and other twentieth-century political activists and radicals, the novel can be seen as continuing the unfinished epic of Black Power set out by Stokely Carmichael and Charles Hamilton. In *Black Power: The Politics of Liberation in America*, the authors argue that "Black Power means that black people see themselves as part of a new force, sometimes called the 'Third World'; that we see our struggles as closely related to liberation struggles around the world."[14] In a sense, the novel can be seen as counter-historical for it situates Martinique in a history of armed resistance and political radicalism that serves as an antidote to departmentalization as it unfolded in the 1950s and 1960s.

In taking up the concerns of Third World solidarity and Black Power, the narrative aspires to a Glissantian Poetics of Relation in which each and every identity is extended through the other. Glissant offers the example of Fanon, one that seems particularly appropriate given Chamoiseau's interest in Fanon as a historical figure as well as Fanonian thought in *Biblique*. However, it is not simply a matter of displacement and return but also of bringing thoughts of others into new networks of thinking and imagining the world. In "The Relative and Chaos," Glissant's explanation of what he means by the turbulence of Relation serves to clarify this point:

> Is it meaningful, pathetic, or ridiculous that Chinese students have been massacred in front of a cardboard reproduction of the Statue of Liberty? Or that in a Romanian house, hated portraits of Ceauşescu have been replaced by photographs cut from magazines of characters in the television series "Dallas"? Simply to ask the question is to imagine the unimaginable turbulence of Relation.[15]

Through the interventions of Balthazar in Third World struggles, Chamoiseau's novelistic discourse is infused with such rhizomatic upcroppings of the resistant imaginary.

Various manifestations of love are presented throughout the story, including the erotic, maternal, fraternal, platonic, sacred, and revolutionary.[16] Rather than historic battles, the novel focuses on the 727 loves of Balthazar and projects its tales of colonial, anticolonial, and decolonial struggles from childhood through to old age. Balthazar's life story functions as a symbolic correlative to collective history as the Martinican self is born in the Middle Passage and reborn through the plantation experience. The story of this culture's neglected childhood is linked to other stories of anticolonial struggle. Erotic and revolutionary ideals of love intersect in ways that resemble the views espoused by Ernesto Che Guevara when he affirms, "Let me say, at the risk of seeming ridiculous, that the true revolutionary is guided by great feelings of love" ("Socialism and the New Man"). Like Guevara, Balthazar's interventions are ambiguous, representing an admixture of benevolence, romantic impulses, self-interest, and lust. More than halfway through the novel, the narrator's over identification with Balthazar as an idealized lover is deflated through the interventions of his adoptive mother figure. Through the presence of Man l'Oubliée, Balthazar learns that he is guilty of a cannibalistic forms of love (*amours-cannibales*) "où il avait tout pris: pris l'esprit et le corps, pris l'odeur et le jeu des regards" (*BDG*, 459) ("where he took everything: took the spirit and the body, took the smell and the play of glances"). In this respect, he shares much in common with Anatole France's Balthasar to whom the star speaks because the man has conquered his lust.[17]

Through his encounters, interactions and exchanges with women, Balthazar learns that sacred, revolutionary, and profane forms of love are entangled. In the essay "Uses of the Erotic: The Erotic as Power," Audre Lorde defines the celebration of the erotic as life affirming:

> The very word *erotic* comes from the Greek word *eros*, the personification of love in all its aspects—born of Chaos, and personifying creative power and harmony. When I speak of the erotic, then, I speak of it as an assertion of the lifeforce of women; of that creative energy empowered, the knowledge and use of which we are now reclaiming in our language, our history, our dancing, our loving, our work, our lives.[18]

Lorde's affiliation of the erotic with women is particularly useful in terms of negotiating Balthazar's transformation from a kind of Don Juan lover of women into a transgender understanding of his own identity, negotiated through communion with women and the transformative power of the erotic.

Man l'Oubliée's multivalent presence in the narrative is particularly significant because she brings together discourses of history and healing through her role as a historical character, a midwife, and a healer named Anne-Clémire. She comes to represent symbolically the forgotten histories of Martinique as well as the need to heal the land and its people through a reconnection to its spiritual sensibilities.[19] Her role as a psychiatric presence and midwife of history is particularly important in this reparative process. In the section titled "Oeuvre et Malédiction," the narrator presents a series of cases that serve to explore embodied histories. Referring to pregnancy as being "en-situation," the narrator refers to the woman's liminal situation between life and death. No longer simply a woman and not yet a mother, she is peopled by a double life. The infant as inhabitant is an ambiguous force, but also one presented as constrained by history. The infant under colonization often threatens the life of the mother and finds its own life threatened by abortion (BDG, 409). When slavery comes to an end, the child who threatens to abort is convinced to remount inside the mother and wait until the full term of pregnancy because Man l'Oubliée tells the infant that the malediction is no longer present and that it is worth trying to live as master of one's own body (BDG, 413). When asked what the malediction might be, she responds with the Creole words "L'estravay, malédisyon fondalnatal" (BDG, 413), which translates as "Slavery: a fundamental malediction." Significantly, the Creole word "fondalnatal" carries the word for birth inside of it. The word "fundamental," already pregnant with meaning, is contained inside the situation of slavery as a kind of analogy to the pregnant woman who is "en-situation." This word play suggests that history of slavery bears its own ambivalent children.

The body as a site of memory is subject to excavation. As a healer, Man l'Oubliée diagnoses the relations between bodily illness and sites of colonial trauma, uncovering repressed memories in order to bring about the recovery of the land and its peoples. When a child named Ti-Roche (Little Rock) falls sick and appears to be dying after nestling against a rock located on a particular sloping hill, the mother goes to investigate the place and comes back with a sense of suffocation, red eyes, and a bitter taste in her throat (BDG, 433). The reason for this horror and illness is explained because this is a terrible place of memory dating back to slavery when the planter would place recalcitrant slaves in an oak barrel whose interior was spiked with nails (BDG, 433). The barrel was pushed down the slope into the river where the unfortunate person inside would be devoured by the nails (BDG, 433). The tortured souls of seven generations of people who underwent this punishment irrigate the slope with their sorrows. Not knowing where to find justice, they inhabit the space and spread the malediction, which infects the body of Ti-Roche. Taking the form of a "Blesse," the child is victim to a disease that rots the body from the inside (BDG, 434). Man l'Oubliée uses her healing knowledge to restore the child, but in other cases the purification of malevolent places of memory suffices to bring about recovery, such as when she honors the victims of a former dungeon (BDG, 443). Elsewhere, Balthazar imitates these gestures of memory (geste de mémoire) when he encounters similar cases in Indochina, the Congo, and the Americas (BDG, 435–36) as well as following the death of Maurice Bishop in Grenada (BDG, 443). Thus, he bears witness to shared sufferings and finds that the gestures of memory provide healing forces in the face of all kinds of imperial maledictions.

These narratives resemble the form of the Creole story, which often features a malevolent force that threatens to consume or destroy the individual, but transform historic and contemporary acts of violence into illnesses that trouble the bodies and minds. Man L'Oubliée's role as a healer is an interesting one for she does not heal her patients through magic so much as a kind of literal or symbolic act psychiatric care. In *Wretched of the Earth*, Fanon's analysis of violence and decolonization is particularly relevant in terms of a narrative model. He observes that public and political acts of violence are often internalized or domesticated as individuals and families come to experience the somatic ill effects of history. The doctor's ability to reconstruct narrative history plays a powerful role in the reparative process as the individual seeks to mend the fractured consciousness through the recovery of memory or a personal reconciliation of how public acts violence intersect with the domestic, the romantic, and the internal dynamics of selfhood. In this context, Man l'Oubliée and her apprentice, Balthazar, function as psychiatrists and their juxtaposed stories can be seen as a creolized narrative response to Fanon. Their narrative presence demonstrates that it is by "living on the borderline of history and language, on the limits of race and gender, that we are in a position to translate the differences between them into a kind of solidarity."[20]

Chamoiseau's reworking of epic as a source to be creolized alongside other genres of storytelling informs his critique of imperialism from conquest and colonization to the new imperialism associated with globalization. Despite the novel's focus on Balthazar Bodule-Jules, a heroic figure of defiance and a freedom fighter in Third World struggles around the world, this is an epic that does not celebrate victory or conquest. Rather, this epic of defeat sets out fruitful ground for a different kind of heroic battle that focuses on the decolonization of the imaginary and the quest for a space of autonomy in face of conquest. The spiritual dimensions of epic play a significant role as the narrative shifts from the terrain of violent combat to the space of imagined solidarities, which are negotiated through a narrative that examines the psychiatric effects of colonization/decolonization, the role of romance as a force that subverts the impulse to imperial conquest, and the creative reworking of *vodou* as a spiritual practice that calls attention to a new kind of kinship relation as the basis for locally related solidarities around the world.

The cycles of flight and violence struggle come to an end when Balthazar confronts L'Yvonnette Cléoste in a new kind of spiritual combat:

> Mon esprit se déchira sur une révélation . . .
> Il allait la combattre et l'anéantir, mais pas avec violence coutumière. Il allait vers elle avec une arme autrement plus puissante que je n'étais pas capable de définir." (BDG, 772)

> (My spirit was wrenched apart by a revelation . . .
> He was going to combat and annihilate her, but not with customary violence. He went toward her with another kind of more powerful weapon that I was not capable of defining.)

Unlike the Bible, the outcome of this final battle is not apocalyptic: the world does not end, but undergoes a pacific transformation as the source of evil disappears. The hero, whose aura reminds the narrator of what Sarah-Anaïs-Alicia must have been like, vanquishes the evil sorceress with his gaze. Consequently, the narrator recognizes that Balthazar is much more than simply a rebel; he is a great warrior.

In this moment of apotheosis, Balthazar conquers his enemy and is reborn spiritually through the infusion of Sarah-Anaïs-Alicia's aura. This description reinforces the importance of *vodou* as a structuring principle of the novel and source of power in the form of spiritual resistance. A closer look at the hyphenated names of the characters of Balthazar Bodule-Jules, Deborah-Nicholas, and Sarah-Anaïs is useful for it points to the ways in which novel encodes hermeneutic clues.[21] All of these names are in some way associated with the creolized spiritual traditions of Vodou and Catholicism, particularly as they pertain to the presence of the sacred child. Balthazar, the name of one of the magi, is related to the concept of paying homage to Christ. Deborah refers to the tradition of the woman warrior in the Old Testament, but also refers to Nicholas, the patron saint of children in the Catholic tradition, and counterpart to the Vodou figure who is father of the Marasa (sacred twins). Anaïs is a sacred child of Erzulie, a *lwa* who is sometimes depicted as the Black Madonna holding an infant in her arms. This intermixing of sacred images reinforces the slippery associations and intermixings of Catholicism and *vodou*.

The use of *vodou* functions as a poetic gesture toward the sacred as part of Chamoiseau's project for remapping the imagined Martinican as a space of resistance. This gesture is similar to the rhizomatic linkages to Third World resistance and Black Power. In this sense, the turn toward a syncretic religious practice, rather than the Christian perspective, suggests the need to recover a creolized spiritual tradition. Creolized spiritual practices enact and infuse acts of imperial resistance (i.e., the importance of *vodou* for the Haitian revolution). The hyphenation of names suggests that these characters are associated with certain *lwas* and certainly characters such as Sarah and Sarah-Anaïs-Alicia seem to be involved in *vodou* practices as they use mirrors to communicate with the spirits. The idea of marriage to the spirits could also explain the fixation on the other world. Rather than a retreat from the real, such characters are profoundly engaged in a religious life. Following the death of her mother, Anaïs-Alicia takes on the longer name that includes that of her mother because she is involved in a relationship to the spirits and to her mother through ancestor worship.

An understanding of *quimbois* and *vodou* helps to explain Balthazar's association with the waters, the forest, and the crossroads with other spheres of resistance, such as the animistic belief in the rain forest as a site of transformative power. As a child, he participates in *quimbois* practices when he undergoes the "bain de la chance," which is intended to bring good luck and restore balance. Balthazar's name affiliates him with the Magi. The Wise Men are related to the *vodou* presence of Simbi. The term "Simbi" originates in West African religion where it refers to water spirits; this belief also informs vodouism. In *vodou*, the Simbi is manifest in several forms, including Simbi Trois Kafou (relating to "trios carrefours" as three intersections), Simbi Dlo (relating to "de l'eau" or water), Simbi Bwa (relating to the "bois" or woods) and Simbi Yandé-Zo or Andezo (meaning "of two waters"), Simbi Anpaka (of plants, leaves and poisons), and Simbi Makaya (magician or sorcerer). In the contemporary world, Simbi is associated with communication, including the Internet and communications at the speed of light, electricity, and nerve impulses. Balthazar brings together these diverse manifestations in his many struggles for resistance and various incarnations throughout the narrative.

Reference to *vodou* explains the final moment of possession or the meaning of the "biblique des derniers gestes" in which Balthazar appears to be possessed by the spirit of Sarah-Anaïs-Alicia (*BDG*, 772). Just as the *lwas* or ancestors can possess the worshiper, this moment of spiritual communion empowers him to take on the role of the sacred child and transgender warrior who is neither male nor female but a third self. Through communion with the ancestors, ordinary life achieves a measure of transcendence. In this respect, the final gesture of the novel is toward the completion of an initiation ritual into a special state called "konesans" ("connaissance" or "knowledge") that includes rituals of openness to communication with the *lwas* and ancestral spirits.[22] This patterning of *vodou* communion with spirits and ancestors may be extended to the pantheon of Third World resistance heroes who appear before the final confrontation. This spiritual revelation intersects with the epic tradition of a parade of heroes, such as appears in the *Aeneid* in Book Six. Whereas epic celebrates the genealogies of "son of so and so," Chamoiseau's epic celebrates the genealogies of affiliation and solidarity through the Poetics of Relation in which each and every identity is extended through the other. Rather than temporal lineages, the narrative discloses a world of anti-imperial struggles as an expansive rhizomatic network that mirrors the earlier configuration of the Martinican landscape.

Like the Bible, *Biblique* offers a myth extending over time and space, over invisible and visible orders of reality. Unlike the Bible, this sacred text is affiliated with uncertainty, creolized spiritual beliefs and practices, the Glissantian myth of chaos, and the Poetics of Relation. The initiatory structure of the narrative unfolds from the textual power of writing/marking/sounding/embodying as a sacred gesture enacted through multiple rituals and processes of affiliation and transformation. Rather than a model of resurrection, Chamoiseau tells a story of expanding apprehension as Balthazar comes to a fuller understanding of himself and his place in the world through creolized spiritual practices and moments of relation. Poetic moments of illumination, visions of love, and epiphanies of nature serve to communicate the sublime aspects of this invisible world order while conflict, resistance, and combat prove means of attaining some degree of autonomy in the visible world. Chamoiseau's novel embodies a "guerilla poetics" that calls attention to the psychic, bodily, and emotional terrain of decolonization. The story of Balthazar, the literal guerilla warrior who takes cover in the land and attacks the colonizer, provides a model for a metaphorical guerilla poetics that is not so much an attack of colonialism as it is a mode for conceptualizing postcolonial relations and new kinds of solidarities.

Through Balthazar's raids on global history, the novel opens up what Homi K. Bhabha refers to as a third space of enunciation, a hybrid vision of local and global postcolonial histories.[23] Through multiple points of connection and linkage among the cultural, geographical, and imagined spaces of Martinique, the text operates as a rhizomatic discourse through which the various anticolonial uprisings can be seen in relation and solidarity. The text gestures toward the missed opportunities and the need for activism. Balthazar's lament gestures toward the failures, shortcomings, and disappointments of independence movements. This lament is worth quoting in full for it evokes the kind of postcolonial solidarity that remains as a potentially powerful source for contemporary global postcoloniality:

> Il eut un sursaut belliqueux et se mit à regretter, une fois encore, de ne s'être pas mieux opposé à l'extermination des Black Panthers, de n'avoir pas vu mourir Malcom X, d'être arrivé trop tard pour le Che ou pour Maurice Bishop . . . Il pensa à ces milliers de peuples qui se battaient dan l'ombre et qu'il avait ignorés, qu'il n'avait pas tenté ou pu rejoindre dans leur combat. Je n'ai rien fait pour les Pygmées. Je n'ai rien fait pour les aborigènes d'Australie, les Indiens de Guyane, les Inuits, les Peuls, les Tsiganes. [. . .] Pas assez nègre en Afrique du Sud. Pas assez musulman en Europe. Pas

assez haïtien à Saint-Domingue. Pas assez tibétain en Chine. Pas assez bosniaque en Serbie. [. . .] Pas assez gay à San Francisco. Pas assez paysan face au béton désertifiant des villes. Pas assez chômeur dans cette merde liberale. Pas assez femme un peu partout. (*BDG*, 734)

(He felt a sudden bellicose fit and began to regret, once again, that he had not been more effectively opposed to the extermination of the Black Panthers, that he did not see Malcom X die, that he had arrived too late to help Che or Maurice Bishop . . . He thought of the thousands of peoples who battled in the shadows and of whom he knew nothing, who he did not attempt to help or couldn't join in their combat. I did nothing for the Pygmies. I did nothing for the Aboriginals of Australia, the Indians in Guyana, the Inuits, the Peuls, the Tziagnes. [. . .] Not enough black in South Africa. Not enough muslim in Europe. Not enough Haitian in Saint Domingo. Not enough Tibetan in China. Not enough Bosnian in Serbia. [. . .] Not enough gay in San Francisco. Not enough of a countryman in face of the cement transforming cities into deserts. Not enough unemployed in this liberal shit. Not enough woman a bit everywhere.)

Exhausted by the fallout of imperialism and the disappointments of Third World radicalism, this tireless figure offers a vision of solidarities negotiated via the local struggles for decolonization and revolts against oppression of all kinds.

Through digression, multiplication of perspectives, linguistic excess, and amplitude, the novel exhausts its own energies and depletes its own resources, providing a fitting poetic correlative to the life of the hero who succumbs to old age and resigns himself to a world where globalization is the new imperialism. This shift is evident as Balthazar looks back on his life and considers how the battlefield has shifted from one of open resistance and violent confrontation to something more subtle and more difficult to pinpoint. The description of Balthazar's responses to the contemporary world order sound very much like the sentiments of an antiglobalization protester:

Il voyait grandir la puissance mafieuse des médias. Il voyait la connaissance scientifique se transformer en arme. Il voyait les technologies neuves se concentrer en mains prédatrices. Il devinait un peu partout des organisations sans visage est sans âme, sans drapeau et sans dieu, qui fructifiaient dans le brouillard des hautes finances. De nouveaux conquérants déployaient leurs griffes cybernétiques dans les espaces du monde. (BDG, 734)

(He saw the mafia-like power of the media expand. He saw scientific knowledge become a weapon. He saw new technologies concentrated in the hands of the predatory. He caught glimpses of organizations everywhere without a face or soul, without a flag and without a god, which profited from the confusion of high finance. New conquerors deployed their cybernetic claws in the spaces of the world.)

The narrator goes on to observe that Balthazar is a witness to disembodied forces that traverse the world like barbarian hordes in order to take advantage of peoples who cannot perceive fully what is taking place (BDG, 734). These forces inhabit the spirits and desires and dominate not only nations or races but also the hundreds of millions of people who consume their products (BDG, 734).

Fanon suggests that decolonization represents the meeting of "two forces, opposed to each other," namely the colonizer and the colonized, which entails the substitution of one species of men for another. Chamoiseau's analysis of globalization sees a comparable opposition between the faceless, dehumanizing forces of commoditization and the individual.[24] While decolonization aims to turn the thing which has been colonized into someone human through the process of self-liberation, globalization can threaten to return the human to a thing-like status.[25] The situation is all the more complex when the processes of decolonization remain incomplete so that overlapping forms of dehumanization coexist or intersect in certain instances. While Balthazar wants to combat these forces in battle, he ends his life in a retreat to a world of poetic vision in touch with memory and nature. Whatever his failures as a rebel, he opens the way for the Warrior of the Imaginary, a figure whose terrain of battle is no longer than of anti-imperial struggle but of psychic decolonization through a Poetics of Relation or the ways in which "each and every identity is extended through a relationship with the Other."[26]

The novel torques the epic tradition and takes the form of what David Quint refers to as the epic of the vanquished. In *Epic and Empire*, Quint observes that "epic draws an equation between power and narrative."[27] When related to the narrative of empire and conquest, epic is seen as a form that shows how all of experience can be assimilated into a pattern in which everything makes sense and interconnects into a meaningful whole. However, epic can also show a tendency to dissolution or narrative wandering when the narrative is one of defeat rather than victory. In postcolonial epic works, such as Salman Rushdie's *Midnight's Children*, Derek Walcott's *Omeros*, or Gabriel Garcia Marquez's *One Hundred Years of Solitude*, epic plays a far more unsettling role, often dissolving into counter-epic or anti-epic as ideologies of the nation collapse. In such works, epic does not follow the linear teleology associated with conquest, but the losers' form of epic, which is affiliated with romance and its "random or circular wandering."[28] Quint argues that the victors "experience history as a coherent end-directed story told by their own power" while the losers "experience a contingency that they are powerless to shape to their own ends."[29]

Where Quint explores epic in relation to romance, Glissant takes up the idea of epic in relation to tragedy. In "Expanse and Filiation," he suggests that tragedy ensues when the epic sense of filiation, legitimacy, or community consent is threatened.[30] By contrast, he suggests that a "modern epic and a modern tragedy would offer to unite the specificity of nations, granting each culture's opacity (though no longer as *en-soi*) yet at the same time imagining the transparency of their relations."[31] Modern tragedy continues to fulfill its revelatory function, but places emphasis on the tragedy of expansion (related to empire and the effacement of the other). In this instance, a sacrifice of a victim-hero is no longer required. Instead, the hero helps the reader to see the world as a web of relations, "pondering it together and recognizing ourselves side by side within it."[32] Rather than imperial expansion, the modern epic celebrates the expanse of the world. Glissant's affirmation that the "the sacred is of us, of this network, of our wandering, our errantry"[33] can be seen in the context of Chamoiseau's narrative structure, in which the epic hero's wandering is redoubled through the discursive space of errant storytelling and circuitous reading processes.

Balthazar, the epic hero, spends his time reminiscing about loves, re-reading love letters and Saint-John Perse's poetry. These literary references give us a clue as to the tensions between romance and epic that inform the novel and are played out in the hero's life. In particular, Perse's *Anabase* is worth noting as an epic influence that Chamoiseau describes as follows:

Anabase. Je n'y vois pas une épopée de la colonisation, même s'il en a les accents qui auraient aimé vos pères, et les mêmes ingrédients. *Anabase* épelle ce que vous croyez être la grandeur: la projection sur le monde; l'extension à l'infini de sa propre légitimité; l'énergie précieuse de la violence; la tentative d'organiser et de dominer les hommes et le monde; la solitude agissante dans une foule bien accordée aux ampleurs d'un projet. Mais tout cela sera traversé par le doute, habité d'une errance qui cherchera à dénombrer tout le Divers du monde. C'est le monde tout entier qui deviendra, pour votre conqérant-poète, le matériau d'un inventaire. Mais, malgré ce doute et cette errance, il restera conquistador.[34]

(*Anabasis*. I do not see an epic of colonization, even if there are accents that your fathers would have loved and the same ingredients. *Anabasis* spells out that which you believe is grandeur: the projection on the world, the infinite extension of its own legitimacy, the precious energy of violence, the effort to organize and dominate men and the world, the active solitude of a crowd that is finely in tune with the scope of a project. But all of this is interlaced with doubt, inhabited by an errantry that seeks to enumerate all the Diversity of the world. It is the world in its entirety that becomes, for your conquering poet, the material of an inventory. But despite this doubt and this errantry, he remains a conquistador.)

Chamoiseau's reference to Perse demonstrates his keen awareness of the relations between imperial power and narrative structure in the epic tradition. Despite the imperial content of the plotting and the attitude of the conqueror-poet, he sees in Perse indications of doubt and wandering, which subvert the imperial impulse in the quest for the diversity of the world. In a reading that owes much to Glissant's "A Rooted Errantry," Chamoiseau argues that Perse's epic is imperial on account of Perse's (as opposed to the conqueror-poet of the poem) need to govern, which manifests itself in sumptuous verse as a means toward a unity of being. The encyclopedic effort to describe the world is its own kind of imperial epic. For this reason, we can see Chamoiseau's decision to write an uncertain, impossible narrative in which the ground is constantly shifting as a refusal to describe and map the world. Instead, the world is seen in its whirling motions and relations. The rain forest relates to the rest of the world. Like a portal, it opens up other relations to the local through affiliated loves, intertwined histories and a network of anti-imperial encounters.

CHAPTER EIGHT

Activism and Tales of Initiation

Chamoiseau's role as an educator, investigative writer, and activist has come to shape not only his political writings but also, in a more diffuse way, his approach to narrative. Chamoiseau's contributions to *Quand les murs tombent: L'identité nationale hors-la-loi? (When the Walls Fall: National Identity Outside the Law?)* (2007), *L'Intraitable beauté du monde: Adresse à Barack Obama (The Unrelenting Beauty of the World: Address to Barack Obama)* (2009), and *Manifeste pour les "produits" de haute nécessité (Manifesto on "Products" of High Necessity)*[1] (2009) offer clearly articulated perspectives on migration, globalization, food production, and the relevance of relational thinking in a changing world order. These literary manifestos belong to a long tradition in French letters, whether we think of the politically oriented writings of the Enlightenment philosophers or the twentieth-century tradition of manifestos so characteristic of literary modernism, particularly of surrealism and existentialism, and, in a Martinican context, the work of Césaire and Fanon.[2] Chamoiseau's manifestos are reflective of a desire to extend the nascent postcolonial work of earlier generations; they are part of the writer's effort to revive and renew the anticolonial moment of solidarity in a contemporary context, such as already found in *Biblique*. The aforementioned treatises to which Chamoiseau has contributed tend to extend Glissantian philosophical concepts to the public domain of social action while his narratives can be seen as offering a more abstract incarnation of his poetico-political concerns about the environment and the world. This chapter begins with an account of the author's activist concerns and then turns to readings of the tales of initiation and alternative paths to enlightenment as represented in *Un dimanche* and *Malfini*.

The Activist as Collaborator: Chamoiseau and Glissant

Chamoiseau and Glissant wrote "Quand les murs tombent: L'Identité nationale hors-la-loi?" (2007) in response to the formation of the Ministry of Immigration, Integration, National Identity and Co-development in France (2007). The authors argue against governmental policies concerning assimilation and the increased policing of migration. Instead, the authors promote a new kind of imagined community that recognizes the human condition as fluid, migratory, and relational. Their argument is directed against certain Enlightenment principles, such as the idea of rational progress; instead, they propose a model of stuttering progress, which involves regressions (such as the sense of a loss of self) and pathologies (a sentiment of exasperation concerning collective feelings of superiority) in order to move forward or beyond outmoded principles of identity (QM, 1). They argue for a psychological and embodied feeling of communal development as a way of being-in-the-world. This phenomenological approach to a theory of relation and human rights sees identity as operating according to a principle of risk:

> C'est que l'identité est d'abord un être-dans-le-monde, ainsi que dissent les philosophes, un risqué avant tout, qu'il faut courir, et qu'elle fournit ainsi au rapport avec l'autre et avec ce monde, en même temps qu'elle résulte de ce rapport. Une telle ambivalence nourrit à la fois la liberté d'entreprendre et, plus d'avant, l'audace de changer. (QM, 1–2)

> (Identity is first of all a way of being in the world, according to what philosophers say; a risk above all that one needs to undertake, which produces a rapport with the other and the world at the same time that it is the result of this rapport. Such ambivalence nourishes at the same time freedom of enterprise as well as, more than ever, the audacity to change.)

At the same time, Chamoiseau and Glissant argue against the imperialistic tendencies underpinning the nation-state, which entails exalting, defending, and (when possible) exporting communal values (QM, 2). In their view, this desire for a single rooted identity is evident in colonization and has resulted in disasters throughout the world. Against this concept of community and nation, they offer the example of post-apartheid South Africa, which they see as embracing a theory of the mixed society that goes beyond the silo-like effect of multiculturalism where multiple ethnicities and cultures are merely juxtaposed (QM, 4).

Their protest against the French government's treatment of illegal immigrants leads them to rework many French concepts about rights and democracy via poetic-philosophical concepts. For example, the democratic space is presented as a field of antagonistic and virulent forces, the least evil of all systems, which demands a constant warrior-like vigilance (QM, 6). The "vigilance de guerrier" ("warrior's vigilance") fits with Chamoiseau's need for the Warrior of the Imaginary in the modern world where economic forces afford opportunities but also introduce potential threats (QM, 6). Regression and advance are allied as is evident in a world where the divide between the rich and poor is intensifying (QM, 7). Yet, at the same time, there is an opportunity to recognize not only the migratory human condition but also the collapse of walled-off concepts of identity. Increasingly, the world is interdependent and interlinked. Invoking a domestic metaphor, they liken the world to a home or household in which a sense of balance depends of the symbiotic equilibrium of all (QM, 7). Juxtaposing the poetics of relation against the concept of walled identities, they see American hegemony in the world, standardization, neocolonial economic imperatives, and the Occidental tradition of domination as sources of danger.

In terms of globalization, Chamoiseau and Glissant see the opportunity to embrace a relational concept of identity and places. Both are seen as open and sustained through relations to the world. This does not imply a sense of rootless existence but of roots that are connected in the shared earth (QM, 18). Just as there were nation states, they declare that there will be nations in relation to one another (QM, 18). Just as there were territories that separated and differentiated, there will be territories that differentiate and join and only differentiate in order to relate and link (QM, 19). Their augury relies on a redefinition of barbarism and civilization in an age when the desire to dominate, dictate laws, build an empire, take pride in superior strength, take pride that one holds the truth will be seen as the surest signs of barbarism in the history of humanities (QM, 19). Instead, they argue for a principle of change through exchange, which diminishes neither the individual nor the nation (QM, 19). Rather than a strict adherence to policies of intermixture or authenticity, they argue for a more flexible, adaptive approach, which recognizes the concept that identity is a mystery we live: "que l'identité serait un mystère à vivre, à vivre au plus large, à vivre au mieux ouvert, et que c'est de vivre ce mystère qui ferait que l'on vit, et qu'on se sent exister" (*QM*, 21) ("that identity would be a mystery to live, to live to the full extent, to live at best openly, and that by living this mystery one would live and feel a sense of existing").

While they recognize that many of their suggestions for better global government sound utopian, they still believe that principles of economic redistribution, ecological good governance, and other global policies for reform should be encouraged by agencies such as the International Monetary Fund and the World Bank (*QM*, 21–22). Their call for a Poetics of Relation is intimately connected with an activist impulse: "La relation à l'autre (à tout l'autre, dans ses présences animales, végétales, et culturelles, et par conséquent humaines) nous indique la part la plus haute, la plus honorable, la plus enrichissante de nous-mêmes" (*QM*, 25) ("Relation to others [to all others, in their animal, vegetable, and cultural presences, and consequently human presences] reveals the highest, most honorable and most enriching part of ourselves"). The treatise ends with a special plea for protest against walled-in ways of thinking that tempt us to accommodate ourselves to the worst, to habituate ourselves little by little to the insupportable and which lead us to live in silence and even to risk complicity with the inadmissible (*QM*, 26). All of this, Chamoiseau and Glissant argue, goes against beauty.

L'Intraitable beauté du monde: Adresse à Barack Obama picks up the theme of aesthetics following the election of Barack Obama. This work takes the long history of the New World, beginning with the Middle Passage, as the basis for a discussion of the shared spaces and concerns of the Americas. Their conception of Obama begins with a utopian description of the many hopes and debates concerning his potential as a leader capable of improving conditions for blacks and other minorities, fighting poverty, ending war, and bridging racial and ethnic divisions (*IB*, 3). In the authors' view, Obama embodies the modern world's capacity for creolization and is one who has heard the *cri du monde* ("cry of the world"), which Glissant has defined in *Traité du Tout-Monde* as a capacity to acknowledge the interrelatedness of traumatic events, local struggles, and creolizing processes at work in the world.[3] Celia Britton notes that Glissant's "cry of the world" attests to the ways in which "the globalization of mass media has meant that local struggles are no longer carried out without the knowledge of the rest of the world."[4] In the authors' view, Obama's upbringing in a Hawaiian mosaic (*IB*, 5) culture and the histories of migration that led to his birth make him a compelling figure: Obama embodies the possibilities for transcontinental fusions of identity. The symbolic potential of Obama's identity also serves as a point of a departure for a diatribe on the conception of race in America (the one-drop rule) and the politics of segregation, particularly as they underpin prevailing conceptions of multiculturalism in America (*IB*, 7, 11). Their revisionary aesthetics celebrates the Glissantian notion of the relational and rejects solitudes, fundamentalisms, ethnic purification, the expulsion of migrants, the cult of consumerism, and the malign aspects of capitalism (*IB*, 28–29). Instead, they call for the recognition of beauty in every place in the world (*IB*, 29). This entails new aesthetic forms and practices. Politically, they call for specific initiatives, such as the cancellation of debt in Africa and other structural adjustments to alleviate disequilibrium on the continent, the establishment of an international tribunal to address economic crimes, and the redistribution of food to needy countries and regions through an international relief agency (*IB*, 31). These political actions are seen as part of a wider aesthetic that recognizes the emergence of new forms of communication, such as sms/chat (*IB*, 47), worldwide creolizing processes, diagenetic models of plurality (*IB*, 51), and the redefinition of power based on a relational approach rather than through the use of force (*IB*, 56, 39). While none of these principles of beauty marks a departure from Glissantian perspectives already articulated, the text is noteworthy in that a number of these principles, as will be seen, inform the aesthetics of *Un dimanche* and *Malfini*. Moreover, this treatise can be usefully read in dialogue with *Écrire* and *Biblique* as indicative of the author's approach to relations among the local and the global, the uses of media and technology, and the abstraction of aesthetic principles derived from the landscape.

Chamoiseau and Glissant have contributed to (other authors include Ernest Breleur, Serge Domi, Gérard Delver, Guillaume Pigeard de Gurbert, Olivier Portecop, Olivier Pulvar, and Jean-Claude William) *Manifeste pour les "produits" de haute nécessité*, which reflects the authors' shared concerns about self-sufficiency, the environment, and the exploitive tendencies of global capitalism. The prefatory quotations from Gilles Deleuze's *L'Image-temps* and Césaire's letter to Maurice Thorez in which he announced his resignation from the French Communist Party (known as a the PCF or Parti communiste français) in 1956 following the suppression of the Hungarian revolution are indicative of the focus on a sense of community based on the needs of the people. While the quotation from

Deleuze refers to the emergence of a sense of the people in slums, camps, and ghettos in conditions of struggle and the consequent need for a political form of art, the citation from Césaire refers to the need for a new direction in politics following the collapse of hopes in a Marxist state. While the former is indicative of the locally derived aesthetic, the latter indicates an awareness of relations to the global politics of emancipation through relations to other places of struggle. The authors of the treatise build on both approaches through their Marxist-oriented critique of global capitalism, which takes particular aim at the culture of consumerism (MPHN, 3) and the economic definition of certain products as "necessary." They introduce the term "haute nécessité" ("high necessity") in order to refer to the poetic and imaginary values of products in terms of a vision of self-sufficiency within the Caribbean: "C'est tout ce qui constitue le coeur de notre souffrant désir de faire peuple et nation, d'entrer en dignité sur la grande-scène du monde" (MPHN, 4) ("It's all that's at the heart of our intense suffering desire to be a people and a nation, to enter with dignity into the great scene of the world"). In this utopian treatise, the authors state their opposition to capitalism and call for a reinstatement of work in the sphere of the poetic or as a means of self-fulfillment, social invention, and self-creation (MPHN, 9). Specifically, they suggest that the oil companies will sink into oblivion if people give up driving cars and adopt other means of transport (MPHN, 8); they argue that there is a need for full employment balanced by creative consumption (MPHN, 8–10); and they call for free, open access to the Internet, books, tales, theater, music, and so forth (MPHN, 10). None of these initiatives is backed up by an indication of how such objectives might be achieved in practical terms (MPHN, 10). Instead, they appeal for politics to be elevated into an art that values the individual and relations among individuals; while they challenge the exploitative tendencies of the market-based approach to the world economy, they commit themselves to a global ecological relation to the world's environmental balances (MPHN, 11–12). This eco-poetical perspective on global politics can be seen as a manifestation of planetary thinking, which evokes the idea of the world as an interdependent ecosystem. While the opposition to the consumption of French goods and products can be situated in terms of the alienating effects of colonial and neocolonial economic production in the overseas departments of France, the desire for a locally based sense of necessity can be seen in terms of the commodification of culture through global capitalism.

Un dimanche au cachot

Chamoiseau's professional experience working with delinquent children shapes the narrative of *Un dimanche au cachot*, which focuses on the author's efforts as educator. One Sunday morning, the author receives a call from Sylvain who runs *La Sainte Famille* ("Holy Family"), a home for orphaned, abused, neglected, and runaway youths. A young girl named Caroline has absconded to a dungeon (the "cachot" mentioned in the title of the work) and refuses to exit or communicate with anyone; Sylvain would like Chamoiseau to convince her to exit from the dungeon. The author agrees to assist; he enters the dungeon where Caroline and Chamoiseau are witnesses to events in the slave past, which focus particularly on the life of a young girl named L'Oubliée (The Forgotten One) who at one time was imprisoned in a plantation dungeon. Like Caroline, L'Oubliée has not received sufficient love and care; both are victims of sexual abuse. In this respect, the account of the relations between the two young girls suggests that the intertwining of histories of trauma can serve to work through both the long histories of suffering in Martinique, both personally and collectively. While the events of the past prove to be proleptic, in looking forward to a post-abolition world that emerges from within the colonial condition, the narrative of the present incorporates analepses as part of its restorative progression. During this narrative, which takes place on a single day, the rhythms of the day from dusk to darkness provide a backdrop for this cycle from "incommencements" ("false starts") to "recommencements" ("fresh starts") through the entanglement of histories past and present. The tensions between fluid and interrupted temporalities drive the narrative and take the form of the contrast between Chamoiseau's prose reverie and the constant punctuation of mobile phone calls that startle the narrator and bring him out of meandering thoughts to the immediate concerns of the helping Caroline in the present. The opening of the narrative sets the stage for the importance of the call to action as the narrator observes, "Quand la corne de lambi sonne c'est déjà l'heure. Ou moins. Ou plus" (*UDC*, 17) ("When the conch shell calls it is already time. Or more. Or less"). The idea of urgency combined with indeterminacy is a fitting beginning for this plot, which returns to the slave past and mediates its disruptive presence. Just as the conch shell sounded the alarm in the past, the mobile phone sounds the alarm in the present: the ringing phone serves as a source of disruption, interrupting the seemingly isolated account of the historical past.

Moreover, through its association with the conch shell, the mobile phone has the potential to signal something new on the horizon: not merely an interruption, the ringing phone might also serve both literally and figuratively as a call to action, which creates a line of communication between inner and outer worlds of experience.

Sunday, typically a day of rest, meditation, and worship, proves to be a time of multiple possibilities and potentialities. For children in this institutional facility, Sunday's are particularly difficult because they remind children of the absence of a family home. A rainy Sunday, like the one on which Sylvain calls, is worse because the children are confined indoors, which has the effect of increasing their feeling of loneliness. Chamoiseau considers the role of Sunday as a day of rest, which brings with it the potential for creativity and melancholia. As a creative writer, he welcomes the uneasy sense of an identity in flux, but the sociologist in him protests against the contemporary world with its hectic workweek, leisure-time diversions, which are promoted in the media, and other forms of escape, such as drugs (i.e., Prozac) that promise a beatific existence (*UDC*, 20). In a combative opening to his tale, he refuses the identity of "outré-mer" and claims that he is ultramarine and ultraperipheral: the anesthetized product of a postcolonial technocracy (*UDC*, 21). He laments the social ills associated with a consumer-oriented culture, tourism, failures to protect the environment, and the rise of bureaucracy (*UDC*, 21). As in *Écrire*, Chamoiseau depicts a community that continues to suffer the ill effects of domination: "Pour tout peuple livré aux dépendances, le dimanche est un metteur en scène qui ne donnent rien à jouer, ni en dedans ni en dehors" (*UDC*, 22) ("For all people who are in a state of dependence, Sunday is [comparable to] a director who does not offer a[n actor a] role to play, neither from within nor from without"). For the oppressed, Sunday represents a day of foreclosed opportunities, but through the narrative process of working through the traumatic past, the day is also shown to be one that has restorative potential. The eventual exit from the dungeon serves as a symbolic rebirth, which echoes the Christian theme of resurrection. Rather than turning to the Messianic promise of a saviour, Chamoiseau figures Caribbean peoples as a community who acts as the agent of its own reclamation and renewal of life.

Chamoiseau adopts a number of masks and discusses the role of disguise as a strategy for survival and self-determination. In a footnote to the text, he provides a possible speculative fiction that he might have written about an exiled hero who loses connection to his gods, genesis, and founding myths (*UDC*, 29). In order to combat European colonization, he dons a tribal mask in order to do battle against the oppressors, but this mask becomes a dungeon: "Mais ce masque se transforme en cachot" (*UDC*, 29) ("But this mask transforms itself into a dungeon"). He becomes caught up in an increasingly desperate struggle of violence and counterviolence. On a certain Sunday, he gets a glimpse of his forgotten face beneath the mask: a face that the hero no longer recognizes, but which remains much the same underneath. The hero no longer knows what to do. Keep the mask and continue to fight to the death in an unending war? Recover what remains of his face and be massacred? Or remain in this uncertain condition and die in the struggle between his mask and his face? Chamoiseau, the narrator, observes that because he is a tragic hero, he attempts to tear off the mask, but in doing so he almost rips out his eyes. He tries to leave the mask in place, but his face (now revived) will no longer accept the mask. In a state of tension, he begins to wander in a manner comparable to Don Quixote on his quest, but he is looking for a way to be present in the world. This "idiotic" fiction, as the author describes it, shows the author's ongoing interest in the role of masquerade (mimicry) and unmasking as central to the quest for decolonization. The violence associated with masquerade suggests that it is far from liberating, but that the act of unmasking is equally futile and potentially suicidal. Thus, the quest for identity requires an ability to negotiate a sense of one's place in the world between acts of masquerade and unmasking.

Multiple masked identities surface in the related worlds of the story. Oubliée (the forgotten girl) serves as a double for Caroline. Both suffer from abandonment and neglect; both undergo a process of transformation; both (we eventually learn) share the name Caroline. Moreover, the dungeon-like space of the slave system provides a metaphorical womb for the transformation of consciousness (*UDC*, 313). This "echoing world" structure is not exactly like the Glissantian concept of "les échos-monde," but Chamoiseau seems to be inspired by the idea that these stories past and present enter into a mutually illuminating dialogue in which one story calls forth aspects of the other. The doubling of the conch shell and the mobile phone reinforces this notion of the stories in a call-response form of echoing stories and personages. In this respect, Oubliée is a relational figure who can be linked not only to Caroline but also to Man l'Oubliée in *Biblique* as well as to the old slave who flees because she too encounters the criss-crossed rock. Oubliée represents the forgotten in history, but she is also paradoxically the character through whom the forgotten is recalled and reconnected. She is mother to marginal women whose knowledge and wisdom are attested to in the fictions of Chamoiseau because they play a role in his memory, enabling him to name and construct the forgotten (*UDC*, 315). The multiple narrative trajectories of the novel encourage a sense that interpretive certainties about the past can never be wholly recovered so that the question is rather one of sensing the relatedness and chain of relations among historical moments (*UDC*, 317). Rather than excavating certain knowledge about the past, Chamoiseau calls for an excavation of uncertainties; this novel then is closer to the realm of fantasy and speculative fiction where equally probable (or improbable) explanations of the world are brought into dialogue. In this sense, his fiction seeks to uncover places, objects, and artifacts that elicit the world that might have been and a culture that might exist. Much like the imagined artifacts of Jorge Borges's "Tlön, Uqbar, Orbis Tertius," he does not seek to recover the original truth but the mysterious doubles or tangible (ir)realities of the imagined past. The spaces and places of this world belong to the shared fictions of Glissant, William Faulkner, Perse, and others who have created fictions in response to these resonant locales. Such excavations involve not only actual objects and artifacts in the world but also entail investigations into symbolic spaces and times (*UDC*, 315).

By combining the sacred, meditative time of Sunday (a time associated with a glimpse of freedom for the slave) with the taboo space of the dungeon, Chamoiseau evokes a disquieting state of meditative tensions. In colonial times, the dungeon was a space of torture and folly; its stones formed a metaphorical stomach that engulfs and consumes the slave (*UDC*, 39). Caroline and Chamoiseau are twins in a dungeon described as a cocoon of reverie and a "utérus fétide" (fetid uterus) (*UDC*, 40), suggesting that this is a space of transformation and nascence for this pair who are diluted and reborn into a "gémellité mortifière" or a "mortified twinning" (*UDC*, 41). This ambivalent, even repellent, description of the mordant space of women's reproductive organs fuses together destructive and creative possibilities. In this respect, the dungeon resembles the "cale" or lower decks of the ship during the Middle Passage as a deathly tomb and a space of horrific rebirth. Like the lower deck, this dungeon swallows the two (*UDC*, 42). Yet, through Chamoiseau's presence as a kind of midwife to history, he helps to transform this into a vital space where Caroline may come to ready herself for a rebirth in the world, moving beyond the malevolent legacies of the past to a more vital relation to the space-time of the present.

The related themes of abortion, spiritual rebirth, and resistance resurface in this narrative as a persistent reminder of Chamoiseau's fascination with the idea of a murderous maternal love that would rather kill the child than see it born into slavery. The ambivalence of maternal love and the ill effects on the child, the subject of Chamoiseau's "Solitude la mulâtresse," resurfaces here in the past-present juxtaposition of Oubliée-Caroline: both abused, given harmful drugs, abandoned, and left enclosed in the dungeon where they adopt the same postures and utter cries. Oubliée plays a maternal role in the life of La Belle ("The Beauty"), easing the suffering she feels because she cares for others in pain (*UDC*, 49). La Belle is aligned with the *bête-longue* (the *Bothrops lanceolatus*) and "sauvemort" (a saving death or abortion) as both represent mortal forces of resistance. The image of swallowing and pregnancy are once again associated when La Belle tells Oubliée not to carry her child to full term because this is a way of feeding the plantation system (*UDC*, 52) or argues that slavery is a form of being without life and should not be perpetuated (*UDC*, 54). Abortion is seen in relation to other strategies of resistance, such as in the opacity of language. La Belle speaks in an African language, which the Oubliée barely comprehends, yet the two are reborn into a common language of mutual understanding. The Creole interface becomes a kind of womb-like space of resistance to the master's language and discourses of power (*UDC*, 52–53). Similarly, the role of plants for healing and poisoning discloses the ways in which solidarity and resistance go hand-in-hand. The old slave who flees shows Oubliée a datura, a poisonous plant sometimes used by shamans for ritual purposes, and warns her that it can "eat the spirit" (*UDC*, 55). Indeed, Oubliée has memories of her mother smoking the plant and the effects of inhaling this soporific when the *béké*'s father gives it to her to smoke and rapes her while the mother gazes at the mango trees, unaware of what is happening. In her drugged condition, she barely recalls or comprehends what has happened. While she recalls the smoking of the datura as a happy event, which produced "tant de bonheur" (so much happiness) on a conscious level (*UDC*, 55), she also yearns for the old man to take on the role of fathering her child, which indicates an intuitive understanding of the trauma that accompanied the poison and a recognition of the good will of the old slave man.

On the whole, the narrative functions as an ambivalent form of resistance, which is articulated through the condition of an uncertain, meditative form of knowing and unknowing. Chamoiseau describes the psychological function of reverie in the life of the abused child as follows:

> La rêverie est un des boucliers de l'enfance brisée. La maltraitance arrête le cheminement de ces petites consciences qui se retrouvent bloquées au-devant d'un abîme: fixes dans le paysage d'une souffrance impracticable. La rêverie devient un baume, un ange bienveillant, mais qui peut se transformer en diable: emporter l'enfant dans une absence définitive. (*UDC*, 40)

> (Reverie is one of the shields of the broken childhood. Maltreatment stops the course of these small consciousnesses, which find themselves stuck in front of an abyss: fixed in a landscape of unbearable suffering. Reverie becomes a balm, a kind angel, but it can also transform into a devil: carrying the child into an inescapable absence.)

To disrupt Caroline's diabolic form of reverie, Chamoiseau tells the story of Oubliée, enabling her to confront trauma indirectly through a positive form of reverie. The discourse as a whole reverberates from this narrative kernel, which takes the form of a collective reverie about the maltreatment of Martinican subjects. The rejuvenation of consciousness through the life of the child past-present serves as an allegorical way of talking about the collective unconsciousness that continues to suffer the post-traumatic effects of slavery and violence.

As a literary mode, reverie serves as a meditation on the pathological condition of inner flight and the destabilizing effects of the drug experience: a reflective engagement with these processes serves as the basis for a process of enlightenment through the revival of the marooned consciousness. Chamoiseau invokes a readerly memory of *L'Esclave vieil homme et le molosse* as an event in time. In dialogue with the proleptic ending of the novella, *Un dimanche au cachot* follows the figure of the marooned slave and the effect of his flight on those who know him: the rippling of one consciousness to another produces a surging counter-discourse. Oubliée experiences the old man's flight as a form of abandonment, resulting in the feeling of a swarming absence (*UDC*, 60). When the *molosse* returns, she experiences his changed appearance as a confusion of senses, which is associated with the destabilizing effects of datura (*UDC*, 60). For his part, the *molosse* wants to vomit and starts to regard the plantation as something beyond rather than as a space or system in which he participates (*UDC*, 61). The master returns and is somehow broken inside (*UDC*, 62), and this sense of displacement is further confounded by the arrival of the porcelain vendor who is an abolitionist. Like the escaping slave, the porcelain vendor has a destabilizing effect on those around him, but he too is shaken and transformed by his encounters on the plantation because he is open to the desire to listen and remake himself through relations with others. Chamoiseau the narrator describes him as understanding that each age has its own infamies and that these are often unrecognized during the time for they appear masked by the prevalent ideologies of the age (*UDC*, 67). The porcelain vendor confronts La Belle, who is imprisoned in the dungeon, and recognizes that she embodies the power of the African presence in the Caribbean (*UDC*, 69). His interchange with Sechou prompts the slave to see himself beyond his current dehumanized state, which prompts an inner dialogue with the escaped slave. He begins to cry, an event the porcelain vendor records in his notebook (*UDC*, 70). For the porcelain vendor, the planter is the only one to have a global view of the plantation, and this reinforces his power over the slaves.

In opposition to this system of domination, Chamoiseau introduces a relational, clairvoyant poetics. In *Quand les murs tombent*, Glissant and Chamoiseau argue for a "poétique clairvoyante du Tout-Monde" or poetic clairvoyance of the Tout-Monde (*QM*, 15), and this principle plays a structuring principle in *Un dimanche au cachot* where Chamoiseau forwards a speculative account of relational identity as already nascent during the colonial period. Specifically, the hiccups in the narrative embody a pivotal moment when the body and the body politic are seized by a force that disrupts a monolithic sense of identity (*QM*, 8). The hiccup is symptomatic of loss and disruptive forces of change. The immobilizing side-effects of the hiccup, however transitory, are a call to presence, an inescapable awareness of the interruptions and transitions taking place in politico bodily processes. The hiccup represents an embodied form of knowledge and a call to action that is both as revolutionary as the conch shell and as mundane as the ring of a mobile phone. Through a narrative chain of action and reaction, consisting of obscure moments of clairvoyance and response, Chamoiseau depicts another kind of fragmentary power, which is grounded in intuition, imaginative affiliations, and surges of consciousness. Oubliée senses that the porcelain vendor perceives the plantation in a way that is similar to and mixes with her own: "Elle croyait voir et entendre avec lui" (*UDC*, 71) ("She believed she saw and understood with him"). The porcelain vendor sees the enslaved persons as solitary and ejected from any form of collective. At the same time, the fact that they are lost together means that they are linked and related (*UDC*, 72). This idea of a chain of consciousness (an alternative to the chains of slavery) is evident in the narrative style, which explores connections among isolated individuals. Oubliée's inner marooning of consciousness is one such example (*UDC*, 72). In this context, the drug experience also has a positive after-effect because it teaches her to know more fully her connections to the ant, herb, water, earth, anoli, and rock (*UDC*, 73). For Oubliée, this form of planetary awareness functions like "une pôglô" (*UDC*, 73), a word of Ethiopian origins that means "a taste of water." The stonemason also participates in this tale of conscience as the one who knows about various rocks as well as the most mysterious rock that reveals the "Pierre Monde" or vision of the world as a composite, creolizing intersection of many voices through time. Like Esternome, the mason knows how to make the mortar that joins fragments together. Unlike Esternome, who helps to build the postcolonial vision and structures of a new form of community in *Texaco*, the mason is both a participant in building colonial structures and a witness to the need to dismantle colonial ways of thought.

In opposition to the imperial desire for a monumental history, Chamoiseau presents an embodied historical narrative of intersections, interruptions, delays, glitches, and relations. William Faulkner's bouts of hiccups are interpreted symptomatically; he is linked to other figures in (post)colonial history who suffer from hiccups during the course of the narrative, including Oubliée, the porcelain vendor, Sechou, and Caroline. Consequently, the motif of the hiccups along the way toward the abolition of slavery is related to processes of self-liberation for the young girl locked in her psychic prison. Like the motif of the hiccup, the multifunctional mobile phone plays an important role in this appellative fiction because it enables several concepts about communication and writing to come together. As a device that supports speech, listening, recording, and writing, the mobile telephone is well equipped for *oraliture* in a modern age. Moreover, it offers a source of dim light, thus calling attention to communication as a method of illumination. As in his other texts, where quotes from authors (*Écrire*) or archival documents (*Texaco*) disrupt the narrative and signal shifting fictional modalities, the mobile phone introduces a similar shifting effect, but in this case it is the construct of Chamoiseau who is disrupted as he is recalled from the space of reverie and narration to the idea of the self as an educator with a specific mission. These call-response mechanisms (the hiccup and the mobile phone) produce a relational history.

The unmasking of the writer and the activity of writing resurfaces as Chamoiseau declares that he invents a world as a speculative fiction about the shadows of the real (*UDC*, 102). He envisions the fiction as a "sidération" that elicits a sidereal time and place (*UDC*, 102). The description of writing is figural, active, and experiential in that it functions as a form of scribbling or a retracing of the world as "un impossible cheminement . . . dans l'impossible" (*UDC*, 102) ("an impossible wandering . . . through the impossible"). The masking and unmasking of multiple selves generates a multiplicity of uncertainties about identity and history. The improbable doubling of L'Oubliée and Caroline is a strategy for forcing the reader to doubt the veracity of the text and to see it as a certain kind of speculative process or experience: a fire that the author builds and lights to enflame the imagination (*UDC*, 247). Moreover, the discourse reinforces the notion of elective affinities, whether through literary alliances, sympathetic connections, or new forms of kinship relations. In this respect, the story of Victor Schoelcher, the ethnographic double for Chamoiseau, serves to show that emancipation can have its origins in the desire to discover more about the world and the experiences of others. The ability to become a good reader of people, situations, texts, and the world, symbolized by the "roche écrite" as the *Pierre-Monde*, is evoked through the improbable marvel of converging narratives, voices, and inscriptions.

Chamoiseau calls attention to the textual relations among his various works on the initiation of consciousness through the use of textual echoes, which resonate in ways comparable to the ringing of the mobile phone, the hiccup and sound of the conch. *Un dimanche au cachot* opens with the question, "Le monde a-t-il une intention?" ("The world, does it have an intention?"), which echoes both *Écrire en pays dominé* and *L'Esclave vieil homme et le molosse* (both of these works pose the same question). Through textual reverberations, Chamoiseau foregrounds the continuities among these discourses about the necessity of confronting the past in order to negotiate a viable present. All of these narratives stage imagined encounters with history and focus on the initiation of a new imaginary; they also posit diagenetic "-scapes" of history, which are fused together in a new cultural topography. With its criss-crossings of narrative trajectories and intertexts, the work can be read as another example of Chamoiseau's *émerveille*. Notably, *Un dimanche* traverses the same imaginative terrain as *L'Esclave* through its return to the story of the slave who flees the plantation, the tale of the *molosse*, and the encounter with the inscribed rock. While *L'Esclave* ended with a premonition of abolition and the decolonization of the imaginary, *Un dimanche au cachot* picks up the story and traces the effects of the slave's flight on others he knew. The theme of emancipation comes to the foreground with the presence of Victor Schoelcher, who appears initially as the unnamed son of a porcelain manufacturer. Recording thoughts in his notebook, this anonymous figure at first plays the familiar role of the ethnographer in Chamoiseau's fiction. When Schoelcher's identity is eventually disclosed, the effect is to show how the work of the imaginary plays a transformative role in history through its resonating presence. This sonorous history dramatizes the ways in which the waves of consciousness and the relational chain of transformations within a community can function as a kind of auditorium, which resonates within the self and world to produce what Glissant refers to as *"a prophetic vision of the past"* where histories of forgotten peoples, accounts of suffering, and intuitions of emancipation are projected onto new planes of existence.[5]

Les neuf consciences du Malfini

Throughout his oeuvre Chamoiseau challenges Western forms of Enlightenment attained through reason and presents alternatives to the violence often associated with rationalization, whether in the case of sanitizing the markets (*Chronique*), police methods (*Solibo*), or urban development policies (*Texaco*). At the same time, he offers a counter-perspective on social development through poetics, such as through the use of language to encourage new forms of associative thought and the manipulation of generic forms and conventions in order to call attention to the mobilization of consciousness. *Les neuf consciences du Malfini* is another of Chamoiseau's conversion narratives, which is part fable and part treatise. This time he turns to the literary tradition of the bird as spokesperson for wisdom, such as found in Aristophane's *The Birds*, the Persian poem by Farid ud-Din Attar, entitled "The Conference of the Birds," and the legend of the figure of the Simurgh, an immortal bird that rests in the Tree of Knowledge, which has fascinated Jorge Borges, Hector Bianciotti, and Mohammed Dib. Similar to *L'Esclave vieil homme et le molosse*, where Chamoiseau represents dog's change of consciousness, this story concerns the enlightenment of a *malfini* (the *Buteo platypterus*, also known as *Mangé poulé* or chicken hawk) or a hawk when confronted by a *colibri* (the generic name for hummingbird, often referred to as a "oiseau-mouche") and *foufou* (an Antillean crested hummingbird: the *colibri huppé* or Orthorhynchus Cristatus). Through a dialogue with the hawk, whom he discovers in his garden following a cyclone, Chamoiseau claims that he enters into a kind of impossible condition where he believes to have perceived what the bird said. The author attributes his ability to understand the hawk's story to his reading of *Alice in Wonderland* and Kafka. Thus, Chamoiseau signals that the narrative belongs to his generic rewriting of the tradition of the marvel, but he also hints at the biocultural or biopolitical aspects of his reading. As in Kafka, a transformation occurs through Chamoiseau's relation to the bird; the relation to the bird takes the form of a marvelous encounter, comparable to Alice's relation to the rabbit and other animals in Wonderland. In the world of the marvel, the division between human and animal dissolves as Chamoiseau responds to the bird within himself.[6] As in *Cachot*, the narrator Chamoiseau highlights the speculative nature of this fiction, which he has heard or imagined what the bird could not say (*M*, 17). The facility to marvel is thus posited as a necessary entry into the conversion narrative for the author as represented in the narrative. This fable concerns the hawk's adventures and initiation of consciousness, particularly through his encounter with a hummingbird named Foufou. The narrative is divided into four main parts, entitled "La chose" ("The Thing"), "Le cri du monde" ("The Cry of the World"), "L'Océan de lumière" ("The Ocean of Light"), and "Récitation sur le vivant" ("Recitation on the Living"), followed by text containing words of wisdom. Thus, the fable becomes the source for a series of sacred meditations passed on to the reader.

Malfini extends Chamoiseau's longstanding interest in birds as metaphors for the liberation of the imaginary.[7] As in *Biblique* and other narratives featuring the Warrior of the Imaginary, the process of enlightenment is presented as a relational chain of radiating effects, emanating, in this instance, through the life of the hummingbird and the flower in the biosphere to the hawk and Chamoiseau as narrator. In this instance, the hawk takes the form of a warrior who learns to questions his solipsistic and imperialistic assumptions about the world. Through his exploration of the hawk's perspective, Chamoiseau addresses issues such as territory, predatory behavior, and violence. The narrator signals that a conversion narrative is about to take place: "Pourtant, il y avait ce trouble... ce désir peut-être d'une autre perspective... un indicible *appel*... C'est alors qu'un hoquet s'empara de ma vie" (25) ("However, there was this trouble... this desire maybe for another perspective... an unspeakable *call*... It's like a hiccup seized my life"). The hawk is thus affiliated with the slave who responds to the call to flight in *L'Esclave* and the young girl in *Un dimanche au cachot* whose narrative is interrupted by hiccups and telephone calls. The titular reference to nine states of consciousness is significant because it corresponds to the Buddhist path to Enlightenment. The title of the work, *The Nine Consciousnesses of the Malfini*, and the inclusion of the words "alaya"[8] and "amala"[9] make reference to key concepts in Buddhist teachings. Buddhism derives from the Sanskrit root "budh," commonly translated as "to enlighten" or "recover consciousness."[10] The Yogacara school of Buddhism refers to eight types of consciousness, which include the seven aspects of individual consciousness (*pravrtti-vijnana*) and the *alaya*. Synthesis takes place through the "alaya," a term that refers to "the indissoluble" (from "a" meaning "not" and "laya" meaning "to dissolve"). The *alaya* is the storehouse consciousness, which acts as the receptacle where the impressions of past experience and karmic actions are stored.[11] At the moment of enlightenment, the *alaya* is transformed into the Mirror-like Awareness or perfect discrimination of a Buddha. Chamoiseau's reference to the ninth consciousness might be seen as a reference to the moment of enlightenment ("awakening"). Indeed, the work as a whole can be seen as concerned with the eight-fold path to enlightenment, which consists of attaining the (1) Right View, (2) Right Resolve, (3) Right Speech, (4) Right Action, (5) Right Livelihood, (6) Right Effort, (7) Right Mindfulness, and (8) Right Meditation.[12] The appendix to the narrative can be seen as an effort to enable the reader to fulfill his or her own quest for enlightenment. That Chamoiseau has the Buddhist notion of the "amala" in mind is evident in the final part of the third section of the narrative, entitled "L'AMALA," through references to the term in the context of the Malfini's recognition of a world that goes beyond mere appearances as well as violent struggles and come to apprehend and practice enlightenment in an intuitive fashion (*M*, 213).

Indeed, the Malfini can be seen as attaining consciousness of the Four Noble Truths through what might be interpreted as a diagnostic process: that life means suffering (diagnosis), the origin of suffering is attachment (identification of causes), the cessation of suffering is attainable (curability), and the discovery of a path to the cessation of suffering (method of treatment). In the course of the narrative, the hawk is transformed from one who brings about suffering to one who helps to ease the suffering of the world as well as contributes to its well-being in a holistic fashion. The hawk's initial state is described as one of "barbarous splendour" ("ma splendeur barbare") (M, 18), characterized by the desire for conquest as well as feelings of hate, jealousy, bitterness, and doubt (*M*, 18). Initially discovery is associated with the colonial encounter whereby the Martinican rain forest of Rabuchon is perceived as "Un inépuisable paradis pour la chasse!" ("An inexhaustible paradise for the hunt") (*M*, 19). The hawk perceives himself as one among many predatory creatures, include eagles, buzzards, and humans (known as "Nocifs" or "Harmful Ones") (*M*, 20). In this state of malediction (the subtitle of a section of the narrative), the cry is associated with the war-like desire to claim and possess territory (*M*, 20). The hawk observes: "J'aime tuer. J'aime frapper les chair chaudes et me repaître de la saveur du sang" ("I like killing. I like striking warm flesh and revel in the taste of blood") (*M*, 21). When the hawk receives the call to awakening, his *alaya* undergoes a transformation, particularly when the predatory bird encounters hummingbirds and realizes that there are planes of existence that have been hitherto invisible to him (*M*, 27). Recognition of suffering in the world comes in many forms, such as witnessing the death and destruction of others as well as ecological disaster. In a Buddhist, sense the Malfini begins to recognize that suffering stems from a desire for attachment and conquest of the earth. Through the presence of Foufou, he comes to realize that there is another way of being in the world, which is to partake in its ceaseless becoming. The cessation of suffering comes about through the cultivation of a sense of dispassion, which entails the dissolution of cravings and attachments to desires and ideas. The discovery of a path to the cessation of suffering is one of self-improvement, which leads to rebirth. For the Malfini, this state of awakening is characterized by a profound sense of connection to all living beings and a turning away from his predatory identity. In the section of the narrative entitled "RENAISSANCE" ("REBIRTH"), the revival of the ecologically devastated Rabuchon, under the influence of the "magician" (Foufou), prompts the hawk to come to terms with his place in the environment, which leads him to encounter the world as a place without territories ("SANS TERRITOIRES") (*M*, 157). As in other narratives featuring the Warrior of the Imaginary, this tale focuses on an adversarial figure (the hawk) who discovers a pacific view of his or her organic place in the world and comes to inhabit the world (rather than desire to conquer it). This transformation is brought about through the recognition of Foufou as a master who is both a dispassionate figure in the Buddhist sense and a Warrior of the Imaginary:

> Toute la sérénité du monde était en moi.
> Je le regardais de loin avec une immense gratitude.
> J'avais enfin compris . . .

Il n'avait pas besoin de disciple. Il n'avait pas besoin d'élève. Il n'avait pas besoin d'honneur. Il faisait juste ce qu'il avait à faire de sa vie, et du mieux qu'il le pouvait. Il n'imposait rien à personne sinon à lui-même et aux batailles qu'il s'ètait choisies. C'était un bien étrange guerrier. (*M*, 181)

(All the serenity of the world was in me.
I looked at him from afar with an immense [sense of] gratitude.
I had finally understood.
He did not need disciples. He did not need students. He did not need honor. He did just what he had to do with his life, as best as he could. He did not impose anything on anyone except on himself and the battles that he chose for himself. He was a very strange warrior.)

This new sense of the world and the role of the warrior is put to the test when a predatory bird, named "Le Féroce" or "The Ferocious One," attacks the hummingbirds and kills Colibri in a wanton act of violence: the hawk enters into battle out of a desire to protect, responding to what he refers to as "the space of self" rather out of a desire for conquest (*M*, 195), but is wounded. Foufou manages to outwit and defeat The Ferocious One, but does so without seeking to harm or destroy the other bird. After the battle, The Ferocious One retreats from the region and lives out his days talking about a hummingbird-dragon (*M*, 202). For his part, the hawk begins to live like Foufou, his master, helping to pollinate plants; in Buddhist terms, this ecological work can be seen as contributing to a sense of the boundlessness of life. Tending plants, the Malfini becomes a gardener, adopting a role comparable to Balthazar in *Biblique*. This transformation of the world into a garden to be tended and inhabited rather than dominated can be seen as a counter-response to the conquest of the Caribbean and the transformation of it into an infernal new Eden of slavery and exploitation. The Malfini's growing awareness of the world as an ecosystem, where the echoes of the cries of the world resound (*M*, 148), stands in contrast to the human emphasis on ecological disaster in the narrow context of economic concerns about banana crops (*M*, 147). Thus, the Malfini's path to enlightenment, which recognizes a world beyond territorial concerns and conquest, via eco-poetics can be read as an allegorical accompaniment to Chamoiseau's views (expressed in treatises and manifestos) on the need for a poetico-political imaginary, which runs counter to the exploitative tendencies of empire and global capitalism in the modern era.

This tale of initiation has resonating effects. Through his encounter with the Malfini, Chamoiseau recognizes that the bird's body (much like the marvelous rock in *L'Esclave*) has become the site of a singing/speaking relation to the world as an indissoluble whole:

> Son corps fut alors empli d'un roucoulement qui se déployait en scansions étranges. Cela me laissa très vite le sentiment d'une liturgie dans laquelle il parlait en chantant, et chantait en parlant. Moi qui avais bien longtemps écouté les oiseaux, je crus reconnaître des modulations de merles, de colibris, de pigeons, de tourterelles, de ramiers . . . Comme si tous les oiseaux du monde avaient chanté en lui. Et pas seulement les oiseaux, mais tout ce qui vivait ici ou ailleurs, capable ou pas d'harmoniser des cris. (*M*, 225)

> (His body was thus filled with a cooing that unfurled in strange scansions. Very quickly this gave me the feeling of a liturgy in which he spoke in singing, and sung in speaking. I who have for a long time listened to the birds, thought I recognized the modulations of blackbirds, hummingbirds, pigeons, turtledoves, woodpigeons . . . As if all the birds of the world had sung in him. And not only birds, but all that lived here or elsewhere, capable or not of harmonizing their cries.)

Through references to the liturgical and singing speech, which might take the form of a kind of chanting, Chamoiseau elicits the sense of a sacred choir of birds, which potentially extends to the entire world of living entities.

Textual and living landscapes converge in the narrative. For instance, the presence of the hummingbirds and their affiliations can be understood in terms of Césaire's influence on revelations in language and nature as well as Glissant's interest in a living landscape. *Les neuf consciences* begins with two epigraphs:

> *Rien n'est vrai, tout est vivant.*
> Édouard Glissant

> *Je me suis toujours étonné qu'un corps si frêle puisse supporter, sans éclater, le pas de charge d'un coeur qui bat.*
> Aimé Césaire (*À propos du colibri*)

(*Nothing is true, everything is living.*
Édouard Glissant

I have always been surprised that a body that fragile could withstand, without exploding, the double-time march of a beating heart.
Aimé Césaire [*On the subject of the hummingbird*])

While the citation of Glissant calls attention to the mutable, unfolding of existence through the world as a living text, Césaire's description of the hummingbird resembles the haiku in its poetic compression of vital and violent energies, evoked through the images of the beating heart, the explosive potential of a body at war, and the surge of the body's very being as a war against the seemingly insurmountable opposing forces in a war against death. Chamoiseau develops these poetic trajectories through his description of the birds and the ways in which they too come to play a role in vital struggles in the Martinican landscape. Notably, the quotation from Glissant is repeated throughout the text as well as in the "Tableau, Répétitions et Gloses du Nocif" ("Scene, Rehearsals and Gloss of the Noxious"), suggesting that the word has a diffuse and pervasive influence throughout the textual landscape as if its presence has proliferated in much the same way as pollination processes are carried out through the hummingbird's travels from flower to flower. The reference to the tableau of scene, rehearsals, and gloss is noteworthy for it suggests that the text might be understood as a sacred drama that is in need of hermeneutic interpretation. In textual terms, this slippage of identities is mediated by the opening sentence to the narrative: "EXORDE—Frère, vivant . . . ô Nocif . . . Je suis l'alarme. Je suis la toute-puissance. Je suis la peur et le danger" (*M*, 17) ("EXORDIUM—Brother, living one . . . O Harmful One . . . I am the alarm. I am the all-powerful. I am fear and danger"). These introductory sentences gesture toward the Western rhetorical tradition of beginning with an introduction that prepares the audience for the oration to come, a tradition that was employed in early sermon traditions also, as well as to the poetry of decadence, specifically the closing lines to Charles Baudelaire's "Au Lecteur" ("To the Reader"), "Hypocrite lecteur,—mon semblable,—mon frère!," which refer to the audience as a dissembling double for the author. These opening sentences, apparently those of the narrator addressed to the reader, are a double for the hawk's call to Chamoiseau. Thus, the narrative foregrounds its duplicities from the start and also calls the reader's attention to the potential perils embodied by the narrative, the reader and the author in the fictional/real world. This slippage between textual and natural, real and imagined, landscapes also elicits the allegorical dimensions of the narrative, which can be taken as both grounded in time and place as well as a free-floating, abstract narration.

Patterns of flight and motion play a particularly strong role in enabling the play between material, textual, linguistic, and symbolic facets of meaning. Initially, the Malfini is unable to grasp what kind of creatures hummingbirds are; he describes a certain "froufrou des ailes" or "rustling of wings" (*M*, 26). He snatches and devours a first hummingbird, but a second escapes him. Soon the predatory pursuit of these creatures turns to wonder as he considers their movements, habits, and relation to their environment. The encounter with the hummingbirds calls attention to what was formerly an invisible aspect of the world (*M*, 27–28). The hawk must learn not simply to take, but also to be overtaken by surprise (*M*, 28). In the hawk's opinion, these birds expend the energy of a volcano for an existence that does not change anything in the order of things (*M*, 29), but eventually he comes to understand that they play a vital role in sustaining the biosphere through their relation to flowers and role in enabling pollination. Two birds in particular catch the Malfini's attention: a hummingbird named Coulibri (which is the generic name for this species) and another whom he calls "Froufrou" (the *colibri huppé* or *Orthorhynchus Cristatus*) and then "Foufou" (the local name for the bird). The slippage from "Froufrou" ("frou-frou" means "to rustle") to the Creole name for the bird "Foufou" calls the reader's attention to the common practice of dropping the "r" when words shift from French to Creole. Thus, the bird reenacts creolizing processes as it comes into contact with the other bird. From the hawk's perspective, the hummingbird's motion, with its darting and spirals, seems to embody folly itself:

> Leurs ailes tournoyaient sur elles-mêmes, en effectuant une spirale verticale, cela sans cesse et sans à-coups, dans une constance qui ne pouvait que confondre l'entendement. Et cette activité démente se déployait avec un tel mystère d'aisance et d'énergie, que ces choses pouvaient, dans une série d'instantanés, fondre à l'horizontale, surgir à la verticale, tournoyer à différents degrés et, pour clore l'insoutenable, se mettre soudain à voler en arrière. (*M*, 30–31)

(Their wings turned on themselves, taking the form of a vertical spiral, without ceasing and without jolting, in a constancy that could only confound understanding. And this demented activity was carried out with such a mystery of ease and energy that these things could in a series of instants melt into the horizontal, spring up in the vertical, turn in different degrees, and to finish off the impossible, go suddenly in flight backward.)

Yet, eventually, this spiraling motion is suggestive of an open relation to the world as the hawk's flight pattern comes to signify a salutary gesture rather than predatory circling (M, 204). While engaged in this open spiraling motion, the hawk decides that he will do his part to support Foufou's relational way of being in the world. For Glissant and Frankétienne, the circle represents the creative *errance* of the postcolonial world.[13] In the world of the criss-crossing marvel, it is not surprising that the flight patterns of Chamoiseau's hummingbird and hawk should embody this natural, intertextual, and scribal form.

From a textual perspective, the hawk's tutelage with Foufou, who serves as a master in the Buddhist sense rather than the colonial one, the narrative might be seen as an allegory of Chamoiseau's relationship to Glissant. In particular, the *Traité du Tout-Monde* (*Treatise on the Tout-Monde*) and *Poétique de la Relation* (*Poetics of Relation*) can be seen to inspire the philosophical perspectives presented in the narrative, the representation of spatiality and the Buddhist motif. The Afro-Caribbean emphasis on genealogy is displaced through the Buddhist notion of lineage, which consists of a group of teachings and/or practices handed down from teachers to students; the latter eventually become teachers and sages in their own right. In this respect, we can see the inclusion of textual references from Glissant's work as a correlative to the spatial and organic relations of the hummingbird. The hawk serves as a mask or guise for Chamoiseau; indeed, the voice of the hawk and the narrator are inseparable. In "Expanse and Filiation," Glissant observes that Buddhism offers a model for the dissolution of self in the world:

> Buddhist mythologies, to offer an almost commonplace comparison, are based on temporal cycles and consider first of all, and uniquely, the individual (himself impermanent or almost so), whose "stories" are of self-perfection through dissolution into the All.[14]

The tendency toward dissolution rather than annihilation or sacrifice is of particular relevance to the Caribbean quest for a postcolonial condition that exceeds perpetual martyrdom, such as is the case with Che Guevara and other "saints" of anticolonial struggle. Ontologically, this way of being in the world supplants the old master-slave paradigm and introduces a collective impetus toward enlightenment. In spatial terms, this Buddhist path is defined by Glissant as follows:

> BUDDHA.—Through a primordial movement of circularity the individual strives in search of perfection towards a dissolution with the All. His successive lives are the cycles ("the histories") of this perfection and do not constitute a linearity. At the end of the process he is reincarnated: he is the same and yet other.[15]

The Buddhist gyre or spiral of motion is of course reproduced by the movement of the hummingbird whose course is so often described as a kind of spiral.[16] In this respect, the Hawk's attentiveness to the pathways and processes of the hummingbird marks a turn from a spectral, predatory perspective to a singular, ruminative, and relational view. The movement toward an expansive or immanent view of one's place in the organic system is brought about through the observation of the hummingbird's participation in the processes of pollination, which are life-giving and reproductive. The master (hummingbird) does not seek to master the cosmic but to dwell within it as an agent who renders service: in biopolitical and spiritual terms, his nourishment is intrinsically related to service. Indeed, the state of awakening itself entails a Glissantian recognition of the chaos of archipelagos in movement (*M*, 85) and mantra-like repetitions and variations on the phrase "Rien n'est vrai, tout est vivant" ("Nothing is true, all is living") (*M*, 230). Malcolm David Eckel notes that in the Buddhist tradition "spaces become sacred by their association with the Buddha or with other sacred persons."[17] In this respect, we can see that the presence of Foufou/Glissant initiates a chain reaction that can be traced through the responses of Malfini/Chamoiseau. Through narrative, Chamoiseau extends the sacred space of the text and the world to the reader.

Malfini is unique in Chamoiseau's oeuvre because it does not entail a strong narrative connection to the slave past or focus on the need to reclaim history. However, this philosophical tale confronts issues of domination and deals with concerns about the Other, which are central to postcolonial criticism. Foufou's deterritorialized relation to plants and role as a sage and warrior offer a model for a nonhierarchical, immanent sense of one's place in the world. Through his dialogue with the Malfini, Chamoiseau becomes bird-like; the author's emphasis on the motions of birds and attentiveness to the environmental as a political model can be seen as an attempt to write with (rather than merely about) nature. In maintaining a stance that is "[n]either identification nor distance, neither proximity nor remoteness," with regard to the Malfini, Chamoiseau is able to "speak *with*, write *with*" the minority without silencing it.[18] Inspired by Kafka, Gilles Deleuze and Félix Guattari claim that "becoming-minoritarian" (which is characterized by the ability to speak with the minority without silencing it) "is a political affair and necessitates a labor of power, an active micropolitics"[19] that subverts the "binary machines" such as "question-answer, masculine-feminine, man-animal, etc."[20] The process of "becoming-animal" binds the writer and the animal with each other; consequently, its political efficacy lies "in the unthinking or undoing of the conventionally human."[21] In this respect, Chamoiseau's Warrior of the Imaginary enters into a quest that is post-human in scope; this figure moves beyond prevailing conceptions of selfhood, language, and being in the world to embrace a relational way of being and becoming in the world. In the context of a post-abolition world, where the slave's body is emancipated from its former commoditized status, the construct of post-human identity is not only appealing but fundamental to the reconstruction of identity for it incorporates both human and nonhuman elements as well as elicits a sense of newness. Thus, Chamoiseau's philosophical reorientation of identity as a quest for being in the world through assemblage and relation can be seen as a way out of the impasse of masking/unmasking as described in *Un dimanche au cachot* where these activities are associated with conquest, the legacies of empire, mimicry, and a sense of alienation. In taking up masquerade as a relational mode of becoming, Chamoiseau the narrator participates in an art of living, which finds expression in a creative relationship to the diversity of the world.[22] As an activist, thinker, and creative writer, Chamoiseau remains steadfastly committed to the politics of place and connection, seeking to establish the beautiful in the world and his work.

NOTES

Chapter 1

1. Wilson Harris, "History Fable and Myth in the Caribbean and the Guianas," *Caribbean Quarterly* 16, no. 2 (June 1970): 16.

2. Errol Hill notes that Lafcadio Hearn observed a masquerade in the carnival on Martinique in 1888 with *diablesses* chanting the question "Jou ouve?" (Is it daybreak?) and receiving the response, "Jou pa'nco ouve." See Hill, *The Trinidad Carnival* (London: New Beacon Books, 1997), 86.

3. Sam Haigh, "From Exile to *Errance*: Dany Laferrière's Cette grenade dans la main du jeune Nègre est-elle une arme ou un fruit?" *The Francophone Caribbean Today: Literature, Language, Culture* (Jamaica: University of the West Indies Press, 2003), 63.

4. Key works in Chamoiseau studies include Lorna Milne, *Patrick Chamoiseau: Espaces d'une écriture antillaise* (Amsterdam and New York: Rodopi, 2006); Maeve McCusker, *Patrick Chamoiseau: Recovering Memory* (Liverpool: Liverpool University Press, 2007); Noémie Auzas, *Chamoiseau ou les voix de Babel: De l'imaginaire des langues* (Paris: Imago, 2009). These works explore the writer's oeuvre in terms of space, time, and language respectively. Special issues of *Antilla*, no. 11, 1988–1989, and *Karibèl Magazine*, no. 3, November–December 1992, have been dedicated to the author. Studies of francophone Caribbean literature attest to Chamoiseau's influence as a theorist and creative writer, including Rose-Myriam Réjouis, *Veillées pour les mots: Aimé Césaire, Patrick Chamoiseau et Maryse Condé* (Paris: Editions Karthala, 2004); Mary Gallagher, *Soundings in French Caribbean Writing Since 1950: The Shock of Space and Time* (Oxford: Oxford University Press, 2002); Delphine Perret, *La créolité: Espace de création* (Martinique: Ibis Rouge Editions, 2001); Dominique Chancé, *L'auteur en souffrance* (Paris: Presses Universitaires de France, 2000); H. Adlai Murdoch, *Creole Identity in the French Caribbean Novel* (Gainesville: University Press of Florida, 2001); Luciano Picanço, *Vers un concept de littérature nationale martiniquaise: évolution de la littérature martiniquaise au XXème siècle: une étude sur l'oeuvre d'Aimé Césaire, Édouard Glissant, Patrick Chamoiseau et Raphaël Confiant* (New York: P. Lang, 2000); Michael Dash, *The Other America* (Charlottesville: University Press of Virginia, 1998); and Lydie Moudileno, *L'écrivain antillais au miroir de sa littérature* (Paris: Editions Karthala, 1997).

5. Édouard Glissant, "Dispossession," *Caribbean Discourse: Selected Essays*, trans. J. Michael Dash (Charlottesville: University Press of Virginia, 1992), 13.

6. Dominick La Capra, *History and Memory after Auschwitz* (Ithaca: Cornell University Press, 1998), 10.

7. McCusker, *Patrick Chamoiseau*, 17.

8. Kathleen M. Balutansky and Marie-Agnès Sourieau, "Introduction," *Caribbean Creolization: Reflections on the Cultural Dynamics of Language, Literature, and Identity* (Gainesville: University Press of Florida, 1998), 3. For more on the instabilities of Creole identity, see H. Adlai Murdoch's introduction to *Creole Identity in the French Caribbean Novel*, pp. 2–7, as well as Wendy Knepper's "Colonization / Creolization / Globalization: The Art and Ruses of *Bricolage*," *Small Axe* 21, no. 1 (Fall 2006): 70–86.

9. Michaeline Crichlow, *Globalization and the Post-Creole Imagination* (Durham: Duke University Press, 2009), 212.

10. Perret, *La créolité*, 264.

11. Gerard Aching, "On Masking and Carnival Time: Some Methodological Considerations," keynote address at the summer symposium "The Arts and Cultural Politics of Carnival," Obermann Center for Advanced Studies, University of Iowa, July 12, 2005. See also Aching's *Masking and Power: Carnival and Popular Culture in the Caribbean* (Minneapolis: University of Minnesota Press, 2002).

12. Milne, *Patrick Chamoiseau*, 27.

13. Milne, *Patrick Chamoiseau*, 25.

14. Born a slave, Toussaint L'Ouverture was an important leader in the Haitian revolution who led troupes to overthrow the plantation owners, abolish slavery, and establish an independent republic.

15. Caryl Phillips, *The Atlantic Sound* (London: Vintage, 2001), 2.

16. V. S. Naipaul, *The Middle Passage* (London: Picador, 2001), 218.

17. Naipaul, *The Middle Passage*, 200.

18. Justin Daniel, *Cinquante ans de departmentalisation outré-mer* (Paris: L'Harmattan, 1997), 11.

19. H. Adlai Murdoch, "Autobiography and Departmentalization in Chamoiseau's *Chémin d'école*: Representational Strategies and the Martinican Memoir," *Research in African Literatures* 40, no. 2 (Spring 2009): 19.

20. Milne, *Patrick Chamoiseau*, 195–96.

21. Saint-John Perse can be seen as participating in the tradition of masquerade; Winspur suggests that Perse introduces a deliberate slippage between extratextual and textual worlds through the projection of the narrator as author. Steve Winspur, *Saint-John Perse and the Imaginary Reader* (Geneva: Droz, 1988), 114.

22. Richard D. E. Burton, "The French West Indies à l'heure de l'Europe: An Overview," *French and West Indian: Martinique, Guadeloupe and French Guiana Today*, ed. Richard D. E. Burton and Fred Reno (Charlottesville: University Press of Virginia, 1995), 5.

23. Richard Price, "The Dark Complete World of a Caribbean Store," *Review* 9, no. 2 (Fall 1985): 217. In 1983, Price noted that 84 percent of a store's goods were imported from outside Martinique.

24. Philippe Lançon, "La geste de Chamoiseau," *Libération*, February 2, 2002 (online version accessible as of March 21, 2007: http://www.liberation.fr/culture/livre/ecrivains/241966.FR.php).

25. Catherine Wells, *L'oraliture dans Solibo Magnifique de Patrick Chamoiseau*, GRELCA Collection Essais 12 (Québec: U. Laval, 1994), 15.

26. Abdellatif Chaouite, "Pour un imaginaire de la diversité: Entretien avec Patrick Chamoiseau," *Allers-retours*, ed. Abdellatif Chaouite and Marie Virolle (Condé sur Noireau: Revues Plurielles / Téraèdre Publishing, 2008), 15–17.

27. Bernadette Cailler offers an excellent analysis of Césaire's influence on Chamoiseau in "Aimé Césaire: A Warrior in Search of Beauty," *Research in African Literatures* 41, no. 1 (Spring 2010): 14–32. In particular, she discusses Chamoiseau's recent work and essay in honor of the poet, entitled "Césaire? Ma liberté," 23/04/2008 BibliObs.com. Shortened version available in *Le Nouvel Observateur*, no. 2268, April 24–30, 2008, 4–5.

28. Chris Bongie has discussed Delsham's work in the following articles: "A Street Named Bissette: Nostalgia, Memory, and the *Cent-Cinquantenaire* of the Abolition of Slavery in Martinique (1848–1998)," *South Atlantic Quarterly* 100, no. 1 (Winter 2001): 215–57; "Exiles on Main Stream: Valuing the Popularity of Postcolonial Literature," *Postmodern Culture* 14, no. 1 (September 2003), accessed online at http://jefferson.village.virginia.edu/pmc/issue.903/14.1bongie.html.

29. Alain Bullo's interview with Chamoiseau confirms details about his studies and stay in France as well as the fact that he worked on both *Chronique des sept misères* and *Solibo Magnifique* while living in France. See Bullo, "Patrick Chamoiseau: *Chronique des sept misères*, de l'oraliture à l'écriture," Facoltà di letter e filosofia, Università Ca' Foscari Venezia, 1994, 36–70.

30. Chancé, *L'auteur en souffrance*, 61.

31. Chancé, *L'auteur en souffrance*, 62.

32. Chamoiseau, *Martinique* (Paris: Richer Hoa Qui, 1995), 7

33. Chamoiseau, "Une semaine en pays dépendent," *Antilla*, no. 552, September 24, 1993, 4–7.

34. Chamoiseau, "Une semaine en pays dominé," *Antilla*, no. 553, October 1, 1993, 5–7.

35. See the joint interview with Chamoiseau and Glissant, *Libération*, December 8, 2005. Maeve McCusker discusses this topic in the opening to *Patrick Chamoiseau*, 1–3.

36. Chancé, *L'auteur en souffrance*, 215.

37. Chancé, *L'auteur en souffrance*, 216.

38. Richard Watts, "'The Wounds of Locality': Living and Writing the Local in Patrick Chamoiseau's *Ecrire en pays dominé*," *French Forum* 28, no. 1 (Winter 2003): 112–13.

39. Arjun Appadurai, *Modernity at Large* (Minneapolis: University of Minnesota Press, 1996), 31.

40. Linda Richards, "Austin Clarke," *January Magazine*, November 2002 (accessed online March 12, 2004, http://januarymagazine.com/profiles/aclarke.html).

41. Caryl Phillips, *A New World Order* (London: Vintage, 2002), 229.

42. Phillips, *A New World Order*, 130–31.

43. Derek Walcott, "A Letter to Chamoiseau," *New York Review of Books*, August 14, 1997 (accessed online August 15, 2004).

44. Maryse Condé, *Crossing the Mangrove* (New York: Anchor Books, 1995), 189.

45. J. Michael Dash, "Martinique is (not) a Polynesian island: detours of French West Indian identity," *International Journal of Francophone Studies* 11, no. 1 and 2 (2008): 135.

46. Richard D. E. Burton argues that Chamoiseau's poetics represent an imaginative marooning and outlines oppositional patterning in Chamoisea's fiction in *Le roman marron: Études sur la literature martiniquaise contemporaine* (Paris: Harmattan, 1997), 92, 151.

47. In "Martinique is (not) a Polynesian island," J. Michael Dash observes that "Chamoiseau's passéisme may be just another escape from contemplating what Bridget Jones had described as a society trapped in some very cosy contradictions" (135).

48. Dash, "Martinique is (not) a Polynesian island," 133. For a critical discussion on the uses of history, see Richard and Sally Price, "Shadowboxing in the Mangrove," *Cultural Anthropology* 12, no. 1 (1997): 3–36.

49. Lucien Taylor, "Créolité Bites: A Conversation with Patrick Chamoiseau, Raphael Confiant, and Jean Bernabé," *Transition: An International Review* 74 (1997) 124–61, 131.

50. Dash, "Martinique is (not) a Polynesian island," 133.

51. Criticism of theories of Creole identity (particularly as articulated in the *Éloge de la créolité*) is varied, but the primary objection is the essentialist emphasis

on a fixed Creole identity rather than an open, fluid process of ongoing creolization. In *Édouard Glissant* (Cambridge: Cambridge University Press, 1995), J. Michael Dash observes that the authors lack a sense of ironic self-scrutiny and the insistence on process that is part of Glissant's thought (23). Consequently, despite "an avowed debt" to Glissant, the Creolists risk "undoing the epistemological break with essentialist thinking" that Glissant has striven to conceptualize (23).

52. A. James Arnold, "The Erotics of Colonialism in Contemporary French West Indian Literary Culture," *New West Indian Guide / Nieuwe West-Indische Gids* 68, no. 1 and 2 (1994): 5–22; Maryse Condé, "Order, Disorder, Freedom and the West Indian Writer," *Yale French Studies* 83, no. 2 (1993): 121–35, 131; Lorna Milne, "Sex, Gender and the Right to Write: Patrick Chamoiseau and the Erotics of Colonialism," *Paragraph* 24, no. 3 (2001): 59–75. Milne responds to Arnold's and Condé's arguments about the forceful male heterosexuality in Chamoiseau's writing by examining the representation of women and eroticism in his work. Milne notes that predatory masculinity is evident in Chamoiseau's writing, but not rewarded or depicted in idealizing terms (62). Therefore, Milne concludes that Chamoiseau is closer to Arnold's and Condé's critical perspective regarding the colonial legacies that inflect some versions of Antillean masculinity (72). See also A. James Arnold, "The Gendering of *créolité*," *Penser la créolité*, ed. Maryse Condé and Madeleine Cottenet-Hage (Paris: Editions Karthala, 1995), 21–40; Price, "Shadowboxing in the Mangrove," 16–20.

53. In articles in *Antilla*, for instance, Chamoiseau wrote in derogatory (sometimes personally insulting) terms about the work of Annie Le Brun and Richard D. E. Burton. These comments seemed to be motivated by personal animosity or ego rather than a sincere interest in dialogue with his critics.

54. These criticisms are garnered from informal conversations with Martinicans about the author in May–June 2003 and the spring of 2005. Some see a discrepancy between the elitism implied in his use of French and Creole and proliferation of literary references and his interest in telling the stories of the poor, working-class persons or those marginalized in colonial or department Martinique. His prose style is found to be difficult and off-putting for the working-class people whom he depicts in his novels. Thus, some wonder whether the author can reach the very readership that he is at pains to represent in his work.

Chapter 2

1. Dominique Deblaine, "Rencontre avec Patrick Chamoiseau," La librarie Mollat, Wednesday February 6, 2002 (accessed online March 15, 2003, at http://www.msha.fr/celfa/recherche/auteur/chamoiseau/chamoiseau.htm).

2. Taylor, "Créolité bites," 140.

3. Taylor, "Créolité bites," 132.

4. Michaël Plumecocq, "Entretien avec Patrick Chamoiseau autour de *Solibo Magnifique*," *Roman 50/90* 27 (June 1999): 133.

5. Plumecocq, "Entretien," 131.

6. François Makandal, Boukman, and François-Dominique Toussaint Louverture are leading figures in the Haitian history of resistance and revolt.

7. Deblaine, "Rencontre avec Patrick Chamoiseau."

8. Stéphanie Bérard, "From the Greek Stage to the Martinican Shores" *Theatre Research International* 33, no. 1 (2008): 48.

9. Bérard, "From the Greek Stage," 47, 43.

10. Stéphanie Bérard, "Le «marronnage» du Théâtre de l'Air Nouveau: Entretien avec Luc Saint-Éloy,'" April 14, 2003, (accessed on May 1, 2005, at http://www.lehman.cuny.edu/ile.en.ile/paroles/saint-eloy_entretien.html).

11. Foreword to *Une manière d'Antigone* (Unpublished manuscript 1975), 4. Cited by Bérard, "From the Greek Stage," 45.

12. Bérard, "From the Greek Stage," 48.

13. Judith G. Miller, "Le Zoulou; Solitude, La Mulâtresse; La Dépossession," *Educational Theatre Journal* 28, no. 4, Reunion: A Self-Portrait of the Group Theatre, December 1976, 561–62.

14. Miller, "Le Zoulou; Solitude, La Mulâtresse; La Dépossession," 561–62.

15. Laghia is a dance that takes the form of a battle.

16. Dash, *The Other America*, 139.

17. Dash, *The Other America*, 139.

18. Chancé, *L'auteur en souffrance*, 5.

19. Anonymous reviewer, "Un nouveau livre de Patrick Chamoiseau: *Manman dlo contre la fee carabosse*," *Antilla*, no. 18, May 15, 1982, 32.

20. Anonymous reviewer, "Un nouveau livre de Patrick Chamoiseau," 32.

21. Jacques Derrida and Avital Rovnell, "The Law of Genre," *Critical Inquiry* 7, no. 1, "On Narrative" (Autumn 1980): 55–81.

22. Homi Bhabha, *The Location of Culture* (London: Routldge, 1994), 38.

23. Subsequently, particularly in novels such as *Texaco* and *Biblique des derniers gestes*, footnotes are introduced with subversive effect in a more sustained fashion.

24. Notably, in Chamoiseau's retelling of "Madame Kéléman," the crabs lose their heads because they try to protect a child from being devoured by a malevolent female figure.

25. In her conclusion to *Patrick Chamoiseau*, Lorna Milne calls attention to the role of displacement and marvels (see 179–206).

Chapter 3

1. Alain Bullo, "Patrick Chamoiseau: Chronique des sept misères, de l'oraliture à l'écriture" (Thesis, Università Ca' Foscari di Venezia, Venice, 1993–94), 59.

2. Édouard Glissant's preface to the 1988 edition of Chronique refers to Chamoiseau as the marqueur de paroles. However, the figure of the marqueur is first introduced by Chamoiseau as a character in Solibo Magnifique.

3. Chancé, *L'auteur en souffrance*, 26.

4. Chris Bongie, *Islands and Exiles: The Creole Identities of Post/Colonial Literature* (Stanford: Stanford University Press, 1998), 399.

5. Patrick Chamoiseau, "Que faire de la parole? Dans la tracée mystérieuse de l'oral à l'écrit," *Écrire la "parole de nuit"; la nouvelle littérature antillaise*, ed. Ralph Ludwig (Paris: Gallimard, 1994), 158.

6. Perret, *La créolité*, 168.

7. *Antilla Spécial*, no. 11, December 1988–January 1989.

8. Pierre Pinalie-Dracius, "Les strategies langagières dans 'Chronique des sept misères' de Patrick Chamoiseau," *Antilla Kreyol* 9 (1987): 17.

9. Pinalie-Dracius, "Les strategies langagières," 18.

10. Pinalie-Dracius, "Les strategies langagières," 21.

11. Marie-Christine Hazaël-Massieux, "Chamoiseau, cet écrivain qui écrit le créole directement en français...," *Portulan, Châteauneuf-le-Rouge: Vents d'ailleurs* 3 (October 2000): 191, 189–202. See also Noémie Auzas, *Chamoiseau ou les voix de Babel*, 192–93.

12. Marion Pausch, "Exprimer la complexité antillaise à l'aide de la tradition orale," *Caribbean Writers / Les auteurs Caribéens: Between Orality & Writing / entre l'oralité et l'écriture*, ed. Marlies Glaser and Marion Pausch (Amsterdam: Rodopi, 1994), 152.

13. Dash, *The Other America*, 118.

14. Raphaël Confiant, "*Chronique des sept misères*: la mémoire restituée," *Antilla*, no. 216, November 12–19, 1986, 13–14. Édouard Glissant, *Antilla*, no. 216, November 12–19, 1986, 15.

15. Confiant, "*Chronique des sept misères*: la mémoire restituée," 13–14.

16. Confiant, "*Chronique des sept misères*: la mémoire restituée," 14.

17. Confiant, "*Chronique des sept misères*: la mémoire restituée," 14.

18. Confiant, "*Chronique des sept misères*: la mémoire restituée," 14.

19. Confiant, "*Chronique des sept misères*: la mémoire restituée," 14.

20. Richard D. E. Burton, "Débrouya pa péche, Or il y a toujours moyen de moyenner: Patterns of Opposition in the Fiction of Patrick Chamoiseau," *Callaloo* 6, no. 2 (1993): 466–81.

21. Valérie Loichot, "Fort-de-France: Pratiques textuelles et corporelles d'une ville coloniale," *French Cultural Studies* 15, no. 1 (2004): 48–60.

22. McCusker, *Patrick Chamoiseau*, 22–46. See page 36 for a discussion of tragedy.

23. Renée K. Gosson, "For What the Land Tells: An Ecocritical Approach to Patrick Chamoiseau's *Chronicle of the Seven Sorrows*," *Callaloo* 26, no. 1 (2003): 219–34.

24. Milne, *Patrick Chamoiseau*, 73–101.

25. Karl Marx, "The Eighteenth Brumaire of Louis Bonaparte," in *Surveys from Exile*, ed. David Fernbach (Harmondsworth: Penguin, 1973), 146.

26. Glissant, *Antilla*, no. 216, 15.

27. Glissant, *Antilla*, no. 216, 15.

28. Glissant, *Antilla*, no. 216, 15.

29. Glissant, *Antilla*, no. 216, 15.

30. Glissant, *Antilla*, no. 216, 15.

31. Lois Parkinson Zamora, "Swords and Silver Rings: Magical Objects in the Work of Jorge Luis Borges and Gabriel García Marquez," *A Companion to Magical Realism*, ed. Stephen M. Hart and Wen-Chin Ouyang (Woodbridge: Tamesis, 2005), 31.

32. Hart and Ouyang, *A Companion to Magical Realism*, 1.

33. Hart and Ouyang, *A Companion to Magical Realism*, 153.

34. Ormerod, "Magic Realism in Contemporary French Caribbean Literature," 220.

35. Dennis Walder, "Writing, Representation and Postcolonial Nostalgia," *Textual Practice* 23, no. 6 (2009): 939–40. See also Svetlana Boym, *The Future of Nostalgia* (New York: Basic Books, 2001), 41, 257.

36. Chamoiseau, "Les nègres marrons de l'en-ville: à propos du driveur," *Antilla*, no. 473, February 21, 1992, 33.

37. On the difference between narcissistic nostalgia and the need to come to terms with the past, see Walder, "Writing, Representation and Postcolonial Nostalgia," 938–39.

38. Auzas, *Chamoiseau ou les voix de Babel*, 210. This critic interprets the interrogation of narrative as typical examples of the authorial pirouette and the resultant effect of narrative relativity.

39. Michel Prat, "Patrick Chamoiseau, un émule martiniquais de Gadda," *Francofonia: Studi e ricerche sulle letterature di lingua francese* 9, no. 17 (1989): 124; Delphine Perret, "La parole du conteur créole: *Solibo Magnifique* de Patrick Chamoiseau," *French Review* 67 (1994): 825; Catherine Wells, "L'oralitéure dans *Solibo Magnifique* de Patrick Chamoiseau," GRELCA Collection Essais No. 12 (Québec:

Laval University, 1994), 19; Adlai Murdoch, *Creole Identity in the French Caribbean Novel* (Gainesville: University Press of Florida, 2001), 218.

40. Beverley Ormerod, "The Group as Protagonist in Recent French Caribbean Fiction," Postcolonial Fictions: Proceedings of the SPACLALS Triennial Conference *SPAN Journal of the South Pacific Association for Commonwealth Literature and Language Studies* No. 36 Vol. 2 1993 (accessed online 5 May 2004 at http://www.mcc.murdoch.edu.au/ReadingRoom/litserv/SPAN/36/Ormerod.html).

41. Yumna Siddiqi, "Police and Postcolonial Rationality in Amitav Ghosh's *The Circle of Reason*," *Cultural Critique* 50 (2002): 175.

42. Michael Holquist, "Whodunit and Other Questions: Metaphysical Detective Stories in Post-war Fiction," *New Literary History* 3, no. 1 (1971): 155.

43. Susan L. Dorff, "The French Connection," *The Armchair Detective* 22, no. 4 (Fall 1989). (Referenced on March 15, 2008, http://www.trussel.com/maig/dorff.htm.)

44. Georges Simenon, *Maigret's Memoirs*, trans. Jean Stewart (New York: Avon, 1963), 126.

45. Jeffrey Nealon, "Work of the Detective, Work of the Writer: Paul Auster's *City of Glass*," *Modern Fiction Studies* 42, no. 1 (1996): 91–92.

46. Murdoch, *Creole Identity in the French Caribbean Novel*, 223.

47. Michael Denning, "Topographies of Violence: Chester Himes's Harlem Domestic Novels," *The Critical Response to Chester Himes*, ed. Charles L. P. Silet (Westport, CT: Greenwood, 1999), 157.

48. Denning, "Topographies of Violence," 157.

49. Denning, "Topographies of Violence," 160.

50. Plumecocq, "Entretien avec Patrick Chamoiseau," 31–32.

51. Lee Horsley, *The Noir Thriller* (Basingstoke: Palgrave, 2001), 23.

52. Horsley, *The Noir Thriller*, 153.

53. Horsley, *The Noir Thriller*, 23.

54. Denning, "Topographies of Violence," 161.

55. Nealon, "Work of the Detective, Work of the Writer," 91–92.

56. Linda Hutcheon, "Irony, Nostalgia, and the Postmodern," University of Toronto English Library, January 19, 1998 (accessed on May 20, 2004, at www.library.utoronto.ca/utel/criticism/hutchinp.html).

57. Bhabha, *The Location of Culture* (New York: Routledge, 1994), 10.

58. Alberto Manguel, "King of the Wheelbarrow," *New York Times Review of Books*, January 16, 2000 (accessed online March 14, 2004, at http://query.nytimes.com/gst/fullpage.html?res=9A01E6D8123BF935A25752C0A9669C8B63&sec=&spon=&pagewanted=all).

59. Beverley Ormerod, "Magical Realism in Contemporary French Caribbean Literature: Ideology or Literary Diversion?" *Australian Journal of French Studies* 34, no. 2 (1997): 225.

60. McCusker, *Patrick Chamoiseau*, 45–46. For a different view on nostalgia, see McCusker, who suggests that the author displaces "the scene of loss from the Africa of *négritude* to the plantation" and interprets the author's nostalgia for origins in the form of "mourning for lost slave traditions of resistance."

Chapter 4

1. Maryse Condé, "*Créolité* without Creole Language?" trans. Kathleen M. Balutansky, *Caribbean Creolization, Reflections on the Cultural Dynamics of Language, Literature, and Identity*, ed. Kathleen M. Balutansky and Marie-Agnès Sourieau (Gainesville: University Press of Florida, 1998), 101–9.

2. Gayatri Chakravorty Spivak, "Subaltern Studies: Deconstructing Historiography," *In Other Worlds: Essays in Cultural Politics* (New York: Metheun, 1987), 205. According to Spivak, strategic essentialism can be seen as the expedient assumption of a temporary unified subject position on the part of subordinate or marginalized social groups, who may temporarily put aside local differences, in order to forge a sense of collective identity through which they band together in political movements. Arguably, in this instance, the assertion of a Creole identity seems to have played such a role, enabling the writers of the treatise to conceive of a new sense of Caribbean identity. While critics rightly critique the notion of Creole identity as essentialist, I would also make a case for the strategic importance of this concept in poetico-political terms at this particular historical moment in the francophone Caribbean.

3. Taylor, "Créolité bites," 136.

4. Taylor, "Créolité bites," 133.

5. Maeve McCusker, "On Slavery, Césaire, and Relating to the World: An Interview with Patrick Chamoiseau," *Small Axe*, 30, November 2009, 79.

6. Richard Bauman, *Story, Performance, and Event: Contextual Studies of Narrative* (Cambridge: Cambridge University Press, 1986), 2.

7. Walter Benjamin, "The Storyteller: Reflections on the works of Nikolai Leskov," in *Illuminations*, trans. Harry Zohn, ed. Hannah Arendt (New York: Schocken Books, 1968), 87.

8. Bauman, *Story, Performance, and Event*, 112.

9. Benjamin, "The Storyteller," 92.

10. Some of the most often cited readings include Christine Chivallon, "*Texaco* ou l'éloge de la 'spatialité,'" *Notre librairie: Revue du livre: Afrique, Caraibes, Ocean*

Indien 127 (1996): 88–107; Kathleen Gyssels, "Du titre au roman: *Texaco* de Patrick Chamoiseau," *Roman 20–50* 20 (1995): 121–32; Cilas Kemodjio, "Ville-poubelle et auto-contamination dans *Texaco* de Patrick Chamoiseau," *Francographies* 8 (1999): 83–101; Veronique Maisier, "Patrick Chamoiseau's Novel *Texaco* and the Picaresque Genre," *Dalhousie French Studies* 57 (2001): 128–36; Serge Dominique Menager, "Topographie, texte et palimpseste: *Texaco* de Patrick Chamoiseau," *The French Review: Journal of the American Association of Teachers of French* 68, no. 1 (1994): 61–68; and Lorna Milne, "From Créolité to Diversalité: The Postcolonial Subject in Patrick Chamoiseau's *Texaco*," *Subject Matters: Subject and Self in French Literature from Descartes to the Present*, ed. Paul Gifford and Johnnie Gratton (Amsterdam: Rodopi, 2000): 162–80. Milne offers an extended discussion of *Texaco* in chapter 4 of *Patrick Chamoiseau: Espaces d'une écriture antillaise*, 103–42, as does McCusker in *Patrick Chamoiseau*, 103–16.

11. For another discussion of ethnography, see Ashley Dawson's "Squatters, Space, and Belonging in the Underdeveloped City," *Social Text* 22, no. 4 (Winter 2004): 17–34.

12. McCusker, *Patrick Chamoiseau*, 110.

13. For a discussion of the creole city, see Roy Chandler Caldwell Jr., "For a Theory of the Creole City: Texaco and the Postcolonial Postmodern," *Ici-Là: Place and Displacement in Caribbean Writing in French*, ed. Mary Gallagher (Amsterdam: Rodopi, 2003), 25–39.

14. Dash, *The Other America*, 144.

15. Dash, *The Other America*, 145.

16. Dash, *The Other America*, 146.

17. James Clifford, *On the Edges of Anthropology* (Chicago: Prickly Paradigm, 2003), 18.

18. James Clifford, "Introduction: Partial Truths," *Writing Culture: The Poetics and Politics of Ethnography*, ed. James Clifford and George E. Marcus (Berkeley and Los Angeles: University of California Press, 1986), 2.

19. Clifford and Marcus, *Writing Culture*, 2–3.

20. Peter Watrous, "Author's Quest for Identity Uncovers Universal Themes," *New York Times*, May 27, 1997.

21. The crossroads appears in *Chronique des sept misères*; in the opening pages of the novel, reference is made to his burial practice. The body of the defeated Zouti (who lost a laghia battle) is found beneath the crossroads crucifix. Ironic reference to crucifix is made in the prologue to Earl Lovelace's *The Dragon Can't Dance*. However, Chamoiseau's narrative figuration might be seen as closer to the work of Kamau Brathwaite and Frankétienne in that it signals a shift between the

word and the world as well as between subjects who collectively give voice to new articulations of the postcolonial condition.

22. Hannah Arendt, *The Human Condition* (Chicago: University of Chicago Press, 1958), 175–75.

23. Michael Hardt and Antonio Negri, *Empire* (Cambridge: Harvard University Press, 2000), 204.

24. Hardt and Negri, *Empire*, 204.

25. Bhabha, *The Location of Culture*, 18.

Chapter 5

1. Mary Louise Pratt, *Imperial Eyes: Travel Writing and Transculturation* (London: Routledge, 1992), 7.

2. Sharon L. Shelley, "Addressing Linguistic and Cultural Diversity with Patrick Chamoiseau's *Chemin-d'école*," *French Review* 75, no. 1 (October 2001): 112.

3. For a contextual discussion of autobiographical fiction in the French Caribbean, see Maeve McCusker's excellent discussion in "'Troubler l'ordre de l'oubli': Memory and Forgetting in French Caribbean Autobiography of the 1990s," *Forum for Modern Language Studies* 40, no. 4 (2004): 438–50.

4. Gallagher, *Soundings in French Caribbean Writing*, 105.

5. Gallagher, *Soundings in French Caribbean Writing*, 106.

6. Julia Watson, "Unruly Bodies: Autoethnography and Authorization in Nafissatou Diallo's *De Tilène au Plateau* (A Dakar Childhood)," *Research in African Literatures* 28, no. 2 (1997): 50.

7. James Buzard, "On Auto-Ethnographic Authority," *Yale Journal of Criticism* 16, no. 1 (2003): 77.

8. Philippe Lejeune, *Les brouillons de soi* (Paris: Seuil, 1998), 125.

9. McCusker, *Patrick Chamoiseau*, 52. In chapter 2 of her monograph, McCusker explores the elusive nature of autobiographical memory in a postcolonial context.

10. Bongie, *Islands and Exiles*, 1998, 13–14.

11. Gallagher, *Soundings in French Caribbean Writing*, 104.

Chapter 6

1. For a discussion of the importance of the marvel in Chamoiseau's oeuvre, see the concluding chapter to Milne's *Patrick Chamoiseau* in which she discusses the poetics of displacement. Milne offers an excellent reading of *Biblique* as a text that embodies the principles of the *émerveille* (199–206).

2. The film won several awards, including the *Prix Sacem* awarded to Jocelyne Beroard for the title song "Ahidjéré," FESPACO's (Festival Pan-African du cinéma et de la télévision de Ouagadougou) *Prix Paul Robeson* in 1995 and the "Best actor" award for Robert Liensol at the 1994 Namur International Festival for Francophone Film.

3. Chris Bongie observes that the film presents a "disturbingly limited understanding of diasporic Atlantic identity" in "A Street Named Bissette: Nostalgia, Memory, and the *Cent-Cinquantenaire* of the Abolition of Slavery in Martinique (1848–1998)," *South Atlantic Quarterly* 100, no. 1 (2001): 221. Richard and Sally Price note that African viewers complained that Béhanzin, a "powerful leader and national hero of resistance, was depicted in the film as a pitiable, broken man who lacked cultural credibility" in "Shadowboxing in the Mangrove," *Cultural Anthropology* 12, no. 1 (1997): 23.

4. Bernabé, "L'Exil de Béhanzin ou la négritude revisitée," 30.

5. Bernabé, "L'Exil de Béhanzin ou la négritude revisitée," 31.

6. Stuart Hall, "The formation of a diasporic intellectual," Interview by Kuan-Hsing Chen, *Critical Dialogues in Cultural Studies* (New York: Routledge, 1996), 490.

7. Bernabé, "L'Exil de Béhanzin ou la négritude revisitée," 28.

8. For an account of one adversarial exchange during this time, see Chris Bongie's discussion of arguments with Annie Le Brun, *Islands and Exiles*, 341–47.

9. *Antilla*, no. 620, February 17, 1995, 4.

10. *Antilla*, no. 620, February 17, 1995, 5.

11. *Antilla*, no. 654, October 27, 1995.

12. Chamoiseau, "Contre la Départmentalisation: autopsie d'un désastre," *Antilla*, no. 676, April 10, 1996, 4–6.

13. Chamoiseau, "Contre la Départmentalisation: autopsie d'un désastre," 8.

14. Chamoiseau, "Contre la Départmentalisation: autopsie d'un désastre," 9.

15. Chamoiseau, "Contre la Départmentalisation: autopsie d'un désastre," 9.

16. Chamoiseau, "Contre la Départmentalisation: autopsie d'un désastre," 9.

17. Chamoiseau, "Contre la mémoire," 31.

18. Chamoiseau, "Contre la mémoire," 27.

19. Chamoiseau, "Contre la mémoire," 30.

20. Chamoiseau, "Contre la mémoire," 31.

21. Stephen Greenblatt, *Marvellous Possessions: The Wonder of the New World* (Oxford: Oxford University Press, 1991), 16–17, 79–80.

22. La librarie Mollat, 2002.

23. Alejo Carpentier, "The Baroque and the Marvelous Real," *Magical Realism. Theory, History, Community*, ed. Lois Parkinson Zamora and Wendy B. Faris (Durham, NC: Duke University Press, 1995), 102.

24. Dash, *The Other America*, 95. At the first Congress of Black Writers in 1956, the Haitian novelist Alexis presented his "Du réalisme merveilleux des Haïtiens." He argued for seeing Haitian culture as creolized rather than neo-African; he saw the marvel as a new narrative method that would reflect the Haitian people's ability to combine the real and the fantastic in their imagination. Dash has also noted that Alexis's definition of magic realism provides a "zonal confluence" or a poetics grounded in the lived realities and complexities of Caribbean identity. See *The Other America*, 94–95.

25. Carpentier, "The Baroque and the Marvelous Real," 104.

26. Carpentier, "The Baroque and the Marvelous Real," 104.

27. Zamora and Faris, "Editors' Note," *Magical Realism*, 75.

28. Carpentier, "The Baroque and the Marvelous Real," 100–101.

29. Carpentier, "The Baroque and the Marvelous Real," 100–101.

30. Carpentier, "The Baroque and the Marvelous Real," 94.

31. For a discussion of the baroque, see Dominique Chancé's "De *Chronique des sept misères* à *Biblique des derniers gestes*, Patrick Chamoiseau est-il baroque?" *MLN* 118, no. 4 (September 2003): 891–93.

32. In chapter 5 of *Patrick Chamoiseau*, Milne focuses on the initiatory aspects of the narrative with a particular emphasis on the role of the Martinican rainforest, which features as a space of initiation in both *L'esclave* and *Biblique*.

33. Victor Turner, *The Forest of Symbols: Aspects of Ndembu Ritual* (Ithaca, NY: Cornell University Press, 1967), 13–14.

34. Christopher Yggdre, "Entretiens avec Patrick Chamoiseau: Devenir des fondateurs... plaidoyer pour un guerrier de l'imaginaire," *Périphériques* 13 (Spring 2000): 10–17 (accessed online on September 20, 2005, at http://www.globenet.org/periph/journal/13/fr1310.html).

35. Yggdre, "Entretiens avec Patrick Chamoiseau."

36. Yggdre, "Entretiens avec Patrick Chamoiseau."

37. Yggdre, "Entretiens avec Patrick Chamoiseau."

38. Chamoiseau, *Écrire en pays dominé*, 309. The word "local(e)" meaning both the local and a specific locale seems to capture what Chamoiseau means when he refers to the *Lieu* as a concept.

39. Perret, *La créolité*, 290. See also Doris L. Garraway's "Toward a Creole Myth of Origin: Narrative, Foundations and Eschatology in Patrick Chamoiseau's *L'Esclave vieil homme et le molosse*," *Callaloo* 29, no. 1 (Winter 2006): 151.

40. Perret, *La créolité*, 281.

41. Chamoiseau describes the slave's experiences, saying "il fait son *je*," referring to the fact that the slave learns to perceive himself from the first-person perspective (as "I") rather than from a third-person, outsider's viewpoint. See Perret, *La créolité*, 90.

42. John Taylor, "Rabelais in Martinique," *Times Literary Supplement*, October 10, 1997, 32.

43. Lorna Milne, "The *marron* and the *marqueur*," *Ici-Là. Place and Displacement in Caribbean Writing in French*, ed. Mary Gallagher (Amsterdam and New York: Rodopi, 2003), 68.

44. Tzvetan Todorov, *The Fantastic: A Structural Approach to a Literary Genre*, trans. Richard Howard (Ithaca, NY: Cornell University Press, 1975), 33.

45. *La folie Célat* (1987) was subsequently published in 2000 as part of a collection titled *Le monde incréé* (Paris: Gallimard, 2000).

46. Dawn Fulton, "*Roman des nous*: the first person plural and collective identity in Martinique," *French Review* 76, no. 6 (May 2003): 1110.

47. Édouard Glissant, *L'Intention poétique* (Paris: Gallimard, 1969), 8.

48. Glissant, *L'Intention poétique*, 8.

49. Ann Armstrong Scarboro emphasizes the importance of a *"prise de conscience*, the inner voice and a call to action" as attributes of the modern-day maroon. "A Shift Toward the Inner Voice and *Créolité* in the French Caribbean Novel," *Callaloo* 15, no. 1 (Winter 1992): 27.

50. The "Pierre-Monde" can be translated as the "philosopher's stone." This ancient symbol originates in Hermetic philosophy and the alchemical arts. For medieval alchemists, the philosopher's stone could transmute base lead into gold. In a spiritual sense, the stone represents the quest for perfection. In taking the Carib stone (probably a petroglyph) as a symbol of creolization, Chamoiseau suggests that a more perfect world order can be attained by embracing the "alchemical" processes of transformation that creolization entails. His concept should also be seen as a response to Glissant's idea of the unpredictable, creolizing aspects of the *Tout-Monde*.

51. Patrick Chamoiseau, "Dans la Pierre-Monde," *Créolisation de la Culture* (Zurich: Pro Helvetia, Fondation suisse pour la culture, 2000), 16.

52. The *émerveille* or *grand merveilleux* plays an essential role in the concept of the *deuxième monde* in *Biblique des derniers gestes* (*BDG*, 538) and *Livret des villes du deuxième monde*. Generally speaking this mode of analysis could also be applied to the role of Bodule-Jules as a rebel figure who becomes a *guerrier* (*BDG*, 773) in a narrative told as a series of *émerveilles*.

53. Watts, "'The Wounds of Locality,'" 115.

54. Watts, "'The Wounds of Locality,'" 116.

55. Appadurai, *Modernity at Large*, 33.

56. Appadurai, *Modernity at Large*, 33.

57. Appadurai, *Modernity at Large*, 33–34.

58. Appadurai, *Modernity at Large*, 34.

59. The section titled "Anabase" is subtitled "En digenèse selon Glissant." This section takes inspiration in equal part from Glissant's concept as defined in *Le traité du Tout-Monde* where the author notes that the genesis of Creole societies in the Americas is founded upon another obscurity, that of the slaveholder (Paris: Gallimard, 1996), 36. Rather than referring to the genesis or creation of the New World, Glissant refers to its hybrid formation or digenesis. See also Glissant's *Faulkner, Mississippi*, trans. Barbara Lewis and Thomas C. Spear (Chicago: University of Chicago Press, 2000), 195.

60. *Poetics*, 11.

61. Chamoiseau, "Contre la mémoire," 30.

62. Chamoiseau, "Contre la mémoire," 31.

63. Chamoiseau, "Contre la mémoire," 31.

64. Chamoiseau, "In the World," 15.

65. Chamoiseau, "In the World," 15–16.

66. Stuart Hall, "Conclusion: The Multicultural Question," *Un/Settled Multiculturalisms. Diasporas. Entanglements. Transruptions*, ed. Branor Hesse (London and New York: Zed Books, 2000), 226; Chamoiseau, "In the World," 13–14.

67. Chamoiseau, "In the World," 13.

68. Chamoiseau, "In the World," 13.

69. Chamoiseau, "In the World," 13

70. Chamoiseau, "In the World," 16.

71. Chamoiseau, "Mon journal de la semaine: Enrayer la violence en Corse," *Libération*, November 27–28, 1999 (accessed online on March 15, 2005, at http://jacbayle.club.fr/livres/Cham_Corse.html).

Chapter 7

1. The description of this film is based on a press release by the screenplay author and director, which was published in "Gazet sifon blé/Lavwa ka bay" or "Bulletin de l'Association pour l'information dans le monde créole," no. 81, January 2004, 5–6 (http://creoles.free.fr/archivesGSB/GSB81.pdf). The film was reviewed by Manuel Norvat, "Ki Nov? Matinik Le cinéma de la mer," http://www.potomitan.info/matinik/matnik11.html.

2. Manuel Norvat, "Ki Nov? Matinik: Le cinéma de la mer," http://www.potomitan.info/matinik/matnik11.html. Accessed August 1, 2005.

3. Patrick Chamoiseau was interviewed about the film under production; see http://www.bondamanjak.com/content/view/2413/81/.

4. Richard Watts, "'Toutes ces eaux!': Ecology and Empire in Patrick Chamoiseau's *Biblique des derniers gestes*," *MLN* 118, no. 4 (2003): 897.

5. With reference to *L'Esclave vieil homme et le molosse*, Milne argues that the forest represents a space affiliated with the resistance to slavery as well as a space of transformation: "mais c'est aussi l'espace des transformations, des découvertes de soi, de l'affirmation d'une identité fortement liée à l'histoire comme à l'espace même de la Martinique et alimentée par des racines multiples et des relations toujours changeantes: une identité «rhizomatique», donc, mais surtout aussi dynamique." See Milne, *Patrick Chamoiseau*, 157–58.

6. Watts, "'Toutes ces eaux!'" 901–2.

7. Watts, "'Toutes ces eaux!'" 903.

8. Heidi Bojsen, "Flashbacks of an Orchid: Rhizomatic Narration in Patrick Chamoiseau's *Biblique des derniers gestes*," *Caribbean Literature and the Environment: Between Nature and Culture*, ed. Elizabeth M. DeLoughrey, Renée K. Gosson, and George B. Handley (Charlottesville: University Press of Virginia, 2005), 214.

9. Michael Niblett, "'The Body Grotesque': The Ecology of Identity in Patrick Chamoiseau's *Biblique des derniers gestes*," *What is the Earthly Paradise? Ecocritical Responses to the Caribbean*, ed. Chris Campbell and Erin Somerville (Newcastle: Cambridge Scholars Publishing, 2007), 103.

10. Niblett, "'The Body Grotesque,'" 102.

11. Niblett, "'The Body Grotesque,'" 115–16.

12. Édouard Glissant, "Distancing, Determining," *The Poetics of Relation*, trans. Betsy Wing (Ann Arbor: University of Michigan Press, 1997), 146.

13. Jana Evans Braziel, "Caribbean Genesis in Caribbean Literature and the Environment," *Caribbean Literature and the Environment*, 112.

14. Stokely Carmichael and Charles Hamilton, *Black Power: The Politics of Liberation in America* (London: Cape, 1968), xiii.

15. Glissant, "The Relative and Chaos," *Poetics*, 138.

16. "Dans *Biblique des derniers gestes*, même si cela paraît partir dans tous les sens, le thème c'est l'amour: tout le processus amoureux, toutes les facettes de l'amour, les différentes formes d'amour sont explorés" ("In Biblique des derniers gestes, even if it seems to go in all directions, the theme is love: the entire process of love, all the facets of love, the different forms of love are explored"), observed Chamoiseau. "Entretien de Savrina Parevadee Chinien avec Patrick Chamoiseau: À travers l'évocation de certains de ses romans, l'auteur revient sur l'acte d'écrire et sur la gestation de son écriture," February 28, 2008 (accessed on May 5, 2008, at http://www.africultures.com/index.asp?menu=affiche_article&no=7396).

17. Cited in Richard L. Harris, *Che Guevara: A Biography* (Santa Barbara: Greenwood, 2011), 129. Anatole France's story "Balthasar" inspired Norman Cameron's play by the same name. As with Chamoiseau, Maryse Condé's *Le dernier roi mage* may also owe a debt to France's short story.

18. Audre Lorde, *Sister Outsider: Essays and Speeches by Audre Lorde* (Berkeley and Toronto: Crossing Press, 1984, 2007), 55.

19. In *Patrick Chamoiseau: Recovering Memory*, McCusker offers a very different interpretation; she observes that "[t]he body is repeatedly figured as vulnerable, abject, scatological, fragmented or excessive, and these states are discursively linked to the trauma of slavery itself" (147). In particular, she views the representation of the female body as "the key site (and sight) of horror, and a constant threat to the integrity of the male" (147). While I agree that there is a tension between the warrior's priaptic conquest of women and anticolonial politics (148), I would argue that Chamoiseau distances himself from Balzathar's unreconstituted masculinity. Indeed, the emphasis on the conversion narrative would seem to offer an implicit critique of "'aggressively heterosexual eroticism'" (149).

20. Bhabha, *The Location of Culture*, 170.

21. The infusion of hyphenated names that refer to Catholic saints and vodou *lwas* as well as the practice of spiritual traditions that resemble vodou, such as the use of mirrors to communicate with spirits, evokes a creolized spiritual world and diasporic sensibility similar to that found in Maryse Condé's *Les derniers rois mages*, a novel that bears the influence of Erzulie Dantor and Erzulie Freda and comparable references to the rebirth of the warrior figure and the presence of the Magi as witness to the birth of a sacred child. In many ways, we might see Chamoiseau's reworking of these themes as a response to Condé, particularly as her novel dealt with the figure of Béhanzin, the exiled African king who was the source for Chamoiseau's first articulation of the poetics of the Warrior of the Imaginary.

22. Margarite Fernádez Olmos and Lizabeth Paravisini-Gebert, *Creole Religions of the Caribbean: An Introduction from Vodou and Santería to Obeah and Espiritismo* (New York: New York University Press, 2003), 107.

23. Bhabha, *The Location of Culture*, 36–39.

24. Frantz Fanon, *Wretched of the Earth*, trans. C. Farrington (1967; rpt. London: Penguin, 2002), 27–28.

25. Fanon, *Wretched of the Earth*, 28.

26. Glissant, "Errantry, Exile," 11.

27. David Quint, *Epic and Empire* (Princeton, NJ: Princeton University Press, 1993), 45.

28. Quint, *Epic and Empire*, 9.

29. Quint, *Epic and Empire*, 9.
30. Glissant, "Expanse and Filiation," *Poetics of Relation*, 52.
31. Glissant, "Expanse and Filiation," 55.
32. Glissant, "Expanse and Filiation," 55.
33. Glissant, "Expanse and Filiation," 56.
34. Chamoiseau, "Méditations à Saint-John Perse," http://www.potomitan.info/atelier/meditations.html, Section 33.

Chapter 8

1. This manifesto has been translated into English as *A Plea for "Products of High Necessity"* by Isabelle Metral for *L'Humanité in English*. See Thursday March 5, 2009: http://www.humaniteinenglish.com/spip.php?article1163.
2. Examples of literary treatises include Aimé Césaire's "En guise de manifeste littéraire" (1942) and *Discours sur le colonialisme* (*Discourse on Colonialism*) (1955), Frantz Fanon's *Peau noire, masques blancs* (*Black Skin, White Masks*) (1952) and Jacques Stephen Alexis's "Lettre aux Hommes Vieux" (1946).
3. Glissant, *Traité du Tout-Monde*, 17–18.
4. Celia Britton, *Édouard Glissant and Postcolonial Theory: Strategies of Language and Resistance* (Charlottesville: University Press of Virginia, 1999), 179.
5. Glissant, "The Known, the Uncertain," *Caribbean Discourse: Selected Essays*, 64.
6. One might refer to Jacques Derrida and David Wills, "The Animal That Therefore I Am (More to Follow)," *Critical Inquiry* 28, no. 2 (Winter 2002): 369–418. Gilles Deleuze and Félix Guattari's discussion of assemblages and "becoming-animal" is also relevant here as Chamoiseau's state of consciousness slips into that of nature and the bird so that he is no longer positioned as merely human but also as a participant in an organic wholeness. See Gilles Deleuze and Félix Guattari, *A Thousand Plateaus: Capitalism and Schizophrenia*, trans. Brian Massumi (Minneapolis: University of Minnesota Press, 1987), 260. The Deleuzo-Guattarian wasp-orchid assemblage offers an exemplar of mutual deterritorialization, which is also evident in Chamoiseau's relation of the hummingbird to the flower. Chamoiseau's clairvoyant relationship to the Malfini might be seen as an example of an assemblage.
7. Chamoiseau's interest in birds can be traced back to the many puns on his name, which contains the word "oiseau" or bird within it. Notably, the nickname *oiseau de Cham* or "bird of Cham." This biblical reference to the story of Noah's son, Cham, and the curse the father placed on Cham's descendants, has been interpreted as the curse of slavery. "Chamoiseau" takes this lexical play further as

composition of his name (consisting of "bird," suggesting flight, and "Ham," suggesting enslavement) defies the binaries of freedom and slavery. *Texaco* contains a relevant episode in which Marie-Sophie's grandfather is imprisoned for his presumed resistance to slavery. Both the slave owner and his fellow slaves are suspicious of his incantory references to birds, assuming some form of curse is being carried out, but the narrator informs us that the jailed man is merely expressing his lifelong fascination with the birds in flight (*T*, 52–53). Perhaps the most pertinent example is the account of the hummingbird myth of origins in *Chronique des sept misères* where the hummingbird is described as a vengeful entity reduced to minuscule size by his enemy who has magical powers (*CSM*, 106–7). The hummingbird cultivates a sharp pointed beak over the centuries in order to take vengeance, but over time forgets his rage and spends his time becoming drunk on the nectar of flowers. Eventually, his heart gives out and he explodes, dissipating into the world of flowers. The theme of dissolution in the world resurfaces in *Malfini*.

8. The term "alaya" is defined as follows: [a]laya (Skt.). 1. Basis, substratum; sometimes used simply as an abbreviation for the Yogcra concept of the 'storehouse consciousness' ([a]laya-vijñna) but also found in Tibetan Buddhist usage as a distinct concept in the sense of the 'ground of being'. These two aspects of the term thus distinguish the ontological and epistemological aspects of the [a]lya-vijñna. 2. The term also occurs in a nonphilosophical sense as a synonym of trsn[a], meaning attachment, clinging, or desire. See *A Dictionary of Buddhism*, ed. Damien Keown (Oxford: Oxford University Press, 2003). *Oxford Reference Online*, Oxford University Press, Brunel University. Referenced on April 29, 2010: http://www.oxfordreference.com/views/ENTRY.html?subview=Main&entry=t108.e73.

9. The "amala" or "amala-vijñna" refers to the "'unsullied consciousness', a term used in Param<a>rtha's system of Yogcra and equivalent in many respects to Buddha-nature or the tathgata-garbha." See *A Dictionary of Buddhism*.

10. According to *A Dictionary of Buddhism*, the term "Buddha" is defined as "an epithet of those who have achieved enlightenment (*bodhi*), the goal of the Buddhist religious life" and "the Buddhas are those who have awakened to the true nature of things as taught in the Four Noble Truths."

11. *A Dictionary of Buddhism*.

12. *A Dictionary of Buddhism*.

13. A. James Arnold, "The Essay And/In History," *A History of Literature in the Caribbean: Hispanic and Francophone Regions*, Volume I, ed. Albert James Arnold, Julio Rodríguez-Luis, and J. Michael Dash (Philadelphia and Amsterdam: John Benjamins Publishing Company, 1994), 563.

14. Glissant, "Expanse and Filiation," 48.

15. Glissant, "Expanse and Filiation," 51.

16. Glissant, "Expanse and Filiation," 48–49.

17. Malcolm David Eckel, *Buddhism: Origins, Beliefs, Practices, Holy Texts, Sacred Place* (Oxford: Oxford University Press, 2002), 65.

18. Gilles Deleuze and Claire Parnet, *Dialogues* (New York: Columbia University Press, 1987), 52, original emphasis.

19. Deleuze and Guattari, *A Thousand Plateaus*, 292.

20. Deleuze and Parnet, *Dialogues*, 2.

21. Steve Baker, *The Postmodern Animal* (London: Reaktion Books, 2000), 104.

22. Chamoiseau, "Pour une imaginaire de la diversité," 17.

SELECT BIBLIOGRAPHY

Works by Patrick Chamoiseau

PUBLISHED BOOKS
Chronique des sept misères. Paris: Gallimard, 1986.
Solibo Magnifique. Paris: Gallimard, 1988.
Texaco. Paris: Gallimard, 1992.
Antan d'enfance. Paris: Gallimard, 1993.
Chemin-d'école. Paris: Gallimard, 1994.
Écrire en pays dominé. Paris: Gallimard, 1997.
L'Esclave vieil homme et le molosse. Paris: Gallimard, 1997.
Biblique des derniers gestes. Paris: Gallimard, 2002.
À bout d'enfance. Paris: Gallimard, 2005.
Un dimanche au cachot. Paris: Gallimard, 2007.
Les neuf consciences du Malfini. Paris: Gallimard, 2009.

WORKS FOR CHILDREN
Chamoiseau, Patrick, and Georges Puisy. *Les Antilles sous Bonaparte: Delgrès.* Fort-de-France: Editions Désormeaux, 1981.
Chamoiseau, Patrick, and Mireille Vautier. *Au temps de l'antan: contes du pays martinique.* Paris: Hatier, 1988.
Chamoiseau, Patrick and Maure. *Émerveilles.* Paris: Éditions Gallimard Jeunesse, 1998.
Chamoiseau, Patrick, and William Wilson. *Le commandeur d'une pluie suivi de L'Accra de la richesse.* Paris: Gallimard Jeunesse, 2002.
Chamoiseau, Patrick, and Thierry Ségur. *Encyclomerveille d'un tueur, 1. L'Orphelin de cocoyer grands-bois.* Tournai: Guy Delcourt Productions, 2009.

SELECTED THEATRICAL WORKS
"Solitude la mulâtresse." Fort-de-France, Schoelcher Library (manuscript).
"L'Époque Delgrès." Fort-de-France, Schoelcher Library (manuscript). 1974.
"Une manière d'Antigone." Paris (manuscript). 1975.
Manman Dlo contre la fée Carabosse. Paris: Editions Caribéennes, 1982.

CREOLE THEORY AND HISTORY

Bernabé, Jean, Patrick Chamoiseau, and Raphaël Confiant. *Éloge de la créolité*. Paris: Gallimard, 1989.

Chamoiseau, Patrick, and Raphaël Confiant. *Lettres créoles: Tracées antillaises et continentales de la littérature Haïti, Guadeloupe, Martinique, Guyane, 1635–1975*. Paris: Hatier, 1991.

VISUAL TEXTS

Delsham, Tony, and Patrick Chamoiseau. *Le retour de Monsieur Coutcha*. Fort-de-France: MGG, 1984.

Chamoiseau, Patrick, Michel Renaudeau, and Emmanuel Valentin. *Martinique*. Paris: Richer-Hoa-Qui, 1995.

Chamoiseau, Patrick, and Jean-Luc de Laguarigue. *Elmire des sept bonheurs: confidences d'un vieux travailleur de la distillerie Saint-Etienne*. Paris: Gallimard, 1998.

———. *Cases en pays-mêlés*. Paris: Editions Hazan, 2000.

———. *Tracées de mélancolies*. Paris: Hazan, 2001.

Chamoiseau, Patrick, and Anne Chopin. *Trésors cachés et patrimoine naturel de la Martinique vue du ciel*. Paris: HC Éditions, 2007.

SELECTED SCREENPLAYS

L'Exil du roi Béhanzin. Dir. Guy Deslauriers. Kréol Productions, 1994.

Chamoiseau, Patrick, and Claude Chonville. *Femmes-Solitude*. RFO, Kréol Productions and Caribbean Vidéo Diffusion, 1995.

———. *Un siècle d'écrivains: Édouard Glissant*. Kréol Productions and FR3, 1996.

———. *Passage du milieu*. Kréol Productions and Les films du Rafia, 2000.

Nord-Plage. Dir. José Hayot. Les films du dorlis and Prodom along with Canal Antilles, 2003.

Biguine. Dir. Guy Deslauriers. Kréol Productions and RFO, 2004.

Aliker. Dir. Guy Deslauriers. Kréol Productions, 2009.

ENGLISH TRANSLATIONS

Creole Folktales. Trans. Linda Coverdale. New York: New Press, 1994.

School Days. Trans. Linda Coverdale. London: Granta, 1998.

Strange Words. Trans. Linda Coverdale. London: Granta, 1998.

School Days. Trans. Linda Coverdale. Lincoln: University of Nebraska Press, 1997.

Chronicle of the Seven Sorrows. Trans. Linda Coverdale. Lincoln: University of Nebraska Press, 1999.

Seven Dreams of Elmira: A Tale of Martinique. Trans. Mark Polizzotti. Cambridge: Zoland Books, 1999.

Solibo Magnificent. Trans. Rose-Myriam Réjouis and Val Vinokurov. New York: Pantheon Books, 1997.

Texaco. Trans. Rose-Myriam Réjouis and Val Vinokurov. New York: Pantheon Books, 1997.

Childhood. Trans. Carol Volk. Lincoln: University of Nebraska Press, 1999.

SELECTED ARTICLES

"En témoignage d'une volupté." *Carbet*, 10, December 1990, 144.

"Reflections on Maryse Condé's *Traversée de la mangrove*." *Callaloo* 14, no. 2 (1991): 389–95.

"Une semaine en pays dépendant." *Antilla*, no. 552, September 24, 1993, 4–7.

"Une semaine en pays dominé." *Antilla*, no. 553, October 1, 1993, 5–7.

"Contre la mémoire et l'histoire." *Antilla*, no. 557, October 29, 1993, 25–31.

"Une semaine en pays dominé." *Antilla*, no. 558, November 5, 1993, 3–5.

"Que faire de la parole? Dans la tracée mystérieuse de l'oral à l'écrit." *Ecrire la parole de nuit*. Ed. Ralph Ludwig. Paris: Gallimard, 1994. 151–58.

Traces-mémoires du bagne. Paris: Caisse Nationale des Monuments Historiques et des Sites, 1994.

"Une semaine en pays dominé." *Antilla*, no. 608, November 18, 1994, 4–5.

"Une semaine en pays dominé." *Antilla*, no. 612, December 16, 1994, 4–6.

"Une semaine en pays dominé." *Antilla*, no. 613, December 23, 1994, 4–6.

"Une semaine en pays dominé." *Antilla*, no. 616, January 20, 1995, 4–6.

"Une semaine en pays dominé." *Antilla*, no. 619, February 10, 1995, 4–6.

"Une semaine en pays dominé." *Antilla*, no. 620, February 17, 1995, 4–5.

"Une semaine en pays dominé." *Antilla*, no. 621, February 24, 1995, 4–5.

"Une semaine en pays dominé." *Antilla*, no. 623, March 10, 1995, 4–5.

"Une semaine en pays dominé." *Antilla*, no. 624, March 17, 1995, 4–5.

"Une semaine en pays dominé." *Antilla*, no. 632, May 12, 1995, 12–13.

"Une semaine en pays dominé." *Antilla*, no. 636, June 9, 1995, 4–6.

"Une semaine en pays dominé." *Antilla*, no. 638, June 23, 1995, 4–5.

"Une semaine en pays dominé." *Antilla*, no. 640, July 7, 1995, 4–6.

"Une semaine en pays dominé." *Antilla*, no. 642, July 21, 1996, 4–7.

"Une semaine en pays dominé." *Antilla*, no. 643, July 28, 1995, 7–9.

"Une semaine en pays dominé." *Antilla*, no. 650, September 29, 1995, 4–6.

"Une semaine en pays dominé." *Antilla*, no. 651, October 6, 1995, 4–5.

"Une semaine en pays dominé." *Antilla*, no. 652, October 13, 1995, 5.

"Les os de la mémoire." *Antilla*, no. 654, October 27, 1996, 15–16.

"Une semaine en pays dominé." *Antilla*, no. 666, January 26, 1996, 4–7.

"Une semaine en pays dominé." *Antilla*, no. 671, March 6, 1996, 4–7.

"Une semaine en pays dominé." *Antilla*, no. 676, April 10, 1996, 4–9.

"Une semaine en pays dominé." *Antilla*, no. 705, November 13, 1996, 23–25.

"Une semaine en pays dominé." *Antilla*, no. 706, November 20, 1996, 20–22.

"Mon journal de la semaine. Enrayer la violence en Corse." *Libération*, November 27–28, 1999.

"De la mémoire obscure à la mémoire consciente." *De l'esclavage aux réparations*. Ed. Serge Chalons et al. Paris: Karthala, 2000. 109–16.

"In the World of the Philosopher's Stone." *The Creolisation of Culture*. Trans. Simon Knight. Zurich: ProHelvetia, Arts Council of Switzerland, 2000.

"Dans la Pierre-monde." *Kapes Kreyol*. www.palli.ch/kapeskreyol/divers/pierre.html (accessed on September 15, 2004).

SHORTER WORKS

Chamoiseau, Patrick, and Rodolphe Hammadi. *Guyane: traces-mémoires du bagne*. Paris: Caisse nationale des monuments historiques et des sites, 1994.

Chamoiseau, Patrick, Gerard Delver, Édouard Glissant et al. "Manifeste pour refonder les DOM." *Le Monde*, January 21, 2000.

Chamoiseau, Patrick. *Livret des villes du deuxième monde*. Paris: Monum Éditions du Patrimoine, 2002.

Chamoiseau, Patrick, Serge Hélénon, and Dominique Berthet. *Les bois sacrés d'Hélénon*. Paris: Dapper, 2002.

Chamoiseau, Patrick, and Édouard Glissant. *Quand les murs tombent. L'identité nationale hors-la-loi?* Paris: Galaade Éditions, 2007.

———. *L'Intraitable beauté du monde: Adresse à Barack Obama*. Paris: Galaade Éditions, 2009.

Breleur, Ernest, Patrick Chamoiseau, Serge Domi, Gérard Delver, Édouard Glissant, Guillaume Pigeard de Gurbert, Olivier Portecop, Olivier Pulvar, and Jean-Claude William. *Manifeste pour les "produits" de haute nécessité*. Paris: Galaade Éditions, 2009.

SELECTED INTERVIEWS

Arsenault, Michel. "Recréer la créolité: Interview with Patrick Chamoiseau." *Le Monde*, 1998.

Baker, Valerie. "Place et role de la ville dans *Texaco* de Patrick Chamoiseau: Entretien avec l'auteur de *Texaco*, Patrick Chamoiseau." Université des Antilles et de la Guyane, 2000.

Broussillon, Odile, and Michèle Desbordes. "Interview P. Chamoiseau Ecrivain Martiniquais." *Notes Bibliographiques Caraïbes*, 48, 1988, 9–22.

Bullo, Alain. "Patrick Chamoiseau: *Chronique des sept misères*, de l'oraliture à l'écriture." *Facoltà di letter e filosofia*. Venice: Università Ca' Foscari Venezia, 1994. Interview, 36–70.

Chancé, Dominique. "Entretien avec Patrick Chamoiseau." *L'auteur en souffrance*. Paris: Presses Universitaires de France, 2000. Interviewed February 1997, 199–216.

Chaouite, Abdellatif. "Pour un imaginaire de la diversité: Entretien avec Patrick Chamoiseau." *Allers-retours*. Ed. Abdellatif Chaouite and Marie Virolle. Condé sur Noireau: Revues Plurielles / Téraèdre Publishing, 2008. 11–30.

Deblaine, Dominique. "Patrick Chamoiseau chez Libraire Mollat." 2002.

McCusker, Maeve. "De la problématique du territoire à la problématique du lieu: Un entretien avec Patrick Chamoiseau." *French Review: Journal of the American Association of Teachers of French* 73, no. 4 (2000): 724–33.

———. "On Slavery, Césaire, and Relating to the World: An Interview with Patrick Chamoiseau." *Small Axe*, 30, November 2009, 74–83.

Morgan, Janice. "Entretien avec Patrick Chamoiseau." *The French Review* 80, no. 1 (October 2006): 186–98.

———. "Re-imagining Diversity and Connection in the Chaos Word." *Callaloo* 31, no. 2 (2008): 443–53.

Pausch, Marion. "'Exprimer la complexité antillaise à l'aide de la tradition orale': Interview avec Patrick Chamoiseau." *Matatu*, 12, 1994, 151–58.

Perret, Delphine. *La créolite: Espace de création*. Martinique: Ibis Rouge Editions, 2001. (This study of Chamoiseau's work draws on numerous interviews with the author.)

Plumecocq, Michaël. "Entretien avec Patrick Chamoiseau autour de Solibo Magnifique." *Roman 20–50: Revue D'Étude du Roman du XXe Siècle* 27, 1999, 125–35.

Réjouis, Rose-Marie. "A Reader in the Room: Rose Myriam Réjouis Meets Patrick Chamoiseau." *Callaloo* 22.2, 1999, 346–50.

Taylor, Lucien. "Créolité Bites: A Conversation with Patrick Chamoiseau, Raphaël Confiant, and Jean Bernabé." *Transition: An International Review* 7, no. 2 (74) (1998): 124–61.

Valhodiia, Jil. "La guerre doit être menée sur le terrain de l'imaginaire: Entretien avec Chamoiseau." *Les périphériques vous parlent* 10 (Spring 1998): 58–63.

Yggdre, Christopher. "Devenir des fondateurs . . . Plaidoyer pour un Guerrier de l'imaginaire: Entretien avec Patrick Chamoiseau." *Les périphériques vous parlent* 13 (Spring 2000): 10–17.

SELECTED WORKS ABOUT CHAMOISEAU

Arnold, A. James. "The Erotics of Colonialism in Contemporary French West Indian Literary Culture." *New West Indian Guide/Nieuwe West-Indische Gids* 68, no. 1 and 2 (1994): 5–22.

Auboy, Miguel. "Avez-vous lu 'Biblique des derniers gestes'? Miguel Auboy rend hommage à Patrick Chamoiseau." March 18, 2007 (retrieved April 15, 2007, from http://remue.net/cont/chamoiseau_aubouy.html).

Auzas, Noémie. *Chamoiseau ou les voix de Babel: De l'imaginaire des langues*. Paris: Éditions Imago, 2009.

Bojsen, Heidi. "Flashbacks of an Orchid: Rhizomatic Narration in Patrick Chamoiseau's *Biblique des derniers gestes*." *Caribbean Literature and the Environment: Between Nature and Culture*. Ed. Elizabeth M. DeLoughrey, Renée K. Gosson, and George B. Handley. Charlottesville: University Press of Virginia, 2005. 213–24.

Burton, Richard. "Débrouya pa péche, Or il y a toujours moyen de moyenner: Patterns of Opposition in the Fiction of Patrick Chamoiseau." *Callaloo* 16, no. 2 (1993): 466–81.

Buzelin, Helene. "Creolizing Narratives across Languages: Selvon and Chamoiseau." *Canadian Literature* 175 (2002): 67–92.

Caldwell, Roy Chandler, Jr. "Creole Voice, Creole Time: Narrative Strategies in Chamoiseau's *Chronique des sept misères*." *Romance Quarterly* 47, no. 2 (2000): 103–11.

———. "For a Theory of the Creole City: Texaco and the Postcolonial Postmodern." *Ici-Là: Place and Displacement in Caribbean Writing in French*. Ed. Mary Gallagher. Amsterdam: Rodopi, 2003. 25–39.

Casas, Olga Janeth. "'L'oraliture' dans *Chronique des sept misères* de Patrick Chamoiseau." *Lettres Romanes* 55, no. 3–4 (2001): 319–29.

Chancé, Dominique. "De *Chronique des sept misères* à *Biblique des derniers gestes*, Patrick Chamoiseau est-il baroque?" *MLN* 118, no. 4 (2003): 867–94.

———. *L'auteur en souffrance*. Paris: Presses universitaires de France, 2000.

Chivallon, Christine. "*Texaco* ou l'éloge de la 'spatialité.'" *Notre Librairie: Revue du Livre: Afrique, Caraïbes, Océan Indien* 127 (1996): 88–107.

Crosta, Suzanne. "Du silence à l´écriture. Les lieux d´être de l´imaginaire créole." *University of Toronto Quarterly: A Canadian Journal of the Humanities* 63, no. 2 (1993): 375–78.

———. *Récits d'enfance antillaise*. Sainte-Foy: Éditions du GRELCA, 1998.

Curtius, Anny Dominique. "La créolité de Chamoiseau: phénomène nouveau ou continuité d'un détour 'negzagonal.'" *Beginnings in French Literature*. Ed. Freeman G. Henry. Amsterdam: Rodopi, 2002. 181–96.

Dash, J. Michael. "Martinique is (not) a Polynesian island: detours of French West Indian identity." *International Journal of Francophone Studies* 11, no. 1 and 2 (2008): 123–36.

Dash, J. Michael. "A Poetics of Liminality: Another Caribbean Fin de Siècle." *The Other America: Caribbean Literature in a New World Context*. Charlottesville: University Press of Virginia, 1998. 134–59.

Dawson, Ashley. "Squatters, Space, and Belonging in the Underdeveloped City." *Social Text* 22, no. 4 (2004): 17–34.

Delcroix, Maurice. "Façons diverses sans faits divers: Marguerite Yourcenar et Patrick Chamoiseau." *Écrire l'insignifiant: dix études sur le fait divers dans le roman contemporain*. Ed. Paul Pelckmans and Bruno Tritsmans. Amsterdam: Rodopi, 2000.

Du Rivage, Francoise. "L'écriture de la folie dans trois romans de Patrick Chamoiseau." *Romance Languages Annual* 9 (1997): 53–57.

———. "*Texaco*: From the Hills to the Mangrove Swamps." *Thamyris* 6, no. 1 (1999): 35–42.

Figueiredo, Euridice. "La Reécriture de l'histoire dans les romans de Patrick Chamoiseau et Silviano Santiago." *Études Littéraires* 25, no. 3 (1992): 27–38.

Fulton, Dawn Hioryun. "Romans des Nous: The First Person Plural and Collective Identity in Martinique." *French Review: Journal of the American Association of Teachers of French* 76, no. 6 (2003): 1104–14.

Gosson, Renee K. "For What the Land Tells: An Ecocritical Approach to Patrick Chamoiseau's *Chronicle of the Seven Sorrows*." *Callaloo* 26, no. 1 (2003): 219–34.

Gyssels, Kathleen. "Du titre au roman: *Texaco* de Patrick Chamoiseau." *Roman 20–50*, 20, 1995, 121–32.

Hazaël-Massieux, Marie-Christine. "Chamoiseau, cet écrivain qui écrit le créole directement en français." *Portulan*. (Châteauneuf-le-Rouge: Vents d'ailleurs, 2000. 189–202.

Jones, Moya. "Chamoiseau and Matura: Translators and Translations." *Palimpsestes*, 12, 2000, 61–70.

Kemodjio, Cilas. "Ville-Poubelle et Auto-Contamination dans *Texaco* de Patrick Chamoiseau." *Francographies*, 8, 1999, 83–101.

Knepper, Wendy. "Re-membering the Last King of Dahomey: Diasporic Desires and Black Masculinities in *Les derniers rois mages* and *L'exil du roi Béhanzin*." *Men and Masculinities in African Film and Fiction*. Ed. Lahoucine Ouzgane and Onookome Okome. London: James Currey, 2010.

———. "The *Émerveille*: Initiating the Warrior of the Imaginary." *The Caribbean Writer as Warrior of the Imaginary—L'Ecrivain caribéen, guerrier de l'imaginaire*. Ed. Kathleen Gyssels and Bénédicte Ledent. Amsterdam: Rodopi, 2008, 51–72.

———. "Patrick Chamoiseau's Field of Play: Fostering a New World Imaginary." *To See the Wizard: Politics and the Literature of Childhood*. Ed. Laurie Ousley. Newcastle: Cambridge Scholars Publishing, 2007. 337–59.

———. "Remapping the Crime Novel in the Francophone Caribbean: The Case of Patrick Chamoiseau's *Solibo Magnifique*." *PMLA* 122, no. 5 (2007): 1431–46.

———. "Patrick Chamoiseau's Seascapes and the Trans-Caribbean Imaginary." *Constructing Vernacular Culture in the Trans-Caribbean*. Ed. Holger Henke and Karl-Heinz Magister. Lanham: Lexington Books, 2008. 155–77.

Kullberg, Christina. "Parole de résistance: L'écriture de Patrick Chamoiseau." *Moderna Språk* 94, no. 1 (2000): 81–90.

Kundera, Milan. "The Umbrella, the Night World, and the Lonely Moon." *New York Review of Books* 38.21, 1991, 46–50.

Lagarde, François. "Chamoiseau: L'histoire, la parenté et la merveille." *Oeuvres et Critiques* 24.2, 1999, 133–48.

———. "Chamoiseau: L'écriture merveilleuse." *Études Françaises* 37.2, 2001, 159–79.

Loichot, Valérie. "Fort-de-France: Pratiques textuelles et corporelles d'une ville coloniale." *French Cultural Studies* 15, no. 1 (2004): 48–60.

Lutus, Liviu. "Fantastique contemporain aux Antilles: L'exemple de Patrick Chamoiseau." *Les Cahiers du Gerf* 26, 2004, 101–12.

Maisier, Veronique. "Patrick Chamoiseau's Novel *Texaco* and the Picaresque Genre." *Dalhousie French Studies* 57 (2001): 128–36.

McCusker, Maeve. "No Place Like Home? Constructing an Identity in Patrick Chamoiseau's *Texaco*." *Ici-Là: Place and Displacement in Caribbean Writing in French*. Ed. Mary Gallagher. Amsterdam: Rodopi, 2003. 41–60.

———. *Patrick Chamoiseau: Recovering Memory*. Liverpool: Liverpool University Press, 2007.

Menager, Serge Dominique. "Topographie, texte et palimpseste: *Texaco* de Patrick Chamoiseau." *French Review: Journal of the American Association of Teachers of French* 68, no. 1 (1994): 61–68.

Miller, Judith G. "Le Zoulou; Solitude, La Mulâtresse; La Dépossession." *Educational Theatre Journal* 28, no. 4, Reunion: A Self-Portrait of the Group Theatre, December 1976, 561–62.

Milne, Lorna. "From Créolité to Diversalité: the Postcolonial Subject in Patrick Chamoiseau's *Texaco*." *Subject Matters: Subject and Self in French Literature from Descartes to the Present*. Ed. Paul Gifford and Johnnie Gratton. Amsterdam: Rodopi, 2000. 162–80.

———. "Sex, Gender and the Right to Write: Patrick Chamoiseau and the Erotics of Colonialism." *Paragraph* 24, no. 3 (2001): 59–75.

———. "The *marron* and the *marqueur*: Physical Space and Imaginary Displacements in Patrick Chamoiseau's *L'Esclave vieil homme et le molosse*." *Ici-La: Place and Displacement in Caribbean Writing in French*. Ed. Mary Gallagher. Amsterdam: Rodopi, 2003. 61–82.

———. "Metaphor and Memory in the Work of Patrick Chamoiseau." *L'esprit créateur* 43, no. 1 (2003): 90–100.

———. *Patrick Chamoiseau: Espaces d'une écriture antillaise*. Amsterdam and New York: Rodopi, 2006.

Murdoch, H. Adlai. "Autobiography and Departmentalization in Chamoiseau's *Chemin d'école*: Representational Strategies and the Martinican Memoir." *Research in African Literatures* 40, no. 2 (Spring 2009): 16–39.

———. "Postcolonial Peripheries Revisited: Chamoiseau's Rewriting of Francophone Culture." *French Prose in 2000*. Ed. Michael Bishop and Christopher Elson. Amsterdam: Rodopi, 2002. 135–42.

———. "*Solibo Magnifique*: Carnival, Opposition, and the Narration of the Caribbean Maroon." *Creole Identity in the French Caribbean Novel*. Gainesville: University of Florida Press, 2001. 197–267.

———. "Inscribing Caribbean 'Oraliture': The Polysemic Discourse of Patrick Chamoiseau." *Multiculturalism and Hybridity in African Literatures*. Ed. Hal Wylie and Bernth Lindfors. Trenton: Africa World Press, 2000. 359–67.

———. "Re-Siting Resistance: Chamoiseau's Articulation of Creole Identity." *Sites: The Journal of Twentieth-Century/Contemporary French Studies* 3, no. 2 (Fall 1999): 315–31.

Niblett, Michael. "'The Body Grotesque': The Ecology of Identity in Patrick Chamoiseau's *Biblique des derniers geste[s]*." *"What is this Earthly Paradise?" Ecocritical Responses to the Caribbean*. Ed. Chris Campell and Erin Somerville. Newcastle: Cambridge Scholars Publishing, 2007. 101–18.

Ormerod, Beverley. "The Group as Protagonist in Recent French Caribbean Fiction." *SPAN .Journal of the South Pacific Association for Commonwealth Literature and Language Studies* 36, no. 2 (1993) (accessed online on September 20, 1994, at http://wwwmcc.murdoch.edu.au/ReadingRoom/litserv/SPAN/36/Ormerod.html).

———. "The Martinican concept of 'creoleness': A multiracial redefinition of culture." *Mots Pluriels* 7 (1998) (accessed online on March 15, 2004, at http://motspluriels.arts.uwa.edu.au/MP798bo.html).

———. "Magical Realism in Contemporary French Caribbean Literature: Ideology or Literary Diversion?" *Australian Journal of French Studies* 34, no. 2 (May–August 1997): 216–26.

Pépin, Ernest. "The Place of Space in the Novels of the Créolité Movement." *Ici-Là: Place and Displacement in Caribbean Writing in French*. Ed. Mary Gallagher. Amsterdam: Rodopi, 2003. 1–24.

Perret, Delphine. "La Parole du conteur créole: *Solibo Magnifique* de Patrick Chamoiseau." *French Review: Journal of the American Association of Teachers of French* 67, no. 5 (1994): 824–39.

———. *La créolité: Espace de création*. Martinique: Ibis Rouge Editions, 2001.

Picanço, Luciano C. *Vers un concept de littérature nationale martiniquaise: évolution de la littérature martiniquaise au XXème siècle: une étude sur l'oeuvre d'Aimé Césaire, Édouard Glissant, Patrick Chamoiseau et Raphaël Confiant*. New York: P. Lang, 2000.

Pinalie-Dracius, Pierre. "Les stratégies langagières dans 'Chronique des sept misères' de Patrick Chamoiseau." *Antilla Kreyol* no. 9, 1987, 17–23.

Prat, Michel. "Patrick Chamoiseau: Un émule martiniquais de Gadda?" *Francofonia: Studi e Ricerche Sulle Letterature di Lingua Francese* 9, no. 17 (1989): 113–25.

Price, Richard and Sally. "Shadowboxing in the Mangrove." *Cultural Anthropology* 12, no. 1 (1997): 3–36.

Réjouis, Rose-Marie. "Mourning the Story(teller): Patrick Chamoiseau's *Solibo Magnifique*." *RBSE* 2, no. 5 (2003): 229–35.

Seifert, Lewis C. "Orality, History, and 'Creoleness' in Patrick Chamoiseau's *Creole Folktales*." *Marvels & Tales* 16, no. 2, 2002, 214–30.

Shelly, Sharon L. "Addressing Linguistic and Cultural Diversity with Patrick Chamoiseau's *Chemin-d'école*." *French Review: Journal of the American Association of Teachers of French* 75, no. 1 (2001): 112–26.

Tcheuyap, Alexi, and R. H. Mitsch. "Creolist Mystification: Oral Writing in the Works of Patrick Chamoiseau and Simone Schwarz-Bart." *Research in African Literatures* 32, no. 4 (2001): 44–60.

Vincenot, Stella. "Patrick Chamoiseau and the Limits of the Aesthetics of Resistance." *Small Axe*, 30, November 2009, 65–73.

Watts, Richard. "'Toutes ces eaux!': Ecology and Empire in Patrick Chamoiseau's *Biblique des derniers gestes*." *MLN* 118, no. 4 (2003): 895–910.

———. "The 'Wounds of Locality': Living and Writing the Local in Patrick Chamoiseau's *Ecrire en pays dominé*." *French Forum* 28, no. 1 (2003): 111–29.

Wells, Catherine. *L'oraliture dans* Solibo Magnifique. Sainte-Foy: Grelca, 1994.

INDEX

absurd/absurdity, 67, 68, 84, 88–89
Aching, Gerard, 8
activism, 5, 14, 22, 24, 28–30, 46, 200, 207, 212–17
adolescence, 13–14, 21, 145–50
Africa and African presence, 6–7, 32, 36, 38, 44, 49, 51, 55, 96, 105, 107, 120, 124, 138, 151, 155–59, 174, 179, 186, 188, 206, 208, 213, 216, 222, 224
anticolonialism, 13–14, 38–39, 193–94, 204, 207–8
Appadurai, Arjun, 27, 28, 29, 30, 31, 115, 178
Arendt, Hannah, 122
autoethnography, 139

Bakhtin, Mikhail, 92, 103, 165
Baudelaire, Charles, 134, 233
Bauman, Richard, 102–3
Béhanzin, 22, 42, 155–56
béké, 43, 73, 89–90, 104–5, 121, 124, 167–72, 189–90
Bernabé, Jean, 19, 27, 30, 64, 95, 156
Bhabha, Homi, 51, 92, 128, 207
Borges, Jorge, 194, 221, 227
Brathwaite, Edward Kamau, 30, 59, 66, 96
bricolage, 24, 76, 113, 150, 186
Bongie, Chris, 62, 140, 241n8, 251n3
Britton, Celia, 215
Buddhism, 229, 235
Burton, Richard D. E., 11, 67

call-and-response, 57, 91, 126, 140
Calvino, Italo, 77, 78, 90, 194
carnival, 3, 33, 34, 39, 40
carnivalesque, 3, 34, 40, 145, 153
Césaire, Aimé, 10, 14, 16, 27, 28, 38–39, 76, 109, 156, 212, 216–17, 232–33
Chamoiseau, Patrick: *Aliker*, 21, 185, 190; *Antan d'enfance/Childhood*, 26, 95, 130, 131, 133–37, 140; *Au temps de l'antan: Contes du pays Martinique/Creole Folktales*, 19, 21, 26, 27, 57, 95, 101–5; *Biguine*, 21, 188; *Biblique des derniers gestes*, 17, 23, 26, 57, 107, 109, 119, 121, 145, 159, 185, 189–93, 199, 201–3, 206, 207, 208, 209; *À bout d'enfance*, 15, 21, 24, 130, 136, 137, 140, 145–52; *Chemin-d'école/School Days*, 19, 21, 26, 95, 130, 138, 140, 142–45, 151; *Chronique des sept misères/Chronicle of Seven Sorrows*, 7, 18, 20, 22, 25, 57, 59–74; *Un dimanche au cachot*, 3, 152, 217–26; *Écrire en pays dominé*, 12, 16, 49, 65, 75, 80, 92, 155, 165, 166, 175–82; *Éloge de la créolité/ In Praise of Creoleness*, 19, 26, 27, 95–100, 152; *Émerveilles*, 145, 148, 159, 162–65; *Encyclomerveille d'un tueur*, 21, 191; *L'Esclave vieil homme et le molosse*, 168–74; *Lettres créoles*, 19, 27, 95, 101–2, 106–11, 174; "L'Époque Delgrès," 16, 28, 33, 35–38, 194–97; *L'Exil du roi Béhanzin*,

21–22, 42, 155, 185, 187; *L'Intraitable beauté du monde: Adresse à Barack Obama*, 215–16; *Livret des villes du deuxième monde*, 194–97; *Les neuf consciences du Malfini*, 228–36; "Une manière d'Antigone," 16, 33, 39, 72; *Manifeste pour les "produits" de haute nécessité*, 216–17; *Manman Dlo contre la fée Carabosse*, 17, 33, 46, 47, 49–56; *Nord-Plage*, 21, 189–90; *Passage du milieu*, 21, 28, 107, 188; *Quand les murs tombent: L'Identité nationale hors-la-loi?*, 213–15, 224; "Solitude la mulâtresse," 43–45; *Solibo Magnifique/Solibo Magnificent*, 18, 20, 62, 77, 78, 82, 83, 84, 85, 88–91; *Texaco*, 5, 7, 8, 15, 20, 26, 27, 38, 41, 60, 95, 108, 109, 111–29, 145, 150, 154, 156, 160, 187, 225, 227

Chancé, Dominique, 19, 48, 62
clairvoyance, 186, 190–91, 199–200, 224
coming-of-age, 57, 130–53, 191
Condé, Maryse, 27, 96, 99, 101, 132
Confiant, Raphaël, 10, 19, 27, 28, 30, 59, 64, 67, 95–96, 100–102, 106–7, 110–11, 121, 132, 174
consumerism, 67, 216–17
creolization (defined), 7–8, 98–101, 148, 160–61, 183, 242–43n51
cric-crac, 56, 61, 91

Danticat, Edwidge, 101, 111
Dash, J. Michael, 29, 47, 114–15, 252n24
Delsham, Tony, 10, 13–15, 22, 34, 47, 59, 89, 149

departmentalization (effects of), 9, 11–12, 16, 59–62, 67–76, 93–94, 98, 112, 131, 154–55, 157, 180, 189–90
Deslauriers, Guy, 21, 42, 187–88, 190
Díaz, Junot, 26
dimorphism, 192
djobeur, 12, 16, 18, 61–78, 94, 98

ecological interests, 22, 28, 127, 176, 184, 192, 196–98, 215, 217, 230–31
eco-poetics, 231
educator, 7, 25, 212, 218, 225
émerveille, 24, 28, 57, 145, 147–48, 152, 158–61, 165–66, 168, 173, 175, 184, 186, 198, 226
ethnography, 18, 62, 116, 118–19, 129, 139, 153
exoticism, 29, 64

fairytales, 53, 148, 171, 198
Fanon, Frantz, 8, 10, 17, 23, 97, 109, 200, 203, 209, 212
Faulkner, William, 221, 225
folktales, 19, 27, 55, 64–65, 101
Frankétienne, 10, 15, 30, 97, 109–11, 235
Fulton, Dawn, 172

Gallagher, Mary, 132, 145, 239n4
genesis, 106, 109, 120–21, 123, 174, 179, 186, 197, 219
genre, 12–13, 49–50, 61, 63, 77–94, 139, 148, 158, 175
Glissant, Édouard, 5–7, 10, 13 ,15, 20, 23–24, 27–28, 30, 35, 44, 56, 59, 65, 67, 69, 78, 97, 99–100, 111, 118–19, 148, 153, 158–59, 164, 167, 171–73, 175, 178–81, 189, 198, 200,

207, 210–12, 213–17, 220, 224, 227, 232–33, 235–36
globalization, 23, 25, 155, 181–83, 197, 204, 208–9, 214–15
Gosson, Renée, 68
griot, 107
Guerrier de l'imaginaire, 3, 7, 22–23, 156, 166, 168, 174, 179, 198–99, 214, 231

Harris, Wilson, 3, 30, 51
Hayot, José, 21, 187, 189–90

Jameson, Fredric, 80
Johnson, Linton Kwesi, 189

Laguarigue, Jean-Luc de, 185
landscape, 24, 46–56, 76, 84, 119, 159–61, 166, 169, 175–76, 178–79, 182, 184, 186, 194, 198, 206, 223, 232–34
language, 7, 10, 26–27, 53–54, 59, 64–66, 69, 90, 96–101, 112, 114, 117–18, 120, 122–24, 126–30, 142–45, 176, 222, 232
Lorde, Audre, 201–2

magical realism, 64, 69–72, 98, 148, 160–61
maroon slave, 4, 16, 32, 37, 39, 42–45, 75–76, 85–86, 93–94, 154, 166, 170–71, 223
marooning of consciousness, 4, 45, 107, 165–66, 170, 172–74, 177, 180–81, 225
Marqueur de paroles, 3, 7, 18, 20, 22–23, 25, 62, 63, 77, 78, 94, 95, 102, 106, 111, 121, 169, 199
masks, masking, and masquerade, 3–10, 25, 47, 51–52, 57, 64–65, 69, 78, 88, 94, 219–20, 225–26, 235, 237

McCusker, Maeve, 7, 29, 68, 100, 113, 139, 239n4, 242n35, 246n22, 248n60, 249n10, 250n3, 250n9, 256n19
Milne, Lorna, 8, 10, 29, 68, 193, 239n4, 243n52, 244n25, 249n10, 250n1, 252n32, 255n5
mimicry, 9, 109, 220, 237
Murdoch, H. Adlai, 9, 84, 239n4, 240n8

Naipaul, V. S., 9, 29
names, 6–7, 54, 69, 87, 128, 143, 205, 256n21
Negritude, 14, 27–28, 36, 56, 96–97
Niblett, Michael, 197–98
nostalgia, 29, 73–74, 92–94, 132, 150–51

oraliture, 20, 49, 57, 95, 102, 107–9, 113, 119, 122, 129, 145, 160, 187–88, 225
Ormerod, Beverley, 70, 79, 93

petroglyph(s), 106, 109, 140, 174
Phillips, Caryl, 9, 26
Pierre-Monde, 23, 175, 178, 181, 183–84, 226, 253n50
Pinalie-Dracius, Pierre, 64–65
Pratt, Mary Louise, 115, 130, 139
Price, Richard (and Sally), 29, 241n3, 251n3
Proust, Marcel, 132–36

quimbois, 71, 82, 85, 90–91, 108, 123, 137, 205–6

Rabelais, François, 26, 81, 86, 89, 117
rebel, 10–18, 32–58, 93, 154, 157, 181, 193, 198, 204, 209
resurrection, 121–22, 194–95, 207, 219

Index 273

revolution, 10, 33, 35, 41, 44–45, 47, 54, 110–11, 138–39, 157, 190, 200–205, 216, 224
rhizome, 24, 179–81, 183, 193, 197, 201, 205–7
riddles, 35, 37, 44, 78, 91
Rushdie, Salman, 26, 210

sacred, 38, 51, 110–11, 120–23, 201, 205–7, 210, 219, 221, 232–33, 235–36, 256n21
Saint-Éloy, Luc, 16, 40–41
Saint-John Perse, 10, 109, 132, 176, 179–80, 210–11, 221
Schoelcher, Victor, 11, 226–27
Schwarz-Bart, André, 16, 42
screenplay, 21, 107, 155, 185–90
slavery: abolition, 4, 6, 22, 35, 76, 112, 120, 161, 218, 225, 226, 237; crime against humanity, 22; representations of, 35, 43, 85–87, 112–29, 167–74, 188, 202–3, 222–25
solidarity, 24, 34, 111, 123, 158–59, 182, 184, 190, 193, 200, 204, 206–7, 212
Spivak, Gayatri Chakravorty, 99, 248n2
storytelling, 25, 49, 56–57, 63, 78–79, 91–92, 101–9, 125, 140, 146, 161–64

Ti-Jean, 104, 108

vodou, 111, 121, 127, 129, 165, 198, 204–6

Walcott, Derek, 27, 30, 59, 66, 210
Warrior of the Imaginary. See *Guerrier de l'imaginaire*
Watts, Richard, 24, 176, 192, 197

Word Scratcher. See *Marqueur de paroles*

zombi (zombie), 43, 45, 56, 71–72, 81–82, 146, 157